Bed, Breakfast & Bike
Northeast

by

Cynthia Reeder

Bed, Breakfast & Bike Northeast
Copyright 2000 by Cynthia Reeder

Cover: *photos by Cynthia Reeder; design by Jean Sullivan*

Maps: *Richard Widhu*

ISBN: 0-933855-21-4
Library of Congress Control Number: 00-134464

Also available:
Bed, Breakfast & Bike Mid-Atlantic
Bed, Breakfast & Bike Western Great Lakes
Bed, Breakfast & Bike Pacific Northwest
RIDE GUIDE: Covered Bridges of Ohio
RIDE GUIDE: North Jersey 2nd Edition
RIDE GUIDE: Central Jersey 2nd Edition
RIDE GUIDE: South Jersey 2nd Edition
RIDE GUIDE: New Jersey Mountain Biking
RIDE GUIDE: Mountain Biking in the New York Metro Area
RIDE GUIDE: Hudson Valley New Paltz to Staten Island 2nd Edition
and
Happy Endings by Margaret Logan

Send for our catalog or visit us at www.anacus.com

Published by

ANACUS PRESS INC.

P.O. Box 156, Liberty Corner, New Jersey 07938

"Ride Guide" and "Bed, Breakfast and Bike" are trademarks of Anacus Press, Inc.

Printed in the United States of America

Preface & Acknowledgments

Who doesn't remember the feeling of freedom they experienced the first time they pedaled a two-wheel bicycle unaided?

Ever since shedding my training wheels as a youngster my bicycle has liberated me, time and time again, from the pressures and routines of everyday life—whether on a quick 10-mile warm-up ride in the neighborhood or on a multi-day or multi-week excursion. Without a doubt, the first time I joined an organized week-long inn-to-inn ride, I was hooked on cycle touring.

To me, there's no better way to let your senses soak up the sights, smells, and sounds of your surroundings. No better way to mix exercise with adventure. No better way to explore remote byways and "blue highways" at your own pace.

And there's certainly no better way to end a day of cycling than to settle in at a convivial inn or B&B where you can exchange travel stories with other adventurous guests and gracious innkeepers.

New England and New York are home to thousands of inviting B&Bs and inns, making the research for this book particularly challenging. I visited every establishment listed in the book and hope to visit all of them again some day; however, I wish that I could have included even more destinations and developed even more cycling routes—but then, this book never would have gone to press. I'd still be exploring the endless lodging and cycling opportunities throughout the Northeastern states.

Many of the recommendations for places to stay, routes to follow, and things to do came from friends and strangers I met along the way while researching and writing this edition of *Bed, Breakfast & Bike*. I'd like to extend a special thanks to the innkeepers and local bike shop owners whose cooperation and advice helped make this project possible. I'd also like to acknowledge the support and contributions of the following friends, family members, and acquaintances who lent abundant support or went out of their way to aid my research:

Mike Andrews
Joan Caine
Joe Cohen
John Coull of Valley Bicycles
Matthew Crews, Eclectic Bicycle, Peterborough
Shari Hymes of BikeHampton

Jim at Action Sports, Old Saybrook
Steve Kamen
Colleen Kelly
Bill Kilday, Battenkill Bike, Manchester
Bobbie Kinn
Harry Koenig
Robert Koshar, Greenwich Bicycles
Mike Miller
Jeff Munk
Pete at Professional Camera in White River Junction
Dale Robinson
Kris Stoltz
Robert Sullivan, Sports Outlet Ski Shop, No. Conway
Haske Van Oijen
John Worth, East Burke Sports
Bruce Harrington, Spokes & Slopes, Peterborough

And a final note of thanks goes to my editor at Anacus Press, Christian Glazar, whose patience and commitment brought the book to life.

Contents

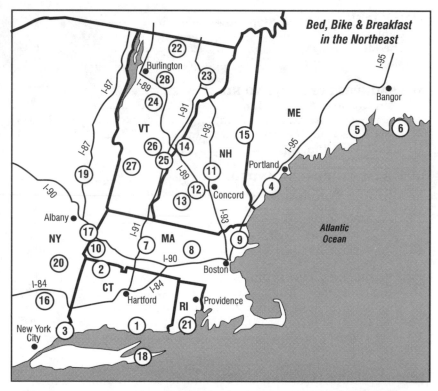

Numbers on map correspond with numbers in the Table of Contents

How to Use This Book

Information About the B&Bs

When it comes to B&Bs, no two establishments are alike—not even remotely alike. They all reflect the individual styles and tastes of their owners. Nevertheless, virtually everyone will find something that tickles their fancy in the selected cyclist-friendly accommodations in this book, from gentrified farms to traditional B&Bs to mountaintop lodges. Some are popular because of their setting, some because of their rich history or distinct architecture. The entry for each inn contains descriptions of ambiance, amenities, and locale to guide your selection.

From a management and hospitality perspective, the lodgings fall, in general, into two different categories: B&Bs, which tend to be smaller, family-run businesses where the innkeeper will greet you at the door and even serve you breakfast, and inns, which are somewhat larger establishments with larger staffs and slightly less personal—albeit hospitable and professional—service. If you're the kind of person who can't live without a TV, phone, and mini-bar in your room and who must have porters, fax machines, and room service on-demand, you probably won't enjoy a stay at a small, intimate, relaxed B&B or inn. That said, many B&Bs and small inns are adding amenities, such as in-room phones with voicemail, and some may even offer a television or a mini-bar in your room. In any event, if there is an amenity that you can't live without it's best to check with the innkeeper before booking a room. Many establishments also have non-smoking policies, so if you're a smoker ask about the smoking policy when you make a reservation.

The heading for each listing includes all contact information, including Web addresses where available, plus rate information. The rate description is based on the rates when I visited the inns in 1999, and is subject to change. Additionally, I have given an indication of the inn's meal plan: B&B indicates that breakfast is included; MAP—Modified American Plan—indicates both breakfast and dinner are included in the rate. Rather than give a specific rate, which can quickly become obsolete, I have instead placed the rates in a range as follows:

Budget: $90 or less
Moderate: $91-140
Deluxe: $141-199
Luxury: $200 and up

Cycling

At least two recommended road rides with maps are included for each inn; however, in many cases innkeepers or local bike shops can make additional recommendations. In several instances, additional routes in a region can be found under another listing for an inn that's within cycling distance.

Descriptions of each ride cover terrain, road and traffic conditions, as well as interesting sites and landmarks along the way. The author rode a touring bike with regular road tires on all routes. However, where road conditions are better suited to either a mountain or hybrid bike it's noted.

The ride cues are well documented and mapped; however, it is a good idea to carry a detailed local map when riding the routes. Sometimes innkeepers will have them on hand; otherwise, they usually can be found at a local gas station, convenience store, bike shop, outdoor recreation or book store, or through a tourist bureau or chamber of commerce. In some areas, maps especially designed for cyclists are available and are included in the section on additional resources. In a few instances, free maps are available from local real estate offices.

Cue Sheets

The cue sheets are presented in a standard format, providing information about mileage, landmarks, and turning points. The abbreviations represent:

Pt.-Pt.	Point-to-point, distance between turns or points of interest
Cum.	Cumulative, total miles from start point
Street/	
Landmark	Description of street names or distinguishing landmarks
Dir.	Direction
L	Left
R	Right
S	Straight
BL	Bear left
BR	Bear right
R,L or **L,R**	Turn in one direction followed by another quick turn in another direction
	Point of interest or highlight

Mountain Biking Opportunities

Due to the growing popularity of off-road cycling, each chapter includes information on local mountain biking opportunities. However, many of the most common destinations, such as ski resorts and state and local parklands and forests, change their guidelines and policies from year to year. In some cases trails may be closed; in others, new trails will be opened. In all cases, it is advisable to check in advance the status of a recommended riding area.

Also, unless you're riding with someone familiar with a particular trail or riding area, good maps are imperative.

Before You Go

Preparing for the Trip

Everyone has his or her own approach to self-guided bicycle touring. Which is precisely the beauty of it. Riders who enjoy easy village-to-village routes and those who prefer strenuous mountain passes alike will discover destinations to their liking in this collection of cue sheets, maps, and descriptions.

The write-up for each inn and related rides includes descriptions of the locale, bike routes, and noteworthy sites along the way. However, riders who like to do more thorough advance planning, or who enjoy delving into regional history, culture and diversions, may want to contact one of the organizations under the **Additional Resources** section before planning their trip.

Most of the routes in this book are designed for recreational cyclists and can be handled by riders in moderately good physical condition. Stronger riders will find that there are a number of longer routes and some with challenging hills. In all cases, the ride descriptions will indicate for which kind of cyclist the route is suited.

In any event, if you haven't been on a bike for a while, you'll find your trip more enjoyable—and more endurable—if you do some training in advance.

Your Cycling Gear

Since the most critical item for a bicycle tour is your bicycle, you'll want to make sure that it's in good repair. If it hasn't been serviced for a while, head down to the local bike shop and have it fine-tuned to make sure everything is in excellent working order. When riding, it's a good idea to carry a tool kit and know how to use it. Likewise, since one of the most common on-the-road equipment problems is a flat tire, carry a pump and a spare inner tube—and know how to replace it.

Most touring cyclists like to mount a bag on their handlebar or rear rack for carrying items such as a camera, snack food, picnic lunch, sun block, and foul weather gear. How much and what you carry in your bag is a matter of personal style and preference.

In any event, carry plenty of water and drink it frequently to avoid dehydration.

What to Wear

What you wear is going to depend on the time of year and where you're riding. Summers in the Northeast tend to be warm, with slightly cooler temperatures at higher altitudes, so a t-shirt and shorts are usually adequate. However, it's always best to be prepared for a change of weather by taking along a windbreaker or lightweight rain jacket. Spring and fall temperatures vary from pleasantly warm to chilly. During these seasons, particularly along the northern coast and in the mountains, the weather can change quickly. Take along a warm sweater or pullover and consider wearing long tights over your bike shorts so that you can peal off or add layers as the day warms up or cools down. What starts out as a chilly morning can turn into a glorious afternoon, and you don't want to be excessively dressed for the warmer part of the day.

Wearing bright colors makes you more visible to oncoming traffic.

Finally, no matter how experienced your are, wear an ANSI- or SNELL-approved helmet.

Safety Tips
- Obey traffic laws
- Ride with traffic, as close to the shoulder as safely possible
- Avoid riding double except on extremely remote roads
- Use extra caution when crossing busy routes or intersections
- Use hand signals to indicate turns
- Cross railroad tracks at right angles
- Watch for sewer grates, pot holes, rocks, wet leaves and other obstacles

---

—Important Disclaimer—

While this book provides as accurate a description of these rides as possible, road conditions and other critical information provided in these pages can change overnight. It is your own responsibility to have a thorough understanding of the routes you ride, the mechanical condition of your bike, and your riding ability. By purchasing this book or borrowing it from a friend, you have released Anacus Press, the authors, and the artists from any liability for injuries you may sustain while using this book as a guide.

Connecticut Inns and Rides

Connecticut may be a small state, but it offers rewarding cycling through landscape rich in history and diversity. As one the country's most prosperous states, Connecticut is populated with well-manicured estates, well-maintained public lands, and pristine villages.

The Long Island Sound forms the southern border of The Constitution State, and amid its gently rolling coastal plains sit two of the featured inns, both of which boast histories as colorful and fascinating as their home state: the **Stanton Inn**, in the well-heeled village of Greenwich, and the legendary **Griswold Inn** in Essex, not far from the mouth of the Connecticut River.

The Sound is a magnet for boating enthusiasts, while its secondary coastal roads attract recreational cyclists who can safely pedal their way along routes overlooked by drivers zooming along busy major highways and interstates. Best of all, riders don't have to pedal far inland to enjoy rural countryside and forested lands that contrast dramatically with the waterfront vistas.

In the northern section of the state, Connecticut's highlands rise above the Connecticut River, which cuts the state in half. The terrain rises gradually from the river's valley to a general elevation of about 1000 feet, with a few peaks amidst the western highlands reaching more than 2000 feet. In this more rugged part of the state, where the Taconic Mountains and Litchfield Hills join the Berkshires, nestles the vintage town of Norfolk, home to the distinguished **Manor House Inn**. Here, cyclists can enjoy miles and miles of unspoiled natural beauty, vast farmlands, and beautiful mountain vistas.

One of the original thirteen colonies, Connecticut is dotted with vestiges of its earliest years. Roadside markers and building plaques provide constant reminders of events that shaped its history. The territory was first claimed by the Dutch in the early 1600s, then later settled by the English, whose influence is still evident in its quintessential New England towns and villages. Although a pivotal state in the American Revolution, and one of the first states to approve the Federal Constitution, only a few skirmishes were fought in Connecticut. Its forges, remnants of which are found along some the cycling routes, turned out critical weaponry for patriot soldiers.

Just about a century after the American Revolution left its mark on the state, another revolution (of less renown) left a different imprint on the state: a bicycling revolution. Albert Pope's Columbia bicycles, which were manufactured in Hartford, fueled a cycling craze. Pope, a pioneer in sports marketing, launched extravagant (for its day) marketing programs that included bicycle races, riding schools, and bicycle clubs.

Today, the cycling craze continues to be fueled through a number of notable road and mountain biking events and well-organized cycling clubs. A state bicycle coordinator in the Department of Transportation and the non-profit Connecticut Bicycle Coalition actively promote and support cycling activities statewide, and are among a number of valuable resources for cyclists.

Resources
Connecticut Office of Tourism
505 Hudson St.
Hartford, CT 06106
(860) 270-8080 or (800) CT-BOUND
www.state.ct.us/toursim/
Distributes Connecticut Vacation Guide, Special Events Calendar, and official highway map. Also publishes official bicycle map, which can be received by special request. However, the map is only marginally helpful; more detailed maps are recommended.

Bicycle Coordinator
Connecticut Dept. of Transportation
2800 Berlin Turnpike, P.O. Box 317546
Newington, CT 06131-7546

Connecticut Department of Transportation
Engineering Record
2800 Berlin Turnpike, P.O. Box 317546
Newington, CT 06131-7546
Publishes detailed county maps.

Connecticut Department of Environmental Protection
Natural Resource Center
165 Capitol Ave., Room 555
Hartford, CT 06106
(203) 566-3540
Publishes topographic county maps.

Connecticut Bicycle Coalition
One Union Place
Hartford, CT 06103
(860) 527-5200
(860) 527-5035, fax
www.ctbike.org
A community of individuals, clubs and businesses dedicated to promoting bicycling in Connecticut. Publishes *The Connecticut Bicycle Directory*, an excellent compendium of cycling-related resources, activities, and 12 route suggestions with cue sheets.

For Off-Road Cyclists
Connecticut Department of Environmental Protection
79 Elm St.
Hartford, CT 06106
(860) 424-3200

Connecticut Chapter of
NEMBA (New England Mountain Bike Association)
P.O. Box 1375
Farmington, CT 06034-1375
http://members.aol.com/joeorto/index.html

The Griswold Inn, Essex, Connecticut

The Griswold Inn

Douglas Paul, Innkeeper
36 Main Street
Essex, CT 06426
Rates: Moderate-Deluxe B&B
Open all year

Phone: (860) 767-1776
Fax: (860) 767-0481
Web: www.griswoldinn.com
E-mail: griswoldinn@snet.net

The Griswold Inn is as old and rich in history as the United States itself. Dating to 1776, the inn—as well as the gem of a village where it sits—embody Americana. Icons of a colorful past, they almost unknowingly transport visitors through their historic earlier days: to a golden era when the Essex waterfront was filled with world-class vessels built in its bustling shipyards; when sea captains built glorious colonial and federal homes on its narrow streets and lanes; when the Griswold Inn welcomed weary travelers arriving by boat and by stagecoach.

Essex, nestled along the banks of the lower Connecticut River just north of where it empties into the Atlantic, was voted number one in Norman Crampton's "The 100 Best Small Towns in America," which noted its "appearance has a storybook-like quality." The International Nature Preservancy calls it "one of the last forty great places left on Earth." Whatever their impressions, visitors find that the "Gris" is an integral part of this classic New England village.

Today, as during its early years, the Gris serves as a popular roadhouse for seaman, overland travelers, and locals alike. In its three museum-like dining rooms and lively, handsome Tap Room they gather to spin yarns, enjoy good food and drink, and partake of its long-standing tradition of sea chanteys, spoon-playing, banjo music, and other foot-tapping entertainment.

Walking through the inn's main rooms is like strolling through a mini museum. Each is filled with an impressive collection of early American artifacts and art, including works by Currier and Ives and Antonio Jacobsen and original prohibition banners. The Steamboat Room, which has a moving turn-of-the-century mural of Essex on the wall, is lined with riverboat memorabilia. The Covered Bridge Room is actually a dining room constructed from an abandoned hand-crafted bridge that once spanned a river in New Hampshire. The Tap Room is a former schoolhouse built in 1738 as one of the first in Essex. The room is dominated by a pot-bellied stove that once warmed the Goodspeed Opera House in East Haddam. And an antique popcorn machine spews out the hot-buttered snack.

In its more than 220-year history, the inn has had only six owners.

Its newest ones, the Paul brothers—Geoffrey, Gregory, and Douglas—bought it in 1995. They hail from the region, respect its legacy and intend to preserve its character. Doug, the on-site manager, admits that there's even a little of his own family's history woven into the inn: His wife worked at the Gris for six summers when she was younger. In any event, the Pauls, as presiding caretakers, are carefully maintaining its original character while updating and refreshing its sleeping quarters.

The Gris has 31 rooms and suites spread across several colonial buildings in the center of Essex. Several of them have fireplaces or private porches off Griswold Square, a tiny park-like setting bordered by a white picket fence and home to several small shops. All of the rooms have private baths, some with old clawfoot tubs and other unique decorative features such as hand-painted murals and antique furniture. The furnishings, nicely suited to the inn's character, offer a mix of period antiques and more traditional country furnishings and accessories, such as four poster beds, oriental rugs and print wallpaper. As a concession to modern-day travelers, the rooms have phones, but guests can request that they be turned off.

The rooms in the three-story main building are more suited to guests who want to experience the lively spirit of the dining room and bar below. They're a little darker, and not as quiet as rooms in the other building.

The recently refurbished Annex, in the separate gambrel-roofed John Hayden House next to the main inn, offers comfortable common rooms with a fireplace, a common TV room, and a mix of colonial and traditional furnishings.

A basic continental breakfast is served by the friendly staff in one of the inn's common dinning rooms. It includes an assortment of teas, coffee, English muffins, fresh fruit, and hot and cold cereals. On Sunday, the Gris upholds a long-standing tradition with its Hunt Breakfast, which features hearty authentic fare such as grits, cheese soufflé, turkey sausage links, home fried potatoes, fried chicken, corn bread, and boiled kidneys.

While in Essex, be sure to stroll the small village and soak up its heritage. Visit the Connecticut River Museum at the former steamboat dock and explore the local history—a history that includes the British navy laying siege to the town and converting the Griswold Inn to its headquarters during the War of 1812. Take in the boating activity on North Cove, or the serene views overlooking Middle Cove. Or simply enjoy the New England charm of this postcard-pretty town with its white clapboard houses decorated with window flower boxes and red, white, and blue bunting.

Bicycling from The Griswold Inn

Essex is conveniently situated within riding distance of several other historic Connecticut River Valley and Atlantic coastal towns, including Old Saybrook, Deep River, Chester, and East Haddam. On the weekends and during the summer tourist season the numbered routes and roads along the Atlantic coast tend to be heavily traveled. The region offers a mix of coastal routes, forest lands, and river roads, with flatter terrain along the Atlantic coast and more undulating routes along the river and inland.

While it's a great place to visit year-round, the best time for riding is on weekdays, late in the spring or in the fall. During leaf-peeping season, however, advance reservations are recommended. For additional regional cycling tips visit the local bike shops or contact **Pequot Cyclists** (www.ctol.net/~knrf/), a 300-member regional cycling club that organizes regular group rides and cycling events in the region.

Local Bike Shops

Clarke Cycles
4 Essex Plaza
(Route 154, at intersection with Route 9)
Essex, CT 06426
(806) 767-2405
ClarkeW251@aol.com
Sales, service, and accessories. Local bike maps. Closed on Sundays.

Action Sports
1385 Boston Post Road
Old Saybrook, CT   06475
(860) 388-1291
staff@actionsportsct.com
Sales, service, and accessories. Organized mountain bike rides leave from shop on Sunday mornings.

Mountain Biking Opportunities

Several state parks in the Essex area offer excellent mountain biking on their trails. In most of them, trails marked with blue blazes are for hikers only. It's best to check with park headquarters to identify trails open to bikers.

Local bike shops also can suggest trails, and weekly group rides depart from Action Sports in Old Saybrook. Or contact the **Connecticut Chapter of the New England Mountain Biking Association (NEMBA)** at P.O. Box 290956, Wetherfield, CT 06129-9956, or http://members.aol.com/joeorto/index.html.

Cockaponset, Connecticut's second largest state forest, covers 15,000 acres and offers more than 20 miles of trails of varying length and difficulty on everything from dirt forest roads to technical singletrack. From Route 9, travel west on Route 148 for about 1.5 miles, then turn left on Cedar Lake Road. Go about 1.5 miles and turn left at Pattaconk Lake sign, and follow to gravel parking lots. Contact Forest Headquarters for a mountain bike trail map: Cockaponset State Forest, Ranger Road, Haddam, CT 06538, (860) 345-8521.

For easier, moderate riding along short trails that skirt the shore, head to smaller **Rocky Neck State Park** in East Lyme, (860) 739-5471, or **Bluff Point State Park** in Groton. Bluff Point, a wildlife preserve, offers views of Fisher's Island and Race Point. Park headquarters, (860) 445-1729, can provide a mountain bike trail map,

The **Devil's Hopyard State Park**, in East Haddam, which features scenic 60-foot Chapman Falls, also allows mountain biking on its trails. Park office: (860) 873-8566.

Other Resources
Connecticut River Valley & Shoreline Visitors Council
393 Main Street
Middletown, CT 06457
(860) 347-0028 or (800) 486-3346
(860) 704-2340, fax
www.cttourism.org

Old Saybrook Chamber of Commerce
146 Main Street
P.O. Box 625
Old Saybrook, CT 06475
(860) 388-3266
(860) 388-9433, fax

Coves, Beaches and Countryside (22.6 miles)
Easy to moderate
This route winds its way past the Turtle Creek Sanctuary and scenic, residential Watrous Cove and along the marinas of Ferry Point to Old Saybrook, taking cyclists through spots overlooked by most visitors to the region.

The Main Street of Old Saybrook, Katharine Hepburn's hometown, is lined with buildings that provide a study in early American architecture. Explore the many scenic yacht-filled coves along its waterfront, where two lighthouses grace the harbor, or relax on one of its beaches. Then return to Essex via secluded, shady Schoolhouse Road and

Westbrook Road, which are dotted with farms and scenic countryside.
The traffic on the numbered roads, and along Old Saybrook's shore-line, tends to be heavier during the summer tourist season and on the weekends. Route 1 around Old Saybrook is always busy, and the tour has been designed to minimize the time on it. Schoolhouse Road has no shoulder, and very little traffic. Route 153 has a nice wide shoulder.

Pt.-Pt.	Cume	Turn	Street/Landmark
0.0	0.0	R	On **Ferry St.** Marina and shipyard at end of street
0.1	0.1	L	Onto **Pratt St.**
0.1	0.2	S	At stop sign. Continue on **Pratt**
0.1	0.3	L	Go part way around circle, onto **West Ave.**, following bike route signs out of town.
0.2	0.5	L	Onto **South Main St.**
0.5	1.0	L	At stop light onto **Rt. 154 S**
1.1	2.1		Saybrook town line
0.1	2.2	L	Onto **Watrous Point Rd.** This turn is easy to miss. If you pass the Saybrook Oil Company you've gone too far.
0.3	2.5		Turtle Creek Sanctuary is on your left.
0.3	2.8	BR	At split in road to stay on **Watrous Pt. Rd.**
0.1	2.9	L	Onto **Azalea Way**
0.0	2.9		Stay to the left at split with Crest Rd.
0.1	3.0	BL	Onto **River Edge Rd.**
0.3	3.3	BL	At River Edge sign, onto unmarked **Otter Cove Dr.**
0.6	3.9	BL	At split in road, dropping down to stop sign
0.0	3.9	L	Onto **Otter Cove Dr.**, which turns into **Ayer's Point Rd.**
0.6	4.5	L	Onto unmarked **Essex Rd.**
0.9	5.4	R	At stop sign onto **Ferry Rd.**
1.3	6.7	S	At stop sign, onto **Route 1.** This is a very busy road. Ride cautiously.
0.7	7.4	L	At major stop sign onto **Rt. 1 West/Rt. 154 South.** Entering Old Saybrook.
0.3	7.7	R	Onto **Stage Rd.**
0.1	7.8	L	Onto unmarked **Main St.**
0.1	7.9	S	Cross over Rt. 1 to stay on **Main St.**
0.2	8.1	R	Onto **Elmwood St.**
0.1	8.2	L	**Oak St.**
0.1	8.3	R	At stop sign onto unmarked **Maplewood St.**
0.1	8.4	L	At stop sign onto unmarked **Lynde St.**

PtPt.	Cume	Turn	Street/Landmark
0.3	8.7	S	At 4-way stop onto **Pennywise Lane**
0.2	8.9	R	Onto **Main St./Rt. 154** at stop sign
0.8	9.7	L	**North Cove Rd.**
0.7	10.4	R	**Cromwell**
0.3	10.7	L	**College St.**
0.1	10.8	R	**Bridge St.** (Just after crossing causeway, you can turn left on Nibang Ave. to explore Lynde Point.)
2.1	12.9	L	**Hartlands Drive,** between 2 stone pillars. (Or, continue straight to have a drink at the Inn)
0.2	13.1	R	**Pratt Rd.**
0.2	13.3	L, R	Left onto **Town Beach Rd.**, quick right on **Ridge Rd.**
0.1	13.4	R	**Rt. 154/Plum Bank Rd.**, which becomes **Hammock Rd.**
1.5	14.9	L	At stop sign onto unmarked **Old Boston Post Rd.** Follow signs to Rt. 1.
0.1	15.0	L	At stop light onto **Rt. 1 West**
0.6	15.6	R	Onto **Schoolhouse Rd.**
2.8	18.4	R	Onto unmarked **Westbrook Rd./Monahan Rd./Rt. 153**
2.6	21.0	S	At stop light, entering Essex on **West Ave.**
1.0	22.0	BR	At stop sign, onto **unmarked street**, keeping Champlin Sq. on your right
0.3	22.3	R	At the square, onto **Main St.**
0.3	22.6		Arrive at The "Gris"

To Gillette Castle (28.2 miles)
Moderate

The route to **Gillette Castle**, in East Haddam, is chock full of things to see and do. The enormous granite structure, designed by actor William Gillette, famous for his performances as Sherlock Holmes, sits on 184 hilltop acres offering spectacular views of the Connecticut River. It is now part of the state park system.

En route, you will ride along the rolling hills of the riverbanks of the Connecticut, through the well-preserved towns of Deep River, Chester, and Ivoryton, and near lush parks and nature preserves.

Chester is home to many artists and artisans as well as The National Theatre of the Deaf, whose award-winning ensemble performs in sign and spoken language. Deep River, once a center for ivory trade, is known for its annual Muster of Fife and Drum Corps, and Ivoryton is home to **Ivoryton Playhouse**, thought to be the oldest summer stock theater in the country.

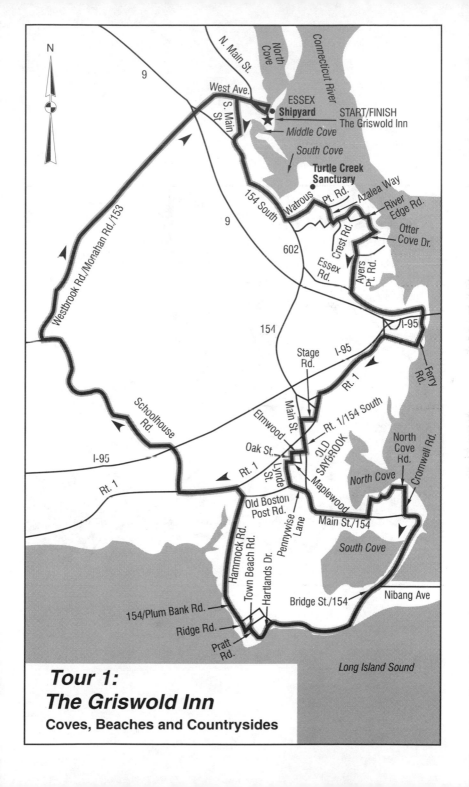

N

9

N. Main St.

North Cove

Connecticut River

West Ave.

S. Main St.

ESSEX
Shipyard

START/FINISH
The Griswold Inn

★ Middle Cove

South Cove

Turtle Creek
Sanctuary

Azalea Way

River Edge Rd.

154 South

Watrous

Pt. Rd.

9

602

Crest Rd.

Otter Cove Dr.

Essex Rd.

Ayers Pt. Rd.

Westbrook Rd./Monahan Rd./153

154

I-95

Ferry Rd.

Stage Rd.

I-95

Rt. 1

Schoolhouse Rd.

Main St.

Elmwood

Rt. 1/154 South

I-95

Oak St.

Rt. 1

Lynde St.

OLD SAYBROOK

Maplewood

North Cove

North Cove Rd.

Cromwell Rd.

Rt. 1

Old Boston Post Rd.

Pennywise Lane

Main St./154

South Cove

Hammock Rd.

Town Beach Rd.

Hartlands Dr.

154/Plum Bank Rd.

Ridge Rd.

Pratt Rd.

Bridge St./154

Nibang Ave

Long Island Sound

Tour 1:
The Griswold Inn
Coves, Beaches and Countrysides

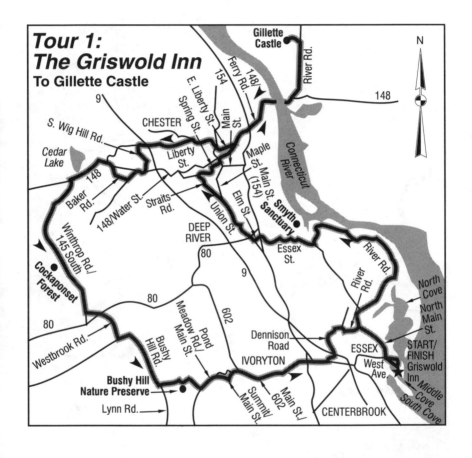

Tour 1:
The Griswold Inn
To Gillette Castle

Gillette Castle

N

Ferry Rd.

River Rd.

148/

154

148

E. Liberty St.
Spring St.

Main St.

CHESTER

Maple St.

Connecticut River

Liberty St.

S. Wig Hill Rd.

Cedar Lake

148

Baker Rd.

148/Water St.

Straits Rd.

Elm St.

Main St. (154)

Smyth Sanctuary

Union St.

DEEP RIVER

Essex St.

Winthrop Rd./ 145 South

80

9

River Rd.

River Rd.

Cockaponset Forest

80

North Cove

North Main St.

80

Westbrook Rd.

Bushy Hill Rd.

Pond Meadow Rd./ Main St.

602

Dennison Road

ESSEX

START/ FINISH Griswold Inn

West Ave.

IVORYTON

Bushy Hill Nature Preserve

Summit/ Main St.

Main St./ 602

Middle Cove

South Cove

Lynn Rd.

CENTERBROOK

Nature lovers will find the Smyth Sanctuary just before entering Deep River and several entrances to the trails and lakes of Connecticut's second largest state forest, Cockaponset, along Routes 148 and 145. The heavily forested 107-acre **Bushy Hill Preserve**, managed by the Essex Conservation Commission, is filled with a cornucopia of animals and plants. At the center of this former pasture land sits an ancient white oak, called the Wolf Tree.

The route covers moderately undulating terrain along quiet backroads, many of which have little or no traffic. Traffic is more congested around the town centers, particularly along Route 602 in Centerbrook.

Pt.-Pt.	Cume	Turn	Street/Landmark
0.0	0.0	R	**Ferry St.** Marina and shipyard at end of street
0.1	0.1	L	**Pratt St.**
0.1	0.2	S	**Pratt St.** Stop sign
0.1	0.3	R	**N. Main St.** at stop sign
0.4	0.7	R	**New City St.**
0.2	0.9	L	**Riverview St.**
0.2	1.1	L	**Maple Ave.**
0.4	1.5	R	**N. Main St.**, which becomes **River Rd**.
3.6	5.1	BR	At stop sign where **River Rd.** becomes **Essex St.**
0.4	5.5		Evelyn S. and Hawthorne L. Smyth Sanctuary is on the right
0.6	6.1	R	**Main St./Rt. 154** Stop sign. Entering Deep River, where you can buy something for lunch or continue to Chester
0.1	6.2	L	**Elm St.** Stop light
0.2	6.4	R	**Union St.** Stop sign
0.0	6.4	S	**Union St.** Stop sign
0.0	6.4	S	Onto **Straits Rd.** at intersection with Maple St.
1.7	8.1	R	Unmarked **Spring St.** Stop sign, where there's a garden in the median on the left. Pass Jennings Pond.
0.5	8.6	L	**Main St.** Stop sign (marked no left turn). Chester has stores, restaurants, coffee shop.
0.1	8.7	R	**Water St./Rt. 148.** Stop sign.
0.7	9.4	S	**Rt. 148.** Cross Rt. 154 at light. **Water St.** becomes **Ferry Rd./Rt. 148**
0.7	10.1	S	**Ferry Slip.** Cross Connecticut River on Ferry. $0.75 for bikes.
0.0	10.1	S	Exit ferry.
0.2	10.3	BL	At stop sign; toward Gillette Castle

Pt.-Pt.	Cume	Turn	Street/Landmark
0.5	10.8	L	**River Rd.**; toward Castle.
0.3	11.1		Enter Gillette Castle State Park.
0.0	11.1	R	Exit parking lot and follow **River Rd.** toward Rt. 148 W.
0.9	12.0	S	**Take ferry** to Rt. 148.
0.7	12.7	S	**Rt. 148/Water St.** Cross Rt. 154
1.2	13.9	R	**East Liberty St.**
0.4	14.3	BR	At V to stay on **East Liberty St.**
0.1	14.4	S	**Liberty St.** Stop sign.
1.4	15.8	L	**S. Wig Hill.** Stop sign.
0.5	16.3	R	**Rt. 148 W.** Stop sign.
0.2	16.5	L	**Baker Rd.**
0.3	16.8	BR	At split in road to stay on **Baker Rd.**
0.4	17.2	L	**Rt. 148 W.** Stop sign.
0.6	17.8		On right is Cedar Lake. (Cedar Lake Rd. leads to Pattaconk Lake; swimming is permitted)
0.3	18.1	L	**Rt 145 S./Winthrop Rd.**
1.7	19.8		Entrance to Cockaponset State Forest on right
0.9	20.7	L	**Rt. 80 East** at split in road.
0.2	20.9	R	**Westbrook Rd.** Stop light.
0.6	21.5	L	**Bushy Hill Rd.**
1.2	22.7	BL	**Bushy Hill Rd.** (Lynn Rd. goes straight) Entrance to Bushy Hill Nature Preserve trails is on the right about 0.5 miles after turn.
0.8	23.5	L	**Pond Meadow Rd./Main St.** Stop sign.
0.7	24.2	R	**Summit/Main St.** Stop sign. Ivoryton Theater is on left.
0.1	24.3	R	**Main St./Route 602**
1.3	25.6	S	**Rt. 602.** Stop light. Continue through Centerbrook, following Bike Route signs. Traffic is congested in this section.
0.3	25.9	L	Onto **Dennison Rd.** at split in road by Essex Ambulance Station (Road sign indicates that Essex is to the right. Go left.)
0.9	26.8	L	At stop sign at V to stay on **Dennison Rd.**
0.2	27.0	R	At T, stop sign onto **River Rd.**
0.9	27.9	R	Stop sign. Go around circle onto **Main St.**
0.3	28.2		Arrive at "The Gris"

Manor House

Diane & Henry Tremblay,
Innkeepers
69 Maple Avenue
Norfolk, CT 06058
Rates: Moderate-Luxury, B&B
Open all year

Phone: (860) 542-5690
Web: www.manorhouse-norfolk.com
Email: innkeeper@manorhouse-norfolk.com

When you tell folks—even those from other corners of Connecticut—that you're going to Norfolk, they're likely to get a quizzical look on their face and ask, "Where?" And that's just the way the locals like it.

A little off the beaten track and delightfully free of fast-food restaurants, multiplex theaters, strip malls—and tourist crowds—this quiet town of about 2000 inhabitants exudes New England charm. In the late 19th century, when it was accessible by railroad, the village experienced a summer resort boom, accompanied by an architectural boom thanks to the healthy bank accounts of its summer residents.

The resort boom is over and the train tracks are gone, but its architectural gems remain, many surrounding the tranquil town green and lining genteel, shady Laurel Way. Another one of these gems sits between the green and Laurel Way on Maple Avenue: Manor House, today an inn with nine guestrooms.

A stately English Tudor-style structure, with rich, exquisite woodwork, Manor House was designed by E.K. Rossiter in 1898 for Charles Spofford, the designer of London's underground and son of Abraham Lincoln's Librarian of Congress. Its colorful history also includes a stint as the home of "Speedometer Jones" in the mid-1900s. An eccentric inventor, whose most acclaimed invention was that all-important device for measuring speed, Jones used to test his ideas in the house and was known to rig it with booby traps.

Hank and Diane Tremblay, escapees from the corporate world, bought the house in 1985 from Hank and Christine Boyle, who had begun restoring it—and ensuring that none of Jones's contraptions remained operational! The Tremblays continued the restoration to create what some consider a romantic getaway; to others it's simply a refreshing, relaxing retreat from the hustle and bustle of everyday life. Built for the leisure class of an earlier era, it's a perfect place to rest after a scenic bike ride. But if guests need further help unwinding, the Tremblays keep a massage therapist on call.

A number of uncommon features and architectural details contribute to the inn's soothing atmosphere, such as the way light shines through the manor's windows, many made of Tiffany stained and leaded glass. In fact, some 20 of these windows were actually house presents from Louis Tiffany to the original owners.

The first floor of the house contains a number of spacious common rooms: a baronial living room, featuring a fireplace with six-foot hearth and a grand piano; a smaller salon/library lined with bookshelves; a sunny enclosed porch and game room; a dining room lined with Tiffany windows that contains a fireplace framed with its original decorative tiles; and a small bar with a television, a guest refrigerator, and several shelves and baskets storing literature about local attractions and activities.

The Manor House occupies a quintessential New England village, but its decor hardly fits the traditional Yankee standard. Rather, its fine Victorian architecture is complemented by a unique collection of Victorian furnishings and accents. Dressmakers' forms hold vintage dresses, decorative sconces and shelves accent the walls, and beaded purses, old photo albums and other tabletop period pieces create Victoriana still lifes throughout the house. At the same time, there are occasional diversions from the Victorian theme, giving the inn a comfortable lived-in feeling.

The sleeping rooms, each of unique shape, size and decorative detail, are located on the second and third floors. Many have grand Victorian armoires and beds with huge headboards, and some have fireplaces and private porches overlooking the expansive lawn and perennial gardens.

Several of the rooms have large tubs with Jacuzzis. In fact, the Country French Room has one in what was once a cedar closet that is nearly the size of a wading pool. The oversized English Room features, in the sleeping room, a tub surrounded by a lace shower curtain through which the mid-day sun shines.

The inn's largest guest chamber, the Spofford Room, measures 30' x 18', and has a huge wood-burning fireplace and private porch. Windows on three sides are dressed with lace curtains and shades, complementing the lace canopied bed, and an intimate sitting area includes unexpectedly comfortable and functional period pieces.

In the morning, guests are treated to a delicious gourmet breakfast in the dining room. The menu changes daily, featuring specialties such as orange waffles, banana pancakes, and French toast. These are complemented by fresh fruit and juices, and honey harvested from the Tremblays' bee hives.

For early risers, the perfect way to start the day is with a short warm-up ride around Doolittle Lake or with a refreshing stroll to Norfolk's village green, which is like taking a trip back in time. You may even catch a glimpse of a horse-drawn carriage carrying children from the nearby Hutterian Fellowship, a sect whose principals and practices are similar to the Mennonites.

Anchoring the green on the south side is Eldridge Fountain, a three-tiered landmark designed by Stanford White. On the opposite end sits Norfolk Library, an impressive Romanesque-style structure with red fish scale tile shingles. Its Great Hall, with fireplace, arched wood beam ceiling, and stained glass windows presents a church-like interior, and among its collections is a plaque depicting Robert Louis Stevenson designed by Homer St. Gaudens. A more modest, colonial-style structure on another side of the green houses the Historical Society Museum. Across from it are the picturesque white Congregational Church and Battell Chapel, a stone structure, both of which feature windows by Louis Comfort Tiffany.

Behind these buildings, on a peaceful estate bequeathed to the Yale Summer School of Music and Art, sits the Music Shed. Known for its acoustics, the site also is home to the Norfolk Chamber Music Festival. The festival is a century-old tradition that today attracts world-class performers such as the Tokyo String Quartet, the Vermeer Quartet, violinist Syoko Aki, and pianists Lilian Kallir and Peter Frankl.

Biking from Manor House

Norfolk sits in the midst of relatively rugged terrain defined by the Litchfield hills and the Berkshire mountains. Due to its location just south of the Massachusetts border, several of the rides weave back and forth between Connecticut and its neighbor to the north.

While most of the bicycling loops around Norfolk involve riding over rolling hills, none of them are very steep or long. In some cases, though, they just seem to keep on coming as you ride to the top of a hill, fly down the other side, and begin pedaling up another one.

All of the roads are paved, with shoulders of varying size. For the most part, traffic is light, with the heaviest (heavy being a relative term) traveled section found along Route 7/Ethan Allen Highway and Route 44. Both of these have good, wide paved shoulders.

For additional suggestions on cycling in the region, contact local bike shops or get a copy of "The Litchfield Hills: Touring by Car, Foot, Boat & Bike" published by the Litchfield Hills Visitors Bureau, which includes four scenic rides between 24 and 39 miles long. A popular annual road bike event in the region is the Tour de Torrington in August. For information, contact Tommy's Bicycles, (860) 482-3571.

Riders who would like to do a longer, more challenging loop can combine the Falling Waters ride with the Umpachene Falls ride from Windflower Inn in Great Barrington.

Bike Shops in the Region

Bike Doctor & Sports Center
97 Church Terrace
Canaan, CT
(860) 824-5577
Sales, service, accessories.

Tommy's Bicycles & Fitness
40 East Main Street
Torrington, CT
(860) 482-3571
Sales, service, accessories.

Other Resources

Litchfield Hills Visitors Bureau
P.O. Box 968
Litchfield, CT 06759-0968
(860) 567-4506
(860) 567-5214, fax
www.litchfieldhills.com
Publishes 36-page "Touring by Car, Foot, Boat & Bike" brochure.

Southern Berkshire Chamber of Commerce
284 Main Street
Great Barrington, MA 01230
(413) 528-1510
www.greatbarrington.org

Berkshire Visitors Bureau
Berkshire Common, Plaza Level
Pittsfield, MA 01201
(800) 237-5747 or (413) 443-9186
www.berkshires.org

Rubel Bike Maps
The Berkshires, Connecticut River Valley, Quabbin Reservoir
P.O. Box 1035
Cambridge, MA 02140
www.bikemaps.com
From Globe Corner Bookstores:
(800) 358-6013 or (617) 723-1676

Mountain Biking Opportunities

Many of the dirt roads around Norfolk make for pleasant off-road cycling.

A number of state parklands permit mountain biking. However, remember that the blue-blazed trails are for hiking only.

Nearby, mountain biking is permitted on **Haystack Mountain**, a 224-acre state park. For more information, contact the Connecticut State Parks Division of DEP, 79 Elm St., Hartford, CT 06106-5127, (860) 424-3200.

Local riders also head to **Nepaug State Forest**, off Route 202 in New Hartford. The Trailheads Mountain Bike Club (for more information inquire at Tommy's Bicycles) meets here for weekly rides. MTB trail maps are available from People's State Forest HQ in Pleasant Valley, CT 06063, (860) 379-2469.

Mountain biking is permitted in the **Mohawk Mountain State Forest**, off Route 4 in Cornwall, CT. In 1999, the final race of the Connecticut Mountain Bike Challenge, "Mohawk Mountain Bicycle Madness" was held at the ski area, (860) 672-6464 or 672-6100.

For additional MTB opportunities in the region see the information included in the section on the Windflower B&B in Great Barrington, Massachusetts.

Doolittle Warm-up (9.9 miles)
Moderate, rolling hills

This sweet little warm-up ride covers rolling hills, through mostly forested land surrounding private Doolittle Lake. The route around the lake is lined with mountain laurel groves and a wonderful mix of wildflowers that bloom in late spring and early summer. Return to the inn via Loon Meadow Drive, which received its name during Norfolk's earliest years when a loon was supposedly spotted along it, and finally along Laurel Way, which provides a glimpse of the handsome "cottages" hidden behind tree-lined properties and drives.

Riders interested in a more challenging ride can turn at the Haystack Mountain access road and ascend one steep mile to the end of the paved road. If you want to combine the ride with a rugged ½-mile hike, a 34-foot stone tower at the top of Haystack (elevation 1716 feet) affords one of the most spectacular vistas of the region. On a clear day visitors catch views of Long Island Sound, the Berkshires, and peaks in Massachusetts and New York.

All roads are paved, with varying degrees of smoothness. There's virtually no traffic.

Pt.-Pt.	Cume	Turn	Street/Landmark
0.0	0.0	L	**Maple Ave.** from drive of Manor House
0.0	0.0	L	**Mills Way**
0.4	0.4	R	**Rt. 44W** at stop sign
0.1	0.5	BR	**Rt. 272N/North St.** at split
0.2	0.7		Turnoff for Haystack Mtn. is on left. One-mile climb on paved road.
1.3	2.0	R	**Ashpatog Rd.** (To your left is the Little Red Schoolhouse, the only one of 11 local schoolhouses from the 1900s to still have its original interior and furnishings intact)
0.8	2.8	BL	Road turns to left and becomes **Doolittle Dr.**
0.8	3.6	R	**Doolittle Dr.**
1.1	4.7	R	**Doolittle Dr.**, just after cemetery
0.7	5.4		Club House for private Doolittle Lake Club is on right
0.6	6.0	BR	**Unmarked road** at T
0.8	6.8	R	**Loon Meadow Dr.** at T
0.5	7.3	L	Unmarked **Loon Meadow Dr.**
1.2	8.5	R	**Rt. 44W** at double stop sign
0.6	9.1	R	**Laurel Way**
0.6	9.7	L	**Maple Ave.**
0.2	9.9		Arrive at Manor House Inn

Hilltop Vistas (36.1 miles)
Moderate to difficult, hilly

This route covers lots of rolling hills through the rugged farmland and scenic countryside of northwestern Connecticut. It offers great vistas of the Litchfield Hills and only a few very short, steep climbs among the many rollers that are interspersed with pleasant flat sections. Riders who enjoy doing long stretches along secondary roads—but not necessarily remote country roads—will like this one. There are few cues and the route is easy to follow.

Just outside Norfolk, off Route 272, the **Hillside Gardens** are open to the public, and just next to them is the entrance to **Dennis Hill Park**, from whose peak visitors can savor a timeless 360-degree view of the surrounding mountains. From 272, riders pick up East Goshen Road, a little-traveled, scenic country lane dotted with farms, stables, historic markers, meadows, and woodlands.

On Route 7 between Goshen and Canaan sits Robbins Swamp, the largest wetland are in the state. And Route 44 between Canaan and Norfolk offers several attractions, including **Beckley Furnace**, which

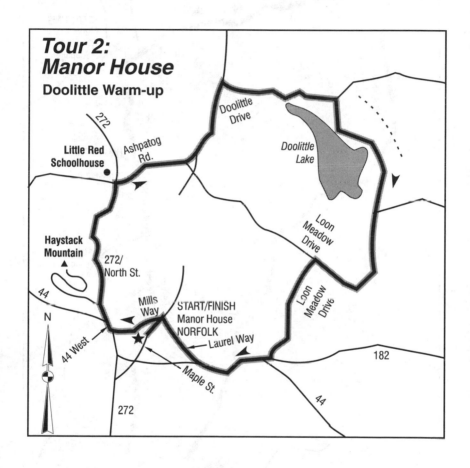

Tour 2:
Manor House
Doolittle Warm-up

272

Little Red
Schoolhouse

Ashpatog
Rd.

Doolittle
Drive

Doolittle
Lake

Haystack
Mountain

272/
North St.

Loon
Meadow
Drive

44

Mills
Way

START/FINISH
Manor House
NORFOLK

Loon
Meadow
Drive

N

44 West

Laurel Way

Maple St.

182

272

44

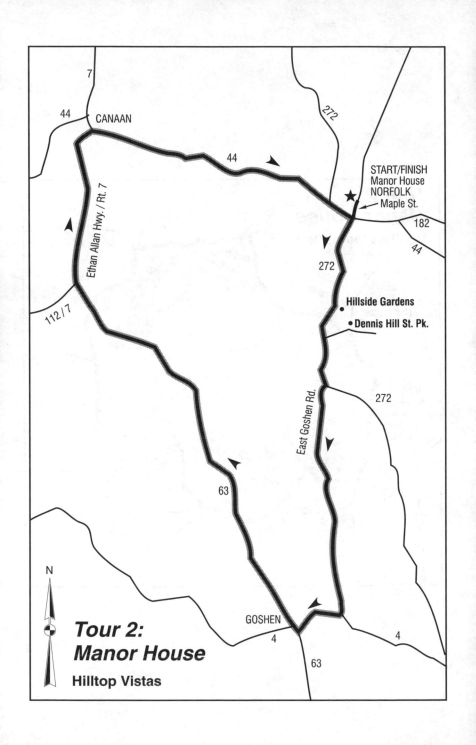

7

44 CANAAN

44 ▸

272

START/FINISH
Manor House
NORFOLK
★ ← Maple St.

182

44

Ethan Allan Hwy. / Rt. 7

112 / 7

272 ▾

Hillside Gardens

• Dennis Hill St. Pk.

272

East Goshen Rd.

▾

63

▾

N

Tour 2:
Manor House

Hilltop Vistas

GOSHEN

4

63

4

was the centerpiece of a much larger installation that served as the core of the region's iron ore business from 1837 to 1918. The water next to the remaining structure makes a great spot to cool off on a hot summer day.

Continuing east on Route 44, the smell of cow manure and fresh fields dominates the route near the expansive Elm Knoll and Laurel Brook farms. Beyond these farms, Freund's Farm Market offers plenty of fresh local products and the kind of unqualified hospitality that characterizes small, rural villages. As customers leave, a painted sign encourages them to return: "We hope you had a good time. Come again and bring a friend."

Most of the route, except for sections of Route 44, are lightly traveled and have good shoulders.

Pt.-Pt.	Cume	Turn	Street/Landmark
0.0	0.0	R	**Maple Ave.** from driveway of Manor House Inn
0.3	0.3	S	Onto **272 S** at stop sign, crossing Rt. 44
0.1	0.4	L	**Rt. 272 S** at stop sign
2.2	2.6		Hillside Gardens on left, next to entrance to Dennis Hill Park. *(For a short detour, enter the park and make the 0.6-mile ride to the top of the hill, where you'll be rewarded with a spectacular view.)*
2.0	4.6	S	**East Goshen Rd.**, at split where Rt. 272 goes left
6.7	11.3	R	**Rt. 4** at stop sign
1.4	12.7	R	**Rt. 63** at yield sign in town of Goshen
11.3	24.0	BR	**Rt. 7 N/Ethan Allen Hwy.** at split
4.5	28.5	R	**Rt. 44E** at stop light in Canaan
2.2	30.7		Turn-off on right to visit Beckley Furnace. Nice spot for picnic/swim, just 0.3 miles down the road.
5.0	35.7	BR	**Rt. 44E**
0.1	35.8	L	**Maple Ave.**
0.3	36.1		Arrive at Manor House Inn

Falling Waters (36.5 miles)
Moderate, rolling hills

Riders who are attracted to water tumbling over layers of rock will enjoy this route which winds its way near waterfalls in the Norfolk area and just over the border in Massachusetts. It also passes through several small Massachusetts settlements, including Clayton, Southfield, Mill River, and Ashley Falls.

Reaching the first of the waterfall attractions, in **Campbell Falls Park**, involves a hike that is worth the effort.

The remote country roads between Campbell Falls and Clayton take riders through lush farmlands and offer a number of rewarding mountain vistas.

In Southfield, a small, neat enclave of colonial houses, a converted **buggy whip factory** houses an 18,000-square-foot antiques market and a small casual cafe. During its heyday the former Turner and Cook Shop turned out the largest number of rawhide whip centers of any plant in the U.S. Later it manufactured belt pins for industrial machines.

The rolling terrain from Southfield leads to Mill River, a thriving settlement in the mid-1800s that was populated by paper mill workers. The mill is long gone, but today—as was the case 100 years ago—what little activity there is in the town seems to revolve around the general store, with its inviting long front porch and yesteryear ambiance.

Just a mile south of Mill River, a short and narrow dirt road leads to **Umpachene Falls**, a cataract that dashes down rock stairs. At its base rests an inviting pool of cool water, perfect for swimming on a hot summer afternoon.

From here the route loops back through Clayton to Ashley Falls, whose quarries once supplied marble for the Boston Customs House and the Court House in New York City. Its main street today is dotted with antique shops. The falls here apparently sit on private property and are not accessible to the public.

Aptly-named Valley View Road is lined with corn fields in front of a scenic mountain backdrop. It also offers access to the tiny Canaan airport, whose grass airstrip provides a break in the neighboring fields.

Canaan offers eating and shopping opportunities before picking up a small road that parallels the Blackberry River. Riders pass a huge stone quarry before reaching the last of the falling water sites next to the Beckley Furnace, once the core of the region's iron ore business.

The route covers lots of rolling hills, with a few notable short steep ascents, and lots of enjoyable descents. All roads are paved, with the majority covering little-traveled side roads without much shoulder. Route 44 is more heavily traveled, but has a good wide shoulder.

Pt.-Pt.	Cume	Turn	Street/Landmark
0.0	0.0	L	**Maple Ave.** from driveway of Manor House
0.0	0.0	L	**Mills Way**
0.4	0.4	R	**Rt. 44** at stop sign
0.1	0.5	S	**Rt. 272N/North St.**
4.1	4.6	L	**Spaulding Rd.**

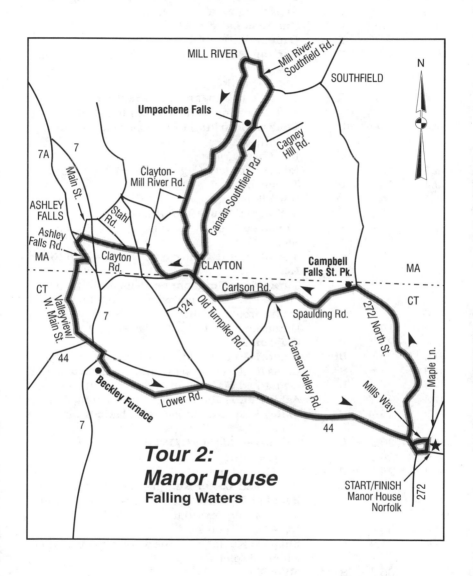

MILL RIVER

Mill River-Southfield Rd.

SOUTHFIELD

N

Umpachene Falls

Cagney Hill Rd.

7A

7

Main St.

Clayton-Mill River Rd.

Canaan-Southfield Rd.

ASHLEY FALLS

Stahl Rd.

Ashley Falls Rd.

MA

Clayton Rd.

CLAYTON

Campbell Falls St. Pk.

MA

CT

Valleyview/ W. Main St.

124

Carlson Rd.

Spaulding Rd.

272/ North St.

CT

44

7

Old Turnpike Rd.

Canaan Valley Rd.

Mills Way

Maple Ln.

Beckley Furnace

Lower Rd.

44

7

**Tour 2:
Manor House**
Falling Waters

START/FINISH
Manor House
Norfolk

272

Pt.-Pt.	Cume	Turn	Street/Landmark
0.2	4.8		Entrance to Campbell Falls trails on right next to parking area
1.7	6.5	L	**Emmons Lane**
0.7	7.2	R	**Canaan Valley Rd.**
0.5	7.7	L	**Carlson Rd.** (just before cemetery), becomes **New St.**
1.2	8.9	R	**Old Turnpike**
0.6	9.5	R	Unmarked **Canaan-Southfield Rd.** at 4-way sign, following signs to Southfield & Mill River
0.2	9.7	BR	**Canaan-Southfield Rd.**, following sign to Southfield
3.2	12.9	L	Road bears right
0.1	13.0		Road bears left, Cagney Hill Rd. goes right
0.1	13.1	BL	To stay on route
1.7	14.8	L	**Norfolk Rd.**
0.4	15.2	L	**Mill River-Southfield Rd.**
0.7	15.9	R	**Unmarked road**, following sign to Mill River Store
1.2	17.1	L	Just after bridge, turn onto **Clayton-Mill River Rd.**
1.0	18.1		**Turnoff for Umpachene Falls** is on the left. Follow dirt road approximately 0.3 miles to picnic area on right.
1.2	19.3	R	Unmarked **Rt. 124** at 4-way stop
3.8	23.1	R	**Clayton Rd.**
0.6	23.7	BL	**Clayton Rd.** at split. (Stahl Rd. goes right)
0.9	24.6	S	Cross Rt. 7 at stop sign, onto **unmarked street**
0.8	25.4	L	Unmarked **Main St.** in Ashley Falls at stop sign
0.3	25.7	L	**Ashley Falls Rd.** at stop sign/flashing light
0.2	25.9	R	**Valley View Rd.**, becomes **W. Main St.** in Canaan
0.3	26.2	L	Unmarked **Main St./Rt. 44**
1.9	28.1	S	At stop sign
0.2	28.3	R	**Rt. 7S** at stop light
0.4	28.7	L	Unmarked **Lower Rd.**, just after bridge.
0.1	28.8		**Beckley Furnace** is on your right. Can swim in the water next to it.
2.0	30.8	R	**Rt. 44E** at stop sign
0.6	31.4	L	**Shepard Rd.** (or continue to Village Green, then left on Maple)
4.7	36.1	S	**Mills Way**
0.1	36.2	R	**Maple Ave.**
0.3	36.5		Arrive at Manor House

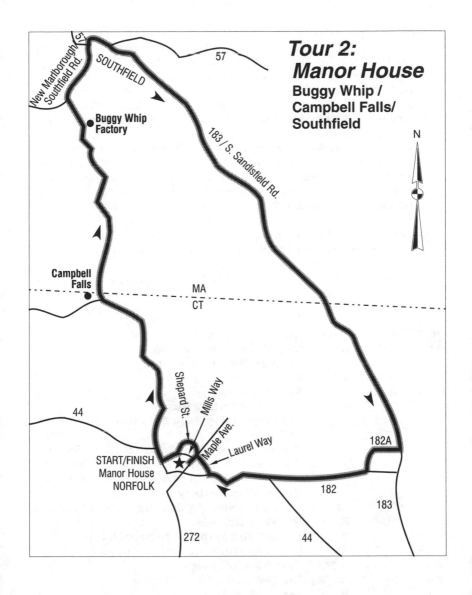

Tour 2:
Manor House
Buggy Whip /
Campbell Falls/
Southfield

N

57
SOUTHFIELD
New Marlborough/
Southfield Rd.
57
Buggy Whip
Factory
183 / S. Sandisfield Rd.
Campbell
Falls
MA
CT
44
Shepard St.
Mills Way
Maple Ave.
Laurel Way
START/FINISH
Manor House
NORFOLK
182A
182
183
272
44

Buggy Whip/Campbell Falls/Southfield (28.4 miles)
Moderate, rolling hills

This picturesque route covers the quiet back roads connecting Norfolk, Southfield, New Marlborough, and Colebrook, with about 50 percent covering terrain in Connecticut, the balance in Massachusetts.

The rolling terrain takes riders past the entrance to two parklands: **Haystack Mountain State Park**, where a mountaintop tower provides spectacular views of mountain peaks in New York, Massachusetts, and Connecticut, and **Campbell Falls Park**, where a scenic waterfall offers another pleasant diversion from the bike route.

A former **buggy whip factory** in the pristine settlement of Southfield boasts 18,000 square feet of antique-filled space, as well as a small cafe. From here, the rolling hills continue through the tiny enclave of New Marlborough to South Sandisfield, passing the entrance to **Sandisfield State Forest**, (413) 528-0904. Within this hardwood forest area are lots of trails and six lakes, ranging in size from 10 to 60 acres. York Lake offers a 300-foot sandy beach and picnic area.

Skirt the tiny enclave of Colebrook, before heading back to Norfolk. Enter Norfolk via "cottage"-lined Laurel Way.

How easy or hard riders find this route will depend on their conditioning. It covers lots of undulating terrain along, for the most part, lightly traveled routes.

Pt.-Pt.	Cume	Turn	Street/Landmark
0.0	0.0	L	**Maple Ave.** from driveway of Manor House Inn
0.1	0.1	L	**Shepard Rd.** at 4-way stop sign
0.4	0.5	R	At stop sign
0.2	0.7	R	**Rt. 44** at stop sign
0.1	0.8	BR	**Rt. 272N/Norfolk Rd.**
0.2	1.0		Entrance to **Haystack Mountain State Park** on left
4.1	5.1		Turnoff for **Campbell Falls** on left. (Ride about 0.5 miles down dirt road and follow the sound of water through the woods to the falls.)
3.9	9.0		**Buggy Whip Factory**
0.5	9.5	BR	Unmarked **New Marlborough-Southfield Rd.**
1.2	10.7	R	**Rt. 57** at stop sign
0.4	11.1	BR	**Rt. 183 S/South Sandisfield Rd.**
11.6	22.7	BR	**Rt. 182A** (Turn is before the sign.)
1.4	24.1	R	**Rt. 182** at stop sign
2.8	26.9	R	**Rt. 44W** at double stop signs
0.7	27.6	R	**Laurel Way**
0.6	28.2	L	**Maple Ave.** at stop sign
0.2	28.4		Arrive at Manor House Inn

The Stanton House Inn

Tog & Doreen Pearson,
Innkeepers   Phone: (203) 869-2110
76 Maple Avenue   Fax: (203) 629-2116
Greenwich, CT 06830
Rates: Budget-Moderate B&B; Suites available
Open all year

The Stanton House Inn, an elegant white colonial structure on tree-lined Maple Avenue, sits just a stone's throw from the center of the tony coastal New York City suburb of Greenwich, Connecticut. In a town that is home to the rich and famous, and where many of the houses are the size of hotels, the Stanton House is one of a kind. It offers the warm comforts of a country manor, and is just a few minutes by foot from top-notch restaurants and shops and a few minutes by bike from an array of cultural and outdoor attractions. In a community that offers few lodging options, the Stanton House is a gem.

And if its walls could talk, tales of its former inhabitants would be endless. Over the years, the stately three-story mansion has changed hands several times. It was built in 1840 by John Sackett on land granted to one of his ancestors in the 1700s, and was expanded by a subsequent owner around the turn of the century to designs by noted architect Stanford White. Today's inn, however, is the namesake of renowned American feminist Elizabeth Cady Stanton. The social reformer's granddaughter Nora Stanton Barney bought the house in 1937. A feisty woman in her own right, she fought the opposition of the town council and converted it to a lodging establishment that catered to returning war veterans.

When former banker Tog Pearson and his wife Doreen took over the house, which had been in Tog's family for a number of years, it needed a face lift. They embarked on a massive restoration project that included upgrading the rambling mansion's infrastructure, including electrical wiring and plumbing, as well as refurbishing and reconfiguring its sleeping quarters. They knocked down walls to create 22 bright, spacious rooms and suites of unexpected shapes and sizes. They installed modern bathrooms, while respecting the inn's classic colonial architecture. They meticulously painted and repaired the house top to bottom, returning it to its original splendor. And they decorated it with an elegant mix of antique and traditional furnishings, including classic oriental rugs and swag window treatments.

On the grounds, among the flowers and grand old trees, they installed a pool where guests can relax and enjoy their surroundings.

The inn's large, first floor common rooms—including two bright parlors and a dining room—have fireplaces, and are separated from the classic center hall entrance by French doors.

Among the guestrooms on the first floor, three have private outside entrances, which means guests do not have to go through the main house to get to their rooms. One of the favorites has a patio next to the garden.

All of the guest quarters feature modern amenities such as air conditioning, phones with voice mail, televisions, and hairdryers. Several of them have a fireplace and many have a wet bar with sink and stocked refrigerator. All are individually decorated using quality fabrics of tasteful florals and other delicate patterns. They also have private baths and, like the rest of the inn, will pass the most stringent white glove test.

The third floor rooms, with their unique layouts and interesting nooks and crannies, are the innkeepers'—and many guests'—favorites. Room 37, a cheery suite with a garden trellis separating the sleeping and lounging areas, also includes a table and chairs next to a wet bar. Room 39 has a pull-out sofa, in addition to the bed, and is filled with bright blue and yellow country prints with painted white wooden and wicker furnishings.

On the second floor, Room 28, a popular corner room at the front of the house, overlooks the pool and features a fireplace and small outdoor terrace. Room 20, a large, comfortable room decorated in off-whites and beiges, includes a fireplace, wet bar with refrigerator, and a microwave oven, and both a charming bath area with an antique iron clawfoot tub and a bathroom with shower.

A self-serve continental buffet breakfast is served each morning at individual round tables in front of the fireplace in the sunny dining room. It includes fresh cold and hot beverages and a large selection of breads and baked goods, including muffins and bagels and cream cheese. On the weekends, hot breakfast items such as eggs and bacon are served.

Bicycling from Stanton House Inn

Greenwich has multiple personalities. It's a coastal town with several impressive private harbors, exclusive yacht clubs, and town beaches for residents and guests. Yet inland it is surrounded by winding roads lined with thickly wooded land, old stone walls, and large gated estates. Located just 30 minutes by train from midtown Manhattan, it's a thriving and desirable suburban haven for commuters and a perfect quick getaway destination for city dwellers. It offers top-notch attractions for nature lovers and culture lovers alike. And the prestigious downtown shopping and dining area, within walking distance of the Inn, contrasts with and complements the quiet rural area that envelopes it.

The inn is located at a perfect starting point for exploring backroads. Without a map or cue sheet, however, riders can easily get lost on the intricate road system that laces the rolling hills of Fairfield County, Connecticut, and adjacent Westchester County, New York. The roads are narrow, with little to no shoulder, and twist and turn pleasantly. Inland there is no way to avoid the hills; it's just a matter of identifying your favorite kind: gently rolling or short, steep ascents and descents. Because the backroads bend so frequently and sometimes sharply—and because there are so many of them—traffic tends to be light and travels cautiously. On straight stretches and major routes, however, traffic is heavier and moves faster.

Along the coast the routes are relatively flat, but also more heavily traveled—particularly during the summer. The best time to ride to the beach is early in the morning on the weekends, or on weekdays.

The area has an active and large cycling community. Several local bike clubs organize frequent rides for cyclists of all abilities. On the weekends you'll likely encounter these brightly-dressed, spandex-clad groups along the routes.

Local Bike Shops

Greenwich Bicycles
40 W. Putnam Ave.
Greenwich, CT 06830
(203) 869-4141
www.greenwichbikes.com
Email: bikeinc@home.com
Sales, service, accessories for road and mountain bikes.

Cycle Dynamics
12 Riversville Rd.
Greenwich, CT
(203) 532-1718
Sales, service, accessories. Roadside service.

Dave's Cycle & Fitness Ct.
78 Valley Rd.
Cos Cob, CT
(203) 661-7736
Sales, service, accessories. Rentals with reservations.

Mountain Biking Opportunities

Mianus River State Park, on the Greenwich-Stamford border, offers novice fire trails and plenty of intermediate technical singletrack. It features scenic rolling hills and old stone walls. Take Stanwich Road to Cognewaugh Road; turn left off Cognewaugh to enter park.

Cranbury Park, in Norwalk, is home to one of Connecticut's oldest and largest mountain biking races, the Jack Rabbit Run. The race is part of the eastern circuit of NORBA's American Mountain Bike Challenge. Once a private estate, the park offers riders five miles of trails on 134 acres surrounding an historic mansion. It contains some nice singletrack and fast downhills. Because it's relatively small, it's difficult to get lost. You won't be alone, however, on the weekends. From Norwalk, take Route 7 north and turn right on Kensett Street, or enter harder trails off Grumman Avenue.

Huntington State Park, off Sunset Hill Road in Redding, has about 20 miles of trails for beginning and intermediate riders. Take Merritt Parkway north to Route 58 north; turn right on Sunset Hill Road and look for two stone pillars and parking on right.

Graham Hills, a 431-acre park in Mount Pleasant, New York, offers about 5 miles of aggressive singletrack for intermediate to advanced riders. Trails are color-coded. Take Taconic State Parkway or Saw Mill River Parkway to Bedford Road/Route 117.

More details on mountain biking in Mianus River State Park, Huntington State Park, and Graham Hills, including maps and cue sheets, can be found in *RIDE GUIDE: Mountain Biking in the New York Metro Area* by Joel Sendek. It is available at local bike shops for $14.95, or by calling Anacus Press at (908) 604-8110 or visiting www.anacus.com.

Two local recreational biking groups, Sound Cyclists Bicycle Club and Westchester Cycle Club (see details below), organize weekly mountain bike rides in the area. Both the Westchester Mountain Biking Association and the Connecticut Chapter of NEMBA can provide additional information on regional events, activities, and trails.

Other Resources

Coastal Fairfield County
Convention and Visitor Bureau
MerrittView, 338 Main Avenue
Norwalk, CT 06851
(800) 866-7925 or (203) 899-2799
www.visitfairfieldco.org

Sound Cyclists Bicycle Club
P.O. Box 3323
Westport, CT 06880
(203) 840-1757
Email: mailbox@soundcyclists.com
www.soundcyclists.com

Connecticut Chapter of
New England Mountain Biking Association (NEMBA)
P.O. Box 290956
Wetherfield, CT 06129-9956
http://members.aol.com/joeorto/index.html.

Westchester Cycle Club
www.westchestercycleclub.org

Westchester Mountain Bike Association
www.wmba.org

Manors, Mansions, and McMansions (20 miles)
Moderate, rolling hills

Ride up, down, and around the estate-lined undulating backroads that surround Greenwich. The roads are narrow and winding, with little to no shoulder and light traffic. Except for 0.3 miles on Mead Road, all roads are paved.

The tour can be combined with a hike and picnic in **Babcock Pre serve.** This 297-acre park, off Lake Avenue, just north of Old Mill Road, includes well-marked trails along ponds, streams, and meadows. There are no food stops along the route, so pick up a picnic and snack items in Greenwich.

Pt.-Pt.	Cume	Turn	Street/Landmark
0.0	0.0	L	**Maple Ave.** from Stanton House Inn parking lot
0.1	0.1	S	**N. Maple Ave.** at stop sign
0.6	0.7	BR	**Husted Lane** at Y
1.1	1.8	S	**Beechcroft Rd.** at stop sign
0.6	2.4	R	**Grahampton Lane** at stop sign
0.0	2.4	L	**Clapboard Ridge Rd.**
0.7	3.1	R	**Dairy Rd.**
0.4	3.5	BR	**DeKraft Rd.**
0.2	3.7	R	Unmarked **Butternut Hollow Rd.**
0.5	4.2	L	**Old Mill Rd.**
0.2	4.4	R	**Lake Ave.** at stop sign

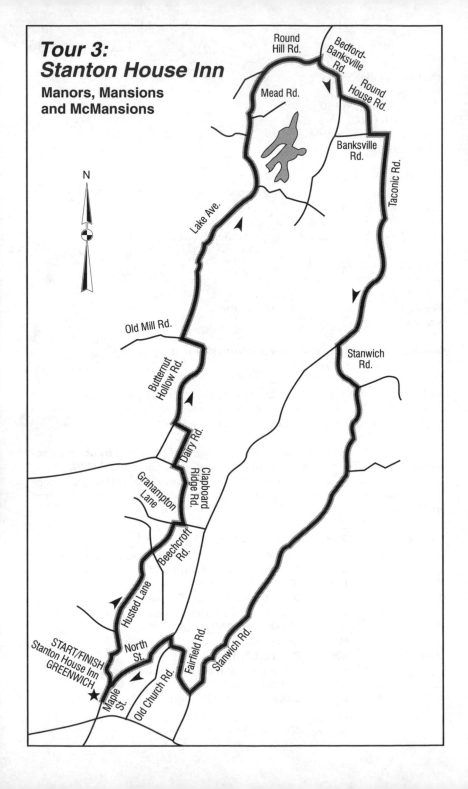

Pt.-Pt.	Cume	Turn	Street/Landmark
1.4	5.8	**BL**	**Lake Ave.**
0.5	6.3	**BR**	**Lake Ave.**
0.7	7.0	**L**	**Lake Ave.**
0.7	7.7	**BR**	**Lake Ave.** Dirt road for 0.3 miles. Becomes **Mead Rd.**
0.7	8.4	**R**	Unmarked **Round Hill Rd.** at stop sign
0.9	9.3	**R**	**Bedford-Banksville Rd.** at stop sign
0.8	10.1	**L**	**Round House Rd.**
0.5	10.6	**L**	**Banksville Ave.** at stop sign. Becomes **Taconic Rd.**
1.8	12.4	**S**	**Taconic Rd.** at stop sign
0.8	13.2	**L**	**Stanwich Rd.** at split
1.6	14.8	**BR**	**Stanwich Rd.**
2.8	17.6	**R**	**Stanwich Rd.**
0.4	18.0	**R**	**Stanwich Rd.** at stop sign
0.1	18.1	**R**	**Fairfield Rd.**
0.8	18.9	**BR**	**Old Church**
0.05	18.95	**L**	**North St.**, then left at stop light onto **North St.**
0.85	19.8	**L**	**N. Maple**
0.2	20.0		Arrive at Stanton Inn

Outdoor and Indoor Museums (19.3 miles)
Moderate, rolling hills

*(**Note:** Can be combined with optional Parks, Ponds, and Reservoirs loops for longer rides.)*

Discover the museum-quality collection of sculptures that dot 168 acres of beautifully tended landscape at the world headquarters of Pepsico. The **Donald M. Kendall Sculpture Gardens** include more than 40 works by major 20th-century artists, including Alexander Calder, Jean Dubuffet, Max Ernst, and Auguste Rodin. In fact, the garden itself, the creation of landscape designer Russell Page, is a work of art—from the more formal gardens near the building to the picnic grove by the pond to the stream garden. Pack a lunch and soak up the serene surroundings.

The ride also passes through the **State University of New York (SUNY)** campus in Purchase, which is dotted with sculptures, including works by Henry Moore and George Rickey. At the center of the 500-acre site sits the **Neuberger Museum of Art**, a 78,000-square-foot facility that houses a number of galleries and is home to more than 6,000 modern American and ancient art pieces, including a permanent collection of African art. Its collection includes works by artists such as Willem de Kooning, Jackson Pollock, Edward Hopper, and Milton Avery. A museum cafe sells a variety of sandwiches, soups, and snacks. The campus also features a four-theater performing arts center where there are year-round professional performances. The building also houses a 4,400-pipe mahogany Flentrop Organ that can float on jets of air and was too big for Carnegie Hall.

Most of the roads are narrow and winding, with moderately rolling hills. Riversville Road, King Street, and Anderson Hill Road tend to have more traffic, but have wider shoulders than the others. The center of Glenville, where there are several stores and traffic lights, is busy.

Pt.-Pt.	Cume	Turn	Street/Landmark
0.0	0.0	L	**Maple Ave.** from Stanton Inn parking lot
0.1	0.1	S	**North St.** at stop sign.
0.2	0.3	R	**Hillside Dr.**
0.3	0.6	R	Unmarked **Ridgeview Rd.** at stop sign
0.2	0.8	L	Unmarked **Ridgeview** at stop sign. (Andrews goes right)
0.4	1.2	L	Unmarked **Parsonage Rd.**
0.8	2.0	R	**Beechcroft Rd.**
0.6	2.6	R	**Grahampton Lane** at stop sign
0.0	2.6	L	**Clapboard Ridge Rd.**
0.9	3.5	R, L	Right at stop, then quick left on **Clapboard Ridge Rd.**
1.0	4.5	R	Unmarked **Round Hill Rd.** at stop sign
1.3	5.8	L	**Porchuck Rd.**
0.5	6.3	L	**Porchuck Rd.**
0.8	7.1	L	Unmarked **Riversville Rd.** at stop sign
1.1	8.2	R	**Sherwood Ave.**
1.1	9.3	R	**King St.** at stop sign
0.4	9.7	L	**Lincoln Ave.** Rough pavement
0.7	10.4	L	**Brigid Flanigan Dr.** on SUNY campus. (To visit the **Neuberger Museum**, turn right here and follow signs.)
0.1	10.5	R	**Lincoln Ave.** at stop sign
1.0	11.5	L	**Brigid Flanigan** (aka **SUNY Loop**) **Rd.** at stop sign
0.1	11.6	BR	To exit SUNY campus
0.1	11.7	S	Cross unmarked **Anderson Hill Rd.** at stop light. Enter **Pepsico campus**.
0.1	11.8	L	Toward visitor parking.
0.3	12.1	R	Enter far end of parking lot. Pick up map for gardens at information booth/restrooms.

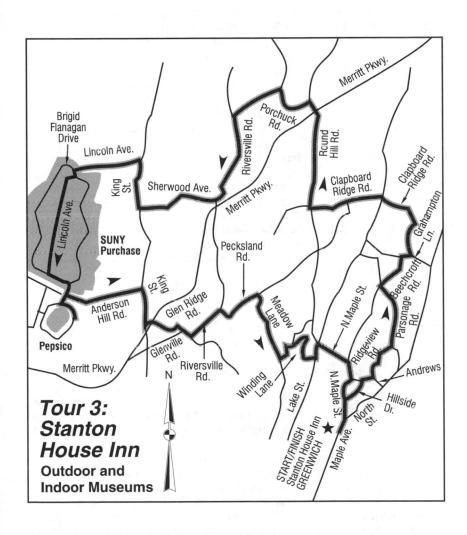

Brigid
Flanagan
Drive

Lincoln Ave.

King St.

Lincoln Ave.

SUNY
Purchase

Pepsico

Anderson
Hill Rd.

Merritt Pkwy.

King St.

Glenville
Rd.

Glen Ridge
Rd.

Riversville
Rd.

N

Sherwood Ave.

Riversville Rd.

Porchuck
Rd.

Merritt Pkwy.

Round
Hill Rd.

Clapboard
Ridge Rd.

Clapboard
Ridge Rd.

Grahampton
Ln.

Merritt Pkwy.

Pecksland
Rd.

Meadow
Lane

Beechcroft
Rd.

Parsonage
Rd.

Winding
Lane

Lake St.

N.Maple St.

Ridgeview
Rd.

Andrews

Hillside
Dr.

N.Maple St.

North
St.

Maple Ave.

START/FINISH
Stanton House Inn
GREENWICH

Tour 3:
Stanton
House Inn
Outdoor and
Indoor Museums

PtPt.	Cume	Turn	Street/Landmark
0.2	12.3	L	Exit parking. Head back to Pepsico entrance road.
0.3	12.6	R	At stop sign to exit Pepsico campus
0.2	12.8	R	**Anderson Hill Rd.** at stop light. *(***For optional Parks, Ponds, and Reservoirs ride, turn left here.)*
0.9	13.7	R	**King St.** at stop light
0.7	14.4	L	**Glen Ridge Rd.** (At the end of the bridge)
0.0	14.4	R	Make quick right onto **Ridge Rd.**
0.3	14.7	S	**Ridge Rd.** at stop sign
0.2	14.9	S	Unmarked **Glenville Rd.** toward center of Glenville.
0.1	15.0	L	**Riversville Rd.** at stop light. (Firehouse is on right.)
0.5	15.5	R	**Pecksland Rd.** (Longer loops rejoin at this intersection)
0.7	16.2	R	**Meadow Lane**
0.3	16.5	BR	**Meadow Lane** at stop sign
0.5	17.0	L	**Winding Lane**
0.8	17.8	L	Unmarked **Lake St.** at T
0.2	18.0	R	**N. Maple**
1.1	19.1	S	**N. Maple** at double stop signs
0.2	19.3		Arrive at Stanton Inn

Parks, Ponds, and Reservoirs (37.5 miles)

Longer Option: Combine with Outdoor and Indoor Museums tour for 49.6 mile ride
Moderate; moderately hilly terrain with one significant climb

If you haven't spent your whole day exploring the cultural attractions of Pepsico and SUNY and want to take in the unspoiled outdoors, this route incorporates an invigorating series of lakes, preserves, and wooded parks.

After climbing the hill on Park Lane, riders are rewarded with a fast descent and an opportunity to walk along the trails of **Cranberry Lakes Park**, or to relax at the base of Kensico Dam in the Kensico Plaza Park. Although the route takes riders across the top of the dam and offers great views of Kensico Reservoir, the best way to view the impressive World War I stone structure itself is from the park below. A detour along a brick access road to the left among the trees, just before crossing the dam, leads to **Kensico Plaza Park** at the base of the dam. Return to the route on the same road.

The route winds along the forested watershed of the reservoir, which supplies water to New York City residents, then through the small town of Armonk, where there are a number of restaurants and food shops. (Just north of town, the long and short routes split.)

About two miles north of Armonk, on Route 128, is **Wampus Pond County Park**, a nice shady park with pond-side picnic tables. Continue toward Mount Kisco and around Byram Lake, skirting the Leonard Park Wildlife Preserve and Butler Memorial Sanctuary

The last park on the route is the **Audubon Park** of Greenwich, a 280-acre wildlife sanctuary that features eight miles of marked trails, a picnic area, interpretive center, and environmental gift shop. More than 35 species of mammals and 160 species of birds have been sighted among its woods, ponds, streams, and meadows. The Audubon Center also provides information on the 127-acre Audubon Fairchild Garden, a wildflower sanctuary established in the early 1900s featuring more than 900 species of flora. Its entrance is just south of the Park, off Riversville Road, on North Porchuck Road.

The route mixes flat stretches with moderately rolling terrain, and includes two notable ascents followed by rewarding descents along tree-lined roads. All roads are paved, except a small section of packed dirt along Byram Lake. Traffic is heavier and faster along Routes 120 and 128, but they offer plenty of room for cyclists to share the road with cars.

Pt.-Pt.	Cume	Turn	Street/Landmark
0.0	0.0	L	**Anderson Hill Rd**. at light, leaving Pepsico campus
1.0	1.0	R	**Rt. 120/Purchase St.** at light
0.3	1.3	BL	Stay on **Rt. 120**
0.8	2.1	L	**Barnes Lane**
0.8	2.9	R	**Lake St.** at stop sign
0.3	3.2	L	**Park Lane.** Will climb for about 1.5 miles.
1.9	5.1	S	**Park Lane** at stop sign
0.6	5.7	L	Onto **Rt. 22** at light. Just after entrance to Cranberry Lake Park.
0.7	6.4	R	**West Lake Dr.**, at light. (On the left just after turn, before passing large pillars, is a brick road that leads to **Kensico Dam Park**)
1.4	7.8	BR	Unmarked **Columbus Ave.** at yield
0.1	7.9	R	**West Lake Dr.**
0.8	8.7	BL	Unmarked **West Lake Dr.**
0.3	9.0	R	**Charles St.**
0.0	9.0	L	**West Lake Dr.**

PtPt.	Cume	Turn	Street/Landmark
0.2	9.2	R	**Stevens Ave./West Lake Dr.** at stop sign
1.3	10.5	S	**West Lake Dr.** at stop sign
0.2	10.7	R	**Nanny Hagen Rd.** at stop sign
1.7	12.4	R	**Rt. 120 S** at stop sign
1.1	13.5	BR	Merge **Rt. 22 S/Rt. 120 S**
0.3	13.8	L	At light, toward **Rt. 120**
0.0	13.8	R,L,R	Make a U-turn around V onto **Old Post Rd.** (Don't continue on Rt. 120)
0.9	14.7	L	Unmarked **Old Post Rd.** at stop sign
0.1	14.8	S	Cross Rt. 22, onto **Old Rt. 22** at light
0.6	15.4	L	**Rt. 128 (Armonk Avenue)** at stop sign
0.8	16.2		*(**For shorter option: Turn right at School St., and follow cues below. Continue straight on Rt. 128 for longer option.)*
4.7	20.9	R	**Rt. 117 N**
0.4	21.3	R	**Byram Lake Rd.** (For optional visit to downtown Mt. Kisco, continue straight on Rt. 117/ E. Main St.)
0.4	21.7	BL	Stay on **Byram Lake Rd.** Nice steady climb.
5.7	27.4	BL	**Cox Ave.**
0.2	27.6	R	**Rt. 22** at flashing light, stop sign
0.1	27.7	L	**Rt. 433/N. Greenwich Rd.** at light
0.7	28.4	BL	**Riversville Rd.**
1.4	29.8	S	**Riversville Rd.** at stop sign. Entrance to Audubon Park of Greenwich is on left.
3.9	33.7	L	**Peckland Rd.**
0.7	34.4	R	**Meadow Lane**
0.3	34.7	BR	**Meadow Lane** at stop sign
0.5	35.2	L	**Winding Lane**
0.8	36.0	L	Unmarked **Lake St.** at T
0.2	36.2	R	**N. Maple**
1.1	37.3	S	**N. Maple** at double stop signs
0.2	37.5		Arrive at Stanton Inn

Shorter Option: Combine with Outdoor and Indoor Museum tour for 40.1 mile ride
Moderate; hilly terrain with two significant climbs

PtPt.	Cume	Turn	Street/Landmark
0.0	16.2	R	**School St.**
0.3	16.5	BR	At Y to stay on **School St.**, which becomes **Cox**
0.7	17.2	BR	**Byram Lake Rd.**

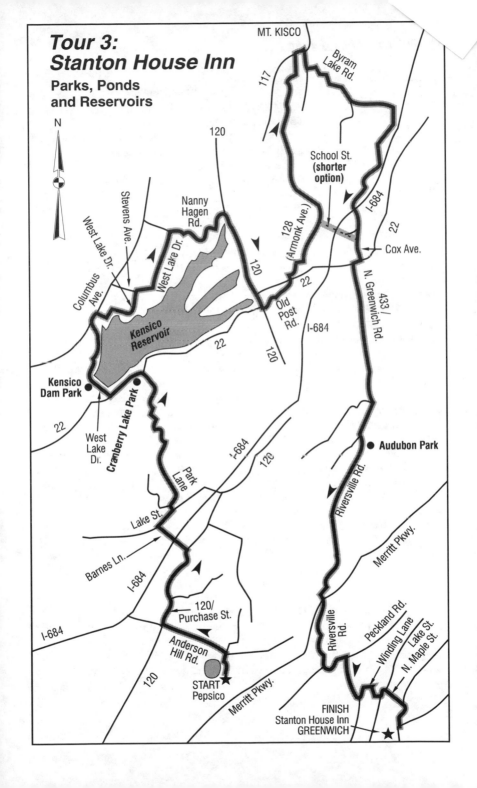

Pt.-Pt.	Cume	Turn	Street/Landmark
0.2	17.4	R	**Rt. 22** at flashing light, stop sign
0.1	17.5	L	**Rt. 433/N. Greenwich Rd.** at light
0.7	18.2	BL	**Riversville Rd.**
1.4	19.6	S	**Riversville Rd.** at stop sign. Entrance to Audubon Center of Greenwich is on left.
3.9	23.5	L	**Pecksland Rd.**
0.7	24.2	R	**Meadow Lane**
0.3	24.5	BR	**Meadow Lane** at stop sign
0.5	25.0	L	**Winding Lane**
0.8	25.8	L	Unmarked **Lake St.** at T
0.2	26.0	R	**N. Maple**
1.1	27.1	S	**N. Maple** at double stop signs
0.2	27.3		Arrive at Stanton Inn

Coastal Parks and More Museums (20.5 miles)
Easy to Moderate, mixes rolling hills with flat terrain

The Greenwich area's cultural and natural delights keep coming. Highlights of this tour include two museums and several parks and beaches.

The **Bush-Holley House Museum**, a classic 1732 saltbox in the historic district of Cos Cob, is the site of the first Impressionist art colony in America. Artists such as John Twachtman, Childe Hassam, Elmer Livingston MacRae, and J. Alden Weir summered here among the woodlands and coastal landscape to pursue open-air painting. The museum includes an impressive collection of 18th-century furnishings and art.

The former bluff-top home of wealthy textile merchant Robert Bruce, now the **Bruce Museum**, presents twelve changing exhibits annually, as well as a permanent natural science exhibit on the ecosystem of Long Island sound and mineral and science galleries with changing interactive exhibits.

Both **Bruce Park** and **Greenwich Point Park** are favorite recreation spots for locals. The 147-acre Greenwich Point features a large beach, as well as boating and picnic facilities and walking trails. Bruce Park, at the base of Bruce Museum, offers grassy spots to relax, tennis courts, horseshoe pits, and plenty of walking paths.

From Ferry Landing at Arch Street, residents can take a 30-minute boat ride to **Great Captains** and **Little Captain Islands**, where there are beaches and picnic areas. The lighthouse on Great Captains, although no longer active, was built in 1863 and resembles a "church lighthouse." All of the Greenwich Beaches are owned by the city and their use is limited to residents with beach cards. Ask the innkeepers for a guest card.

The first several miles of the ride involve climbing moderate hills, then the terrain levels out along the coast for pretty easy riding. There is a steep, winding descent on Cat Rock Road. Traffic tends to be heaviest on summer weekends around Old Greenwich and Greenwich Point. However, many residents cycle in these areas, so autos travel cautiously.

Pt.-Pt.	Cume	Turn	Street/Landmark
0.0	0.0	L	**Maple Ave.** from Stanton Inn parking lot
0.1	0.1	S	**North St.** at stop sign
0.2	0.3	R	**Hillside Dr.**
0.3	0.6	R	Unmarked **Ridgeview Rd.** at stop sign
0.2	0.8	L	Unmarked **Ridgeview** at stop sign (Andrews goes right)
0.4	1.2	R	Unmarked **Parsonage Rd.** at stop sign.
0.3	1.5	L	**North St.** at light. Busy road.
0.4	1.9	R	**Doubling Rd.**
0.6	2.5	R	**Hill Rd.**
0.4	2.9	L	Unmarked **Stanwich Rd.** at stop sign
0.6	3.5	R	**Cat Rock Rd.**
0.9	4.4	L	**Cat Rock Rd.** at Y. Be careful on steep, winding descent.
0.9	5.3	L	Unmarked **Valley Rd.** at stop sign
0.2	5.5	R	**Palmer Hill Rd.**
0.1	5.6	R	**Sheep Hill Rd.** (next to deli)
0.7	6.3	L	**Sound Beach Ave. ext.**
0.5	6.8	S	**Sound Beach Ave.** at light. Cross Putnam Ave.
0.4	7.2	R	**Sound Beach Ave.**
0.1	7.3	L	**Forest Ave.**
0.4	7.7	R	**Tomac Ave.** at stop sign
0.4	8.1	S	**Tomac Ave.** at stop sign
0.3	8.4	R	**Shore Rd.** at stop sign
0.5	8.9	S	**Shore Rd.** at stop sign
0.8	9.7		Enter **Greenwich Point Park**
0.0	9.7		Exit Greenwich Point Park, at booth
0.7	10.4	L	**Sound Beach Ave.**
0.9	11.3	L	**West End Ave.** at light
0.3	11.6	L	**Riverside Ave.** at yield sign
0.8	12.4	R	**Riverside Ave.**
0.4	12.8	L	**Riverside Ave.** onto RR bridge
0.2	13.0	L	**Lockwood Rd.** at stop sign
0.3	13.3	L	**Lockwood Lane** at stop sign
0.3	13.6	S	Cross Putnam at light onto **Sheep Hill Rd.**
1.2	14.8	L	**Palmer Hill Rd.** at stop sign

Pt.-Pt.	Cume	Turn	Street/Landmark
0.1	14.9	L	**Valley Rd.** at stop sign
0.4	15.3	S	**Valley Rd.** at stop sign
0.6	15.9	L	**River Rd. ext.**
0.2	16.1	S	**River Rd. ext.** Cross busy Putnam Ave.
0.7	16.8	L	**Strickland Ave.** at T. **Bush Holley Museum** is in front of you.
0.3	17.1	L	**Sound Shore Dr.**
0.5	17.6	L	Unmarked **Indian Field Rd.** at light. Cross over I-95.
0.3	17.9	S	**Indian Field Rd.**
0.2	18.1	R	**Davis Ave.**
0.4	18.5	L	**Bruce Park Dr.** at stop sign
0.3	18.8	S	**Museum Dr.**, to entrance to **Bruce Museum**
0.3	19.1	R	**Steamboat Rd.** at light. (Go straight on Arch St., just beyond motel to get ferry to Great Captains and Little Captain Islands and beaches.)
0.2	19.3	R	**Bruce Park Ave.** at light
0.1	19.4	L	**Mason St.**
0.1	19.5	BR	**Milbank St.**
0.8	20.3	BR	At split before light
0.0	20.3	S	Cross Putnam Ave. at light onto **Maple Ave.**
0.2	20.5		Arrive at Stanton Inn

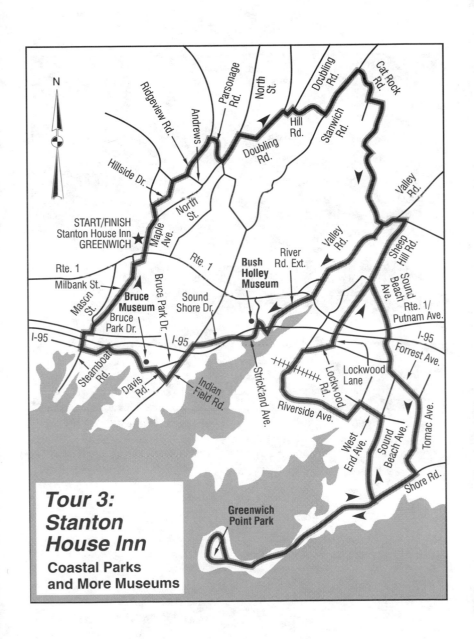

N

START/FINISH
Stanton House Inn
GREENWICH

Ridgeview Rd.

Parsonage Rd.

North St.

Doubling Rd.

Cat Rock Rd.

Andrews

Hill Rd.

Stanwich Rd.

Hillside Dr.

Doubling Rd.

North St.

Valley Rd.

Maple Ave.

Rte. 1

Rte. 1

Valley Rd.

Milbank St.

River Rd. Ext.

Bush Holley Museum

Sheep Hill Rd.

Mason St.

Bruce Museum

Bruce Park Dr.

Sound Shore Dr.

Sound Beach Ave.

Rte. 1/ Putnam Ave.

I-95

Bruce Park Dr.

I-95

I-95

Forrest Ave.

Steamboat Rd.

Davis Rd.

Indian Field Rd.

Strickand Ave.

Lockwood Lane

Lockwood Rd.

Riverside Ave.

West End Ave.

Sound Beach Ave.

Tomac Ave.

Shore Rd.

Tour 3: Stanton House Inn

Coastal Parks and More Museums

Greenwich Point Park

Captain Jefferds Inn, Kennebunkport, Maine

Maine Inns and Rides

As the country's most northeastern frontier, Maine has long been a magnet for people of strong independent spirit. It's known for its rugged land, rugged coastline, and population of rugged individualists.

It is perhaps lesser known as a land of romance—the kind of romance that fills a remote forested mountain or a craggy coastline where the ocean dances with the mountains.

For centuries Maine's industry has been dominated by logging, fishing, and agriculture. The dominance of these industries is giving way slowly—very slowly—to more modern industries. Yet its extensive forests and long Atlantic coastline continue to shape its appeal to vacationers and adventurers.

The state offers thousands of miles of spectacular cycling in remote areas with few towns and distractions, as well as in not-so-isolated areas, such as the coastal towns highlighted in this section. The three featured inns and the towns in which they reside are among the highlights of Maine's coast. However, a warning is due: these wonderful spots can get busy in the height of the tourist season, so the best time to visit would be at either the beginning or end of the season.

The **Captain Jefferds Inn** in historic Kennebunkport on the southern coast defines the splendor of this small port town once inhabited by wealthy sea merchants and captains. The town is now the summer home of President George Bush and a popular vacation destination. Strike off from Kennebunkport to explore scenic small fishing ports or the sandy beaches of Goose Rocks and Fortunes Rocks. Enjoy the fresh lobster catches and chowder that are served up by virtually every restaurant in town.

Further north in the town of Camden, the setting for the movie *Peyton Place*, a lively trio keeps **The Maine Stay** in ship-shape and serves up memorable Down East hospitality. Rides from this inviting inn on the edge of 5,500-acre Camden Hills State Park feature fantastic coastline, spectacular mountain views and scenic lakes. The town itself, voted one of the best places to live in America, possesses a sophisticated atmosphere and a scenic harbor filled with schooners.

Continuing north, amidst the highest coastal mountains and headlands on the Eastern Seaboard, sits Bar Harbor, home of **Manor House Inn**. The main attraction at Bar Harbor, however, is Acadia National Park, one of the most visited national parks in America. It boasts some of the most dramatic, rugged coastline in the country, as well as an intricate system of 50 miles of auto-free former carriage roads and 27 miles of paved roads for cycling. The inn itself is barely a stone's throw from the park's entrance and actually includes several buildings: an elegant restored mansion that's on the National Register of Historic Places, the original Chauffeur's Cottage and two newer Garden Cottages.

Resources
Department of Economic & Community Development
Maine Office of Tourism
59 State House Station
Augusta, ME 04333-0059
(207) 287-5710
(207) 287-2010, fax
www.state.me.us./

Bicycle Coalition of Maine
P.O. Box 5275
Augusta, ME 04332
(207) 865-4842 or 288-3028
www.bikemaine.org
BCM members receive *Maine Cyclist* newsletter; e-mail news and updates; listing of cycling resources in Maine including local clubs, bike shops, etc., information on issues and events.

Captain Jefferds Inn

Pat and Dick Bartholomew, Innkeepers

Jane Bartholomew, Host	Phone: (207) 967-2311;
P.O. Box 691	(800) 839-6844
5 Pearl Street	Fax: (207) 967-0721
Kennebunkport, ME 04046	Web: www.captainjefferdsinn.com
Rates: Moderate-Luxury,	E-mail:
in season, B&B	captjeff@captainjefferdsinn.com
Open all year, except Dec. 15 -30	

Historic Kennebunkport's streets are lined with well-manicured, gracious inns, mansions, and estates that once served as homes for wealthy merchants or as symbols of success for seafaring captains of yore. Captain Jefferds Inn today serves as a wonderful tribute to its early years and exudes a natural elegance befitting the town's heritage.

Daniel Walker built the impressive Federal-style mansion in 1804 as a wedding present to his daughter and her new husband Captain William Jefferds, and it stayed in the Jefferds family until 1884. Apartments in the carriage house were first rented seasonally by one of the previous owners in 1944, but it wasn't converted to a working bed and breakfast until prior owner Warren Fitzsimmons purchased it in 1983.

Dick Bartholomew, who was a large animal veterinarian, and his wife Pat, a microbiologist, combed the east coast for three years looking for the perfect property before "becoming charmed by this inn," adding that their recent renovations are the "product of (their) thoughts, history, inspiration, and imagination." Since purchasing it in 1996, they have meticulously refurbished and re-decorated the inn top to bottom in the spirit of their favorite places.

The Bartholomews run the inn with the assistance of their energetic daughter Jane, whose warmth and hospitality matches her parents—and their environs. Inndog Kate, a personable golden retriever, helps entertain guests and loves the fresh-baked cookies and treats as much as they do.

All of the inn's common areas and guestrooms are immaculately appointed with fine furnishings, including many family antiques and period reproductions. At the end of the day, guests tend to gather in front of the fireplace in the main living room, in the sunny garden room at the back of the house, or on its adjacent terrace. Tea, hot mulled cider, homemade lemonade and fresh-baked sweets are served in the garden room every afternoon.

Six of the inn's 16 guestrooms have fireplaces and all have private baths. In addition to the individually decorated rooms in the three-story mansion, there are several spacious suites in the carriage house with breezy screened-in porches. The rooms are decorated with quality furnishings, which include fourposter and canopy beds, and interesting architectural features. The Florida room, for example, has a skylight over the bed and trapezoidal doors overlooking the garden, and the Vermont suite, named after the innkeepers' home state, has exposed wood beams and an antique clawfoot tub in the bath. The in-room amenities and special touches include air conditioning, down-filled comforters, fresh flowers, and small bottles of liqueur.

Three-course gourmet breakfasts are served by candlelight in front of a warm fire, or on the terrace in the summer. These hearty meals include fresh fruit, a hot entrée, and fresh-baked muffins, breads, or coffee cakes, and feature specialties such as Pineapple Bread Pudding with Bourbon Sauce and Apricot-stuffed French Toast.

In the evening, walk through Kennebunk's historic district or to one of the restaurants in town, or simply relax with a book from the inn's library.

Bicycling from Captain Jefferds Inn

From Captain Jefferds cyclists can pedal along Maine's magnificent southern coastline, with its beaches, salt marshes, and rocky capes. Or they can ride to small fishing villages like Cape Porpoise, sandy beaches such as Goose Rocks or Gooch's, or along rural inland roads.

During the busy summer season, Kennebunkport is crowded with tourists and automobiles. Local drivers and tourists alike are accustomed to sharing the popular coastal route with cyclists; however, friendliness towards cyclists varies on other roads. The terrain is relatively flat with pleasant rolling hills and no significant climbs. The best and most enjoyable time of year to visit the region by bike is early in the season, or after Labor Day. During tourist season, ride early in the morning.

Cape-Able bike shop provides local cycling information, and the Kennebunkport Chamber of Commerce publishes in its *Welcome* magazine several short, easy rides around the town.

Local Bike Shop

Cape-Able Bike Shop
Townhouse Corners, 83 Arundel Rd.
Kennebunkport, ME 04046
(207) 967-4382
Sales, service, repairs, and accessories. Road, mountain, hybrid, and tandem rentals. Local maps and route suggestions.

Mountain Biking Opportunities

There are a number of easy, gentle mountain biking options on bridle paths and dirt roads around the Kennebunks (which is comprised of four villages: Kennebunk, Kennebunkport, Cape Porpoise, and Goose Rocks Beach). A pleasant ride follows the bridle path along the Mousam River in Kennebunk: it's off the entrance road to Sea Road School. Other paths are in Wonderbrook Park, off Summer Street, and the old train line behind Cummings Market in West Kennebunk.

For more serious off-road biking head to the rocky trails around **Mount Agamenticus**, to the south of Kennebunkport and east of Ogunquit. To access trails: From Ogunquit, enter Agamenticus Road/ Clay Hill Road off Main Street. Or follow Pine Hill Road to Route 1, then turn right on Mountain Road near Cape Neddick. From Mountain Road, continue until road turns to dirt and park. This forested area is dotted with ponds, marshes, streams and a stone wall. Atop the 691-foot mountain is an American Indian burial site and the tomb of St. Aspinquid, a Pawtucket medicine man who converted to Christianity and watches over the mountain. The beautiful but difficult and technical trails around Folly Pond are steep in places. On the west side of the mountain, near the base of a former ski resort, are more gentle rolling trails. Local group rides often meet on the weekend.

In the spring and fall, the York Parks and Recreation Department holds two mountain bike challenges for novice to expert riders, (207) 363-1040.

Other Sources and Services

Kennebunkport Chamber of Commerce
P.O. Box 740
Kennebunk, ME 04043
(207) 967-0857
kkcc@maine.org
www.kkcc.maine.org

Goose Rocks and Cape Porpoise (17 miles)
Easy

This gentle route takes riders along the rural back roads of the Kennebunks and its spectacular, varied coastline.

From Kennebunkport ride to Arundel, home to the Kennebunkport Historical Society—and Cape-Able bike shop. This area is named after the literary work of Kenneth Roberts, who contributed to much of Kennebunk's renown prior to President George Bush's arrival on the scene.

At the intersection of Route 9 and Goose Rocks Road notice on your left the "Clock Farm" with its unique clock tower. From here ride to Goose Rocks, whose more than two-mile long sweep of sandy beach is popular with swimmers and walkers alike and offers great birdwatching at its southeast end.

Cape Porpoise, with its white steepled church and fleet of lobster boats, represents the quintessential working Maine harbor, from which one catches a glimpse of the tiny lighthouse on Goat Island. It is also home to an alfresco seafood restaurant that offers what some think are the best views in the region.

From Cape Porpoise to Kennebunkport the road winds along the oft-photographed coastline, passing the summer home of former President Bush, Blowing Cave, and Spouting Rock.

All of the roads are paved, with traffic tending to be heavier and faster on North Street and Route 9. The best time to ride is early in the day.

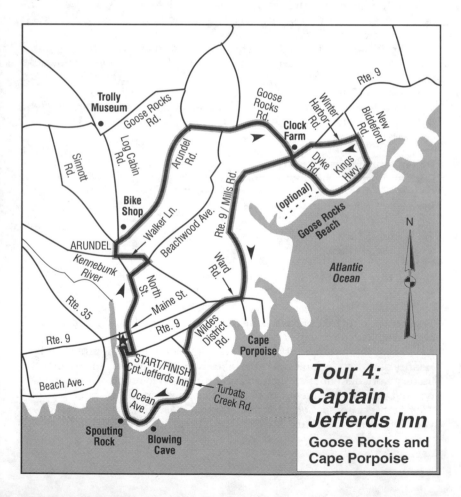

Tour 4: Captain Jefferds Inn
Goose Rocks and Cape Porpoise

Pt.-Pt.	Cume	Turn	Street/Landmark
0.0	0.0	R	**Pleasant St.** from garage of Captain Jefferds Inn
0.0	0.0	L	**Green St.**
0.1	0.1	L	**Maine St.** at stop sign
0.3	0.4	BR	**North St.**
0.9	1.3	BR	**Beachwood Ave.**
0.4	1.7	L	Unmarked **Walker Ln.**
0.3	2.0	R, R	**Log Cabin Rd.** at stop sign; then quick right onto **Arundel Rd.** (Cape-Able Bike Shop will be on your right just after second turn.)
2.2	4.2	BR	Unmarked **Goose Rocks Rd.** at stop sign at Y
2.0	6.2	S	**Dyke Rd.** at stop sign (cross Rt. 9)
0.6	6.8	BL	**Kings Hwy.**, and follow along beach. *(For optional side trip, bear right and follow road to end, 0.8 miles, where there's a path to the beach)*
0.7	7.5	L	**New Biddeford Rd.**
0.7	8.2	L	**Winter Harbor Rd.**
0.6	8.8	L	**Rt. 9/Mills Rd.** at stop sign
3.2	12.0	L	**Unmarked road** at stop sign. *(For optional 1-mile side trip to the pier in Cape Porpoise, continue straight and go over bridge.)*
0.0	12.0	R	Immediate right onto **Langsford Rd.**, past church
0.2	12.2	R	**Ward Rd.**
0.3	12.5	L	**Wildes District Rd.**
1.1	13.6	L	Unmarked **Turbats Creek Rd.**, just before the firehouse
0.0	13.6	L	**Turbats Creek Rd.** at stop sign
3.4	17.0		Arrive at **Pearl St.**

Coast to Country to Coast (41.1 miles)
Easy terrain

Make this loop a day-long excursion, take a swim at one of the many beaches, savor the beautiful scenery, explore some of the many coastal and inland attractions and distractions.

The ride begins with the popular sites along Ocean Avenue—the Bush family compound, Blowing Cave, and Spouting Rock—then through the unspoiled lobstering village of Cape Porpoise, scenery so spectacular that riders won't mind doing it twice if they do the Goose Rocks/Cape Porpoise loop.

From Goose Rocks ride along beautiful Fortunes Rocks, another beach popular with swimmers, walkers, and windsurfers, to the beautiful natural areas of Biddeford Pools. This area is dominated by the Rachel Carson National Wildlife Preserve, the Audubon Conservancy, and East Point Sanctuary, and its mile-wide tidal basin attracts many species of shore birds.

Pedal along the scenic rural roads to Arundel, where the Seashore Trolley Museum offers a diversion. On River Road, pass the Landing School of Boatbuilding and a herd of Belted Galloways, which kids call "Oreo Cookie" cows.

Cross the Kennebunk River and ride along the outskirts of Kennebunk, a town of glorious Federal-style houses. The Wedding Cake House, probably the most photographed house in the state, is adorned with Gothic filigree woodwork dripping from it like icing, the work of a shipbuilder who, in the 1840s, decorated the plain Georgian home beneath to surprise his bride on their wedding day.

Sea Road takes riders back to Kennebunkport and along Mother's and Gooch's beach, past the Franciscan Monastery and through the town's lively shopping district, with its many boutiques, galleries, and restaurants.

All roads are paved, and traffic is seasonal. The busier coastal and numbered roads tend to have wider shoulders than the inland roads, many of which have none.

Pt.-Pt.	Cume	Turn	Street/Landmark
0.0	0.0	L	**Pearl St.** from parking of Captain Jefferds Inn
0.0	0.0	L	**Ocean Ave.** at stop sign
3.4	3.4	R	**Unmarked Rd.** just before firehouse. Becomes **Wildes District Rd.**
1.2	4.6	S	**Rt. 9E** at stop sign
0.2	4.8	S	To go over bridge onto **Pier Rd.** in Cape Porpoise
0.7	5.5		Arrive at end of Pier Rd. where there are a number of eateries. Turn around to return via Pier Rd.
0.7	6.2	R	**Rt. 9E** at stop sign
2.8	9.0	R	**Dyke Rd.** The clock barn is opposite Dyke Rd.
0.7	9.7	BL	At split in road. Ride along **Goose Rock Beach** or take a swim
0.7	10.4	L	**New Biddeford Rd.**
0.8	11.2	S	Toward **Rt. 9**
0.1	11.3	R	**Rt. 9E** at stop sign
0.8	12.1	R	**Scadlock Mill Rd.** Just after the "Entering Biddeford" sign.

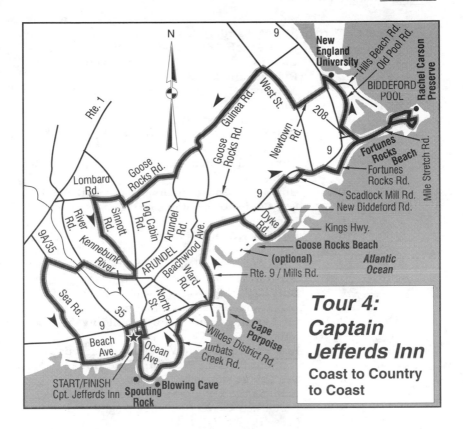

Tour 4:
Captain
Jefferds Inn
Coast to Country
to Coast

Pt.-Pt.	Cume	Turn	Street/Landmark
0.4	12.5	**R**	Unmarked **Rt. 9E** at stop sign
0.6	13.1	**R**	**Fortunes Rock Rd**. Another opportunity to go swimming or enjoy a sandy beach.
1.7	14.8	**R**	**Mile Stretch Rd.** Pass Rachel Carson Wildlife Refuge
1.0	15.8	**BR**	In Biddeford Pools area
0.2	16.0	**BR**	Unmarked **Orcutt Blvd.**
0.5	16.5	**R**	**Ocean Ave.** and follow coast
0.6	17.1	**R**	**Unmarked street** at stop sign
0.0	17.1	**L**	**Unmarked street** at stop sign
0.2	17.3	**L**	**First St.**
0.2	17.5	**L**	**Unmarked street**
0.2	17.7	**S**	**Unmarked street**
0.0	17.7	**BR**	**Lester B. Orcutt Blvd.**, pass post office and a few shops. Becomes **Yates St.**
0.4	18.1	**R**	Unmarked **Mile Stretch Rd.**
0.9	19.0	**R**	**Rt. 208/Bridge Rd.**
0.7	19.7	**BR**	**Old Pool Rd.** (Before junction of Rt. 9)

Pt.-Pt.	Cume	Turn	Street/Landmark
1.3	21.0	L	**Hills Beach Rd.** at stop sign. New England University Campus is in front of you
0.4	21.4	L	**Rts. 9W** and **208S**
0.1	21.5	R	**Newtown Rd.,** which has a rough asphalt surface.
1.5	23.0	R	Unmarked **West St.** at stop sign
1.5	24.5	L	**Guinea Rd.** at 4-way stop. West St. Market is in front of you.
2.3	26.8	R	Unmarked **Guinea Rd.** (After bend in road. Easy to miss)
1.0	27.8	BR	Unmarked **Goose Rocks Rd.** at yield
1.5	29.3	R	**Log Cabin Rd.** at stop sign
0.2	29.5	L	**Lombard Rd.**
0.8	30.3	L	**Sinnott Rd.** at stop sign
2.3	32.6	R, R	Right at stop, then quick right onto **River Rd.** Cape-Able Bike Shop is off Arundel Rd. to your left.
1.5	34.1	L	**Durrells Bridge Rd.** at 3-way stop sign. A farm with unusual belted Galloway cows is next to the **Landing School of Boatbuilding** on your right.
0.4	34.5	R	**Rts. 9A W and 35 N.** Very busy road. Ride with caution. Pass the **Wedding Cake House**.
0.9	35.4	L	**Sea Rd.** at stop light. *(To visit town of Kennebunk continue straight for about 1 mile)*
2.4	37.8	S	Unmarked **Beach Ave.** at stop light. Cross Rt. 9.
2.8	40.6	R	**Rt. 9** at stop light
0.3	40.9	R	**Ocean Ave./Shore Dr.**
0.2	41.1		**Pearl St.** and Captain Jefferds Inn on your left.

The Maine Stay

**Peter and Donny Smith
and Diana Robson, Innkeepers**
22 High Street
Camden, ME 04843
Rates: Budget-Moderate, B&B
Open all year

Phone: (207) 236-9636
Fax: (207) 236-0621
Web: www.mainestay.com
E-mail: innkeeper@mainestay.com

The Maine Stay, which sits grandly in Camden's historic district, is one of the most hospitable places to stay in Maine, in one of the Pine Tree State's most attractive seaside locations. Often voted a top vacation destination in the Northeast—and one of the best places to live—Camden is a place where contrasts cohabit gracefully: where age-old mountains offering four-star views meet the blue-green sea; where sturdy lobster boats share the harbor with shining yachts; where cow-filled pastures give way to forested rugged coastline; where outdoor enthusiasts mingle with artists and artisans.

Just a short walk from Camden's shops and Penobscot Bay harbor, The Maine Stay is operated by an energetic trio. It has, according to *Country Inn* magazine, "three of the liveliest innkeepers on the coast." Retired Navy Captain Peter Smith, his wife Donny, and her identical twin Diana "keep the place shipshape and delight guests with their enthusiasm." Sometimes, they also delight them with their musical talent. Known as the Maine Stay Merry Muffin Makers, a Barber Shop quartet minus one, they will (with a little prodding) sashay from the kitchen to the dining room and break into perfect harmony.

Their stately white clapboard house, like 61 other buildings in the impressive 65-acre High Street Historic District, is listed on the National Register of Historic Places. Originally built as a two-story house in 1802 by a carpenter and housewright, subsequent owners added an additional story and a half and an ell connecting the house to a large carriage barn. Today, the wood-framed post and beam structure, with its gabled slate roof, is an eclectic yet elegant mix of Federal, Greek Revival, Gothic, and Italianate architectural elements.

The house is nestled at the base of Mt. Battie, from whose peak Camden native daughter Edna St. Vincent Millay was inspired to write "Renascence." The 800-foot-high mountain dominates Camden Hills State Park, which boasts some 30 miles of scenic trails, including one that originates in the inn's backyard. The inn's wooded glen, with a brook running though it and an occasional animal nibbling on the tulips, is a perfect spot for guests to relax or explore.

Inside, guests tend to gather in front of the fireplace in one of the two tastefully furnished sitting rooms on the first floor, or in the kitchen next to the 1800s Queen Atlantic cast-iron stove. Unlike most inns, the Maine Stay welcomes guests in its informal kitchen. They can help themselves to the cookie jar or hot beverages, such as herb teas, gourmet hot chocolate and coffee. Or they can strike up a conversation with the congenial innkeepers as they whip up one of their favorite recipes. The kitchen also houses the innkeepers' computer, from which they'll print out one of their cataloged recipes or a trip guide (for cyclists and non-cyclists alike) featuring local attractions. In a separate TV room, guests also find a useful collection of reference materials and books on the region.

The inn features eight individually furnished guestrooms and suites, six of which have private baths. Rooms in the main house are named after the art on the walls. A favorite, the Clark Suite, is the namesake of English artist Graham Clark. Four of his hand-painted lithographs hang on the walls of this cheery two-room suite, which has bookshelves and a fireplace bordered by lovely decorative tiles. The Stitchery Room, actually two interconnected rooms on the third floor, features the twins' stitchery projects. One room has a queen bed, and the smaller one has a high antique iron twin bed. The art highlight of the Kilham Room is one of several renderings of the Maine Stay (used in an L.L. Bean catalogue) created by nationally-known local artist Anne Kilham. The Rackham room is adorned with ten original, turn-of-the-century illustrations by Arthur Rackham, illustrator of many children's books including *Peter Pan* and *Wind in the Willows*. Three windows in this room overlook the wooded garden.

The Carriage House Room, a large chamber on the ground floor at the back of the house, is considered very private and romantic. It has a queen bed, lots of books, a Vermont Castings stove, and French doors that open onto a stone patio.

Guests are treated to a hearty breakfast, served either family-style at a long harvest table in the main dining room, or at individual tables in the sunny breakfast room overlooking the garden. Early risers will find a fresh pot of coffee in the kitchen at 5:30 a.m. Each day, the inn alternates between a plentiful buffet and a served hot breakfast. These fresh, healthy meals include a variety of options to suit any appetite. Specialties include baked apples, Gramma's pancakes, quiche, waffles with warm maple or blueberry syrup, granola (made fresh every two days), and fresh fruit salad with yogurt.

Good-humored innkeepers and small special touches—such as chocolate-filled candy dishes, hair dryers in the baths, and a "lucky bag" (actually a basket) of toiletries in the upstairs hall, in case guests forget something—have earned the Maine Stay a well-deserved reputation for providing Down East hospitality at its best.

Bicycling from Maine Stay Inn

Camden, known as the place "where the mountains meet the sea," offers a broad range of cycling options, from the more gentle routes along the coast to hillier routes through and around the mountains. This combination also offers breathtaking scenery and diverse attractions.

Route 1 tends to be busy with faster moving traffic. Many of the back roads have no shoulder, but little traffic, particularly in the off-season. In fact, outside the season cyclists can practically have the roads to themselves.

Peter, a cyclist himself, rode 15 miles a day to work when he was stationed in Japan. He has on hand a number of suggested bicycle tours around Camden, or he'll print out a map from his computer and highlight pleasant cycling routes. He also recommends that cyclists take the ferry from Lincolnville to Islesboro to explore its 35 miles of passable roads.

Several road and mountain bike rides are organized during the week by local cycling groups. Check bike shops for details.

Local Bike Shops

Brown Dog Bikes
53 Chestnut Street
Camden, ME   04843
(207) 236-6664
browndog@midcoast.com
Sales, services, accessories. Rents road, mountain, hybrid, and tandem bikes. Weekly rides for local club meet here.

Maine Sport Outfitters
P.O. Box 956 (Route 1)
Rockport, ME   04856
(207) 236-7120 or (888) 236-8797
(207) 236-7123, fax
mainespt@midcoast.com
Sales, service, accessories. Rents mountain and hybrid bikes. Weekly rides for local club meet here. Also organizes kayaking and fishing adventures.

Mountain Biking Opportunities
The **Camden Hills** Off Road Bicycling Association has convinced state officials to let bikers use two trails in the park. If successful, more trails could be added. Maps are available at the Park Visitor Center, off Route 1 just north of the inn, (207) 236-3109

The **Camden Snow Bowl** ski area on Ragged Mountain offers a nice selection of single- and doubletrack trails, including plenty of technical riding. The Snow Bowl also is the site of the Fiddlehead/Maine Sport Cyclo-Cross USCF-sanctioned race. Parking is off Barnestown Road: from Camden, take Mechanic Street (or John Street) to Hosmer Pond Road, following signs to Snow Bowl. You can also enter trails off Rollins Road.

Spruce and **Pleasant Mountains**, just west of Rockport, are also favorite local off-road riding areas. Ask at local bike shops for details.

Other resources
Camden-Rockport-Lincolnville Chamber of Commerce
P.O. Box 919
On the Public Landing
Camden, ME   04843
(800) 223-5450 or (207) 236-4404
www.camdenme.org
Email: chamber@camdenme.org

Camden Hills Off Road Bicycling Association
(Fiddlehead Cycling Club)
P.O. Box 900
Camden, ME   04843
(207) 236-2383 or 4592
Email: wbc@acadia.net
Weekly training series and club rides. Mountain biking and cyclo-cross race series.
Also can call Maine Sport Outfitters at (207) 236-7120 for information.

Killer Warm-up: To the Top of Mt. Battie (5.6 miles)
Challenging

Head to the summit of Mt. Battie and experience the magnificent view that inspired Edna St. Vincent Millay to write:

> *All I could see from where I stood*
> *Was three long mountains and a wood*
> *I turned and looked another way*
> *And saw three islands in a bay*

This challenging little ride follows the paved Camden Hills State Park toll road to the top of the 800-foot mountain, where there's a look-out tower and spectacular views of Penobscot Bay and beyond. See why this is called the place "where the mountain meets the sea."

Pt.-Pt.	Cume	Turn	Street/Landmark
0.0	0.0	L	From Maine Stay driveway onto **Rt. 1N**
1.3	1.3	L	Enter **Camden Hills State Park**, turn left after entering the park for climb to top
1.5	2.8		Arrive at **top of Mt. Battie**; turn around to return the way your came
1.5	4.3	R	**Rt. 1 S**
1.3	5.6		Maine Stay Inn is on your right

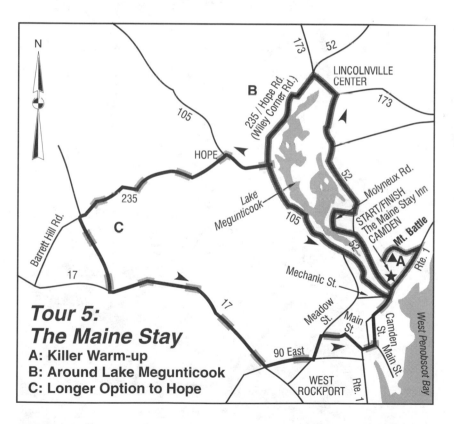

**Tour 5:
The Maine Stay**
A: Killer Warm-up
B: Around Lake Megunticook
C: Longer Option to Hope

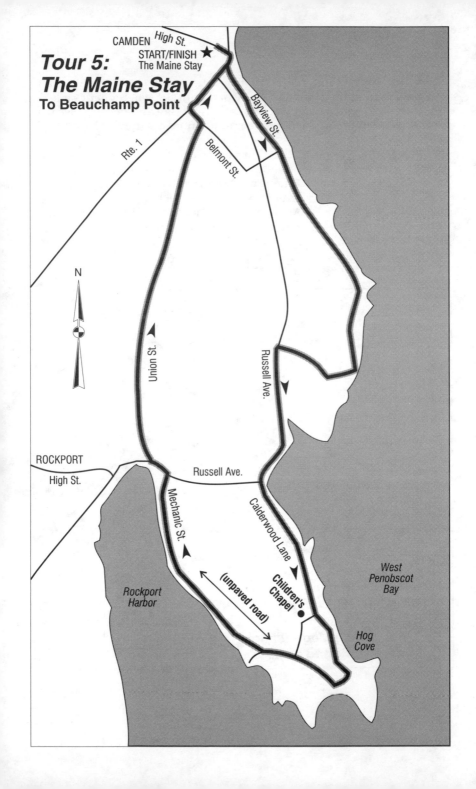

To Beauchamp Point (6.8 miles)
Easy

*(**Note:** Can be combined with Lake Megunticook Loop for moderate 23-mile ride.)*

For a leisurely warm-up ride, enjoy this scenic ramble along Camden's harbor and the rocky coast to the unspoiled village of Rockport. On the return, pass under the Camden/Rockport arch, a notable landmark which during the '60s read "Welcome to Peyton Place."

Just outside town, pass pebbled Laite Beach, a hidden swimming and picnicking area, and continue skirting the ocean, pedaling through woods and farmland. Along the way, pass a herd of Belted Galloways, unusual cattle called the "Oreo cookie cows" because they are black on both ends and white in the middle, at the Aldemere farm. The simple wooden Children's Chapel on Vesper Hill sits on a serene spot overlooking the water and is surrounded by a flower garden that's open from sun up to sun down. Rockport, a gathering place for artists and musicians, is home to the Rockport Opera House, Anne Kilham and Maine Coast Artists Galleries, and the Maine Photographic Workshop. Its Marine Park harbor, a good picnic spot, boasts a view of Indian Island lighthouse, a statue of honorary harbor master Andre the Seal, and an antique narrow gauge steam engine like the ones that once hauled lime from the surrounding region to a trio of old kilns.

This easy route covers a few gentle rolling hills (but the scenery is so spectacular you won't event notice them) and includes about one mile on packed dirt. There is little traffic, except along Route 1 through town.

Pt.-Pt.	Cume	Turn	Street/Landmark
0.0	0.0	**R**	**Rt. 1 S**
0.3	0.3	**L**	**Bayview St.**
1.7	2.0	**L**	Unmarked **Russell Ave.** at stop sign
0.6	2.6	**L**	**Calderwood Lane**
0.6	3.2		Turn right at stone marked Vesper Hill to visit **Children's Chapel,** then return to Calderwood Lane
0.3	3.5	**BR**	Onto **unpaved road**
1.1	4.6	**BR**	Onto unmarked **Mechanic St.**, paved
0.2	4.8	**L**	Unmarked **Russell Ave. (Anne Kilham Gallery** is at 142 Russell)
0.1	4.9	**S**	**Union St.** to return to Camden *(Bear left here to visit the town of Rockport. 0.2 miles to the center of town, then left over the bridge to Marine Park.)*
1.4	6.3	**BL**	**Belmont St.** at stop sign

PtPt.	Cume	Turn	Street/Landmark
0.0	6.3	**R**	**Rt. 1 N** at stop sign
0.4	6.7		(Turn left on Mountain St./Rt. 52 at flashing light to do ride around Lake Megunticook)
0.1	6.8		Arrive Maine Stay Inn

Around Lake Megunticook (16.4 miles, with 29.9 mile option)

Easy to moderate, with option for more challenging longer loop

This route takes riders around scenic, peaceful Lake Megunticook and, at its northern tip, Norton Pond, both of which provide beaches for fresh water swimming. The 1,108-acre lake is surrounded by mountains and dotted with islands.

For riders who would like to combine the ride with a hike, the trailhead for Maiden Cliff is off Route 52 just after leaving Molyneaux Road. Follow old logging trails and a small stream through the woods and open rock ledges to the summit of the 800-foot cliff that overlooks the lake and mountains to the west. Route 235 affords great mountain views. The roads are paved, with relatively good surfaces; many of them do not have shoulders, but traffic is light.

PtPt.	Cume	Turn	Street/Landmark
0.0	0.0	**L**	Leaving driveway for Maine Stay Inn
0.1	0.1	**R**	**Mountain St./Rt. 52 N** at flashing light
1.6	1.7	**L**	**Molyneaux Rd.**
0.7	2.4	**BR**	Stay on **Molyneaux Rd.**
1.6	4.0	**L**	**Rt. 52N** at stop sign
1.9	5.9	**BL**	Stay on **Rt. 52N/Camden Rd.** at Y
1.4	7.3	**L**	**Rts. 52 N** and **173 N** at stop sign. Lincolnville General Store is in front of you.
0.7	8.0	**L**	**Rt. 235 S**, becomes **Hope Rd.** (aka **Wiley Corner Rd.**)
2.9	10.9	**L**	**Rt. 105 E** toward Camden at stop sign at Y *(Turn right here to pick up optional Hope loop for longer ride.)*
5.1	16.0	**L**	**Mechanic St.** at stop sign in Camden
0.1	16.1	**L**	**Rt. 1 N** at stop sign
0.3	16.4		Arrive at Maine Stay Inn

Longer Option to Hope (18.9 miles)

This longer option takes riders over lots of rolling hills and a few challenging climbs as they travel through rural and forested areas, passing lots of lakes, including Hobbs Pond, Alford Lake, Fish Pond, Grassy Pond, and Mirror Lake. Route 235, south of Hope, presents some nice climbs along Hatchet Mountain and Simmons and Barrett Hills. Again, all of the roads are paved with good road surfaces, and varying shoulders. Busier Route 17 has a wide shoulder.

Pt.-Pt.	Cume	Turn	Street/Landmark
0.0	0.0	**R**	**Rts. 105 W/235 S** toward Hope at stop sign at Y
1.2	1.2	**L**	**Rt. 235 S** at split in road at Hope General store
4.8	6.0	**BL**	Stay on **Rt. 235 S**, where Barrett Hill joins the route
2.2	8.2	**L**	**Rt. 17E**, toward Rockland, at stop sign
5.4	13.6	**L**	**Rt. 90 E** at stop light in town of W. Rockport
1.4	15.0	**L**	**Meadow St.**
0.8	15.8	**R**	**Main St.** at stop sign
1.3	17.1	**S**	**Main St.** at stop sign (cross Rt. 1)
0.1	17.2	**L**	**Camden St.**
0.7	17.9	**R**	**Rt. 1 N** at stop sign, toward Camden
0.5	18.4	**S**	Continue on **Rt. 1** at flashing light
0.5	18.9		Arrive at Maine Stay Inn

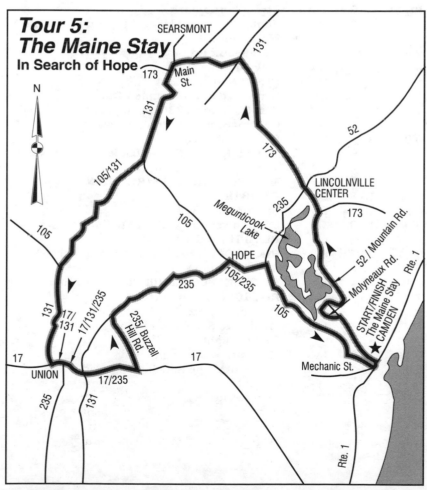

**Tour 5:
The Maine Stay**
In Search of Hope

In Search of Hope (43.3 miles)
Challenging

This challenging route offers lots of hill climbing and beautiful scenery through forests and farmlands, and skirts several picturesque quiet lakes. Pass through the small towns of Searsmont and Union. Route 173 offers a nice climb along Levenseller Mountain. From Searsmont to Union Routes 101 and 131 parallel the St. George River, a popular destination for paddlers, and Sennebec Pond at the base of Appleton Ridge. The Pond's northern wetlands are home to an array of waterfowl including wood ducks, mallards, black ducks, and blue heron. Route 235 between East Union and Hope offers another series of sweet climbs along Barrett and Simmons Hills and Hatchet Mountain.

All roads are paved, with varying shoulder widths.

Pt.-Pt.	Cume	Turn	Street/Landmark
0.0	0.0	R	From driveway at Maine Stay Inn onto **Rt. 1 S**
0.1	0.1	R	**Mountain Rd.**
1.6	1.7	L	**Molyneaux Rd.**
0.7	2.4	BR	Stay on **Molyneaux** at split.
1.6	4.0	L	**Rt. 52 N** at stop sign
1.9	5.9	BL	Stay on **Rt. 52N/Camden Rd.** at Y
1.4	7.3	L	**Rts. 52 N** and **173 N** at stop sign. Lincolnville General Store is in front of you.
0.9	8.2	S	Stay on **Rt. 173 N**
5.1	13.3	L	Stay on **Rt. 173N**, also **Back Belmont Rd.** at stop sign
1.7	15.0	L	**Main St. N/Rt. 131S/Rt. 173 N**
0.8	15.8	BL	**Rt. 131S**
0.5	16.3	BL	Stay on **Rt. 131S**
3.0	19.3		Continue south on **Rt. 131**
7.0	26.3	L	**Rts. 17E/131 S**
0.4	26.7	S	**Rts. 17E/131S/235N** at flashing light
0.6	27.3	S	**Rts. 17E/235N**
2.1	29.4	L	**Rt. 235N/Buzzell Hill Rd.** toward Hope
7.1	36.5	R	**Rts. 105E/235N** in Hope
1.2	37.7	S	Continue on **Rt. 105E**
5.2	42.9	L	**Mechanic St.** in downtown Camden at flashing light
0.1	43.0	L	**Main St.** at stop sign
0.3	43.3		Arrive at Maine Stay Inn

Manor House Inn

Mac Noyes, Innkeeper
106 West Street
Bar Harbor, ME 04609
Rates: Budget-Moderate,
low season;
Moderate-Deluxe, peak, B&B
Closed December - March

Phone: (800) 437-0088 or (207) 288-3759
Fax: (207) 288-2974
Web: www.acadia.net/manorhouse
E-mail: manor@acadia.net

Manor House Inn, a huge, elegant Victorian mansion, serves as the perfect home base for exploring one of America's most spectacular national parks. Located on historic, tree-lined West Street, it's within walking distance of the many shops and restaurants in downtown Bar Harbor and just a mile away from Acadia National Park's Park Loop and Carriage Roads.

The restored mansion, which is on the National Register of Historic Places, is full of antiques, oriental carpets on beautifully polished floors, and Victorian period accessories and floral wallpaper. The three-story manor, known as Boscobel, was originally built in 1887 as the summer house of Colonel James Foster. Today, the inn is comprised of the mansion, the original Chauffeur's Cottage, built in 1897, and two newer Garden Cottages, all situated on an acre of pleasantly landscaped grounds and gardens.

Bar Harbor native Mac Noyes bought the inn in 1989, after having arranged financing for a number of inns in his previous career as a banker. A high energy, multi-talented inn owner, he did the needed restoration, repair, and decorating work himself.

The common rooms in Boscobel feature the original maple floors, working fireplaces, a baby grand piano, and lots of room for guests to socialize with each other, or find their own corner. A small but comfortable TV and reading room is tucked away on the third floor. From the way the towels are folded to the guest bathrobes in each room to the decorative dishes of potpourri, small touches and attention to detail create a warm, comfortable atmosphere.

All of the sleeping rooms in the mansion have queen- or king-size beds and private baths, and many have working fireplaces. Like the rest of the house they're furnished with beautiful period pieces such as large hand-carved wooden beds and dressers. An attractive, roomy suite on the third floor, perfect for a family, includes a garden view room with queen bed, another room with two twin beds and a sitting area. Rooms 2 and 7 also have private sitting areas. Room 4, a spacious chamber with fireplace, is furnished with antique oak furnishings, including a rocking chair, dresser, and desk, white lace curtains, and a stuffed chaise lounge.

The Chauffeur's Cottage offers three rooms and suites with private entrances: two on the first floor, and a "Honeymoon Suite" that covers the entire second floor. This spacious suite includes a bedroom with king-size bed and skylight window, sitting room with fireplace, stained glass windows, full bath, and a porch.

Afternoon tea, featuring hot and cold beverages and fresh baked goods, is served in the former butler's pantry on the first floor of the mansion. In the fall, to take the chill off, Mac puts out hot cider and baked goods such as pumpkin cookies. Guests can enjoy the sumptuous treats in one of the common rooms or on the huge wrap-around porch which is full of wicker furniture (including a swing) and flower pots. The inn doesn't serve alcohol, but does allow guests to consume their own favorite spirit or brew.

In the morning, a breakfast buffet is laid out in the butler's pantry and guests can dine next to the fireplace in the dining room at the large formal table, a smaller table by the window, or at one of the tables in the living room. Cyclists can fuel up on a hearty meal of home-baked goods (Mac cooks too), such as fresh blueberry muffins and cranberry bread, fruit salad and cereals. Each day a different hot entree, such as quiche, blueberry French toast, or eggs Florentine, is served. The inn's signature dish is Breakfast Bread Pudding with apple cider sauce.

Biking from Manor House Inn

Bar Harbor sits on the eastern side of Mount Desert Island, most of which is covered by Acadia National Park. The island got its name when explorer Samuel de Champlain ran aground on it in 1604. He dubbed it the *L'Ile des Monts Deserts*, French for "the island of bare mountains." Here, riders find the highest coastal mountains and headlands on the Eastern Seaboard and some of the most dramatic scenery and rugged, natural beauty in the Pine Tree State. Cyclists experience miles and miles of spectacular vistas in a way that most park visitors can't imagine.

Acadia offers some 50 miles of picturesque auto-free dirt carriage roads and 27 miles of paved roads suitable for cycling. During high season, mid-June to Labor Day, auto traffic is heaviest (some 4 million people visit the park annually). Very early in the season and late in the season, however, cyclists practically have these roads to themselves.

The western half of Mt. Desert Island, or the "quiet side" as locals call it, is more rural, less visited, and dotted with marshes, coves, and an occasional village. This side's largest town, Southwest Harbor, has less than 2,000 inhabitants and ranks among the top 10 commercial fishing harbors in Maine, and boat building is the main industry.

Due to Mount Desert's northern coastal location, temperatures tend to be moderate in the summer. The high temperatures in July and August range between 70 and 80 degrees; in the spring and fall, they're in the 50s and 60s. Be prepared for changes in temperature and dress in layers.

The Park Loop Road, which presents 20 miles of moderate to difficult riding, is a popular ride with experienced cyclists. Well marked and easy to follow with a park map, it includes several long climbs, including a tough climb up Champlain Mountain.

Local bike shops, Park Headquarters, and innkeeper Mac Noyes can provide additional suggestions and tips for cycling on the island.

Local Bike Shops
Bar Harbor Bicycle Shop
141 Cottage Street
Bar Harbor, ME   04609
207-288-3886
www.barharborbike.com
Sales, service, clothing, and accessories. Rents mountain and tandem bikes and accessories, such as panniers, car racks, and trailers.

Acadia Bike
48 Cottage Street (across from Post Office)
Bar Harbor, ME   04609
207-288-9605
Sales, service, accessories. Rents regular and tandem mountain bikes and accessories. Also rents kayaks and canoes.

Mountain Biking Opportunities
Due to fragile soil conditions and erosion problems, off-road riding is not permitted in Acadia. Hiking trails and private carriage roads are off-limits. However, the public carriage roads and fire roads offer an abundance of enjoyable mountain biking on more than 50 miles of dirt and crushed stone paths that wind through the heart of the park.

Other resources
Biking on Mount Desert Island
By Audrey Minutolo, Down East Books, Camden, ME
(800) 766-1670
18 routes on paved and carriage roads through Mt. Desert. Author's family owns Bar Harbor Bike Shop.

Acadia's Biking Guide and Carriage Road Handbook
Tom St. Germain, Parkman publications. Collection of short loops on paved and carriage roads. Available at Park Information offices.

Mount Desert Island Bicycle Association
P.O. Box 531
Bar Harbor, ME   04609
(207) 288-3028 or 3886
Publishes free "Bicycling in Acadia" brochure, which highlights three safe routes from Bar Harbor.

Acadia National Park
P.O. Box 177
Bar Harbor, ME   04609-0177
(207) 288-3338
www.nps.gov/acad/anp.html

Bar Harbor Chamber of Commerce
93 Cottage Street
Bar Harbor, ME   04609
(207) 288-5219 or 2404
(800) 345-4619 or (800) 288-5103, winter

Park Loop Coastal Highlights (13 miles)
Moderate
This short excursion is full of picture postcard scenes. It allows riders to combine breathtaking highlights of Acadia's rocky eastern coastline with a ride along flat, quiet Schooner Head Road where they get a great view of Champlain Mountain and pass a beaver pond.

Just after entering the park (there's no fee for bicyclists), go up a short hill past Sand Beach, where a grindstone that was part of a lumber schooner that ran aground in 1911 served as a mount for a machine gun during WWI to protect the island from landings by German saboteurs. Next, pass Thunder Hole, where the ocean hurtles into a 55-foot canyon with a roar, then ride around the tip of Otter Point and savor the sweeping views of Otter Cove.

As you ride downhill on Route 3, Dorr Mountain and The Tarn, a small lake, are to the left. Also pass Jackson Laboratory, an internationally-renowned center for genetic research, which presents lectures and films explaining its work three times a week.

All roads are paved with good road surfaces, and the volume of traffic depends on the season. On Route 3 the traffic is heavier and faster than on the other roads.

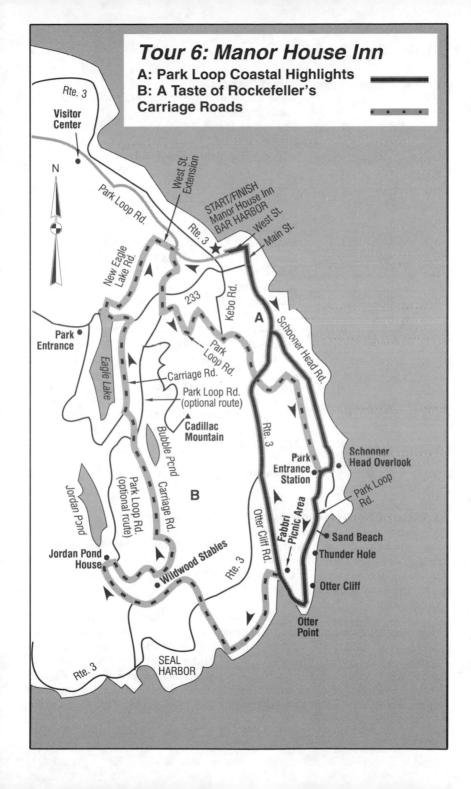

Pt.-Pt.	Cume	Turn	Street/Landmark
0.0	0.0	R	**West St.** from driveway of Manor House Inn
0.1	0.1	R	**Main St./Rt. 3**
1.5	1.6	L	**Schooner Head Rd.** at Ocean Drive-In Restaurant and Dairy Barn
0.3	1.9	BL	Stay on **Schooner Head Rd.** at Y
2.2	4.1	R	Toward Park Loop Road. For a view similar to Champlain Mountain Overlook, but a little closer to sea level, turn left here and go 0.1 miles to the **Schooner Head Overlook.**
0.1	4.2	L	Enter **Park Loop Road**
0.5	4.7		Entrance for **Sand Beach** on left. Take a swim here if you don't mind the numbing water, which is only about 50 degrees at the warmest.
0.9	5.6		**Thunder Hole** is on your left
0.7	6.3		Approaching Otter Cliffs do not follow signs to Bar Harbor. Stay on **Park Loop** and enjoy the view near the 110-foot-high cliffs, the highest headlands on the Atlantic coast north of Rio de Janeiro.
0.8	7.1	R	Go through parking area for Fabbri Memorial Picnic Area
0.1	7.2	L	Unmarked **Otter Cliff Rd.** at stop sign, following sign for Bar Harbor and Rt. 3.
1.7	8.9	R	**Rt. 3 W** at stop sign
4.0	12.9	L	**West St.** at end of Main St.
0.1	13.0		Arrive at Manor House Inn

A Taste of Rockefeller's Carriage Roads (25.3 miles)

Moderate, with 6 miles on packed dirt

Like the loop above, this one includes the spectacular highlights of the eastern coastal road of Acadia. It combines them with six scenic miles through forested land on the park's carriage roads.

On Park Loop Road, take in Sand Beach, Thunder Hole, and Otter Creek Cove.

On the Carriage Roads, get a taste of the details and workmanship that went into designing and building the elaborate 50-mile system between 1913 and 1940. Get an up-close look at the Jordon Pond Gate Lodge and magnificent hand-cut stone bridges that blend harmoniously with their environment and which few park visitors see. Ride past Bubble Pond and Eagle Lake, the largest body of fresh water in the Park, covering approximately 425 acres and averaging 50 feet in depth. Enjoy lunch or a snack at Jordan Pond House, the island's only tea house, which is known for its big, brown, and feather-light popovers and homemade ice cream. From its back lawn, soak up the view of Jordan Pond, framed by the cliffs of Penobscot Mountain, the "Bubbles," and the Pemetic Mountain.

A hybrid or mountain bike is preferable for the carriage roads, but not necessary for the six miles on this route, which is mostly on solid packed dirt. As one Park Ranger points out: Before the mountain bike craze everyone rode road or touring bikes. Nevertheless, skinny racing tires would not be appropriate.

Riders who would like to stay on paved roads and cycle the entire challenging park loop should stay on Park Loop Road at Jordan Pond House.*

Pt.-Pt.	Cume	Turn	Street/Landmark
0.0	0.0	L	From Manor House Inn onto **West St.**
0.3	0.3	S	Cross Rt. 3 onto **West St.** extension
0.8	1.1	L	**Park Loop Rd.**, following sign to Sand Beach
1.3	2.4	L	Following **Park Loop Rd.** to Sand Beach at stop sign at split. Becomes one way.
5.3	7.7		Detour to the left off Park Loop Road (just before entrance booth) and go 0.2 miles for the amazing views from **Schooner Head Overlook**
0.1	7.8	S	Enter **Acadia National Park**. No fee for cyclists.
0.5	8.3		Entrance for **Sand Beach** to your left..
0.9	9.2		**Thunder Hole** is on your left
0.7	9.9		As the road approaches Otter Cliffs do not take the turn off to the right for Bar Harbor. Continue to the top of Otter Cliffs and enjoy the bird's eye view. You're on the highest headlands on the Atlantic coast north of Rio de Janeiro.
0.3	10.2		**Otter Point**
4.9	15.1		**Wildwood Stables** is on your right.
1.0	16.1	R	Enter **Carriage Road** just before the Jordan Pond Gate Lodge. Just in front of you on the left is the **Jordan Pond House**. Good stop for a view of the pond and lunch or a snack of one of their famous popovers. (*Riders who would like to do the entire, more challenging, loop road, continue straight here.*)
1.2	17.3	S	Do not turn off toward Seal Harbor.
2.7	20.0	S	At end of Bubble Pond, pass the parking lot (on your left) and cross the Loop Rd. to continue on the **Carriage Road.**

Pt.-Pt.	Cume	Turn	Street/Landmark
0.4	20.4	**BR**	**Carriage Road** toward Bar Harbor and Eagle Lake
1.9	22.3	**R**	Exit the Carriage Rd. system through the parking lot, and turn right on **Rt. 233/Eagle Lake Rd.**
0.2	22.5	**L**	At "Entering Acadia National Park" sign, onto unmarked **New Eagle Lake Rd.** (aka **New Mills Meadow**)
1.1	23.6	**S**	Continue straight. Do not go over Duck Brook bridge.
0.8	24.4	**L**	Unmarked **West St.** extension at stop sign
0.6	25.0	**S**	Cross Rt. 3, onto **West St.**
0.3	25.3		Arrive at Manor House Inn

*To the inn from Park Loop Road: Pass Bubble Pond, climb along the side of Cadillac Mountain, and after a short downhill bear right at the fork in Park Loop Road. Pick up the one-way road, passing the Gorge Path, then take the first unmarked road on the left, Kebo Road, which joins Eden in Bar Harbor. Then turn right onto West Street. Or bear left at the fork in Park Loop Road and return the same way you entered, via the West Street extension.

The Quiet Side (47.2 miles)
Challenging

(Note: *Can be shortened to 32 miles by beginning in Town Hill, where you can park your car at the firehouse.)*

This route, a popular training ride for local cyclists, cuts through the rural countryside and small villages and harbors of the western "Quiet Side" of Mount Desert Island, an area often overlooked by visitors to the region.

Crooked Hill Road, lined with farms, including one with a stone barn, leads to Town Hill, the kind of village where life centers around the commons and firehouse. Indian Point Road, which has no shoulder, is a serene byway lined with evergreen forests.

Along Route 102 traffic tends to move faster, and riders pass through the small towns of Seal Cove and West Tremont, before reaching Tremont (derived from *trois monts*, French for three mountains), where lobstering is the primary industry.

Next on the route: Bass Harbor Head Lighthouse, built in 1858, which marks the entrance to Blue Hill Bay. Then Wonderland, the natural rock National Seawall, and the wonderfully unpretentious town of Southwest Harbor. The second largest town on Mount Desert, fishing and boat building are its primary industries. It's home to a number of restaurants, cafes, and shops, including a bike shop.

Ride along Echo Lake, the only freshwater lake in the park where swimming is permitted, then through Somesville, the first settlement on the Island and now a National Historic District. From Town Hill retrace the route to Bar Harbor.

There are a number of rolling hills. All roads are paved, but some, particularly Route 102, have a fair amount of traffic (for these parts), especially during the high season. The best bet: get an early morning start.

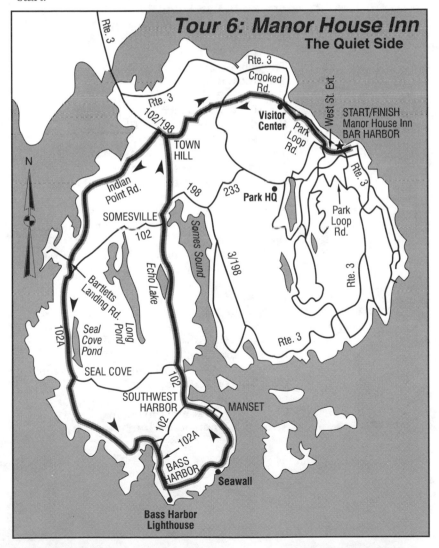

Pt.-Pt.	Cume	Turn	Street/Landmark
0.0	0.0	**L**	**West St.** from driveway of Manor House Inn
0.3	0.3	**S**	Cross Rt. 3 to unmarked **West St.** extension at yield sign
0.9	1.2	**R**	**Park Loop Road** at stop sign at T
1.8	3.0	**R**	At stop sign near Visitor Center
0.1	3.1	**L**	**Rt. 3**
0.3	3.4	**L**	**Crooked Rd.**
4.8	8.2	**R,L**	Right onto **Rts. 102/198** at stop sign; then immediate left at Y at Town Hill Market
0.3	8.5	**L**	**Indian Point Rd.**
1.7	10.2	**BR**	Stay on **Indian Point Rd.**
4.0	14.2	**L**	**Bartletts Landing Rd.** at stop sign
0.2	14.4	**BR**	**Rt. 102** at Y, following signs for Bass Harbor Lighthouse
3.8	18.2		Turn off for **Seal Cove**
4.8	23.0	**BR**	**Rt. 102A** at fork, following signs for Bass Harbor
0.2	23.2	**R**	**Rt. 102A** at stop sign
0.7	23.9	**BL**	**Rt. 102A**, follow sign for Bass Harbor Lighthouse
0.8	24.7		To view the picturesque **Bass Harbor Head Lighthouse**, leave 102A and go 0.4 miles down the road. Prettiest view is from trail off left side of parking lot.
2.4	27.1		Pass **National Seawall.** (About 1 mile after the seawall, make an optional turn to the right to visit the quaint village of **Manset**, headquarters of famed boat builders **Hinckley Co.**)
2.8	29.9	**R**	**Rt. 102** at stop sign at T, following signs to Ellsworth and Southwest Harbor
1.3	31.2	**S**	**Rt. 102**
4.5	35.7		Enter Somesville
1.2	36.9	**S**	**Rt. 102**
2.1	39.0	**R**	**Crooked Hill Rd.**
4.8	43.8	**R**	**Rt. 3** at stop sign.
0.3	44.1	**R**	Enter **Acadia National Park**
0.1	44.2	**L**	**Park Loop Rd.** at stop sign
1.8	46.0	**L**	Follow signs to Bar Harbor
0.8	46.8	**S**	Cross Rt. 3 onto **West St.**
0.4	47.2		Arrive at Manor House Inn

Massachusetts Inns and Rides

Massachusetts, a state whose history was shaped by pilgrims, pioneers and patriots, is a pedaler's paradise.

From the fishing ports and sandy beaches on its North Shore to the rolling hills and cultural attractions of the Berkshire Hills—from the Norwottuck Rail Trail in Amherst to the quiet, history-lined lanes surrounding Stow—New England cycle touring doesn't get much better.

Each of the featured cyclist-friendly inns from these four corners of Massachusetts boasts distinctly different—yet authentic—Yankee architecture and atmosphere. All of them also claim lively pasts. Oh, if their walls could speak, what tales they could tell.

Allen House and **Amherst Inn,** Victorian sisters, sit across from the former Emily Dickinson homestead on Main Street of the bustling university town of Amherst. The region surrounding this popular town near the Connecticut River is bestowed with two descriptive nicknames: Pioneer Valley (promoted by the local tourism machine) and Happy Valley (used by proud locals). Just a couple blocks from the inns riders can pick up the paved Norwottuck Trail, a fine example of a Rails-to-Trails conversion. Or, they can head off into the smile-inducing, history-invoking countryside of Happy Valley.

In the southwestern corner of the state, the **Windflower Inn**, a sprawling classic Federal-style manor, is a perfect starting point for exploring the treasures of the Berkshires. Nearby Stockbridge offers a number of wonderful museums, while those who prefer to fill their day with serious cycling can tackle Mount Washington and visit Bash Bish Falls.

The **Miles River Country Inn**, a rambling Colonial house surrounded by 30 acres of meadows, woodlands, and marshes, represents a classic Boston North Shore estate. From the end of its long shady drive, riders can head for sandy beaches and picturesque port towns or rolling country roads lined with lush fields and forests.

About the same distance from Boston, but to its west, in a region legendary for its American Revolution battles and Nashoba Valley apple orchards, the **Amerscot House B&B** is tucked along a quiet country road in Stow. The circa 1734 red clapboard center chimney house even predates by almost a century the days when Ralph Waldo Emerson, Henry David Thoreau and Louisa May Alcott lived in nearby Concord.

No matter which of these four inns you visit, you'll ride past spots that inspired artists and that shaped early American history. You'll also find bike shops, clubs and other cyclists willing to share their knowledge of the area.

Mountain bikers and road bikers alike will find strong support organizations in Massachusetts. In fact, the New England Mountain Bike Association (NEMBA) is based in Cambridge and the Massachusetts Bicycle Coalition is an excellent resource for cycling-related activities in the state. Each July it sponsors MassBike, a week-long 400-mile tour around the state that covers scenic and historic towns from Eastern Massachusetts to the Berkshires and back.

Resources
Massachusetts Office of Travel and Tourism
State Transportation Bldg.
10 Park Plaza, Suite 4510
Boston, MA 02116
(800) 227-MASS or (617) 973-8500
(617) 973-8525, fax
email: vacationinfo@state.ma.us
www.mass-vacation.com
Publishes free *Massachusetts Getaway Guide,* Massachusetts Bicycle Guide, and "Bicycle Touring in Massachusetts" brochure.

Massachusetts Dept. of Environmental Management (DEM)
Division of Forests and Parks
100 Cambridge St.
Boston MA 02202
(617) 727-3180
www.magnet.state.ma.us/dem/parks
Manages over 280,000 aces of public land for protection and a variety of recreational activities including cycling

MassBike/Bicycle Coalition of Massachusetts
44 Bromfield St., Suite 207
Boston, MA 02108
(617) 542-BIKE or 542-2453
(617) 542-6755, fax
www.massbike.org
Cycling advocacy group that sponsors annual 400-mile week-long tour of the state.

New England Mountain Bike Association
P.O. Box 380557
Cambridge, MA 02238
(617) 497-6891 or 776-4686
Email: mtb-newengland@cycling.org
www.nemba.com

The Allen House

599 Main Street
Amherst, MA 01002
(413) 253-5000
http://www.allenhouse.com
Email: allenhouse@webtv.net

The Amherst Inn

257 Main Street
Amherst, MA 01002
(413) 253-5000

Ann and Alan Zieminski, Innkeepers
Rates: Budget-Moderate, B&B
Open all year

The Allen House and its sister B&B, The Amherst Inn, are ideally located just a few blocks from everything in this lively college town: Within a few cycling minutes are the bustling Town Common, several college campuses, and the 8.5-mile long Norwottuck Rail Trail, a great jumping off point for local riding.

The two inns, just several hundred yards apart (with a bike shop between), are classic stick-style Victorians that have been lovingly restored by energetic innkeepers Ann and Alan Zieminski. Stepping through their doors is like stepping back in time. In fact, the Zieminskis' historically accurate recreation of Aesthetic Movement decor in the Allen House earned them an Historic Preservation Award in 1991, and its original hand-carved cherry wood fireplace mantels are catalogued by New York's Metropolitan Museum of Art.

Alan, a former biochemist who lived in The Allen House as a student before buying it, absorbed its history and is responsible for the collection of period furnishings that fill the 18-room hostelry. Ann, a former dental hygienist, shares Alan's passion for delving into the history of their "painted ladies"—and their surroundings. Due to their inquisitive nature, the Zieminskis are also full of ideas for things to do and see in the Pioneer Valley.

The Allen House, built in 1886, is directly across the street from the Emily Dickinson homestead, and the three acres on which it sits were once part of the Dickinson family's farmland. The Amherst Inn was built in 1849 by Colonel Kingman, a former state senator whose oldest daughter was a friend of Amherst's famous poet.

Each of the inns has seven guest rooms, all with private baths. Despite their yesteryear qualities, the inns have been modernized with central air conditioning and in-room phones and modem jacks. The rooms are individually furnished with period pieces and accessories. There's lots of lace, floral wallpaper, lavish window treatments, accent pillows, oriental rugs, and fluffy down-filled comforters and pillows.

Afternoon and evening refreshments are served at guests' convenience between four o'clock in the afternoon and 10 o'clock in the evening. The Allen House's upstairs veranda with its ornate railing and rocking chairs is a favorite spot for guests to put up their feet and relax at the end of a day of touring. Or they can relax in front of the parlor fire. The Amherst Inn has two breezy porches that invite guests to unwind—one screened and one open-air.

Breakfast, also served at guests' convenience (even in bed, by special request), features a bountiful five-course meal with fresh seasonal fruit and homemade delights such as pumpkin bread, Swedish pancakes, or eggs Benedict. These morning repasts will satisfy even the hungriest cyclist.

Bicycling from The Allen House and Amherst Inn

Amherst and the "Five College" area boast an active and enthusiastic cycling community. And for good reason. The Pioneer Valley, along the Connecticut River and bordered by the Berkshire Hills, offers a wonderful array of scenic and varied cycling terrain for road and off-road enthusiasts alike. It's also a region rich in natural, cultural, and educational attractions.

The Norwottuck Rail Trail, one of two wide paved trails in the state's Forests and Parks System, provides 8.5 miles of traffic-free riding. Plans call for connecting it to the Northampton Bikeway, which begins on the opposite side of the Connecticut River in Northampton. The rural backroads surrounding Amherst carry light traffic. Numbered routes and town centers have heavier traffic patterns.

Valley Bicycles, which has a retail store on Main Street between the two inns, includes cue sheets for a number of local rides on its web site. So does Southampton Bicycle Center. During the riding season, the Franklin-Hampshire Freewheelers conduct organized rides in the area, and the local colleges boast an active bicycle racing community.

Local Bike Shops

Valley Bicycles
319 Main St.
Amherst, MA 01002
(413) 256-0880 or (800) 831-5437
Email: valleybike@aol.com
www.amherstcommon.com/valleybike/
Sales, service and accessories for road and mountain bikes. Rents hybrids, tandems, suspension mountain bikes, and trailers. Workshops and route information.

Bicycle World Too
63 South Pleasant St. (rear)
Amherst, MA 01002
(413) 253-7722
Sales, service and accessories.

UMASS Bike Co-op
Student Union Building
University of Massachusetts Campus
Amherst, MA
(413) 545-0647
www.umass.edu./rso/bikecoop
Provides bike repairs, tool rentals and sells parts and accessories.

Southampton Bicycle Center
247 College Highway/Route 10
Southampton, MA
(413) 527-9784 or (800) 527-9784
(413) 527-9250
http://virtual-valley.com/sohobike/index.html
Sales, service, accessories. Route information and maps.

Valley Bicycles
8 Railroad Street (Trailside shop)
Hadley, MA
(413) 584-4466

Mountain Biking Opportunities

They're everywhere! To the east and west of the Connecticut River, tens of thousands of acres of forest and state parklands get mountain bikers' mouths salivating and legs quivering.

Local bike shops, park headquarters, and the New England Mountain Bike Association (NEMBA) are good sources of trail information. Trail maps and information also can be purchased at some local book stores.

The **Amethyst Brook Conservation Area,** in Amherst, has a number of marked trails for moderately skilled mountain bikers. Entrance is off Pelham Road at the eastern end of Main Street.

South of Amherst, the **Holyoke Range** and **Skinner State Parks** cover nearly 3,000 acres along the spine of the Mt. Holyoke Range. The terrain is varied, but full of gnarly, unmarked trails. There's even a new technical course between the local and upper access trails in the Range.

The best bet is to pick up a map. The Notch Visitors' Center, (413) 253-2883, for Holyoke is on Route 116 between South Hadley and Amherst. Ranger Bill Danielson is the resident expert on mountain biking. For information on Skinner, call (413) 586-0350.

Mt. Toby Reservation, in Sunderland, boasts one of the highest points in the Pioneer Valley. It's managed by UMASS Department of Forestry, (413) 545-2110 or 2665, and offers moderate to difficult riding. The trailhead is located off Park Road. Take Route 116/Sunderland Road north; turn right on Silver Lane, then right on Park.

Wendell State Forest, which includes 7,566 acres of forested hills and the **Metacomet-Monadnock Trail,** is laced with trails of varying degrees of difficulty. The eastern side of the Forest tends to be flatter. The clear water of 10-acre Ruggles Pond makes an inviting swimming spot. Trail maps available at ranger station, (413) 659-3797. Take Route 63 north to Millers Falls; follow Wendell Road over the railroad bridge, then pick up Montague Road and follow signs.

Nearby **Erving State Forest's** 4,500 acres offer miles of easy to moderate riding on forest roads, snowmobile and hiking trails. Take Route 2 to Erving Center; turn at the fire station and follow signs. Trailhead at Laurel Lake, which invites riders to take a swimming break. Stop at forest headquarters south of Route 2 for maps.

Other Resources

Greater Springfield Convention & Visitors Bureau
1500 Main Street, P.O. Box 15589
Springfield, MA 01115-5589
(413) 787-1548 or (800) 723-1548
(413) 781-4607
www.valleyvisitor.com

Amherst Area Chamber of Commerce
409 Main Street
Amherst, MA 01002
(413) 253-0700
Email: chamber@amherstcommon.com
www.amherstcommon.com

Franklin-Hampshire Freewheelers
www.freewheelers.org

Bicycle and Road Map
The Berkshires, Connecticut River Valley, Quabbin Reservoir
Rubel Bike Maps
P.O. Box 1035
Cambridge, MA 02140
www.bikemaps.com
From Globe Corner Bookstores:
(800) 358-6013 or (617) 723-1676

Massachusetts DEM
Forest & Parks, Regional Headquarters
P.O. Box 484, Commonwealth Avenue
Amherst, MA 01004
(413) 545-5993
(413) 545-5995, fax
www.magnet.state.ma.us/dem/region4.htm

Connecticut River Roundabout (31 miles)
Easy to moderate

(Note: *Can be combined with optional Deerfield loop for longer ride.)*

Pack a picnic and pick one of the many scenic points along the way to dine al fresco.

Pedal the gentle, scenic Norwottuck Rail Trail to the Elwell Recreation Area, where a 1,492-foot iron bridge crosses the Connecticut River and Elwell Island, home to an array of rare plant species. The trail passes through the mile-long Hadley Common and offers beautiful views of the Holyoke Range from the bridge.

Ride through the vintage town of Hatfield and its Main Street lined with large colonial homes. Savor the open country road north of Hatfield lined with lush meadows and rich farm lands as you follow the Connecticut River. During the harvest season the route is dotted with fruit and vegetable stands. Pick your own berries, or snap a picture of the large wooden tobacco barns.

On the return to Amherst, stop for a dip in Puffer's Pond.

The route is relatively flat, with just a few gentle hills. All roads are paved, and most are lightly traveled except for approximately 0.5 miles along Damon Road near its junction with Routes 5 and 10. The numbered routes have heavier traffic and good shoulders, and traffic is more congested on East Pleasant and Main Streets in Amherst.

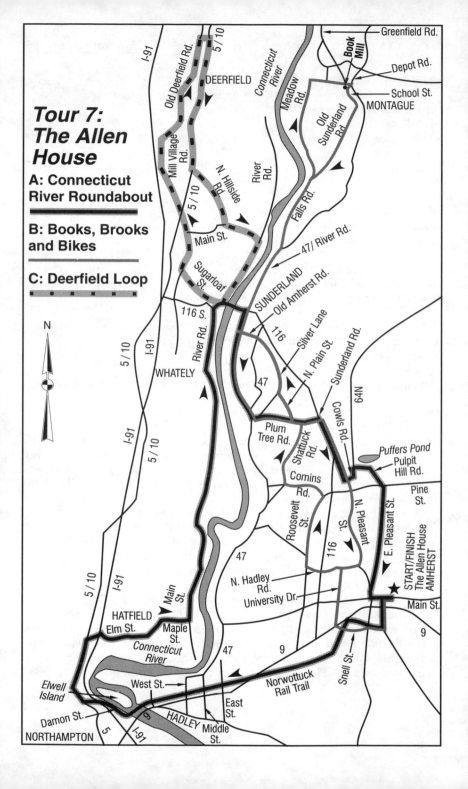

Pt.-Pt.	Cume	Turn	Street/Landmark

Start from Amherst Inn:

Pt.-Pt.	Cume	Turn	Street/Landmark
0.0	0.0	**L**	Onto **Webster St.** as you exit Inn
0.1	0.1	**L**	Onto unmarked **Spring St.**
0.1	0.2	**R**	Unmarked **Dickinson St.**
0.1	0.3	**S**	At stop sign cross Rt. 9 and enter **Amherst campus**

Pick up cue sheet below at 0.6 miles, from entrance to Amherst campus.

Start from Allen House:

Pt.-Pt.	Cume	Turn	Street/Landmark
0.0	0.0	**L**	Outside door of Allen House, onto **Whitney St.**
0.2	0.2	**R**	Stop sign. Right onto **Rt. 9**
0.4	0.6	**L**	Enter **Amherst campus** at intersection of Dickinson St.
0.0	0.6	**BL**	Follow signs toward tennis courts.
0.2	0.8	**S**	Road turns to gravel
0.1	0.9	**BL**	**Dirt road.**
0.0	0.9	**R**	At stop sign, onto paved **bike path**.
4.1	5.0	**S**	Cross East St. at stop sign
0.4	5.4	**S**	Cross Middle St. at stop sign. Valley Bicycles' trailside shop and ice cream stop are at this juncture.
0.4	5.8	**S**	Cross West St. at stop sign
0.8	6.6	**S**	Cross Crosspath Rd. at stop sign.
0.3	6.9	**S**	Enter the old railroad bridge and cross the Connecticut River
0.3	7.2	**R**	Onto **Damon St.** at stop sign. End of bike trail. Very busy road with no shoulder. Keep the faith. This misery will be short-lived.
0.9	8.1	**R**	Stop light. **Rts. 5/10.** Again very busy. Cycle with caution for next half-mile.
1.7	9.8	**R**	Turnoff for Hatfield. Cross Interstate on bridge on unmarked **Elm St.**, which later becomes **Maple St.**
2.2	12.0	**BL**	Onto **Main St.**, which becomes **River Rd.** outside Hatfield.
4.4	16.4	**S**	Hadley town line
3.6	20.0	**BR**	To stay on **River Rd.** *(**Turn left on Sugarloaf St. for Deerfield side trip)*

PtPt.	Cume	Turn	Street/Landmark
0.4	20.4	R	At stop sign to cross Connecticut River on **Rt. 116S**
0.5	20.9	R	At stop light onto **Rt. 47/S Main St.** Becomes **River Rd.** in Hadley
2.7	23.6	L	**Plum Tree Rd.**
1.5	25.1	R	**Rt. 116** at T
0.8	25.9	L	Onto **Sunderland Rd.** (116 continues straight) following signs to Cowls Sawmill and Lumber
0.5	26.4	L	Onto **Cowls Rd.** at sawmill.
0.3	26.7	L	Onto unmarked **Rt. 64 N.** Also **Montague Rd.**
0.2	26.9	R	**Pulpit Hill Rd.** Entering region of Mill River Recreation area.
0.3	27.2	R	Right onto **Mill St.** Entering Mill River Recreation Area
0.2	27.4	S	Stop sign
0.5	27.9	S	Crossroad after the waterfall. Cross unmarked State St., where Mill St. becomes unmarked **Sand Hill Rd.** *To go swimming, turn left and go 0.2 miles to Puffer's Pond swimming area. No fee.*
0.6	28.5	L	Onto unmarked **Pine St.** at stop sign
0.0	28.5	R	Quick turn onto **E. Pleasant**
2.0	30.5	L	Onto **Main St.**
0.3	30.8		Arrive at Amherst Inn
0.4	31.2		Arrive at Allen House

Books, Brooks, and Bikes (36 miles)
Easy to moderate

(Note: Can be combined with optional Deerfield loop for longer ride.)

The motto at the Bookmill in Montague is: "Books you don't need in a place you can't find." Once you *do* find this little hideaway, however, it's a great place to enjoy a riverside lunch on its terrace or at one of the picnic tables.

This gentle scenic route through Pleasant Valley (also referred to by locals as Happy Valley) offers bucolic farm and pastureland settings along the Connecticut River. On the left just north of the Route 116 and 47 intersection in Sunderland sits what is supposedly the oldest sycamore tree in New England.

All roads are paved, except 0.8 miles on Shattuck, and are relatively quiet. There is, however, heavier, faster moving traffic on Routes 116 and 48, which have good shoulders. The terrain is gentle, with just a few small easy grades.

Pt.-Pt.	Cume	Turn	Street/Landmark
From Allen House:			
0.0	0.0	L	Outside door of Allen House, onto **Whitney St.**
0.2	0.2	R	Stop sign. Right onto **Rt. 9**
0.4	0.6	L	Enter **Amherst campus** at intersection of Dickinson St.
0.0	0.6	BL	Follow signs toward tennis courts.
0.2	0.8	S	Road turns to gravel
0.1	0.9	BL	**Dirt road**
0.0	0.9	R	At stop sign, onto paved **bike path**
0.9	1.8	L,R	Exit bike path to the left, and go right on **Snell St.**
0.2	2.0	BR	**University Dr.**
0.1	2.1	S	**University Dr.** at light (Cross Rt. 116)
1.2	3.3	L	**N. Hadley Rd./Mass. Ave.**
0.7	4.0	R	At T onto **N. Maple St./Roosevelt.** Becomes **Meadow**
1.7	5.7	L	**Russellville Rd.**, becomes **Comins**
1.0	6.7	R	**Shattuck Rd.**
0.4	7.1		Shattuck turns to dirt for 0.8 miles. Becomes **S. Plain**
1.2	8.3	L	**Plum Tree Rd.**, at T
0.3	8.6	R	**N. Plain Rd.**
1.3	9.9	R	**Silver Lane** at T
1.0	10.9	L	**Old Amherst Rd.**
0.9	11.8	R	**River Rd./Rt. 47** at T
0.4	12.2	S	Cross Rt. 116 at light, continue north on **Rt. 47**
1.3	13.5	L	**Falls Rd.** at Y
1.6	15.1		Waterfall on right
0.2	15.3	L	**Meadow St.** at Y
2.7	18.0	R	**Meadow St.** at Y
0.6	18.6	R	**Greenfield Rd.** at Y

PtPt.	Cume	Turn	Street/Landmark
0.1	18.7	R	**Depot Rd.** (cross river) Bookmill on right
0.2	18.9	R	**School St.**
0.4	19.3	R	**Old Sunderland Rd.** at stop
1.9	21.2	L	**Meadow Rd.** at stop. Becomes **Falls Rd.**
1.7	22.9	R	**Rt. 47S** at stop
1.4	24.3	S	Cross Rt. 166 at light. Stay on **Rt. 47S/Main St.** (**Turn right and cross bridge to pick up Deerfield loop)
2.7	27.0	L	**Plum Tree Rd.**
1.5	28.5	R	**Rt. 116** at T
0.8	29.3	L	**Sunderland Rd.**
0.9	30.2	S	**N. Pleasant St.** at light
1.8	32.0	R	**Massachusetts Ave.** at light
0.5	32.5	L	**University Dr.**
1.2	33.7	S	At stop light onto **Snell**
0.3	34.0	S	At stop sign, cross E. Pleasant St.
0.0	34.0	L, R	Left to enter **bike path**, then right (east) on path
0.9	34.9	L	Exit bike path and pass tennis courts to exit campus at **College St./Rt. 9**
0.9	35.8		Retrace route to Inn.

Deerfield loop (13.8 miles)
Easy

Village Street in historic Old Deerfield is lined with houses dating to the early 1700s. Known today for its private schools and quintessential New England surroundings, the town has a rich early history.

South Deerfield was the site of both the Bloody Brook Massacre of 1675, when Indians siding with King Philip massacred settlers, and of the Deerfield Massacre of 1704 when it was burned by the French and their Indian allies.

The Deerfield Inn has an elegant cafeteria with outdoor tables, and the village museum, Memorial Hall, is one of New England's oldest. It houses a collection of early American furnishings, paintings, textiles, and Indian artifacts. Mill Village Road is lined with huge maple, sycamore, and shagbark hickory trees.

The terrain is fairly flat, with a few easy grades. All roads are paved, and traffic is a little heavier on Routes 5 and 10.

From Montague loop: Cross bridge; after traveling 0.8 miles on Route 116 turn right on Sugarloaf Street.

From Hatfield loop: Turn left on Sugarloaf Street.

Pt.-Pt.	Cume	Turn	Street/Landmark
0.0	0.0		Intersection of Rt. 116 and Sugarloaf St. Take **Sugarloaf** toward Deerfield.
1.0	1.0	R	**Main St.**
1.6	2.6	S	Cross Rts. 5 & 10. Road becomes **Mill Village Rd.**
2.2	4.8	L	Stay on **Mill Village Rd.**
1.1	5.9	L	**Old Deerfield St.** at triangle
0.7	6.6	BR	**Old Deerfield**
0.3	6.9	R	**Rts. 5 & 10** at T
3.0	9.9	L	**N. Hillside Rd.** at Y
1.5	11.4	L	**Hillside Rd.** at T
0.9	12.3	R	**River Rd.** at T
1.5	13.8	L	**Rt. 116** toward bridge. Cross Connecticut River, and turn **right** on **Rt. 47/Main St.**

Amerscot House, Stow, Massachusetts

Amerscot House

Doreen and Jerry Gibson
61 West Acton Road
P.O. Box 351
Stow, MA 01775
Rates: Moderate, B&B
Open all year

Phone: (978) 897-0666
Fax: (978) 897-6914
Web: www.amerscot.com

The American and Scottish flags hanging side by side outside the Amerscot House give away the origin of its name. Doreen and Jerry Gibson blend her Scottish hospitality with his American affability to create an inviting, comfortable B&B tucked off a quiet, rural road in Stow, Massachusetts.

Stow, one of the state's earliest colonial towns, doesn't attract the kind of tourist traffic evident in nearby historic Concord. To the contrary, it's the quiet, remote kind of hamlet where on Friday nights the convenience store is closed by 9pm and the main activity is Scottish country dancing at one of town's churches. (In fact, the Gibsons, who are regulars at these foot-tapping affairs, are happy to take along their guests.)

Stow—and the Amerscot House—sit at the foot of four hills that dominate the surrounding landscape: Spindle, Marble, Birch, and Pilot Grove. This local fact, and hundreds of others, are documented in a more-than-20-years-old term paper by the Gibson's son Ian that sits among the reading materials in each guest room. The report is filled with tidbits of information about how the circa 1734 red clapboard center chimney colonial structure evolved over the years—including the story of how in its early years "Skunky" White, a neighbor, saved it from burning to the ground.

The Gibsons, who bought and began updating the property in 1972, are delighted to walk guests around the house and share their knowledge of its past. As Jerry installs guests in the first floor chamber at the front of the house, originally the master bedroom, he's likely to explain that its private bath was once the borning—or birthing—room and that its private entrance was known as the "coffin door" because it was the only doorway wide enough for a casket. Or, on the second floor, he might point out a small patch of char on the exposed wood in the cozy loft off one of the suites that was caused by the famous fire documented by Ian.

In total, Amerscot has three guest accommodations. All of them have fireplaces and are decorated with country antiques, hand-made quilts, and area rugs that cover the wide-plank floors. They also feature homey touches such as vases of fresh flowers and modern amenities not often found in small B&Bs, including televisions (hidden in armoires) and private telephones with modem connections.

The Buchanan Room, a first floor corner room with king-size bed, is named in honor of the Gibson family, part of the Buchanan clan. The Lindsay Suite, one of two suites on the second floor, is named for Doreen's father's family. Its furnishings include a queen-size bed with lace canopy, and stuffed armchairs and a desk in a separate sitting room. Its marble-walled bathroom houses a Jacuzzi, shower, and a fireplace. The other second floor suite, the McLean Room, is named for Doreen's mother's family and contains a queen-size fourposter bed. An adjacent loft room with twin beds makes the suite perfect for a family or small group traveling together.

The Amerscot also features a separate Barn Room which can be used for an event or conference for up to 25 people.

Guests tend to gather in one of the common areas on the first floor: in front of the fireplace in the family room, which is lined with bookshelves housing materials about local history and attractions; around small tables and blooming plants in the adjoining, sunny greenhouse; or at the dining room table next to the fireplace in the dining room. While relaxing, guests can sip complimentary sherry or enjoy warm tea and biscuits that sit on the counter between the kitchen and family room.

The Gibsons, who previously operated an inn in Boothbay Harbor, Maine, for 10 years, converted their house to a B&B in 1990. As seasoned innkeepers, they know how to make guests feel at home without being intrusive. Doreen and Jerry enjoy getting to know their guests, sharing stories with them (particularly during what they call the "breakfast buzz"), and helping them plot their explorations in the area.

Guests enjoy breakfast family-style with the Gibsons at the long table next to the fireplace in the dining room. The fare is fresh, healthy, and plentiful—from fresh fruit salad to the inn's signature homemade granola and Baked Orange French Toast.

Former runners who recently took up cycling, the Gibsons provide bike storage space in their garage and can help plan alternate routes to the ones listed here.

Cycling from Amerscot House

Stow sits amidst rural countryside in the Nashoba Valley's rich apple growing region just west of Boston. Linking the elegant, historic towns in the area is rolling terrain dotted with old farmhouses, orchards, stables, lakes, and pastures. These towns feature classic colonial architecture and offer glimpses into the early days of American history, including the site of the first battle of the American Revolution. They also provide an opportunity to roam along terrain that inspired literary artists such as Louisa May Alcott, Henry David Thoreau, Ralph Waldo Emerson, and Nathaniel Hawthorne.

Most of the roads are lightly traveled and the terrain is varied enough to offer enjoyable cycling for riders of all abilities.

The Gibsons can offer route suggestions and the Nashoba Valley Pedalers Bike Club has regularly scheduled organized rides in the area, including some with starting points in the Stow and West Acton area. The Charles River Wheelmen, which organizes an annual *Climb to the Clouds* event in July, with 35 to 100-mile routes and a climb up Mt. Wachusett, also includes several cue sheets for the area on its website.

Local Bike Shops
The Bikeway Source
11 South Rd.
Bedford, MA 01730
(781) 275-7799
www.bikewaysource.com
Sales, service, accessories, and rentals. Organized rides, repair clinics, and tours.

Frank's Spoke 'n' Wheel
119 Boston Post Road (Route 20)
Sudbury, MA 01776
(978) 443-6696
(978) 443-6139, fax
www.spoke-n-wheel.com
Sales, services, accessories.

Pedal Power Bike & Ski
176 Great Road (Route 2A)
Acton, MA 01720
(978) 263-3197
(800) 479-3197
Sales, service, and accessories.

Mountain Biking

Stow is surrounded by hundreds of acres of groomed fire roads and wooded areas with interesting singletrack. Finding them, however, may take the insight of a knowledgeable local rider. Two regional bike clubs, the Nashoba Valley Pedalers and the Minuteman Road Club, organize off-road rides in the area. In fact, the Minuteman Road Club sponsors an annual Pumpkin Mash Mountain Bike Race in Stow.

For nearby off-road cycling check out the **Delaney Pond** area. From Stow, take Route 117 west and turn right on Harvard Street. Parking is on the left.

Another popular riding area north of Stow is 950-acre **Great Brook State Park** in Carlisle, (978) 369-6312. There are some 20 miles of trails of predominantly easy-to-moderate levels of difficulty; many of them, however, are multi-use. Within the park there's also a working dairy farm and seasonal ice cream stand. Take Route 128 north to Exit 31B. Route 225 west to Carlisle Center, then turn north on Lowell Road. Trail maps are available from the Park Office.

Other Resources

Greater Merrimack Valley Convention & Visitors Bureau
22 Shattuck Street
Lowell, MA 01853
(978) 459-6150 or (800) 443-3332
(978) 459-4595
www.lowell.org

Concord Chamber of Commerce
2 Lexington Road
Concord, MA 01742
(978) 369-3120

Eastern Massachusetts Bicycle and Road Map
Rubel Bike Maps
P.O. Box 1035
Cambridge, MA 02140
www.bikemaps.com
From Globe Corner Bookstores:
(800) 358-6013 or (617) 723-1676

Nashoba Valley Pedalers
(508) 266-INVP
www.ultranet.com/~nvp/

Charles River Wheelmen
www.crw.org
(617) 325-BIKE

Minute Man Road Club
(508) 881-3603
www.minutemanroadclub.com

Nashoba and Fruitlands via Nagog Hill and Harvard (40.3 miles)

Moderate; rolling hills

The route covers lots of gently rolling hills, shady country lanes and quiet backroads through the heart of Massachusetts' apple growing region.

About five miles into the route, riders climb a short moderate hill that provides splendid views of Nagog Pond. Tree-lined, undulating country lanes lead to Harvard, an elegant, historic colonial town with a beautiful brick library, general store, classic white church, and village green.

On Prospect Hill Road outside the town of Harvard sits the Fruitlands Museum, (978) 456-3924, which offers spectacular 50-mile panoramic views of the mountains and valley formed by the collision of continents millions of years ago. The Museum is actually several museums in one surrounded by 200 acres of woodlands, meadows, and pine barrens laced with nature trails. The four main museum structures house: the Fruitlands Farmhouse, childhood home of Louisa May Alcott, which now houses letters and memorabilia of Transcendentalist movement leaders such as her father Bronson Alcott, Emerson, and Thoreau; The Shaker Museum of furniture, crafts, and products; The Picture Gallery, two collections of paintings by landscape artists, many of the Hudson River School, and of early folk art portrait artists; and The Indian Museum, which documents the story of New England natives from more then ten thousand years ago to the present. The Museum's Tea Room and patio offer breathtaking landscape views as well as full luncheons and desserts.

The Nashoba Valley Winery sits amid 55 orchard-covered acres on Wattaquaddock Hill Road. Known for its fruit wines and pick-your-own orchards, the winery offers tastings and weekend tours. It also recently released its own line of microbrewed beers. A restaurant in the winery's farmhouse is a popular destination for fine food. For information call (978) 779-5521 or, on the Internet, visit nashobawinery.com.

With the exception of the section along Route 110 after leaving the Fruitlands Museum, there is little traffic along the route. As the names of many of the roads imply (Nagog Hill, Prospect Hill, Wattaquaddock Hill) there are lots of hills. But none of them are steep or terrible. And what goes up creates a pleasant ride down.

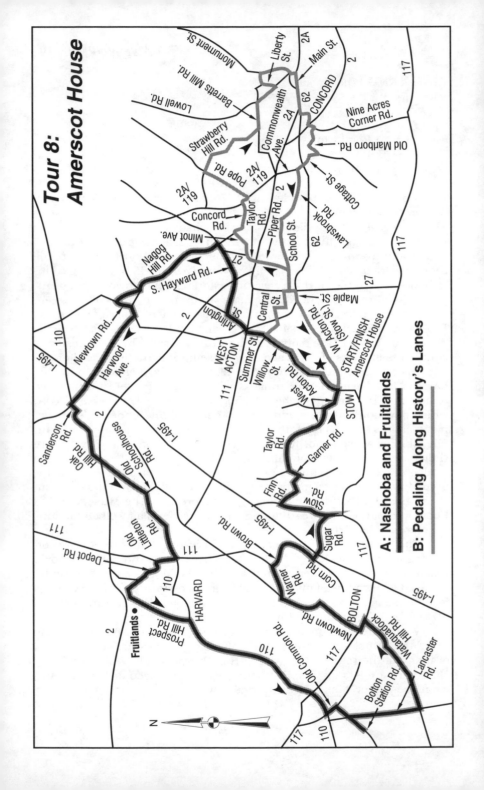

Tour 8:
Amerscot House

A: Nashoba and Fruitlands

B: Pedaling Along History's Lanes

Pt.-Pt.	Cume	Turn	Street/Landmark
0.0	0.0	R	**W. Acton Rd.** from drive of Amerscot B&B. Changes name to **Willow St.**
2.5	2.5	L	**Central St.** in W. Acton
0.3	2.8	S, R	Go through light, then make quick right onto **Arlington St.**
0.5	3.3	R	**Hayward Rd.**
1.2	4.5	L	Unmarked **Main St./Rt. 27** at stop sign
0.8	5.3	L	**Nagog Hill Rd.**
3.1	8.4	L	**Newtown Rd.** at T at end of Nagog Hill Rd.
0.6	9.0	R	**Harwood Ave.**
0.6	9.6	BL	Stay on **Harwood**
2.1	11.7	L	Cross tracks onto **Sanderson Rd.**
0.2	11.9	R	**Oak Hill Rd.**, which becomes **Old Littleton Rd.**
2.8	14.7	BR	At Y, where Old Schoolhouse joins road
0.4	15.1	S	**Old Littleton Rd.** at stop sign
1.4	16.5	R, R	Onto **unmarked street** in center of Harvard, then right onto **Rt. 111 N** at yield sign (or explore Harvard first)
0.4	16.9	L	**Depot Rd.**
0.6	17.5	BL	At Y
0.5	18.0	L	Unmarked **Prospect Hill Rd.** at stop sign
0.9	18.9		**Fruitlands Museum and Tea Room** offer great views
1.0	19.9	R	**Rt. 110W** at stop sign
3.2	23.1	S	**Rt. 110** at stop light, crossing Rt. 117
0.8	23.9	R	**Rt. 110**
0.7	24.6	L	**Old Common** at flashing light
0.3	24.9	R	**Bolton Station Rd.**
0.4	25.3	S	**Lancaster Rd.** at stop sign
1.5	26.8	BL	At Y onto unmarked **Wattaquaddock Hill Rd.**
2.3	29.1		**Nashoba Winery** and restaurant
0.4	29.5	L	**Rt. 117 E** at stop sign
0.2	29.7	R	**Newtown Rd.**
1.8	31.5	R	**Warner Rd.**
0.9	32.4	R	**Brown Rd.**, which becomes **Corn Rd.**
1.5	33.9	L	**Sugar Rd.**
1.2	35.1	L	**East End Rd.** at yield. Becomes **Stow Rd.**
1.3	36.4	R	**Finn Rd.**
0.9	37.3	L	**Garner Rd.** at T
0.3	37.6	R	**No Name** at split
0.1	37.7	BR	**Taylor Rd.**
2.1	39.8	BR	**Unmarked Rd.** at stop sign

Pt.-Pt.	Cume	Turn	Street/Landmark
0.4	40.2	L	**W. Acton Rd.**
0.1	40.3		Arrive at Amerscot B&B

Pedaling Along History's Lanes (21.9 miles)

Easy to Moderate

This relatively easy loop takes riders to the historic town of Concord, scene of the first battle of the American Revolution. There riders can visit Minute Man National Historical Park and the North Bridge, site of the "shot heard 'round the world," the Minute Man Statue by sculptor Daniel Chester French, and The Old Manse, former home of Nathaniel Hawthorne and Ralph Waldo Emerson. Just south of town (but off the bike route) is Walden Pond, made famous by Henry David Thoreau. Cyclists also can enjoy tea at the circa 1716 Colonial Inn, which reputedly has a resident ghost, or enjoy the shops and restaurants in town.

Riders interested in taking in a little more history can pick up the 5.5-mile Battle Road Trail, a multi-use interpretive trail that connects historic sites and natural areas in the Minute Man National Historical Park, (978) 369-6993 or www.nps.gov/mima, between Concord and Lexington. From the center of Concord, follow Lexington Road to Old Bedford Road to pick up the trail.

While traffic tends to be a little heavier around the town of Concord, particularly along Route 62, for the most part there is little traffic along the route.

Pt.-Pt.	Cume	Turn	Street/Landmark
0.0	0.0	R	**W. Acton Rd.** from drive of Amerscot B&B
2.3	2.3	R	Unmarked **Summer St.** at 4-way stop sign
0.1	2.4	R	**Central St.** at stop sign at T
1.2	3.6	R	**Unmarked street** at stop sign.
0.1	3.7	L	**School St.** at stop sign before bridge
0.5	4.2	L	**Piper Rd.**
0.8	5.0	S	Cross Rt. 2 onto **Taylor Rd.** at stop sign
0.4	5.4	R	**Minot Ave.**
0.7	6.1	R	Unmarked **Concord Rd.** at stop sign
0.8	6.9	R	**Rt. 2A E/Rt. 119** at stop sign at T. Busy!
0.1	7.0	L	**Pope Rd.**
1.2	8.2	R	**Strawberry Hill Rd.**
1.0	9.2	BL	At fork to stay on **Strawberry Hill Rd.**
1.0	10.2	L	Unmarked **Barretts Mill Rd.** at stop sign
0.6	10.7	R	**Lowell Rd.** at flashing light/4-way stop
0.7	11.5	L	**Liberty St.** *Use caution* crossing highway

Pt.-Pt.	Cume	Turn	Street/Landmark
0.4	11.9	R	Continue on **Liberty St.**
0.1	12.0	R	**Monument St.**
0.4	12.4		Pass **The Manse**
0.5	12.9	L	**Lowell Rd.** in center of Concord
0.1	13.0	R	**Main St.**
0.7	13.7	BL	**Rt. 62/Main St.**
0.7	14.4	L	**Old Road** to Nine Acres Corner
0.1	14.5	R	**Old Marlboro Rd.**
0.7	15.2	R	**Cottage St.**
0.3	15.5	L	Main St./Rt. 62W
0.1	15.6	BR	**Commonwealth Ave.** at light, and cross RR tracks
0.3	15.9	BL	**Lawsbrook Rd.** at split
1.5	17.4	BL	**School St.** at split
1.7	19.1	L	**Main St.** at light
0.1	19.2	R	**Maple St.**
0.1	19.3	L	**Stow St.**
0.2	19.5	BR	**Stow St.**, which becomes **S. Acton Rd.**
2.3	21.8	R	**W. Acton Rd.** at stop sign
0.1	21.9		Arrive at Amerscot B&B

Miles River Country Inn, Hamilton, Massachusetts

Miles River Country Inn

Gretel & Peter Clark, Innkeepers
823 Bay Road/Box 149   Phone: (508) 468-7206
Hamilton, MA 01936   Web: www.milesriver.com
Rates: Budget-Deluxe, B&B
Suites: Deluxe-Luxury
Open all year

From virtually every direction the roads leading to Hamilton, Massachusetts, are lined by stables, polo fields, and horse-filled pastures. These equestrian trappings lead one to believe that a different kind of riding is more common than bicycling. But, spend a few days in this namesake of Alexander Hamilton and you'll witness a steady stream of cyclists on the country roads that lace the estates area of Boston's North Shore.

One of these sprawling estates, The Miles River Country Inn, sits at the end of a long pasture-lined lane, hidden from the town's main road. A rambling 24-room, white Colonial building, the inn has served as the Clark family's home for 30 years. First attracted to the area because of Gretel Clark's equestrian interests, she and her husband Peter first opened their doors to traveling strangers in 1991 when they converted their home to a B&B after their children were grown. They've had a steady stream of overnight guests ever since.

Named after the river that flows past the property, the inn is surrounded by 30 acres of peaceful meadows, woodlands, and marshes, offering a host of quiet spots to explore at the end of a long day of cycling. In fact, the wonder of the expansive and varied landscape equals—perhaps even surpasses—the authentic Colonial charm of the main house.

Over the years, the Clarks have lovingly resuscitated and enhanced the gardens—ten of them in all—and two ponds. Gretel has even documented the effort in an essay included among the local information and things-to-do files in the first floor library.

From the formal "Secret Garden" to the more natural plantings by the ponds, guests are treated to a spray of contrasting seasonal colors, sights, and sounds. A broad array of annuals and perennials populate the property. So does an impressive array of wildlife and avians, including blue heron, egret, great horned and screech owls, Canadian geese, and a variety of ducks. As for four-legged inhabitants, beavers, otters, muskrats, deer, red fox, and possum can be spotted on different parts of the property.

On this property teeming with life, visitors also will find an assortment of domesticated creatures. Gretel's chickens, for example, provide fresh eggs for breakfast. Her bees provide the source for the golden honey served with her fresh-baked goods. Inn cat Milana "will sleep with any Tom, Dick, or Harriet" according to the house notes in each guest room. If guests are allergic, however, she'll be quarantined.

Four of the uniquely laid-out guest rooms have fireplaces (there are 12 fireplaces throughout the house) and all but two have private baths. Like the rest of the house, the decor reflects the Colonial style of the house and includes many authentic early American pieces inherited from Peter's ancestors. Guest quarters are furnished with pieces such at fourposter beds, oak dressers, clawfoot tubs, and area rugs. Accents such as vases of dried and fresh flowers enhance the homey atmosphere. All of the rooms offer pleasant and unique views of the grounds—even The Nook, a cozy third-floor garret room which shares a bath on the landing with Bryn's Room on the opposite side of the floor.

When rented together, the Hearthside and Lilac Rooms create a sunny spacious suite perfect for a small family or group traveling together.

All rooms, several of which are accessible from unexpected corridors or passageways, offer bright, comfortable quarters reflecting the down-to-earth yet refined character of the inn's owners.

When they're not out wandering the grounds, guests can relax in one of several inviting large common rooms, including a glassed-in porch, living room with piano, or book-lined library.

Breakfast is served family-style at the dining table off the huge country kitchen, where guests can chat with Gretel as she whips up fresh pancakes on the griddle or fries eggs just brought in from the hen house. She'll even provide a lesson on determining exactly how fresh the egg on the frying pan is. (If it's got three distinct rings between the center of the yoke and the edge of the white, it doesn't get any fresher.) Breakfasts are healthy and filling, without being excessively heavy or overwhelming. Guests can choose from fresh fruit, some of which comes from the orchards, juices, yogurt, a variety of cereals, fresh baked goods, or hot plates such as pancakes, French toast, or eggs and bacon.

Lively and diverse conversation usually revolves around guests' vacation adventures, origins, and interests. They also might help each other understand the local dialect where town names like Peabody (p b'dy) and Newbury (nu-bree) abound. Gretel and Peter, who are well-traveled and enjoy many hobbies and interests, keep the conversation moving. They're also happy to recommend both popular attractions in the region and those that the casual tourist would never see.

Bicycling from Miles River Country Inn

Miles River Country Inn is located in a rural area just 25 miles from Boston and a short distance from its North Shore beach towns and working waterfronts, making it a perfect base for exploring scenic coastline, as well as lightly traveled inland roads and historic New England villages. The region offers an abundance of cyclist-friendly roads and terrain to suit riders of all abilities. Away from the shoreline, the roads offer plenty of quiet, pleasant riding; however, areas near popular beach resorts attract traffic during the height of the tourist season.

The Clarks keep a file of highlighted maps of rides in the region (not all of them begin at the inn) between 10 and 50 miles long. Bob at Bay Road Bikes just down the road in South Hamilton also keeps on file a huge selection of cue sheets, predominantly favorite loops by local bike clubs. He's happy to share suggestions for routes. The shop is also home of The Essex Velo Club, which organizes rides for beginner, intermediate, and advanced riders and conducts cycling seminars.

North Shore Cyclists, another regional club, also conducts regular organized training rides in the area. The club sponsors an annual Blazing Saddles Century each August, with 25-mile, 100-kilometer, and 100-mile options.

Local Bike Shop

Bay Road Bikes
52 Railroad Avenue
South Hamilton, MA
(978) 468-1301
(978) 468-0232, fax
www.bayroadbikes.com
Sales, service, and accessories. Organized group rides.

Mountain Biking Opportunities

The area surrounding Miles River Country Inn is full of off-road biking opportunities for cyclists of all abilities. Two local bike clubs, Essex Velo Club and North Shore Cyclists, organize regular mountain bike rides and special events.

Within three miles of the inn are both the 225-acre **Appleton Farms Grass Rides**, (978) 356-5726, off Cutler Road, and **Bradley Palmer State Park**, (978) 887-5931. Bradley Palmer, which is off Asbury Street in Topsfield, has a broader variety of trails, from easy to difficult. The Massachusetts Forest and Park Service publishes trail maps for it and a number of other nearby state parks that permit mountain biking on their trails. The **Hood's Pond** area, **Georgetown Rowley State Forest**, off Route 97 in Georgetown, and neighboring **Willowdale State Forest**, off Ipswich Road near Topsfield, (978) 887-5931, offer a variety of trails, as does the **Boxford State Forest**, south of Boxford. Willowdale and Georgetown Rowley's woods trails include fairly flat sections and are ranked easy to moderate, while Boxford has a wider variety, with some challenging sections.

Another popular spot with local riders is the **Dogtown** area, near the Cape Ann Sportsmen's Club, between Gloucester and Rockport.

Other Resources

North of Boston Convention & Visitors Bureau
17 Peabody Square
Peabody, MA 01960
(978) 977-7760 or (800) 742-3506
(978) 977-7758, fax
email: info@northofboston.org
www.northofboston.org

The Trustees of Reservations
Castle Hill
P.O. Box 563, 290 Argilla Road
Ipswich, MA 01938-2647
(978) 356-4351
(978) 356-2143, fax
www.thetrustees.org
For info about Crane Beach, Crane Wildlife Refuge, and Castle Hill

Cape Ann Chamber of Commerce
33 Commercial Street
Gloucester, MA   01930
(978) 283-1601 or (800) 321-0133
(978) 283-4740, fax
www.cape-ann.com/cacc

Essex Velo Club
P.O. Box 2246
South Hamilton, MA   01982
(978) 468-1301
www.ecvcycling.org

North Shore Cyclists
(978) 352-2524
www.astseals.com/nsc/

Eastern Massachusetts Bicycle and Road Map
Rubel Bike Maps
P.O. Box 1035
Cambridge, MA 02140
www.bikemaps.com
From Globe Corner Bookstores:
(800) 358-6013 or (617) 723-1676

Little Neck and Crane Beach (29.2 miles)

Moderate

History buffs and outdoor enthusiasts alike will enjoy this relatively easy ride through Bradley Palmer State Park, (978) 887-5931, and the historic town of Ipswich and its sprawling acres of salt marshes and sandy beaches.

Ipswich, settled in 1630, claims to be "The Birthplace of American Independence" because the cry "no taxation without representation" was first heard here. However, some of its most notable moments in history came during the Salem witch trials: Several of the accused were jailed near its Meeting House Green. Today, its downtown and historic neighborhoods boast an array of carefully restored and maintained colonial architecture.

East of town, its Great Neck peninsula rises above Ipswich Bay, offering spectacular ocean views, and its dune-edge Crane Beach is considered by many to be one of the best beaches north of Boston.

Pack your swimsuit, buy a picnic lunch in Ipswich, and plan to explore the beach and more than 2,000 acres along the Essex and Ipswich River estuaries that were once part of the estate of industrialist and plumbing magnate Richard Crane. The spectacular Crane properties, today operated by the Trustees of Reservations, (978) 356-4351, include sandy white four-mile long Crane Beach; Crane Wildlife Refuge, a group of several small islands and marshland; and Castle Hill, a 59-room Stuart-style mansion designed by David Adler. The hilltop structure's sweeping landscape was designed by Arthur Shurcliff/Olmstead Brothers. A wide, undulating tree- and statuary-lined, half-mile-long lawn, known as the Grand Allee, connects the mansion and a cliff overlooking the ocean. The grounds are open to the public and the Great House is open for tours several days a week.

Both the 721-acre Bradley State Park, at the beginning of the ride, and Crane Beach offer an array of trails for riders who like to mix hiking or walking with riding.

Overall the route is relatively flat; however, winds coming off the ocean can make up for the flatness in certain sections. Traffic is light, except near the beach during the height of the tourist season. Routes 133 and 1A have heavier traffic than the back roads; however, there is a wide shoulder on 133 and drivers are cyclist-conscious on 1A, which passes in front of the inn. A half-mile section of Cutler Road is unpaved. The most significant climb covers ¼ mile up the drive to Castle Hill, which rewards riders with spectacular views.

Pt.-Pt.	Cume	Turn	Street/Landmark
0.0	0.0	L	**Rt. 1A S** at end of drive of Miles River Country Inn
0.3	0.3	R	**Rock Maple**
0.7	1.0	R	Unmarked **Cutler Rd.** at stop sign (unpaved for 0.5 miles)
1.5	2.5	L	**Highland St.**
0.7	3.2	R	Onto **Bradley Palmer State Park Rd.**
1.5	4.7	L	To exit park
0.2	4.9	R	**Asbury St.**
0.2	5.1	R	**Topsfield Rd.** at stop sign. Becomes **Market St.** in Ipswich
4.4	9.5	S	Onto **N. Main St.** At top of hill stay to the left of the Meeting House Green
0.3	9.8	R	**East St.** at stop sign
0.2	10.0	L	**Jeffrey's Neck Rd.**
0.4	10.4	BL	**Jeffrey's Neck Rd.**
1.7	12.1	BR	**Little Neck Rd.**
1.4	13.5	BL	On **Bayview Rd.** to follow the coast. Becomes **Clark, Colby,** then **High Ridge** *(Optional detour: To explore Little Neck, go to the right and up a hill, then across the causeway.)*
1.9	15.4	BR	**Jeffrey's Neck Rd.** at yield sign
1.8	17.2	L	**Water St.**
0.3	17.5	L	Unmarked **Green St.** and go over bridge
0.1	17.6	R	**Turkey Shore**
0.3	17.9	L, L, R	Left on **unmarked street**, quick left onto unmarked **Woods**, then right onto **Old England Rd.**
0.1	18.0	R	Unmarked **Rocky Hill Rd.**
0.1	18.1	L	**Argilla Rd.**
3.7	21.8	-	**Castle Hill** is on your left
0.2	22.0	-	Entrance to **Crane Beach**. (Mileage to next cue is based on turning around at this point)
2.3	24.3	L	**Northgate Rd.**

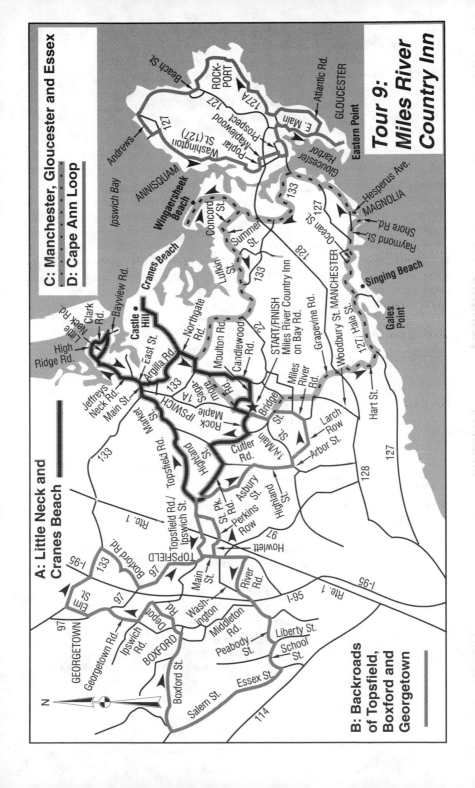

Tour 9: Miles River Country Inn

A: Little Neck and Cranes Beach ▬▬▬

B: Backroads of Topsfield, Boxford and Georgetown ▬▬▬

C: Manchester, Gloucester and Essex ▬▬▬

D: Cape Ann Loop ▬▬▬

N

START/FINISH Miles River Country Inn on Bay Rd.

GEORGETOWN
BOXFORD
TOPSFIELD
IPSWICH
ANNISQUAM
ROCKPORT
GLOUCESTER
MANCHESTER
MAGNOLIA

Ipswich Bay
Gloucester Harbor
Eastern Point
Gales Point
Singing Beach
Cranes Beach
Wingaersheek Beach
Castle Hill

Elm St.
Georgetown Rd.
Ipswich Rd.
Depot Rd.
Boxford Rd.
Washington Rd.
Middleton Rd.
Peabody St.
Liberty St.
School St.
Boxford St.
Salem St.
Essex St.
Main St.
River Rd.
Topsfield Rd./Ipswich St.
Topsfield Rd.
St. Pk. Rd.
Asbury St.
Perkins Row
Howlett
Highland St.
Cutler Rd.
Market St.
Main St.
Jeffreys Neck Rd.
High Ridge Rd.
Little Neck Rd.
Clark Rd.
Bayview Rd.
East St.
Argilla Rd.
Northgate Rd.
Lufkin St.
Concord St.
Summer St.
Rock Maple
Sawmill Rd.
Moulton Rd.
Candlewood Rd.
Bridge St.
1A/Main St.
Larch Row
Arbor St.
Highland St.
Hart St.
Grapevine Rd.
Woodbury St.
Hale St.
Miles River Rd.
Raymond St.
Shore Rd.
Ocean St.
Hesperus Ave.
Atlantic Rd.
E. Main
Prospect
Maplewood
Washington St. (127)
Poplar
Beach St.
Andrews

Rte. 1
I-95
I-95
Rte. 1
114
133
97
97
95
26
1
97
22
133
1A
128
127
127
133
127A
127
128

Pt.-Pt.	Cume	Turn	Street/Landmark
0.7	25.0	R	**Rt. 133** at stop sign
0.6	25.6	L	Unmarked **Candlewood Rd.**
2.1	27.7	R	**Moulton Rd.**
1.2	28.9	L	**Rt. 1A S** at stop sign
0.3	29.2		Arrive at Miles River Country Inn

Backroads of Topsfield, Boxford and Georgetown (48 miles)
Moderate terrain

This modified version of a training route used by local cyclists winds through backroads lined with rolling fields and lush forests. It cuts through Bradley Palmer State Parks, and loops around Boxford and Georgetown Rowley State Forests, all of which offer a variety of hiking and mountain biking opportunities. Swimming is permitted in Hood Pond, off Route 97 north of Topsfield. During the fall, the area offers splendid fall foliage.

The quintessential New England towns of Topsfield, famous for its annual county fair (supposedly the oldest in the nation), and Boxford dot the route. Both towns were settled in the early 1600s and today are marked by their large town greens and fine examples of 17th-century architecture.

Overall, the route covers lightly traveled roads, with heavier traffic on the numbered routes. All roads are paved. Except for a short hill on Howlett Street and Perkins Row in Topsfield, the route covers moderate terrain, distinguished by gently rolling hills. Due to its length, the ride is best suited to conditioned cyclists. For a short, 20-mile ride, riders can follow cues to and from Topsfield, cutting out the sections that go through Boxford and around Georgetown Rowley State Forest.

Pt.-Pt.	Cume	Turn	Street/Landmark
0.0	0.0	L	**Rt. 1A S** at end of drive of Miles River Country Inn
0.3	0.3	R	**Rock Maple**
0.7	1.0	R	Unmarked **Cutler Rd.** at stop sign (unpaved for 0.5 miles)
1.5	2.5	L	**Highland St.**
0.7	3.2	R	Onto **Bradley Palmer State Park Rd.**
1.5	4.7	L	To exit park
0.2	4.9	R	**Asbury St.** at park exit
0.2	5.1	L	**Topsfield Rd./Ipswich St.** at stop sign
1.3	6.4	S	Cross Rt. 1 at light to continue on **Ipswich St.**

Pt.-Pt.	Cume	Turn	Street/Landmark
0.9	7.3	S	**Main St.** at stop sign
1.4	8.7	R	**Salem Rd.**
0.1	8.8	R	Unmarked **River Rd.** (If you cross the bridge you've gone too far)
1.3	10.1	L	**Washington**
1.6	11.7	R	**Peabody St.**
1.2	12.9	R	**Liberty St.** at stop sign
0.4	13.3	L	**School St.**
0.9	14.2	R	**Essex St.** at stop sign. Names changes to **Salem St.**
4.8	19.0	R	**Boxford St.** at stop sign
2.8	21.8	BR	**Unmarked road**
0.9	22.7	L	**Middleton** at 4-way stop
0.4	23.1	S	**Depot Rd.** at stop sign, crossing Elm St.
1.3	24.4	L	**Pond St.**
0.3	24.7	L	**Ipswich Rd.**
0.7	25.4	R	**Georgetown Rd**.
1.2	26.6	L	**Rt. 97** at stop sign at T
0.8	27.4	R	**Elm St.**
0.8	28.2	R	**Rt. 133 E** at T
2.5	30.7	R	**Boxford Rd.**
2.4	33.1	L	**Rt. 97**
3.2	36.3	L,L	Turn onto **E. Common**, then quick left to ride along the green; road becomes unmarked **Howlett St.**
1.1	37.4	L	**Perkins Row**
1.4	38.8	R	Unmarked **Ipswich St.** at T
0.3	39.1	R	**Asbury Rd.**
2.8	41.9	BR	At stop sign
0.2	42.1	BR	**Highland St.** at split. Becomes **Arbor St.**
1.3	43.4	L	**Main St./Rt. 1A**
0.2	43.6	R	**Larch Row**
1.6	45.2	S	**Larch Row** at stop sign
0.7	45.9	L	**Miles River Rd.**
0.7	46.6	L	**Bridge St.** at stop sign
0.4	47.0	R	**Rt. 1A** at stop sign
1.0	48.0		Arrive at Miles River Country Inn

Manchester, Gloucester, and Essex (29.5 miles)
Moderate

This scenic route offers a smorgasbord of New England attractions, everything from rural country roads to scenic coastline to charming historic villages and museums. More adventurous riders, and those wishing to do extra mileage, will find plenty of opportunities to divert from the route to explore sandy beaches and other attractions. Or, the ride can be combined with the optional Cape Ann loop.

Manchester, the first coastal town on the route, has enjoyed a reputation over the years as a choice fishing village, fine woodworking center, and summer retreat for diplomats seeking to escape the heat and humidity of Washington. Today, the shoreline of this fashionable village is populated by their elegant vacation "cottages." Take time to explore the estates area around Proctor and Masconomo (the name of the chief of the Agawam Indians who once lived here) Streets to South Point, or take a swim at Singing Beach where the squeaky sand sings under your feet.

Continuing along the coast, ride around the beach at Kettle Cove, where you can look across at Coolidge Point, the estate of President Calvin Coolidge's family. Then ride through the tiny unpretentious town of Magnolia where there are several good restaurants.

East of Magnolia on Hesperus Avenue sits Hammond Castle, built by inventor John Hays Hammond, Jr. in the mid-1920s on a rocky cliff overlooking the reef of Norman's Woe (which was immortalized by Longfellow in his poem "The Wreck of the Hesperus.") Built of Rockport granite and resembling a 16th-century European castle, it features a Great Hall that is 100 feet long with a 60-foot domed ceiling, and houses a 10,000 pipe organ.

Gloucester, a bustling commercial center and working harbor, emits the pungent smell of sea bounty and its streets are lined with seafood restaurants and lobster houses. When Samuel de Champlain sailed into its harbor in 1604 he christened it "Le Beauport," the beautiful harbor. At what is now Stage Fort Park, the Pilgrims established the second American settlement in 1623, naming it after Gloucester, England. Today Gloucester also is a popular whale watching center and home to a Whaling Museum.

From Gloucester, riders can continue along the optional Cape Ann loop or head back to the Miles River Inn via Essex, an antiquing center with a 300-year history of shipbuilding and clam harvesting. A Shipbuilding Museum, (978) 768-7541, on Main Street features dioramas, full-scale models, and multi-media exhibits. The return trip also provides an optional ride to Wingaersheek Beach and its spectacular views of the Essex and Ipswich Bays.

All of the roads are paved and, for the most part, except along the coast during the tourist season, have little traffic. Traffic also can be congested in the town of Gloucester. A portion of Concord Street has a rough surface, but little traffic. Except for the optional ride to Wingaersheek Beach the route is relatively flat with some moderately rolling hills.

Pt.-Pt.	Cume	Turn	Street/Landmark
0.0	0.0	L	**Rt. 1A S** from drive of Miles River Country Inn
1.0	1.0	L	**Bridge St.**
0.3	1.3	BL	At Y to stay on **Bridge St.**
0.5	1.8	R	**Woodbury St.**
0.7	2.5	S	Cross Rt. 22 onto **Woodbury St.**, which becomes **Rubbly Rd.**
0.6	3.1	L	Unmarked **Grapevine Rd.** at stop sign. Becomes **Hart St.** after it crosses Rt. 128
3.5	6.6	L	**Rt. 127/Hale St.** at stop sign
1.9	8.5	BR	**Central St.**
0.2	8.7	R	**Rt. 127**
0.1	8.8	L	**Rt. 127/Summer St.**
			For optional out-and-back ride to Singing Beach & Gales Point, continue straight
1.4	10.2	R	**Ocean St.**, which goes around Kettle Cove
0.8	11.0	R	**Rt. 127** at stop sign
0.4	11.4	R	**Raymond St.** toward Magnolia
0.4	11.8	R	**Shore Rd.** at yield sign
0.6	12.4	S	Follow pedestrian sign
0.1	12.5	R	Pick up unmarked dirt road (**Hesperus**) by stone pillar
0.2	12.7	R	Unmarked **Hesperus Ave.**
1.6	14.3	R	Unmarked **Rt. 127 N** at stop sign
1.4	15.7	L	**Rt. 133W**
			Continue straight to explore Gloucester or to ride optional Cape Ann loop (see cues below)
2.5	18.2	R	**Concord St.** following sign toward Wingaersheek Beach
1.2	19.4		*Optional turnoff for beach. Approx. 3-mile hilly ride to beach.*
2.1	21.5	BR	Stay on **Concord** (Summer goes to left)
0.8	22.3	R	**Lufkin St.**
0.6	22.9	R	**Rt. 133W** at stop sign
1.3	24.2	R	**Rt. 133W**

Pt.-Pt.	Cume	Turn	Street/Landmark
3.1	27.3	L	Candlewood
0.4	27.7	R	Sagamore Rd.
1.5	29.2	L	Rt. 1A S/Bay Rd. at stop sign
0.4	29.6		Arrive at driveway to Miles River Country Inn

Cape Ann Loop (20.8 miles)
Moderate

This loop begins near Stage Fort Park in Gloucester and skirts the coast around Cape Ann. Attractions along the way include several artists colonies, lighthouses, and a number of swimming beaches. The **Rocky Neck Art Colony** in East Gloucester claims to be the oldest continuously operating art colony in America. Painters such as Winslow Homer, Milton Avery, and John Sloan—and many lesser-known artists—have painted in Gloucester.

Between Gloucester and Rockport, home of the **Bearskin Neck artists' colony**, riders pass Good Harbor, Cape Hedge, and Long Beaches, where they can take a dip in the ocean or explore the side streets among the summer cottages. An optional side trip approximately 3 miles into the route leads to the **Eastern Point Lighthouse** and **Beauport**, (508) 283-0800, the former summer retreat of collector and interior designer Henry Davis Sleeper, perched on the rocks overlooking Gloucester Harbor. Now a museum, its hours of admission vary by season and tours are available. The detour to the lighthouse is a 2.8-mile round trip.

From Rockport, continuing along Route 127, the route goes through Pigeon Cove, Lanesville, Bay View, and Riverdale. Points of interest on this section include **Granite Pier, Halibut Point State Park,** and the picturesque village of Annisquam, which for 200 years served as a fishing and shipbuilding center.

All roads are paved and marked by gently rolling hills. Traffic is season-dependent and a little congested as riders wind their way through Gloucester to avoid busy Route 128.

Pt.-Pt.	Cume	Turn	Street/Landmark
0.0	0.0		Intersection of Rts. 133 and 127 in Gloucester
1.4	1.4	BR	Main St.
0.2	1.6	R	E. Main St., toward Rocky Neck, at light
0.6	2.2	BR	E. Main, which becomes Eastern Pt. Rd.
1.0	3.2		Optional turnoff for Eastern Point Lighthouse and Beauport House

Pt.-Pt.	Cume	Turn	Street/Landmark
0.5	3.7		Becomes **Atlantic Rd.**
2.1	5.8	**S**	**Rt. 127A N** at stop sign.
1.0	6.8	**BL**	At Y
3.7	10.5	**L**	**Unmarked street** in center of Rockport
0.1	10.6	**R**	**Beach St.**
0.5	11.1	**R**	**Rt. 127** at stop sign
2.6	13.7	**BL**	**Unmarked street** at split
0.7	14.4	**L**	**Andrews**
1.4	15.8		Optional right turn here to visit **Annisquam village**
3.0	18.8	**L**	**Poplar St.** *Be careful* crossing traffic
0.4	19.2	**R**	Unmarked **Maplewood**
0.6	19.8	**R**	**Prospect** at stop sign
0.2	20.0	**L**	**Washington**
0.3	20.3	**R**	**Unmarked street**
0.1	20.4	**R**	**Rt. 127 S**
0.4	20.8	**R**	**Rt. 133W**

Windflower Inn, Great Barrington, Massachusetts

Windflower Inn

Barbara & Gerald Liebert and
Claudia & John Ryan, Innkeepers
684 South Egremont Road
Great Barrington, MA 01230
Rates: Moderate-Deluxe, B&B
Open all year

Phone: (800) 992-1993; (413) 528-2720
Fax: (413) 528-5147
Web: www.windflowerinn.com
E-mail: wndflowr@windflowerinn.com

This turn-of-the-century gentleman's retreat, with its spacious common rooms, wrap-around porch, and expansive lawn, is the kind of place where you can put up your feet and relax your weary muscles after a long day of cycling.

The Windflower Inn, a Federal style country inn built in the late 1800s, has been operated since 1980 by seasoned innkeepers Barbara and Gerald Liebert (formerly of the Tulip Tree Inn in Vermont) and their daughter Claudia and her husband John. Their warm tranquil lodgment, which defines country comfort, sits on 10 acres just outside the historic Berkshire town of Great Barrington. Claudia is an outgoing, hospitable host and resident chef. John tends to the grounds and gardens, which include perennials surrounding the inn's private pool, and organic vegetables, berries, and herbs used in Claudia's culinary delights. While gardening, John is kept company by inndogs Cody, a mixed breed, Lucy, a springer spaniel, and Anna, an Airedale.

Great Barrington boasts lots of small shops, boutiques, and inviting restaurants, and during the summer the region attracts lovers of the nearby Tanglewood Music, Jacob's Pillow Dance, and Berkshire Theater festivals. In September it's the site of one of the Berkshires' most popular one-day parties and athletic events: The Great Josh Billings Runaground. The biking-canoeing-running triathlon is the longest-running event of this type and attracts thousands of participants and spectators. Later in the fall, the region is a popular destination for leaf peepers.

Wildflower's two large living rooms with fireplaces, stuffed chairs, and sofas offer plenty of cozy spots for guests to curl up with a book, share experiences with other guests, or play one of the many board games or the piano. Although tea and fresh homemade baked goods are served in the afternoon, snack containers—like a candy jar full of gumdrops and a basket of fresh apples—beg to be raided all day long.

The wide entrance to the main living room is framed by two huge, white Federal columns, and an exquisite staircase leads from it to the guest rooms on the second floor.

Six of the 14 rooms have fireplaces; all are air-conditioned and have private baths, many with clawfoot tubs. They're furnished with a mix of antiques and country furnishings and several have window seats and doors that open onto porches. Room 12, one of the favorites, has a huge wood-burning stone fireplace, a fourposter bed with Laura Ashley linens, and opens to the side porch. Room 1 provides spacious accommodations with both a queen-size and twin beds, dressing room, and fireplace. Room 7 has a fireplace, canopy bed, and bay window with seat.

A full, hearty breakfast is served in the oversized dining room, which also has a fireplace. It includes fresh fruit, juices, cereals, homemade breads and pastries, as well as hot dishes such as French toast (also made from homemade breads), specialty pancakes, quiche, and eggs and bacon.

Bicycling from Windflower Inn

The gentle rolling hills of the Berkshires dotted with small, historic towns and villages create a delightful mix of diverse riding terrain and worthwhile attractions. When it comes to cycling, this area has something for everyone. In the towns and on numbered routes traffic is a little heavier than on the back roads, but the busier routes have good shoulders for riding. During the fall leaf-peeping season traffic tends to be a little heavier.

It hardly matters which back roads around Windflower Inn riders choose to cycle; they'll find pleasant cycling and scenery everywhere, and lots of opportunities to soak up early American history at sites immortalized by artists such as Norman Rockwell, Arlo Guthrie, and Nathaniel Hawthorne.

Both Claudia and the Chamber of Commerce Information Booth on Main Street in Great Barrington can provide information on additional cycling routes in the area.

Local Bike Shops

Berkshire Bike & Blade
326 Stockbridge Rd.
Route 7 North in Barrington Plaza
Great Barrington, MA   01230
413-528-5555
Rents mountain bikes and hybrids. Sales, service, accessories for road and mountain bikes.

Harland B. Foster
15 Bridge St.
Great Barrington, MA
413-528-0564
Sales, service, accessories.

Other Resources
Berkshire Visitors Bureau
Berkshire Common, Plaza Level
Pittsfield, MA 01201
(800) 237-5747 or (413) 443-9186
www.berkshires.org

Southern Berkshire Chamber of Commerce
284 Main Street
Great Barrington, MA 01230
(413) 528-1510
www.greatbarrington.org

The Berkshire Book: A Complete Guide
Jonathan Sternfield
Berkshire House, Great Barrington

The Berkshires, Connecticut River Valley, Quabbin Reservoir
Rubel Bike Maps
P.O. Box 1035
Cambridge, MA 02140
www.bikemaps.com
From Globe Corner Bookstores:
(800) 358-6013 or (617) 723-1676

Mountain Biking Opportunities
Several areas managed by the state's Department of Environmental
Management, (617) 727-3180, allow mountain biking on their trails,
including **Beartown, Mt. Washington, October Mountain,** and
Pittsfield State Forests.
    Beartown State Forest in Monterey, (413) 528-0904, has dirt roads,
logging roads, ORV and snowmobile trails for easy to difficult riding.
The Appalachian Trail, which intersects the forest's trails, does not allow bikes. Swimming is available on 35-acre Benedict Pond. The main
entrance is off Blue Hill Road.
    Mt. Washington, (413) 528-0330, offers 30 miles of moderate to
difficult trails, including a tough climb to Mt. Everett summit. Within
the forest is Bash Bish Falls. From Route 23, take 41 South and follow
signs.
    October Mountain State Forest, in Lee, (413) 243-1778, is the larg-
est state forest in the state. Rocky logging roads and ATV trails are open
to bikes. The trailhead is at the park's headquarters. From Mass Pike
take 20 West, then right on Center Street and follow signs.

Pittsfield Forest, (413) 442-8992, offers plenty of technical climbing along the Taconic Ridge. The trailhead is off Circuit Road.

Kennedy Park, in Lenox, provides easy to moderate riding on about 6 miles of single- and doubletrack trails. Enter behind the shopping center on Route 20. Maps are available from the town of Lenox, (413) 637-5530, or at Arcadian Shop.

To Umpachene Falls (29.3 miles)
Moderate

Ride along quiet Housatonic Valley back roads that connect South Egremont, Sheffield, Mill River, and Great Barrington. Pedal past the site where Captain Daniel Shay, who had fought at Bunker Hill, and his band of rabble rousers fought their last battle against the government in an uprising over taxation and their inability to pay their debts with a worthless new currency after the Revolutionary War. Also pass the site of the oldest, and newest, covered bridge in the state. A new one was built in 1998 to replace the original bridge that burned to the ground in 1994.

The Umpachene Falls is a great place to picnic or swim beneath the cascading falls. Another place to swim along the route is just a few miles before you get back to the inn: About a mile after turning on Routes 23/41, the road crosses the Green River. Just before the bridge there's a trail that winds along the river, where there are several natural pools and stretches of pebbly beach.

All routes are paved and the terrain is marked by gentle rolling hills. Except for the short stretches on Routes 7, 23, and 41, the traffic is light. Boardman Road, although paved, has some rough sections.

Pt.-Pt.	Cume	Turn	Street/Landmark
0.0	0.0	R	**S. Egremont Rd./Route 23 W**
0.4	0.4	BL	Cross highway, follow sign to Sheffield on **Button Ball Lane**
0.1	0.5	L	Unmarked **Sheffield South/Egremont Rd.** at stop sign
3.6	4.1	R	**Rt. 7S** at stop sign
0.3	4.4		Off unmarked bridge road on your left is the oldest **site of a covered bridge** in the state.
0.8	5.2	L	**Maple**
0.9	6.1	BR	**Hewins Rd.** at fork
3.0	9.1	L	Sharp left onto **Alum Hill Rd.**
1.4	10.5	L	**Mill River Rd./Clayton Rd.** at stop sign
1.0	11.5	BL	To stay on **Mill River/Clayton Rd.** at split for Konkapot Rd., which goes to the right

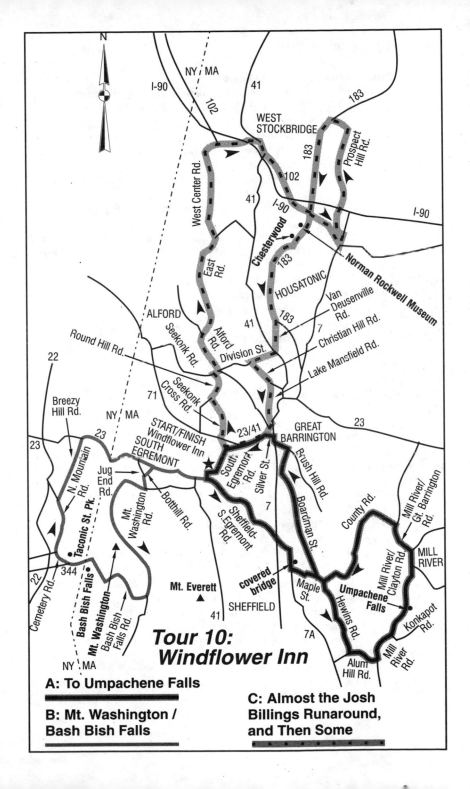

Tour 10: Windflower Inn

A: To Umpachene Falls

B: Mt. Washington / Bash Bish Falls

C: Almost the Josh Billings Runaround, and Then Some

Pt.-Pt.	Cume	Turn	Street/Landmark
1.6	13.1		To visit **Umpachene Falls**, go right on unpaved **Umpachene Falls Rd.** Just after bridge, enter parking on your right and follow the sound of water.
1.3	14.4	R	**Mill River/Clayton Rd.**, over bridge
0.1	14.5	L	Immediately turn left onto unmarked **Mill River Rd.** in middle of Mill River, following sign to Sheffield
0.4	14.9	BL	**Mill River/Great Barrington Rd.** at split
1.3	16.2	BL	Unmarked **County Rd.**, toward Sheffield
4.6	20.8	S	Stay on **County Rd.**, where Hewins Rd. joins it
0.1	20.9	L	**Boardman Rd.**, which becomes **E. Sheffield Rd.**
4.8	25.7	L	**Brush Hill Rd.**
0.3	26.0	R	**Rt. 7 North**
0.5	26.5	L	**Silver St.** at Mahaiwe Cemetery
0.4	26.9	L	**Rt. 23W/41 S.** To your left is **Newsboy Monument**
2.4	29.3		Arrive at Windflower Inn

Mt. Washington/Bash Bish Falls (24.3 miles)
Challenging

This is the perfect tour for anyone who likes hill climbing. Both the ascents up Mount Washington Road and Breezy Hill offer more than two miles of challenging climbing. Over the course of the route, riders climb a total of about 2,000 feet. But the payoffs are fantastic. Ride through thickly-wooded forests and catch amazing views of Jug End Mountain and Taconic Mountain and a valley dotted with expansive farms. Bash Bish Falls Road winds its way downhill along the Bash Bish Brook gorge, sometimes with sharp curves. The trail to the falls is well marked and worth the trip. According to legend, Indian Princess White Swan lives behind the falls. Cool off by taking a dip in the *cold* water below the chuting falls or continue to Taconic State Park, which has a spring-fed swimming hole called Ore Pit Pond.

The entire ride is on paved roads, with some patches of rough payment, through a sparsely populated area. Take the descent from Mount Washington slowly; there are some bumps and cracks in this steep, winding road.

Pt.-Pt.	Cume	Turn	Street/Landmark
0.0	0.0	R	**Rt. 23** from parking lot of Windflower Inn
0.3	0.3	BL	Stay on **Rt. 23**
2.3	2.6	L	**Botthill Rd.**
0.4	3.0	L	Unmarked **Jug End Rd.** at T
0.6	3.6	R	**Mt. Washington Rd.** at stop sign
5.6	9.2		Entrance to **Mt. Everett Reservation**
0.2	9.4	R	Unmarked **Bash Bish Falls Rd.** (Although there is only a country church here, this intersection is the town of Mt. Washington.)
3.2	12.6		Enter parking lot on your left and park your bike. To walk to the falls, follow the trail marked with blue arrows. Climb the rocks at the edge of the lot to get a great view of the valley and mountains. (Road becomes **Rt. 344** when you reach the New York border.)
1.1	13.7		Second parking lot leading to Bash Bish falls.
0.7	14.4	R	Continue on **Rt. 344. Taconic State Park** will be on your right, across from Depot Deli.
0.1	14.5	R	**Cemetery Rd.**
0.1	14.6	R	**N. Mountain Rd.**
2.0	16.6	R	**Breezy Hill Rd.**
2.9	19.5	R	**Rt. 23**
4.8	24.3		Arrive at Windflower Inn

Almost the Josh Billings Runaground, and Then Some (41.7 miles)
Moderate

The Berkshire Hills, a WPA Guide first published in 1938, describes Lenox and Stockbridge as "Berkshire in its best dress suit and evening gown." Time has not altered that description.

This route, which covers a modified version of the 27-mile course of the popular Josh Billings Runaground athletic event, takes riders through well-dressed towns and landscape and offers plenty of educational and recreational diversions. The event is named after Josh Billings, the pen name of local humorist and hayseed philosopher Henry Wheeler, whose style supposedly gave birth to the word "josh". The route has been changed slightly to avoid heavy traffic areas, and additional mileage is added to create a loop.

Enjoy gentle, remote backroads and bucolic hills from the Inn to Stockbridge, passing by the small village of Alford, once known for its marble quarries. In Stockbridge, check out the Old Mission House, eat at the famous Red Lion Inn, or track down the site of the former Alice's Restaurant, memorialized in song by Arlo Guthrie.

Along Prospect Hill, visit the exquisite Naumkeag (which means "place of rest" in Mahican) Estate, once the residence of former ambassador Joseph Choate. Then pass a replica of Nathaniel Hawthorne's Little Red House, across from one of the entrances to Tanglewood, as you ride along scenic Stockbridge Bowl/Lake Mahkeenac. At the end of the lake, from Gould Meadow, sit down and soak up the serenity of the massive grassland and seven-mountain view.

On route 183, Pass Kripalu, one of the largest yoga and holistic health centers in the U.S. At the site of the Norman Rockwell museum, cyclists are allowed to ride on its 36 acres, much as the famous artist and his wife Molly did years ago. Or visit the Chesterwood Estate and Museum—the summer residence of Daniel Chester French, sculptor of the Lincoln Memorial, features his studio and sculpture gardens.

Pt.-Pt.	Cume	Turn	Street/Landmark
0.0	0.0	L	**S. Egremont Rd./Rt. 23 East**
0.9	0.9	L	**Seekonk Cross Rd.**
0.3	1.2	S	At stop sign to stay on **Seekonk Cross Rd.**
1.9	3.1	BR	At fork **Round Hill Rd.**
0.9	4.0	R	Unmarked **Seekonk Rd.** at stop sign
0.3	4.3	L	Unmarked **Alford Rd.**
1.9	6.2	BR	**East Rd.** at fork
4.1	10.3	BL	**West Center Rd.**
4.0	14.3	R	**Route 102E** at stop sign
1.3	15.6	R	**Route 102E** at stop sign/flashing light
0.2	15.8	BL	Stay on **102**
4.6	20.4	L	**Main St./Route 102** at stop sign in Stockbridge
0.4	20.8	L	**Pine St.** (across from Red Lion Inn)
0.1	20.9	BL	**Prospect Hill Rd.**
5.2	26.1	L	**Rt. 183S** at stop sign
3.9	30.0	S	Continue on **Rt. 183 S** at stop sign/flashing light
0.7	30.7		Entrance to **Norman Rockwell Museum**
0.3	31.0		Entrance to **Chesterwood Estate and Museum**
3.1	34.1	S	Unmarked **Van Deusenville Rd.** at stop sign in Housatonic

PtPt.	Cume	Turn	Street/Landmark
1.2	35.3	**R**	Unmarked **Division St.** at stop sign. (On the left, Guthrie Center, in the **Old Trinity Church,** was the sight of the famous party that preceded Arlo Guthrie's garbage "dump" which landed him in jail.)
0.1	35.4	**S**	**Division St.** at flashing light
0.7	36.1	**L**	**Christian Hill Rd.** at flashing light at top of hill
1.3	37.4	**R**	**Lake Mansfield Rd. Lake Mansfield** is a nice picnic and swimming area.
0.9	38.3	**L,R**	At T, left, then quick right onto **Brainard**
0.1	38.4	**L**	On unmarked **Taconic Rd.** at T, then under RR
0.2	38.6	**R**	**Rt. 23W** at flashing light (town of Great Barrington is to your left)
0.2	38.8	**R**	**Rt. 23W**
2.9	41.7		Arrive at Windflower Inn

Moose Mountain Lodge, Etna, New Hampshire

New Hampshire Inns and Rides

The tagline in New Hampshire's tourism brochures sends a blaring invitation to cyclists. "The road less traveled" is more than a marketing ploy; it's the truth. When it comes to vacation destinations, New Hampshire is undeniably overshadowed by neighboring states that more aggressively court leisure travelers.

This should bring smiles to the faces of touring cyclists and wings to their cycling shoes. What could be more inviting than long stretches of lightly traveled scenic roadway? Speaking of scenic terrain, New Hampshire claims that 83 percent of the state is covered by trees and that the rest is under water. Exaggeration or not, this translates into hundreds of thousands of acres of natural beauty.

In spite of all the state's aesthetic appeal, or perhaps because of its rugged mountainous beauty, the Granite State is sparsely populated. Its largest cities and towns are in the southern part of the state. Towns become few and far between the closer one gets to the Canadian border in the remote Great North Woods Region north of the White Mountains.

Tucked away on Foss Mountain, among the foothills of the White Mountains, sits **Snowvillage Inn.** This remote hideaway near the Maine border offers unobstructed views of the Presidential Mountains and peaceful riding along quiet backroads.

Another off-the-beaten-track getaway, the **Moose Mountain Lodge**, offers mesmerizing views of Vermont's Green Mountains from its mountainside perch. Outdoors enthusiasts who relish getting away from all signs of civilization will enjoy the cycling—and hiking (the Appalachian Trail crosses its property)—on the quiet roads and paths surrounding the lodge. Nearby attractions included on the cycling routes include the college town of Hanover, Enfield Shaker Village, and Mascoma Lake. One of the routes follows the Connecticut River, which forms the state's border with Vermont.

In the Lakes Region of the state, southwest of grand Lake Winnipesaukee, the **Black Swan Inn** offers a perfect starting point for exploring the smaller, scenic Newfound Lake and the Shaker Village at Canterbury.

In the southern part of the state, two quintessential, unspoiled New England towns are home to two inns with colorful pasts. Both the **Colby Inn** in tiny Henniker, not far from the state capital of Concord, and the **Hancock Inn**, in Hancock, reflect the peaceful, slow-paced ambiance of their communities—the kind of communities filled with white-steepled churches, town gazebos, and general stores that transport visitors back in time, and where everyone knows everyone else.

Resources

New Hampshire
Office of Travel and Tourism Development
172 Pembroke Rd., P.O. Box 1856
Concord, NH 03302-1856
(800) FUN IN NH
www.visitnh.gov
Publishes New Hampshire Visitor's Guide, Guidebook, and highway map.

Division of Parks and Recreation
same address
(603) 271-3556
(603) 271-2629, fax
www.nhparks.state.nh.us

State Bicycle Coordinator
Department of Transportation
1 Hazen Drive, P.O. Box 483
Concord, NH 03302-0483
(603) 271-3344

Granite State Wheelmen
9 Veterans Road
Amherst, NH 03031

-or-

Two Townsend Avenue
Salem, NH 03079
(603) 898-5GSW

New Hampshire Mountain Bicycling Association
P.O. Box 103
Ashland, NH 03217
(603) 236-4666, 968-7840 or 236-4174

Black Swan Inn

Janet Foster, Innkeeper
354 West Main Street
Tilton, NH 03276
Rates: Budget-Moderate, B&B
Open all year

Phone: (603) 286-4524
Fax: (603) 286-8260

The Black Swan Inn is a warmly decorated three-story former mill owner's mansion that sits on four acres overlooking the Winnipesaukee River where, with a permit, guests can fish. Victorian through and through, it is surrounded by flower gardens and an expansive lawn shaded by old oak and maple trees.

Innkeeper Janet Foster has run the Black Swan Inn for 15 years. She has created a comfortable, homey atmosphere where guests can curl up on a stuffed chair in front of one of the fireplaces, contribute to the progress of the jigsaw puzzle in the salon, or tap on the ivories of the baby grand piano in the music room. A common guest refrigerator is stocked with sodas and mixers, and filled candy dishes tempt guests with a sweet tooth. Outside, visitors can relax in the garden or on one of the inn's two porches.

A legacy of Tilton's prosperous days of yesteryear and of the mansion's original owner, the elegant 1880s structure features exquisite deep mahogany, walnut, and oak woodwork. Its high ceilings generate a sense of space, while the decor and accessories create a cozy, warm environment. Beautifully crafted leaded stained glass windows line the alcoves in the main salon, as well as a favorite guestroom on the second floor.

On the first floor of the mansion are a number of rooms where guests mingle: the main salon, a music room, and a large dining room with an adjacent sitting area with a fireplace. Seven individually furnished guestrooms—three with private baths—are located on the second and third floors. All of the rooms are decorated with interesting Victorian accessories and furniture, including plenty of antiques and period pieces. Two additional suites with private baths are located in a separate carriage house. They feature a number of in-room amenities, such as a TV and telephone; guests in the main house must share the phones and TV in common areas.

One of the favorite guestrooms is Victoria, a spacious, romantic chamber on the mansion's second floor. The sun beams through the stained glass windows and lace curtains of its alcove. It has a queen-size sleep sofa, in addition to a queen-size bed draped with quality lace-trimmed linens and a fluffy comforter. This inviting room is decorated in a soothing mauve, green, and ivory color scheme and has a private bath with shower.

While most of the rooms are accessible from the staircase off the side entrance of the house, the most private room is at the top of a second stairway at the front of the house.

In the morning, Janet's true talents as a hostess and chef are on display. She sets an exquisite breakfast table, with plenty of tabletop conversation pieces, and serves up culinary breakfast delights such as home-baked breads, specialty pancakes, waffles, and omelets. If guests simply prefer to have the fresh fruit bowl and some cold cereal, that's okay, too.

The inn sits on Main Street just a short walk from downtown Tilton, a small, quirky town that is off the beaten track. Though it lacks the kind of shops that cater to tourists, it does possess a few curiosities worth checking out. For example, Tilton boasts more statues than any other American town of its size. The most prominent of these, without a doubt, is the peculiar 55-foot-high granite Tilton arch, which dominates a hilltop park and, technically, resides in the town of Northfield. This replica of a Roman memorial, and the lion carved from Scottish granite that sits beneath it, were given to what was then the town of Sanbornton Bridge in 1869 by Charles E. Tilton, the town's wealthiest citizen and a descendant of its first settler. The town was subsequently renamed in his honor. The eccentric forefather apparently never wanted to lose sight of the arch. His mansion, now the library of the Tilton prep school, provides a direct view of the imposing arch from its hilltop site on the opposite side of town.

Tilton also is home to a number of refurbished antique train cars owned by railway aficionados. Janet can provide details about the eclectic group of collectors who own them and their unique hobby.

The town is not far from the popular vacation destination of Lake Winnipesaukee, a Shaker village, and several other tourist attractions, and it is surrounded by an abundance of lightly-traveled back roads.

Bicycling from Black Swan Inn

Tilton is situated in New Hampshire's Lakes Region, which boasts more than 270 lakes and ponds amidst its rolling hills and heavily forested mountains. For the most part, cycling from the inn covers gently rolling terrain on little-traveled back roads. Longer, steeper climbs are found on the Newfound Lake loop. Traffic is relatively heavy along Routes 3 and 11 and through the town of Franklin. All routes are paved and pass through scenic, rural countryside where small towns—not much more than crossroads—dot the terrain. It's a great region for combining water sports or hiking with cycling.

Local Bike Shops
Klaus' Ski & Sport
560 US Highway 3
Belmont, NH   03220
(603) 524-3535
(603) 524-8159, fax
Sales, service, accessories.

Piche's Ski & Sports
671 US Highway 3
Belmont, NH   03220
(603) 527-3551
Sales, service, accessories.

Other Resources
Lakes Region Association
P.O. 589G6
Center Harbor, NH   03226
(800) 60-LAKES or (603) 253-8555
(603) 253-8516, fax
www.lakesregion.org

Newfound Region Chamber of Commerce
Bristol, NH   03222
(603) 744-2150

Greater Laconia/Weirs Beach Chamber of Commerce
Laconia, NH   03246
(603) 524-5531 or (800) 531-2347

Mountain Biking Opportunities
Gunstock, a popular ski resort off Route 11A in Guilford, provides plenty of mountain biking for riders of all abilities. Its trails offer great views of Lake Winnipesaukee and the White Mountains. The Gunstock Mountain Biking Center, located in the Guest Services Lodge, is open in the summer and fall and rents front-suspension bikes. Guided tours and instructional sessions can be scheduled. For more information call (800) GUNSTOCK or (603) 293-4341, or visit www.gunstock.com.

The **Orange Cove Trail**, in the **Mt. Cardigan State Park** area, has relatively easy singletrack and doubletrack trails. It's off Route 118, northwest of Tilton.

For additional suggestions, check with the local bike shops and look for information about the Bristol-based **White Mountain**

Mudskippers mountain biking club. Or contact the Sea Coast NH Chapter of the **New England Mountain Bike Association** (NEMBA) through its web site (http://24.1.69.170/snemba).

Canterbury Shaker Village (25.5 miles)
Moderate

Cycle over quiet back roads and gently rolling hills through the quintessential New England village of Canterbury Center to the historic Canterbury Shaker Village (603-783-9511, www.shakers.org). Founded in 1780 as the sixth of 19 Shaker communities, the Canterbury village at its peak in the mid-1800s included 100 buildings on 4,000 acres. Today, a cluster of 23 buildings sits on 694 hilltop acres, surrounded by fields, gardens, and trails. The well-preserved, picturesque site—one of the last remaining Shaker villages—provides a glimpse into a simpler way of life and an earlier time. An award-winning restaurant, the Creamery, serves Shaker-inspired four-course candlelight dinners, followed by a tour of the village, on weekends. Lunch is served during the day and the village's homemade ice cream delights aficionados of the creamy, cool treat.

Except for 0.3 miles on Twin Bridge Road, all roads are paved, with a number of gentle rollers and a few short climbs. Traffic is very light.

Pt.-Pt.	Cume	Turn	Street/Landmark
0.0	0.0	R	From Black Swan parking onto **Main St./ Rts. 3 North/11 East**
0.2	0.2	R	**Rt. 132 South** at light
7.2	7.4	L	Stay on **Rt. 132 South** at Y; follow signs to Shaker Village
0.9	8.3	L	Unmarked **Center Rd.**
1.0	9.3	S	**Baptist Rd.** at Canterbury Center; follow signs to Shaker Village
3.9	13.2	L	**Shaker Rd.** at stop sign at T
1.0	14.2		**Shaker Village**
5.2	19.4	L	**Shaker Rd.** (also **South Rd.**)
1.5	20.9	L	**Twin Bridge Rd.** (unpaved for 0.3 miles)
0.3	21.2	R	Unmarked **Shaker Rd.**
1.0	22.2	L	**Bay Hill Rd.**
0.4	22.6	S	At stop sign onto **Bay Hill Rd.**
1.2	23.8	BR	Stay on **Bay Hill Rd.**
0.9	24.7	R	**Elm St.** at stop sign
0.4	25.1	R	**Park St.** at stop sign
0.1	25.2	L	**Main St. Rts. 3 South/11 West**
0.3	25.5	L	Parking at Black Swan

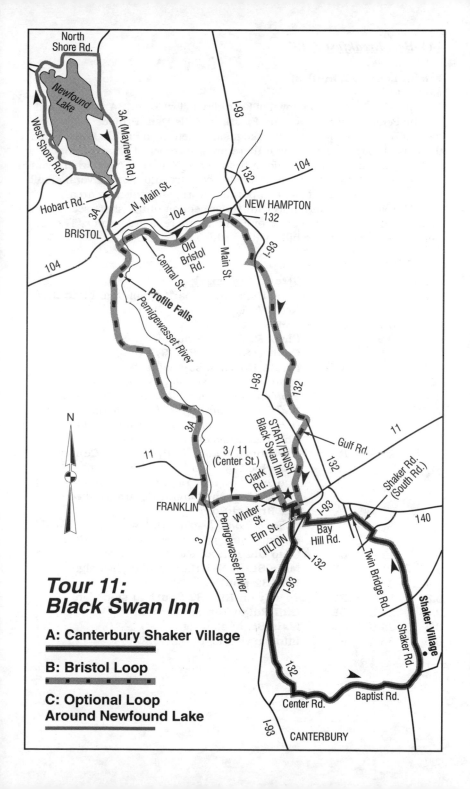

North Shore Rd.

Newfound Lake

West Shore Rd.

3A (Mayhew Rd.)

I-93

132

104

Hobart Rd.

N. Main St.

104

NEW HAMPTON
132

BRISTOL

3A

Old Bristol Rd.

Main St.

I-93

Central St.

Profile Falls

Pemigewasset River

104

N

11

3A

3 / 11 (Center St.)

104

132

START/FINISH
Black Swan Inn

Gulf Rd.

11

Clark Rd.

132

Shaker Rd. (South Rd.)

FRANKLIN

Winter St.

I-93

140

3

Elm St.

Bay Hill Rd.

Twin Bridge Rd.

TILTON

132

I-93

Pemigewasset River

Shaker Village

**Tour 11:
Black Swan Inn**

132

Shaker Rd.

Shaker Village

A: Canterbury Shaker Village

B: Bristol Loop

**C: Optional Loop
Around Newfound Lake**

Center Rd.

Baptist Rd.

I-93

CANTERBURY

Bristol Loop (35.4 miles)

Moderate

After passing through the town of Franklin, follow Route 3A, which parallels the Pemgewassett River and **Franklin Falls Dam Project**, to the tiny town of Bristol. Along the way, take a slight detour to **Profile Falls**. From the Bristol town square, where there are a number of shops, a market, and a restaurant, continue along the river to New Hampton, where you turn south, traveling through unspoiled country and along several small lakes, including **Hermit Lake**, a popular warm water fishing area.

All roads are paved, and with the exception of the short section on Routes 3/11 and in the center of Franklin, there is little traffic. The terrain covers gently rolling hills, with nothing too steep.

Pt.-Pt.	Cume	Turn	Street/Landmark
0.0	0.0	R	From Black Swan parking lot onto **Main St./Rts. 3/11**
0.1	0.1	L	**Winter St.**
0.8	0.9	L	**Clark Rd.** at stop sign
0.9	1.8	R	**Central St.**, also **Rts. 3/11**
2.1	3.9	R	**Rt. 3A North** at stop light
10.9	14.8		*Can leave route here for short detour to Profile Falls. Turn right onto Profile Falls Rd. At 0.1 miles, turn right, then right again after 0.2 miles onto dirt road, which leads to trailhead. Falls are 5-minute walk.*
2.1	16.9	R	Off Central Square in Bristol onto **Central St.**, which goes downhill and over metal bridge. If you reach the intersection of Rt. 104 you've gone too far. Central St. becomes **Old Bristol Rd.** ** *For optional loop around Newfound Lake continue straight to intersection with Rt. 104*
2.5	19.4	L	Onto **Old Bristol Rd.** at stop sign
2.3	21.7	BR	**Main St.** in New Hampton at yield sign
0.4	22.1	BR	**Rt. 132 South**
6.8	28.9	R	To stay on **Rt. 132 South** at stop sign
2.6	31.5	BR	**Gulf Rd.** at Y in Sanbornton
3.4	34.9	R	**Main St.** at stop sign
0.5	35.4	L	Into parking lot of Black Swan

Optional Loop Around Newfound Lake (21.3 miles)
Moderate, some hilly sections

Newfound Lake, with its rugged shoreline, is nestled among bucolic forests and mountains. It sits to the east of **Cardigan State Forest**. On the lake's southwestern shore the 204-acre **Wellington State Park**, (603) 744-2197, features a beautiful half-mile-long, crescent-shaped sandy beach among the pines—a great spot for a picnic, a swim, or a walk along its scenic trails.

Along the north shore are **Hebron Marsh Wildlife Sanctuary** and **Paradise Point Nature Center**, as well as trailheads for the **Ridge Lakeside Trail** and **Plymouth Mountain Trail**.

The route is paved, but narrow and winding in places. With the exception of the northern section, where there are lots of hills, including a significant climb, the portion that skirts the shoreline is moderately flat.

Pt.-Pt.	Cume	Turn	Street/Landmark
0.0	0.0	S	Turnoff for **Central St.** *(cume 16.9 on Bristol Loop cue sheet above)*
0.1	0.1	L	At stop sign on Central Square onto **Rt. 104**
0.0	0.1	R	Quick right onto **N. Main St.**
1.9	2.0	L	**Hobart Rd.**
0.1	2.1	S	Cross Rt. 3A at stop sign, onto **W. Shore Rd.**
2.1	4.2	R	Continue on **W. Shore Rd.**
5.7	9.9	R	**N. Shore Rd.** at yield sign
2.3	12.2	R	**Mayhew Rd.** at stop sign
9.0	21.2	R	Onto **Rt. 3A**, at Central Square in Bristol
0.1	21.3	L	Onto **Central St.** *(Continue over metal bridge per Bristol Loop cue sheet above)*

The Colby Hill Inn, Henniker, New Hampshire

Colby Hill Inn

Ellie & John Day and
Laurel Day Mack, Innkeepers
The Oaks, P.O. Box 779
Henniker, NH 03242
Rates: Moderate-Luxury, B&B
Open all year

Phone: (800) 531-0330; (603) 428-3281
Fax: (603) 428-9218
Web: www.colbyhillinn.com
E-mail: colbyhillinn@conknet.com

The rambling farm complex that today is Colby Hill Inn has played many roles and served numerous community needs in its 200-year history, from stagecoach stop and tavern to cattle farm to meeting house and church.

Today, the farmhouse, weathered barns, and carriage house comprise a comfortable, antique-filled inn and restaurant that reflects the same unspoiled colonial charm and small town hospitality as its home, the riverside village of Henniker.

Henniker, named after a wealthy merchant friend of the governor who chartered the town in 1768, claims to be the only town in the world with the name. Located on the meandering Contoocook River, which attracts kayakers and fly fishermen, and home to Pats Peak Ski Area, it's a perfect destination for sports enthusiasts, including bicyclists. This, however, seems to be a well-kept secret, since the town has not suffered the invasion of commercial tourism.

Inndog Delilah often greets guests on the front porch, followed by a congenial welcome by one of the Days in the old-fashioned lobby. Ellie and John Day, taken by the "warm feeling" of the inn, bought it in 1990. They've retained its historic, comfortable, yet unpretentious feel. The farmhouse, in addition to guest rooms on the first and second floors, features a parlor with a fireplace and an old working cylinder phonograph; a reading gameroom that opens onto the garden; and a gardenside dining room with floor-to-ceiling windows.

Items to occupy one's eyes—and mind—are everywhere. Unique antiques and collectibles abound, such as an eclectic arrangement of Victorian conversation pieces in the first floor hall that includes a dress stand, beaded pocket books, and period lamps. And books and magazines are found throughout: in the gameroom, on tables in the halls, and in the guestrooms.

Guests are free to roam the Inn's five-acre property, which includes a swimming pool, croquet, volleyball and badminton areas, and a whimsical garden complete with white Adirondack chairs, a classic fountain, a gazebo among the apple trees, herbs, and well-tended perennials.

There are plenty of cozy spots inside and outside to relax, read, write, or daydream. For guests interested in exploring Henniker's hidden treasures, the inn is barely a stone's throw from a path that leads to a picture-perfect covered bridge, open only to pedestrians and cyclists, that now belongs to New England College.

The old barn that serves as a passageway to the inn's secluded swimming pool also provides plenty of room for bike storage, amid lots of relics.

Colby Hill has 16 individually-decorated guest rooms in the farmhouse and converted carriage house, all with private baths and some with woodburning fireplaces. Rooms have either twin, queen-, or king-size beds. Room #1 in the main house features a fireplace, antique dresser, tables, and desk, and a brass bed with white eyelet bed ruffle and eyelet-trimmed bedspread, and, like all of the rooms, lots of small decorator touches, such as fringed lamp shades and a brocade accent pillow with tassels.

The guest rooms are television-free, but there are several nods to modern day conveniences, such as central air conditioning, telephones, and data ports.

A bountiful breakfast, which includes creative specialties such as scrambled eggs with boursin over puff pasty, is served to inn guests in the dining room.

In the evening, the candlelit dining room is open to the public, and executive chef Michael Mack and sous chef Dana Hansen turn out memorable dinners in one of the area's best restaurants. Guests can treat their palates to appetizers such as applewood-wrapped shrimp or Jonah crab vol-au-vent; the inn's signature Chicken Colby Hill entree, sesame encrusted swordfish, or filet mignon served with fresh grilled summer vegetable ragout and roasted red potatoes; and finish with a delicious homemade dessert and after-dinner cordial.

Bicycling from Colby Hill Inn
The secluded backroads in the Henniker area offer plenty of quiet, serene riding through small well-preserved historic villages, past covered bridges, along winding rivers and quiet lakes, and through the region's farm and forested lands. Bring a camera.

A mix of flat and hilly terrain offers great cycling for riders of all abilities. The busier routes, 202/9 and 103, offer wide, smooth shoulders.

For additional local cycling tips visit one of the local bike shops or get a copy of the "Outdoor Guide to Henniker/Hillsborough," published by The Henniker Rotary Club. It offers suggestions for four local road loops and three off-road trails, as well as tips for hiking, fishing, canoe-

ing, kayaking, and swimming, and a number of winter sports. Access it
online at http://rotary.henniker.nh.us; write the club at P.O. Box 695,
Henniker, NH 03242; or pick up a free copy at local merchants, banks,
town library, or the police station.

Local Bike Shop
Cyclesmith
10 Main Street
Henniker, NH   03242
(603) 428-8035
Mountain bike specialists: sales, service, accessories and rentals. In
addition, there are a number of fine full-service shops in Concord.

Other Resources
Granite State Wheelmen
Two Townsend Avenue
Salem, NH 03079
(603) 898-5GSW

NH Division of Parks & Recreation
Bureau of Trails
P.O. Box 1856
Concord, NH 03302-1856
(603) 271-3254
www.nhparks.state.nh.us

Mountain Biking Opportunities
Opportunities to ride your bike off-road abound. Henniker is filled with
trails made by dirt bikes and snowmobiles. The surrounding state parks,
mountains, and fields offer everything from unmaintained roads and
trails to well-maintained paths—everything from wide and easy to extremely technical singletrack with lots of rocks and roots.

The **Hopkinton-Everett Reservoir** and **Clough State Park** area
features a 30-mile trail network managed by the NH Trails Bureau, (603)
271-3254. The annual EFTA-sanctioned "Second Start Enduro" is held
at Hopkinton-Everett, which offers diverse terrain, bridges, rivers, and
swimming areas, including a 140-acre river pool in Clough. A map is
available at the Stark Pond parking lot. Take Route 114 S to 77E; in
Dunbarton, turn right on Ray Road, then right at Stark Pond.

Bear Brook State Park, ten miles east of Concord, offers some 50 miles of trails throughout 9,600 acres of forested land. You'll find terrain for all abilities with lots of ponds, brooks, and marshes and opportunities for swimming, hiking, canoeing, fishing, and wildlife spotting. At least one rider reports seeing a moose here. Trails are well marked and maps are available at the main entrance and other locations throughout the park. From Route 202, take 28 South. Park entrance is on left after about 6 miles. For park information, call (603) 485-9874.

Fox State Forest offers 22 miles of trails. Some wide, relatively easy trails lead back to the parking lot. From the center of Hillsborough, go north on School Street (which becomes Center Road) about 3 miles to the entrance, which is on the right.

Mt. Sunapee State Park offers lift-assisted access to its ski trails. For more information, call (603) 763-2356 or visit www.mtsunapee.com.

For additional suggestions or details, check with local bike shops, some of which offer organized weekly mountain bike rides, or the Sea Coast NH Chapter of the **New England Mountain Bike Association** (NEMBA) at its web site (http://24.1.69.170/snemba).

Henniker Warm-up (21.4 miles)
Easy to moderate

A scenic loop that provides a view of Pats Peak from Route 114 and skirts the Weare Town Forest and Hopkinton Reservoir. Overall gentle terrain with a couple hills: a long uphill grade on Route 114 and a short climb just after turning on Route 77. Busier routes, 114 and 202/9, have broad paved shoulders and tend to carry more traffic during commuting hours. There are narrow paved or gravel shoulders on Route 77 and no shoulder—and virtually no traffic—on Sugar Hill and Old Concord Roads.

Pt.-Pt.	Cume	Turn	Street/Landmark
0.0	0.0	L	**Western Ave.** in front of Colby Hill Inn
0.5	0.5	R	**Rt. 114 South** at flashing light/stop sign
7.0	7.5	L	**Rt. 77 East**
4.0	11.5	L	**Sugar Hill Rd.**
1.5	13.0	BL	**Stumfield Rd.** at fork
1.6	14.6	L	**Rts. 202/9** at stop sign
2.3	16.9	L	**Old Concord Rd.**
3.9	20.8	S	Flashing light/stop sign in Henniker
0.5	21.3		Colby Hill Inn

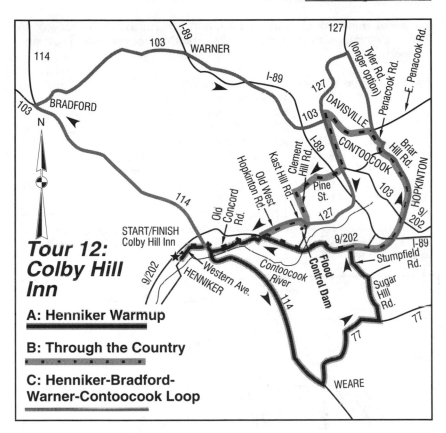

**Tour 12:
Colby Hill
Inn**

A: Henniker Warmup

B: Through the Country

**C: Henniker-Bradford-
Warner-Contoocook Loop**

Henniker-Weare-Deering-Hillsborough Loop (29.8 miles)
Moderate, rolling hills

Cycle through the small towns of Weare and Deering, and historic, colonial Hillsborough, the birthplace of President Franklin Pierce. The undulating roads connecting the villages are lined with miles and miles of unspoiled countryside and forestland, with scenic hills forming frequent backdrops. Route 149 between South Weare and Hillsborough twists and turns and travels up and down, delivering scenic pleasure around virtually every corner: stone-fenced cemeteries, mountain views, an abundant deer population, and a large waterfowl feeding and nesting area in the wetlands of Perkins Pond Marsh. The return to Henniker on Western Avenue winds along the bass- and trout-filled Contoocook River.

Route 114, which includes a long moderate climb, has a good paved shoulder, and there's a short (0.2-mile), steep climb after turning on Route 149. Route 149 is full of rollers. Experience some traffic in the village of Hillsborough and on the short stretch along Routes 202/9 before turning on to the solitude of gentle Contoocook Falls Road and Western Avenue.

Pt.-Pt.	Cume	Turn	Street/Landmark
0.0	0.0	L	**Western Ave.** in front of Colby Hill Inn
0.5	0.5	R	**Rt. 114 South** at flashing light/stop sign
6.7	7.2	S	Stay on **Rt. 114 S/Rt. 77**
4.3	11.5	BR	**Rt. 149,** toward Deering at V
0.1	11.6	R	Sharp right to stay on **Rt. 149**
1.1	12.7	S	To stay on **Rt. 149/Deering Ctr. Rd.**
7.1	19.8	S	Enter Deering
3.2	23.0	BR	To stay on **Rt. 149**
0.9	23.9	R	**Rts. 9/202 East** at stop light in Hillsborough
1.6	25.5	R	Onto **Contoocook Falls Rd.** (toward Bear Hill Motel). Road changes name to **Western Ave.**
4.3	29.8		Arrive at Colby Hill Inn

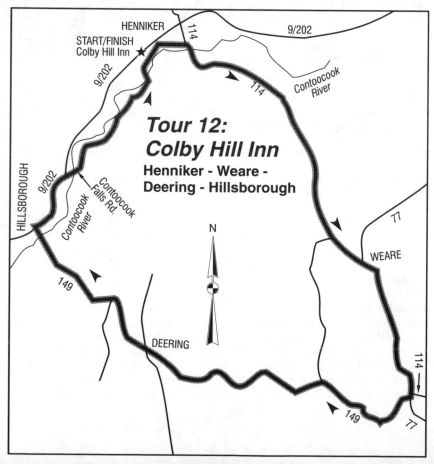

Tour 12:
Colby Hill Inn
Henniker - Weare -
Deering - Hillsborough

Through the Country (26.2 miles, or 30.6 with extra loop)
Moderate; rolling hills

This route takes you through the quiet, unpretentious town of Hopkinton, the crossroads of Davisville, and skirts covered bridge towns of Contoocook and West Hopkinton. In between, pedal through miles of remote countryside. An optional loop to Snyders Mill (don't blink, you'll miss it) adds about four miles of rural terrain to the route.

Except for a short stretch on Routes 202/9, which has a wide, smooth shoulder, there's little traffic on the route. There are a few small hills along the way, just as names of the roads, and their crossroads, hint: Briar Hill, Clement Hill, Kast Hill.

Pt.-Pt.	Cume	Turn	Street/Landmark
0.0	0.0	L	In front of Inn onto **Western Ave.**
0.5	0.5	S	**Concord Rd./Old Concord Rd.** at flashing light/stop sign
3.8	4.3	R	**Rt. 202/9 East** at flashing light/stop sign
3.2	7.5	R	Take exit on right to follow **202/9 East**
1.5	9.0	L	**Rt. 103 West**
0.0	9.0	R	Quick right onto **Briar Hill Rd.** at yield sign at the Y
3.2	12.2	BR	Unmarked **Penacock Rd.** at yield sign at Y
0.9	13.1	L	**Dustin Rd.** (E Penacock goes right) ***Go straight onto Tyler Rd. for longer option*
2.3	15.4	L	**Rt. 127 South** at stop sign. ***Longer option rejoins route here.*
0.1	15.5	L	**Rts. 127/103 South** at stop sign. Country Corner Store of Davisville is on your right.
2.0	17.5	R	**Pine St.** (If you cross the bridge you've gone too far. Pine St. is next to Hopkinton Fire Station)
2.3	19.8	L	**Clement Hill Rd.**
1.5	21.3	L	Go through **Rowell Covered Bridge**
0.0	21.3	BR	**Rt. 127 S** at yield at Y and then cross **Hopkinton Flood Control Dam**
0.4	21.7	R	Unmarked **Kast Hill Rd.** at T
0.2	21.9	L	**Kast Hill Rd. at Y.** (Changes name to **Old W. Hopkinton Rd.** after 0.6 miles)
1.8	23.7	S	**Old Hopkinton Rd.** at stop sign
0.2	23.9	S	Cross Rts. 202/9 at flashing light/stop sign
0.0	23.9	R	Quick right onto **Old Concord Rd.**
1.8	25.7	S	**Western Ave.** at stop sign/flashing light in Henniker
0.5	26.2		Colby Hill Inn

Cues for longer option:

Pt.-Pt.	Cume	Turn	Street/Landmark
0.0	0.0	S	**Tyler Rd.**
3.5	3.5	L	Unmarked **Rt. 127** at stop sign
3.2	6.7	S	Where Dustin Rd. enters **Rt. 127** from the left.

Henniker-Bradford-Warner-Contoocook Loop (36.7 miles)
Moderate; rolling hills

The gentle terrain and rolling hills of this popular local training loop takes you through quaint New England villages and pretty countryside. As with the other rides in the Henniker area, riders pass scenic lakes and wind along and over small brooks and rivers.

Scenic 402-acre Lake Massasecum, known for its smallmouth bass, pickerel, and yellow perch, sits next to Route 114. Elm Brook Park off Route 127 offers a swimming area with a sandy beach and an elevated wildlife-viewing observation deck that overlooks a natural wetland.

Traffic is light, with broad paved shoulders on Route 114, narrower paved shoulders on Route 103, and gravel or no shoulder on Route 127 and Old Concord Road.

0.0	0.0	L	**Western Ave.** in front of Colby Hill Inn
0.5	0.5	L	**Route 114 North**
9.3	9.8	R	**Rt. 103**
8.1	17.9		Warner village center
9.9	27.8		Davisville, Rt. 127 intersection
1.0	28.8	BR	Onto **Maple St./Rt. 127** at Contoocook's Fountain Square
2.7	31.5		Pass entrance to Elm Brook Park
1.2	32.7		Cross **Hopkinton Dam**
0.4	33.1	R	Unmarked **Kast Hill Rd.** at T at end of bridge
0.2	33.3	L	**Kast Hill Rd.** at Y. (Changes name to **Old W. Hopkinton Rd.** after 0.6 miles)
1.8	35.1	S	**Old Hopkinton Rd.** at stop sign
0.2	35.3	S	Cross Rts. 202/9 at flashing light/stop sign
0.0	35.3	R	Quick right onto **Old Concord Rd.**
1.8	37.1	S	**Western Ave.** at stop sign/flashing light in Henniker
0.5	37.6		Colby Hill Inn

The Hancock Inn

Linda & Joe Johnston, Innkeepers
33 Main Street, P.O. Box 96
Hancock, NH   03449
Rates: Moderate-Deluxe, B&B
Open all year, except Christmas Day

Phone: (800) 525-1789 outside NH,
or (603) 525-3318 in NH
Web: www.hancockinn.mv.com
E-mail: innkeeper@hancockinn.mv.com

Hancock, New Hampshire, with its steepled church, white gazebo, general store, four-room schoolhouse, town pond, and historic colonial homes, typifies picturebook New England. Like numerous Americana scenes along a former cow path that's now Main Street, the huge Federal home built in 1789 to celebrate George Washington's inauguration invites visitors to take a nostalgic trip through time. The white-columned clapboard building with a long front porch houses Hancock Inn, the oldest continually operating inn in the state. Since Washington's first year in office, it has hosted a wide range of guests—from rum runners to dignitaries.

Passages from the information book found in each guest room stir images of its early days: "The ballrooms of yesteryear have long since been converted to guest rooms, but if you sit in the common room late at night, you can almost make out the sounds of the saws and hammers that accompanied the birth of a nation, or the rustle of silk skirts, the laugher, and light tap, tap, tap of a generation who danced the quadrille during its growth."

Linda and Joe Johnston, seasoned innkeepers, bought the slightly peeling and neglected inn in 1991 and revived its original beauty. But they didn't take an out-with-the-old, in-with-the new approach. With a careful preservationist's hand, they restored and enhanced the inn's authentic colonial charm, while eliminating its most dreary features. In doing away with the smoke and darkness of the inn's former tavern, for example, they created a comfortable fireside gathering room with a bar, wing-backed chairs and even an antique checkerboard. On its walls Linda emulated the murals of primitive artist Rufus Porter, whose colorful frescoes cover the walls of one of the inn's most unique guest rooms.

The circa-1824 mural that winds its way around the fireplace, windows, and doors of the Rufus Porter room depicts a rural New England landscape of gentle hills dotted with trees and a village of red and white houses.

Another guest room, the Moses Eaton Room, is the namesake of the 19th-century stencil artists, Moses Eaton Junior and Senior, whose works were discovered under layers of wallpaper.

All of the inn's eleven rooms reflect its colonial character, decorated in rich colors, with wide-planked floors, area rugs, stencil trims (done by Linda), period furnishings, and hand-sewn quilts. Each room has a fourposter or canopy bed, private bath, and a number of other "modern" improvements: cassette player with classical tapes, telephone, and air conditioning. Hidden under a calico quilt cozy, guests find a TV with a warning that says "Please do not touch unless you wish to return to the 20th century" and a note from the innkeepers indicating they're embarrassed to admit they have them in the rooms. The John Freeman Eaton room has, in addition to its bathroom, a claw-foot soaking tub tucked under a corner window in the sleeping room between a wooden stand holding a jar of bath salts and an oak wash stand draped with plush towels.

In the fall of 1998, the Johnstons began construction to add four new rooms to the back of the inn.

Breakfast includes a variety of hot and cold items served in a sunny dining room overlooking the garden. The tasty, creative hot dishes live up to the Hancock Inn's reputation for serving fine food; its restaurant has been named one of the top 25 in the country by the American Association of Restaurant Scientists. In the evening, guests dine next to the fireplace of the elegant, candlelit dining room, where Chef David McCarty turns out savory classic favorites and original "new" New England Cooking. The house favorite is cranberry pot roast, adapted from a Shaker recipe and served at the inn for more than 20 years, served with mashed potatoes and steamed fresh vegetables seasoned with fresh herbs. Other specialties include appetizers such as butternut ravioli, Lobster Napoleon, and roasted eggplant stuffed mushrooms, Nantucket seafood chowder, and entrees such as toasted duckling with orange caraway sauce, herb-crusted lamb, and pork chops glazed with honey and served with sweet potato cakes and apple chutney.

Biking from The Hancock Inn

The Monadnock Region is marked by plenty of quiet back roads dotted by lakes and ponds. From the inn, the network of secondary roads includes gently rolling hills with a few short stretches on packed dirt. Cyclists of all abilities will find enjoyable cycling from The Hancock Inn. Some routes are winding and narrow, but offer great scenic beauty around every corner.

Local Bike Shops
Spokes & Slopes
Depot Square
Peterborough, NH 03458
(603) 924-9961
Sales, service, accessories, maps. Rents mountain, road, touring, and tandem bikes, and Burley trailers.

The Eclectic Bicycle
76 Grove Street
Peterborough, NH 03458
(603) 924-9797
Sales, services, accessories and rentals.

Other Resources
Eastern Mountain Sports (EMS)
1 Vose Farm Road
Peterborough, NH 03458
(603) 924-7231
Maps, supplies.

Monadnock Bicycle Touring Center
(603) 827-3925
Custom-planned tours

Cycling the Backroads of Southern New Hampshire
by Linda Chestney
Nicolin Fields Publishing

Greater Peterborough Chamber of Commerce
P.O. Box 401
Peterborough, NH 03458
(603) 924-7234
(603) 924-7235, fax

Mountain Biking Opportunities
Pisgah State Park, 13,000 wooded acres in the southeastern corner of the state, offers a combination of state park roads and trails with a fair amount of climbing on double- and singletrack trails. Trail maps are available at trailheads. From Route 9, take NH 63 south to Chesterfield. Next to town hall, turn left onto Old Chesterfield Road. Follow signs for Pisgah State Park. After 0.2 miles, turn right onto Horseshoe Road; go 1.5 miles to the parking lot, where there is information and maps. For information, contact Pisgah State Park at (603) 239-8153.

Near Greenfield, the **Wind Mountain** trail features a grueling climb, with a fantastic view on top, for advanced riders. To get to the trailhead for the 8-mile ride: If entering Greenfield on Route 31 from the south, there's a farm on the left with a road across from it. Turn right onto the road and take the next right. Park at the end of the road, where the trail starts.

For other recommendations check with Spokes & Slopes in Peterborough and see references to the Weare and Hopkinton areas in the section on Colby Hill Inn.

Harrisville/Dublin Loop (31.6 miles)
Moderate; rolling hills and a couple short, steep climbs

Highlights of this loop include Harrisville, the intact 19th-century textile community that Linda Johnston calls "magical" and Dublin, settled in the mid-1700s by Scottish colonists and now home of *Yankee Magazine* and *The Old Farmers Almanac*. Passing the exquisite mansions with stone walls and boat houses along Dublin Lake, one glimpses traces of why this once popular resort attracted writers such as Emerson, Longfellow, Thoreau, and Twain.

The loop includes a number of ponds and lakes, including Skatutakee Lake, Harrisville Pond, Child's Bog, Seaver Reservoir, Chesham Pond, Dublin Lake, and Halfmoon Pond, near Boston University's Sargent Camp. The Camp, which offers "Experiential Management Training Programs," sits on 850 acres and includes an extensive hiking trail system. The route also passes the entrance to Monadnock State Park near the trailhead to Pumpelly Trail, by Dublin Lake.

The ride includes rolling hills in the beginning and end sections, with flat stretches along the lakes. There's a short stretch of packed dirt on Sargent Camp Road and some rough pavement along MacVeagh, from which riders catch views of Mount Monadnock, supposedly one of the most climbed mountains in the Northeast. Except for a one-mile stretch on relatively busy Route 101, this is truly a back roads tour.

Pt.-Pt.	Cume	Turn	Street/Landmark
0.0	0.0	R	**Rt. 123 W** out of Hancock Inn parking lot
0.1	0.1	L	**Rt. 137 S** toward Dublin
0.3	0.4	L	**Middle Hancock Rd.**
1.4	1.8	R	**Vatcher Rd.**
0.7	2.5		Road becomes **Windy Row Rd.** where it bears left
0.5	3.0	R	**Sargent Camp Rd.**
1.4	4.4	S	**Hancock Rd.** at stop sign
2.6	7.0	BR	Stay on **Hancock Rd.**, as you ride along the north shore of Skatutakee Lake.

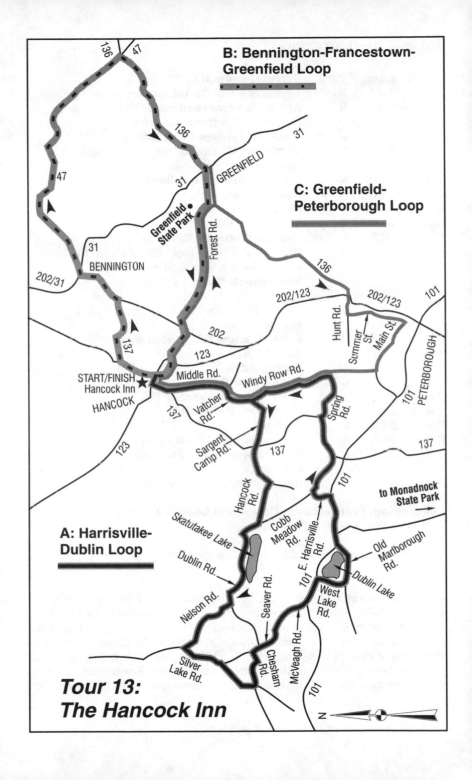

B: Bennington-Francestown-Greenfield Loop

C: Greenfield-Peterborough Loop

Greenfield State Park

136

47

31

GREENFIELD

31

47

31

BENNINGTON

202/31

137

123

Forest Rd.

START/FINISH
Hancock Inn

HANCOCK

Middle Rd.

Windy Row Rd.

202

123

202/123

Hunt Rd.

Sumner St.

Main St.

202/123

101

PETERBOROUGH

101

Vatcher Rd.

Sargent Camp Rd.

137

Spring Rd.

101

137

137

A: Harrisville-Dublin Loop

Hancock Rd.

Skatutakee Lake

Dublin Rd.

Seaver Rd.

Nelson Rd.

Cobb Meadow Rd.

E. Harrisville Rd.

101

West Lake Rd.

McVeagh Rd.

Chesham Rd.

Old Marlborough Rd.

Dublin Lake

to Monadnock State Park

Silver Lake Rd.

101

*Tour 13:
The Hancock Inn*

N

Pt.-Pt.	Cume	Turn	Street/Landmark
1.7	8.7	R	Unmarked **Dublin Rd.** at stop sign
0.5	9.2	R	At Y onto **unmarked road**. Follow signs to Nelson, and enter Harrisville.
1.9	11.1	L	Unmarked **Silver Lake Rd.**
2.4	13.5	L	Unmarked **Chesham Rd.** at stop sign. Follow sign toward Harrisville.
1.1	14.6	R	Unpaved **Seaver Rd. South**
0.4	15.0	S	Road changes name to **MacVeagh**
1.8	16.8	L	**Rt. 101 E** at stop sign
0.6	17.4	R	**West Lake Rd.**
0.8	18.2	L	**Old Marlborough Rd.** at stop sign
1.1	19.3	R	**Rt. 101 E** at stop sign. Do not take the hard right, which goes onto Snow Hill Rd. **Monadnock State Park** is on your right shortly after making the turn
1.2	20.5	L	**East Harrisville Rd.** The first left after Dublin General Store
0.8	21.3	R	**Cobb Meadow Rd.** at stop sign
1.2	22.5	L	**Rt. 137 N** at stop sign
1.4	23.9	BR	**Spring Rd.** at Y
1.2	25.1	L	**Windy Row Rd.** at stop sign
2.6	27.7		Road becomes **Vatcher Rd.**
0.8	28.5	R	Unmarked **Middle Rd.**
0.4	28.9	L	**Link Rd.**
0.6	29.5	R	Unmarked **Rt. 123 W** at stop sign.
1.9	31.4	L	**Rt. 123 W** at stop sign, toward center of Hancock
0.2	31.6		Hancock Inn is on your right

Bennington, Francestown, Greenfield Loop (22.1 miles)
Moderate terrain with rolling hills

(**Note:** *Can be combined with end of Peterborough Loop to create 32-mile loop.*)

Ride around Crotched Mountain, passing through the tiny, picturesque villages of Bennington, Francestown, and Greenfield, with the Federal- and Gothic Revival-style churches, town halls, and meeting houses that typify the architecture of the Monadnock region. In Bennington, the Monadnock Paper Mills, which began making paper from flax by hand in 1819, is one of the country's oldest paper mills. Francestown, once known for its soapstone quarries, features grandiose late 18th- and early

19ᵗʰ-century homes and buildings. The cupola-topped Town Hall once housed the Francestown Academy, whose graduates included President Franklin Pierce. In Greenfield, the meeting house, built in 1795, is one of the oldest in the state.

Between Greenfield and Hancock pass the Greenfield Park, which offers picnicking, hiking and swimming, and the old County Covered Bridge.

All roads are paved and traffic is light.

Pt.-Pt.	Cume	Turn	Street/Landmark
0.0	0.0	**L**	Onto **Rt. 137 N** from Hancock Inn parking lot
0.1	0.1	**L**	**Rt. 137 N,** toward Bennington at split in road
1.0	1.1	**BR**	Stay on **Rt. 137 N** at Y
1.9	3.0	**L**	**Rt. 202 E** at stop sign
1.1	4.1	**BR**	**Rt. 47 S** at Y
0.3	4.4	**S**	Stay on **Rt. 47 S** at stop sign in center of Bennington
7.0	11.4	**BR**	**Rt. 136 W** at Y in Francestown
4.4	15.8	**R**	**Rt. 136 W** at stop sign
0.7	16.5	**BR**	Onto unmarked **Forest Rd.** at Y, follow signs toward Hancock and Greenfield State Park. ***(For longer route bear left and follow Rt. 136W toward Peterborough, picking up cues from mile 7.0 on Peterborough loop)*
3.7	20.2	**S**	Cross Rt. 202 at stop sign and flashing light, to stay on **Forest Rd.**
0.5	20.7	**BL**	Onto **unmarked road** at Y, following signs to Rt. 123
0.7	21.4	**BR**	**Rt. 123 N** at stop sign
0.5	21.9	**L**	**Rt. 123 N** at stop sign, entering town of Hancock
0.2	22.1		Hancock Inn is on your right

Greenfield/Peterborough Loop (22.4 miles)
Easy to Moderate; gentle small rolling hills and one short, steep climb

Follow lightly traveled back roads through the small town of Greenfield to Peterborough, the largest town in the region with a population of nearly 6,000. It's also home to the country's oldest and largest artists' retreat, the MacDowell Colony. Eat lunch in one of the restaurants in the downtown area or pick up fixings for a picnic lunch. Follow quiet rural roads past Sargent Camp back to Hancock.

Pt.-Pt.	Cume	Turn	Street/Landmark
0.0	0.0	**L**	From parking lot of The Hancock Inn
0.1	0.1	**BR**	**Rt. 123 S** at Y, following sign toward Peterborough
0.6	0.7	**BL**	Unmarked **Forest Rd.**, following sign to Greenfield at split in road
1.0	1.7	**S**	Cross Rt. 202 at stop sign/flashing light to stay on **Forest Rd.**
3.6	5.3		Entrance to **Greenfield State Park.**
0.2	5.5	**L**	**Rt. 136 East** to visit town of Greenfield
0.7	6.2		Arrive at flashing light by the church & cafe
0.0	6.2		Turn around and go back on **Rt. 136W** toward Peterborough
0.8	7.0	**BL**	Stay on **Rt. 136** at Y, toward Peterborough
4.9	11.9	**R**	**Rts. 202E/123N** at stop sign. *Do not* go toward Peterborough
0.1	12.0	**L**	**Hunt Rd.**
0.0	12.0	**L**	Quick left at stop sign onto **Hunt Rd.**
0.5	12.5	**L**	**Summer St.** at stop sign at end of Hunt Rd.
1.9	14.4	**R**	**Main St.** in Peterborough.
0.2	14.6		**Main St.** becomes Union St.
1.4	16.0	**R**	**Windy Row Rd.**
3.9	19.9		Becomes **Vatcher**
0.6	20.5	**L**	Unmarked **Middle Rd.** at stop sign
1.5	22.0	**R**	**Rt. 137 N** toward Hancock
0.3	22.3	**BR**	At yield sign at top of hill, onto **Rt. 123**
0.1	22.4		Hancock Inn is on your left

Moose Mountain Lodge

Kay & Peter Shumway, Innkeepers
P.O. Box 272
Etna, NH 03750
Rates: Budget, MAP & B&B
Open June 15-Oct. 20; Dec. 26-Mar. 10

Phone: (603) 643-3529
Fax: (603) 643-4119
E-mail: meeze@aol.com

Sitting on the porch at Moose Mountain Lodge one stops imagining what it's like to be sitting on top of the world. The "99-mile view" of the Connecticut River Valley and Green Mountains gives new meaning to "breathtaking." The sunsets are spellbinding. The fiery tableau of colors in the fall is captivating.

Perched on the side of Moose Mountain among 350 acres of woods and wildflower-filled meadows, the Lodge offers a wonderfully isolated retreat from the activities and sounds of distant towns. The most disturbing sounds here are the morning wake-up call of chirping birds and the buzzing of hummingbirds circling the feeders on the porch. And the quiet rural roads below are a cyclist's heaven.

Kay and Peter Shumway bought the rustic log inn in the mid-seventies after falling in love with the view. When it was built in 1938 as a downhill ski lodge, there was a mile-long tow rope along the mountainside below the lodge. The tow rope is long gone, but today the mountain trails that run through the property make it a popular destination for cross-country skiers in the winter.

In the summer the trails are perfect for mountain biking or hiking. Note, however, that biking is forbidden on The Appalachian Trail, which runs near the property. The Shumways' Weimaraner Tula (which means "sweet little bundle" in Norwegian) knows his way through the trails and is happy to take guests for a hike.

The unassuming and amiable Shumways, who moved to Moose Mountain from South Salem, New York, have created a warm, inviting atmosphere where guests truly feel at home.

Signs of their refreshing highlander lifestyle are abundant. Peter cultivates a huge vegetable garden, the source of fresh ingredients for Kay's healthy and distinctive meals. Four angora goats supply Kay with the mohair she spins during her free time. A pond provides the perfect place to take a dip after a long day of cycling. And Sylvia the pig ... well, she provides a good photo opportunity.

The Lodge's living room, with its giant stone fireplace, large cushioned furnishings, baby grand piano, bookshelves, and game boards, is a cozy spot to curl up with a book or share conversation—or a singalong—

with other guests. The back porch, filled with wicker and wooden chairs and tables, provides the ideal vantage point for colorful evening sunsets or the blaze of fall colors. A small refrigerator on the porch is stocked with cold refreshments. A cookie jar holds fresh-baked cookies and a fruit bowl provides snacks for health-conscious visitors.

There are 12 guestrooms with queen, twin, or built-in bunk beds. Kay, who has many hobbies, including wood turning, built some of the beds from hand-hewn timbers. No overly frou-frou decorations in these rooms; instead, warm, earthy furnishings befit the log and stone building that envelopes them.

The shared bathrooms are spotlessly clean, with special touches such as fresh wildflowers and Kay's Ole, her own skin cream, on the vanities. Moose-themed decorative pieces dot the house. In one of the bathrooms, hand-stenciled moose border its white curtains.

Guests dine together around two oversized wood tables, lending to the familial feeling of Moose Mountain Lodge. (Kay made the 7-foot round table.) A fireplace and chairs at one end of the dining room invite guests to enjoy a pre-dinner drink. Although the Shumways don't have a liquor license, they're happy to chill guests' alcoholic beverages.

Peter and Kay believe that the best food is the freshest food, and Kay's wholesome meals incorporate ingredients straight from the garden and other local sources. She's even compiled her favorite recipes in *The Moose Mountain Lodge Cookbook*. The hearty breakfasts feature plenty of homemade items, from granola to maple syrup to a wide variety of fresh-baked goods and variations on traditional breakfast items: Swedish bread, Norwegian waffles, blueberry muffins (with fresh blueberries, of course). For dinner Kay serves up delights such as salmon with salsa sauce or baked crab with plenty of fresh vegetables on the side, including salad and snow peas from the garden, lentils with cashews, or fresh corn on the cob. And the desserts that come from the kitchen, particularly the homemade ice cream, are impossible to pass up.

Biking from Moose Mountain Lodge

Moose Mountain Lodge is off the beaten track. Consequently, the back roads that dominate this area of the Granite State are little traveled. Peter will share additional route information, local maps, and a *New Hampshire Atlas & Gazetteer* with cyclists wanting to study alternative routes and the terrain before striking out.

On the short stretches on New Hampshire Routes 4, 4A, and 10 and along Route 5 in Vermont, riders will experience more traffic, but the smooth wide shoulders are paved. In and around the towns of Enfield and, in particular, Hanover, exercise caution near the main commercial areas.

Some of the roads, as noted, are unpaved or have rough surfaces, but can be covered on a sturdy road or touring bike. The region is marked by lots of rolling hills, some steeper than others, and the many unpaved roads are perfect for exploring by mountain bike.

Local Bike Shops

Tom Mowatt Cycles
213 Mechanic St.
Lebanon, NH   03766
(603) 448-5556
(603) 448-6327, fax
www.sover.net/~tmc/
Sales, service, accessories. Racing, touring, and mountain bikes.

Omer and Bob's
7 Allen Street
Hanover, NH   03755
(603) 643-3525
(603) 643-3568, fax
Sales, service, and accessories. Mountain and road bike rentals.

CMC Cycles
12 Dunster Dr.
Hanover, NH   03755
(603) 643-4700
Sales, service, accessories.

Other Resources

Hanover Chamber of Commerce
Hanover, NH   03755
(603) 643-3115

Lebanon Chamber of Commerce
Lebanon, NH   03766
(603) 448-1203

Mountain Biking Opportunities

Explore the trails on Moose Mountain, or one of the local bike shops can provide suggestions for mountain biking trails in the region. In fact, Tom Mowatt Cycles includes suggested trails on its web site.

The **Orange Cove Trail**, in the **Mt. Cardigan State Park** area, has relatively easy singletrack and doubletrack trails. Take Route 4 west to NH 118 and follow signs for Mt. Cardigan Park for about 3 miles. Turn left after the bridge and follow the road for approximately 0.2 miles to the beginning of the trail.

Farnum Hill Reserve, just southwest of Lebanon, offers several loops to its north and south peaks. From Routes 10 and 4, about 1 mile west of Lebanon, go left on Saxton Hill Road, then left on Old Kings Highway. The trail starts at intersection of Old Kings Highway and Poverty Land Road.

In the West Lebanon area, there are intermediate single- and doubletrack trails near **Sachem Village**. From the intersection of Routes 120 and 10 in Hanover, go south on Route 10 approximately 1.8 miles and turn left on Gould Road, toward Sachem Village. If driving, park along this road.

Mt. Sunapee, about 30 miles away, provides lift-served mountain biking on its ski trails from July until the beginning of September, and on weekends through mid-October. For details call (603) 763-2356 or visit www.mtsunapee.com.

Shaker Village and a Trio of Lakes (33.9 miles)
Moderate, rolling hills with a few short climbs; about 6 miles on unpaved or rough surfaces

Travel along isolated rural and lakeside roads common to this part of the Granite State. Hanover Center Road, which has lots of rollers, leads to unpaved Goose Pond Road, with its solitude and pristine lake views. Along a short stretch on Route 4, there are two country stores where you can pick up lunch items. Pass Crystal Lake before traveling along the southwestern side of **Mascoma Lake** to the **Enfield Shaker Village**, where you'll find a museum and museum shop. Enjoy a swim or picnic along Mascoma Lake before returning to the Inn via an easy, gradual three-mile climb along Rudsboro Road.

Note: Mileage begins at the bottom of the dirt road to Moose Mountain Lodge, at the intersection of Old Dana and Ruddsboro Roads.

Pt.-Pt.	Cume	Turn	Street/Landmark
0.0	0.0	R	**Ruddsboro Rd.** (paved)
2.0	2.0	R	Unmarked **Hanover Center Rd.** at stop sign
5.5	7.5	R	**Goose Pond Rd.**
7.5	15	BR	Unmarked **Goose Pond Rd.**
2.7	17.7	R	**Rt. 4 West**
0.5	18.2	L	**Unmarked road** (Mascoma Valley Regional High School is on the right.)
0.2	18.4	L	**Jones Hill Rd.** (short, steep climb)

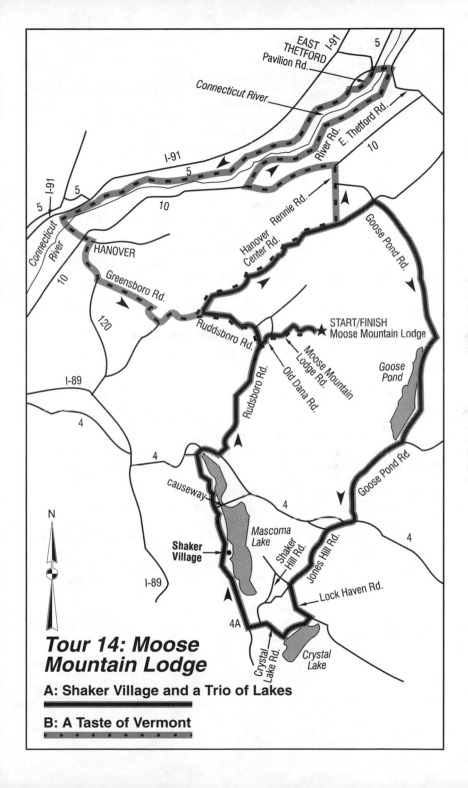

EAST THETFORD
Pavilion Rd.
I-91
5
Connecticut River
River Rd.
E. Thetford Rd.
I-91
5
10
I-91
5
5
10
Connecticut River
HANOVER
10
Hanover Rennie Rd.
Hanover Center Rd.
Greensboro Rd.
120
Ruddsboro Rd.
START/FINISH
Moose Mountain Lodge
Goose Pond Rd.
Goose Pond
I-89
4
Rudsboro Rd.
Moose Mountain Lodge Rd.
Old Dana Rd.
Goose Pond Rd.
4
causeway
4
Mascoma Lake
Shaker Village
Shaker Hill Rd.
Jones Hill Rd.
4
N
I-89
Lock Haven Rd.
4A
Crystal Lake Rd.
Crystal Lake

Tour 14: Moose Mountain Lodge

A: Shaker Village and a Trio of Lakes

B: A Taste of Vermont

Pt.-Pt.	Cume	Turn	Street/Landmark
2.0	20.4	L	Unmarked **Lockhaven Rd.** at stop sign
1.2	21.6	R	**Crystal Lake Rd.**
1.9	23.5	BL	Unmarked **Shaker Hill Rd.** at stop sign
0.3	23.8	R	**Rt. 14A North** at stop sign
2.2	26.0	S	**Shaker Village and Museum** on your right
0.9	26.9	S	Public beach at causeway/Shaker Bridge, to your right
1.5	28.4	S	Baited Hook Restaurant. Good place for lunch or snack
0.4	28.8	R	Past boat ramp; before main road turns left. Road drops down to right
1.2	30.0	R	**Rt. 4 East** (busy route)
0.4	30.4	L	**Ruddsboro Rd.** (just before fire station)
3.5	33.9	R	**Old Dana Rd.**

A Taste of Vermont
(32.9 miles, with several short optional side trips)
Moderate, with a few short steep hills

The further from the Connecticut River, the hillier the roads. Route 10 in New Hampshire and Route 5 in Vermont have more traffic than the quiet back roads around Etna, but they both have wide, paved shoulders, and Route 5, in particular, offers fantastic views.

This route offers several short side trips to picturesque villages. Enjoy the rolling hills from Ruddsboro Road to quiet, traffic-free River Road. Then cross the Connecticut River (or first make a side-trip to the quaint village of Lyme or the picturesque town of Norwich) and enjoy the scenic panoramas of New Hampshire as you travel south.

The Ledyard Bridge, once easy to cross, has recently been expanded to handle more auto traffic. Ride cautiously across it, and up a small hill to the center of the bustling town of **Hanover**, home of Dartmouth College and the center of learning and culture in the region. Visit the **Webster Cottage Museum** or the **Hood Museum**, check out the program at Hopkins Center, or just relax on the Green or enjoy the shops and restaurants.

Note: *Mileage begins at the bottom of the dirt road to Moose Mountain Lodge, at the intersection of Old Dana and Ruddsboro Roads.*

Pt.-Pt.	Cume	Turn	Street/Landmark
0.0	0.0	R	**Ruddsboro Rd.**
2.0	2.0	R	Unmarked **Hanover Center Rd.** at stop sign at T
4.1	6.1	BL	**Rennie Rd.**
1.3	7.4	L	Unmarked **Goose Pond Rd.** at stop sign
0.5	7.9	L	**Rt. 10 South**
2.6	10.5	R	**River Rd.**
5.4	15.9	L	**E. Thetford Bridge** at stop sign. Cross Connecticut River. *(For a detour to Lyme, turn right here and follow E. Thetford Rd. to Lyme, approximately 1.3 miles, and return via same route.)*
0.5	16.4	L	**Rt. 5.** Stop sign in E. Thetford (100 yards to the right is a general store/deli.)
0.1	16.5	L	**Pavilion Rd.** At "Sweet Corn/Flowers/Vegetables/Plants/Etc." sign.
1.0	17.5	L	**Rt. 5** at stop sign
7.0	24.5	L	**Unmarked road**, at sign for Hanover *(To visit the town of Norwich, continue straight on Rt. 5. After visiting Norwich, leave on Rt. 5, then take Ledyard Bridge to cross the Connecticut River to Hanover.)*
1.2	25.7	L	At stop sign to cross **Ledyard Bridge**. Use caution in crossing road; route is busy
0.5	26.2	R	Onto **Main St.** at stop light at top of hill. Hanover Green is diagonally to your left; Hanover Inn in front of you
0.1	26.3	L	At next stop light (at Municipal Office) onto **unmarked street**/Lebanon St. Pass Leverone Field House
0.5	26.8	S	**Rt. 120 South**, at busy intersection with light
0.8	27.6	L	**Greensboro Rd.** at stop light
1.9	29.5	L	At Y, following sign to Etna/Hanover Center
1.4	30.9	R	**Ruddsboro Rd.**
2.0	32.9	L	**Old Dana Rd.**

Snowvillage Inn, Snowville, New Hampshire

Snowvillage Inn

Kevin Flynn, Innkeeper
Stewart Road, Box 68
Snowville, NH 03832-0068
Rates: Budget-Deluxe, B&B
MAP rates available
Open all year

Phone: (800) 447-4345; (603) 447-2818
Fax: (603) 447-5268
Web: www.snowvillageinn.com
E-mail: snowvill@nxi.com

Snowvillage Inn is one of those blissful, get-away-from-it-all destinations that vacationers dream about. As visitors ascend the long, winding drive to the inn, they get just a hint of the inn's magnificent environs. Once they step onto the rambling retreat's screened porch and experience its unforgettable view, they realize what makes this hideaway so special. The amazing, unobstructed vista of the White Mountains, including Mount Washington and the whole Presidential Range, is at once mesmerizing and soothing.

The 18-room inn was originally built in 1916 as a private retreat for historical writer Frank Simonds. It was converted to an inn in 1948 by Swiss natives Max and Greta Pluss—even though their original intent was to turn it into a chicken farm!

Today, seasoned innkeeper Kevin Flynn and chef Laurel Tessier uphold the Plusses' tradition of providing warm, hospitable lodging, combined with fine country dining. After operating the Mill House Inn in Long Island, New York *(see page 205)*, Kevin bought Snowvillage Inn in 1994.

Located on 10 hillside acres on Foss Mountain, the inn is comprised of three buildings encircling a beautifully-landscaped lawn dotted with hammocks, chairs, a bird house, and award-winning perennial gardens.

The Carriage Barn, converted to a guesthouse by the Plusses, houses eight individually-decorated, pine-paneled rooms. The Chimney House, a more recent barn-style annex, features a two-story atrium entrance, guest lounge with fireplace, and four guestrooms with fireplaces. The gabled main house houses the restaurant, a huge common room with fireplace, and eight guestrooms, as well as a mountainview porch with cushioned wicker furniture. All of the sleeping rooms have private baths and are named after authors, with the Robert Frost room in the main lodge being one of the favorites. Through the white lace cafe curtains of its twelve windows lies the same spectacular White Mountain view as from the side porch.

The decor throughout Snowvillage Inn's three buildings is a mix of traditional American and colonial, with hints of the European influence of its previous owners—particularly in the wood-paneled dining room where touches of Tyrol abound.

The huge living room is lined with bookshelves and cozy corners where guests can curl up on a sofa, settee, window seat, or rocking chair. Homey touches, such as vases of wildflowers on the fireplace mantel, add to the warmth of the room—as do inn pets Max, a black lab named after the first innkeeper, and Beemer, a gray cat. Game tables for checkers and chess are set up in the living room and lounge, where there's also a piano. And for serious star gazers, there's a telescope on the porch.

A hearty breakfast, featuring specialties such as cream cheese-stuffed French toast with apricot jam and fresh baked muffins, is served in the dining room with its serene mountain views.

In the evening, folks travel from miles away to enjoy the inn's fine cuisine. The friendly staff serves savory dishes seasoned with fresh herbs and garnished with edible flowers from the garden.

Despite the indoor comforts of Snowvillage Inn, the best part is what lies outside. The cross-country trails outside the inn's front door can be used for mountain biking or hiking, and the hike to the top of Foss Mountain provides spectacular 360-degree views. According the innkeeper, it's just as spectacular during a full moon as during the daylight.

Biking from Snowvillage Inn

Innkeeper Kevin Flynn is an avid cyclist, and his young daughters Caitlin and Maggie share his enthusiasm for the sport. He can provide suggestions for both off-road and road tours, and has compiled a number of route sheets for cyclists of varying abilities and interests.

The region is marked by rolling hills, with plenty of steeper hills for experienced riders. Except for the major routes in and around the center of Conway, there is little traffic. Several groups in the area, including Red Jersey Cyclery and White Mountain Wheel People, organize weekly rides. Contact Red Jersey or check *The Mountain Ear*, a local paper, for meeting places and times.

Local Bike Shops

The Bike Shop
Mountain Valley Mall Blvd.
North Conway, NH   03860
(603) 356-6089
Sales, service, accessories, and repairs. No rentals.

Sports Outlet Ski Shop
South Main Street
North Conway, NH 03860
(603) 356-3133
356-3133
Sales, service, accessories. Custom frames. Mountain bike rentals.

Red Jersey Cyclery
Junction Routes 16 & 302
Glen, NH
(603) 383-4660
(603) 383-0805, fax
www.redjerseycyclery.com
Sales, service, accessories, repairs. Rentals, weekly rides, and tours.

Other Resources
White Mountain Wheel People
P.O. Box 225
Bartlett, NH 03812
www.ncia.net/users/toad/wheel.html
Email: skier@ncia.net

White Mountain Attractions Assn.
Box 10
North Woodstock, NH 03262
(603) 745-8720 or (800) FIND-MTS
www.whitemtn.org
Regional tourism bureau. Free information, maps and guides.

Mountain Biking Opportunities
The abundance of old logging roads, mountain trails, and country paths
provides plenty of mountain biking opportunities in the Snowville area.
Just outside the inn, try the cross-country ski trails or ask Kevin for
route sheets for several local rides.

A **Mountain Biking Map** of the Mt. Washington Valley, a rock
hopper's mecca, is available at local bike shops, outdoor gear stores,
and trail heads.

A number of White Mountain ski resorts to the north and west of
Snowville Inn offer lift-serviced biking, including **Attitash Bear Peak,
Loon Mountain,** and **Waterville Valley**. **Cranmore Resort**, in North
Conway, opens its diverse trails to mountain bikers, but no longer of-
fers lift service. Call (800) 786-6754 or visit www.cranmore.com.

Attitash, in Bartlett, offers a broad range of mountain biking opportunities and activities, including its Masters of Dirt Dual Slalom and Trial Series, Women's Mountain Bike Weekend, and The Pedaling Bear Classic, a stop on the Trail 66 race series. A bike patrol and trail crew develops and services its trail network. Private tours and guided instruction are available. The bike shop provides service and rents front- and full-suspension bikes. Call (603) 374-2368 or visit www.attitash.com.

Loon Mountain, in Lincoln, offers everything from easy, flat trails through the woods to a lift on the Mountain Skyride for those who want to tackle the 1,200-foot vertical downhill, single- and doubletrack of Bear Claw. Loon's Mountain Bike Center provides service, repairs, and bike rentals. For additional details: (603) 745-8111 or www.loonmtn.com.

A little further away is the scenic recreation trail at **Franconia Notch** and Cannon Mountain, (603) 745-8391 or (603) 823-5563. **Great Glen Trails**, at Pinkham Notch in Gorham, offers scenic trails and hosts a NORBA-sanctioned race in May, as well as a number of other races throughout the summer, including a 24-hour race. For information on Great Glen, call (603) 466-2333 or visit www.mt-washington.com. **Waterville Valley's** 30-mile marked trail network incorporates parts of its cross-country ski trails, old logging roads, fire roads, gnarly singletrack, and hiking trails. It also offers chairlift access to the top of Mount Snow, mountain bike clinics, organized rides, competitions, and a Dirt Camp. Call (800) 468-2553, or check out www.waterville.com.

Madison/Conway Loop (23.4 miles)
Moderate

*(**Note:** To eliminate the climb up Stewart Road, begin ride at Crystal Lake)*

Experience quintessential New England scenery, from the white steepled church reflecting in Crystal Lake to the quaint Eaton general store to the mountain views along Route 113. Pass scenic Purity Lake and King Pine Ski area near East Madison, and a blacksmith shop that offers demonstrations on East Madison Road. Except for a short section on Route 16 in Conway, the ride covers quiet back roads. Overall it features rolling hills, with one long hill on East Madison Road and an uphill climb along Brownfield Road and Stewart Road.

Pt.-Pt.	Cume	Turn	Street/Landmark
0.0	0.0	L	Out of Snowvillage Inn driveway onto **Stewart Rd.**
0.6	0.6	L	**Brownfield Rd.**
1.0	1.6	L	**Rt. 153 South**, toward Eaton (at Crystal Lake parking lot)

Pt.-Pt.	Cume	Turn	Street/Landmark
4.2	5.8	**R**	**East Madison Rd.**, which becomes **Madison Village Rd.**
4.3	10.1	**S**	**Rt. 113 North** at stop sign
4.7	14.8	**R**	**Rts. 16 East/113 North** at stop sign
1.9	16.7	**R**	**Rt. 153 South/Pleasant St.** at stop light in Conway
5.1	21.8	**L**	**Brownfield Rd.** (at Crystal Lake parking lot)
1.0	22.8	**R**	**Stewart Rd.**
0.6	23.4	**R**	Drive of Snowvillage Inn

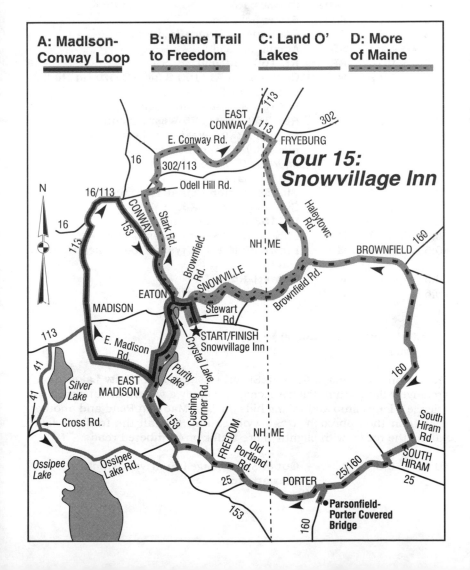

Maine Trail to Freedom (38.7 miles)
Moderate

Ride remote back roads past scenic lakes to Kezar Falls, Maine, then enjoy the off-the-beaten-track return to Snowville via the picturesque village of Freedom. Lots of rolling hills with little to no traffic on most of the route.

Pt.-Pt.	Cume	Turn	Street/Landmark
0.0	0.0	**L**	Out of Snowville Inn driveway onto **Stewart Rd.**
0.6	0.6	**R**	**Brownfield Rd.**
6.2	6.8	**S**	Continue on **Brownfield Rd.**
1.7	8.5	**BL**	At split in road
0.6	9.1	**BR**	**Rt. 160 South** at Y
10.1	19.2	**R**	Continue on **Rt. 160 S** (also **S. Hiram Rd.**) at stop sign at T
0.7	19.9	**L**	**Rt. 160 South** at stop sign
0.1	20.0	**R**	**Rts. 160 South/25 West** at stop sign
2.6	22.6	**S**	Stay on **Rt. 25 West** at split from 160 South *(Parsonsfield-Porter covered bridge is ¼ mile on Rt. 160, to the left)*
3.6	26.2	**R**	**Old Portland Rd.**
2.2	28.4	**R**	**Elm St.** at stop sign at T in Freedom
0.0	28.4	**L**	**Cushing Corner Rd.** at Y
2.1	30.5	**R**	**Rt. 153 North** at stop sign
6.8	37.3	**R**	Stay on **Rt. 153** at bend in road
0.5	37.8	**R**	**Brownsfield Rd.** (Crystal Lake Beach is on left)
0.3	38.1	**R**	**Stewart Rd.**
0.6	38.7	**R**	Driveway for Snowville Inn

Land o' Lakes (33.7 miles)
Moderate

Ride along portions of Crystal, Silver, Ossipee, and Purity Lakes along relatively flat terrain. Pack a picnic and enjoy a waterside lunch. Experience a long climb and rolling hills on East Madison Road and another climb on the approach to Snowville Inn. Overall the traffic is light along the route, with slightly more traffic on numbered roads.

0.0	0.0	**L**	Out of Snowville Inn driveway onto **Stewart Rd.**

Pt.-Pt.	Cume	Turn	Street/Landmark
0.6	0.6	L	**Brownfield Rd.** at stop sign
1.0	1.6	L	**Rt. 153 South**, toward Eaton (at Crystal Lake parking lot)
4.2	5.8	R	**East Madison Rd.**, which becomes **Madison Village Rd.**
4.3	10.1	L	**Rt. 113 South** at stop sign
1.9	12.0	L	**Rt. 41 South**
3.8	15.8	L	**Cross Rd.**, next to entrance to Lumber Mill
0.3	16.1	L	**Ossipee Lake Rd.**
5.1	21.2	BR	**Ossipee Lake Rd.** at Y
2.2	23.4	L	**Eaton Rd./Rt. 153 N** at stop sign
8.7	32.1	R	**Brownsfield Rd.** (at Crystal lake parking lot)
1.0	33.1	R	**Stewart Rd.**
0.6	33.7	R	Drive for Snowvillage Inn

More of Maine (29.6 miles)
Moderate

This is an easy to moderate ride paralleling the winding Saco River to Fryeburg, Maine, and returning via quiet back roads. All roads are paved and most of them have little or no traffic, although the numbered state routes have some traffic. Route 302, where traffic is heaviest, has a wide shoulder. There are some rolling hills and a climb to Snowvillage Inn; otherwise the terrain is gentle. Enjoy this tour through a little-visited corner of New Hampshire and Maine.

0.0	0.0	L	Out of Snowvillage Inn driveway onto **Stewart Rd.**
0.6	0.6	L	**Brownfield Rd.**
1.0	1.6	R	**Rt. 153 North**, toward Conway (at Crystal Lake parking lot)
2.4	4.0	R	**Stark Rd.**
3.1	7.1	R	**Rt. 113**
0.0	7.1	R	**Odell Hill Rd.**
0.7	7.8	R	**Rt. 113**
0.3	8.1	L	**Rt. 302** at flashing light
0.9	9.0	R	**East Conway Rd.**
5.6	14.6	R	**Rt. 113 South**
1.3	15.9	R	**Rts. 302/113** at T in Fryeburg
0.9	16.8	L	**Haleytown Rd.**
5.4	22.2	R	**Brownfield Rd.** at T
6.8	29.0	L	**Stewart Rd.**
0.6	29.6	R	Driveway to Snowvillage Inn

Chimnie House at the Cromwell Manor Inn, Cornwall, New York

New York Inns and Rides

Ever since early explorers first spotted the shores of what is today New York State, its grand waterways and inlets have ranked among its richest assets and most alluring attractions. The state's long arteries and great natural harbors have beckoned adventurous souls and industrious entrepreneurs for centuries, shaping its colorful history and multi-faceted character.

Much of the state's history-rich and most fertile land lies west of the Hudson River, including the rugged Adirondack and Catskill mountains and land bordering two of the Great Lakes. Virtually every corner of the Empire State (a moniker derived from George Washington's reference to it as the "Seat of the Empire") offers an abundance of cycling opportunities. However, the inns and rides featured in this section are based in the great Hudson Valley that dominates the eastern section of the state, and along the eastern tip of Long Island.

The three featured inns along the Hudson River are situated among what many seasoned cyclists view as a biking Mecca. The 306-mile long waterway, whose beauty inspired the famed Hudson River School of landscape painters, offers plenty of inspiration for cyclists too. The mountains and hills that rise above it form diverse terrain, offering a wide range of cycling opportunities for riders of all abilities.

The northernmost of these inns, **The Westchester House**, sits on a small street not far from Saratoga's historic race track and attractive downtown area. This popular cycling region, just north of the state capital, is so well-suited to cycling that the League of American Bicyclists has held two of its huge annual GEAR events here in the last 10 years.

The **WhistleWood Farm B&B** is tucked away on a small country lane on the outskirts of the well-known mid-Hudson Valley village of Rhinebeck. Originally settled in 1713, the town's streets are dotted with colonial establishments whose beginnings pre-date America's independence. During the Gilded Age, the region attracted the barons of American commerce, who built sprawling, opulent estates along the riverbank, many of which operate as museums or parks today and offer welcome spots for cycling breaks or lunch.

Perched on a small, pastoral hill in the unpretentious hamlet of Cornwall, the **Cromwell Manor Inn** beckons visitors to soak up the quiet country atmosphere of the Hudson Highlands. The southernmost of the three Hudson River Valley inns, it's a short, scenic bike ride from the massive compound of West Point Military Academy and Museum and the fertile farmlands of Orange County. Cycling routes on lightly traveled roads offer a range of diversions, including an outdoor sculpture museum and the state's oldest winery.

The tony vacation retreat of East Hampton is home to the **Mill House Inn**. From the Mill House, riders can strike out for one of the prime Atlantic Ocean beaches in the region or for the more forested routes near Cedar Point and Northwest Harbor. Fishing villages, wineries, lighthouses, and maritime museums are among the attractions that dot the routes and offer perfect breaks from riding—if sunbathing and swimming don't consume all your time off the saddle.

Resources

New York State Division of Tourism
P.O. Box 2603
Albany, NY   12220-0603
(800) CALL NYS or (518) 474-4116
www.iloveny.state.ny.us

Hudson Valley Regional Information
(800) 232-4782

New York State
Office of Parks, Recreation and Historic Preservation
Albany, NY   12238
(518) 474-0456
www.nysparks.state.ny.us

New York State Bicycle Program Manager
DOT, Building 4
1220 Washington Ave.
Albany, NY   12232-0424
1-888-BIKENYS or (518) 457-8307
www.dot.state.ny.us/pubtrans/bphome.html

New York Bicycling Coalition
43 Fuller Rd.
Albany, NY   12205
(518) 478-7818
www.nybc.net

New York Mountain Bike Coalition
P.O. Box 784
Syracuse, NY   13209-0784
www.ggw.org/NYMBC/

Cromwell Manor Inn

Dale & Barbara O'Hara
Angola Road
Cornwall, NY 12518
B&B Rates: Moderate-Luxury
Open all year

Phone: (914) 534-7136
Web: http://bbonline.com/ny/cromwell

Most visitors to the northeastern corner of Orange County, New York, head to the imposing and overwhelmingly impressive site of the oldest military academy in the U.S. at West Point. If, however, they follow the Hudson River just a few miles north, they'll discover the tiny, unspoiled village of Cornwall, home of Cromwell Manor Inn. In stark contrast to West Point's formality and grandeur, Cornwall exudes informality and simplicity.

The town today embodies an observation by English navigator and explorer Henry Hudson, when he anchored his vessel *Half Moon* at what is now Cornwall Bay in 1609 and recorded in the ship's log: "This is a pleasant place to build a towne on." Had he discovered the seven-acre hilltop site of Cromwell Manor, with its mountain views and mellow pastures, he surely would have written, "This is a pleasant site to build a house on."

The Cromwell Manor, from its perch off a quiet country road, is surrounded by rural delights. A path mowed through a field directly across the road from the inn leads to the Museum of the Hudson Highlands at Kenridge Farm, an environmental education center on a 177-acre historic farm. A smaller path beyond the inn's goldfish pond leads to neighboring Jones Farm & Country Store, which for five generations has served the area with homegrown produce, fresh eggs, maple syrup, honey, preserves, and homemade baked goods. Behind the inn, yet another path leads to an opening among the wild flowers that reveals, beyond the peach orchard, spectacular unobstructed mountain views.

In addition to a serene setting, Cromwell Manor Inn offers guests lodging in two distinctly different buildings. The centerpiece of Dale and Barbara O'Hara's property, which is listed on the National Register of Historic Places, is a grand circa 1829 Greek Revival mansion built by David Cromwell, a descendant of England's seventeenth-century Lord Protector Oliver Cromwell. The stately, white-columned brick structure seems at the same time perfectly suited to its environs and incongruous to its understated neighbor, The Chimnie, which sits at the base of the manor's sloping lawn. If the mansion fits the description of a country "estate," The Chimnie could best be described, by contrast, as a country "cottage."

The two buildings also reflect two diverse personalities in their decor. Between them, guests can choose from a variety of sleeping quarters that meet a broad range of tastes and budgets.

The Manor houses nine guest rooms, all individually decorated with a mix of antiques, distinct period furnishings, and elegant architectural features such as high ceilings with intricate wood moldings. Some rooms are decorated in bright, cheery floral prints and light color palettes, while others feature deep, rich color schemes and traditional Schumacher and Waverly print wallpapers. Many of the rooms have huge wood-burning fireplaces, including the oversized Arcarian Suite, which also has an oversized bathroom. The suite features an antique brass bed and an array of antique furnishings. In its spacious bath are a 6-foot-long, wood-rimmed soaking tub, separate shower stall, and a unique antique barber shop double-pedestal sink that creates his-and-her basins.

Another favorite room is the extremely oversized Oliver Cromwell Suite, which also has an extremely oversized (15' by 17') bathroom. This magnificent suite, which has a private entrance, is decorated in bright English garden print fabrics and features a queen-size canopy bed, woodburning fireplace and a comfortable sitting area. Its capacious bath offers a Jacuzzi for two, a separate shower, double sinks, and a bidet.

The unassuming Chimnie building, built in 1764, houses four inviting sleeping rooms that transport guests back in time to the Colonial period in which the house was constructed. It's decorated with primitive country furnishings, and its original architectural features have been preserved to create a warm, rustic retreat. The rooms feature original wide-plank floors, wood beam ceilings, diamond-paned windows, exposed brick and stone walls, and built-in wooden cupboards. Unlike the more traditional fabric prints of the Manor house, The Chimnie's rooms feature stenciled walls, country quilts, and white lace-trimmed curtains and beddings.

On the first floor, the Bedingfield contains a huge wood-burning fireplace with original mantel, a queen-size cannonball-style bed, and a separate sitting room with a large couch and several tables and reading lamps. The Hambleton room also features a wood-burning fireplace with original mantel and a mahogany queen-size sleigh bed. At one end of the room, in a wood and stone alcove next to the fireplace, sits an antique clawfoot soaking tub inviting guests to create a pool of bubbles and relax.

The two second-floor rooms, which share a bath, are perfect for a family or guests traveling together. The larger room houses a queen-size bed beneath its 20' cathedral ceiling featuring the original hand-hewed exposed beams and hand-pegged joints. The bright, smaller adjoining room features a queen-size sleigh bed.

In the morning guests are likely to be awakened by the roosters next door on Jones Farm (actually, contrary to conventional thinking, the Jones roosters crow almost any time of day) in a call to enjoy breakfast in the Manor's dining room or on the veranda. The inn's full country breakfast includes delights such as Hudson Valley baked apples and Cromwell Manor quiche.

Biking from Cromwell Manor Inn

Cornwall sits along the shores of the Hudson River in a valley formed by the Schunnemunk Mountains and the Hudson Highlands. The further from the river riders go, the higher the ridges get. However, the routes mapped from the Cromwell Manor avoid the more challenging mountains to the south and west and follow gentle to moderately hilly terrain along the Hudson River and inland along the fertile tableland that attracted early settlers and today remains dotted with sprawling farms.

The region also boasts a number of historic sites, museums, and natural attractions that make worthwhile sidetrips or excursions. Speaking of history, Orange County is one of the original counties of the Province of New York and derives its name from King William III, who was a prince of the House of Orange. Going even further back in history—way back—the earliest carbon dated human settlement in North America, more than 12,500 years old, is found in the county. In fact, mastodons once roamed the territory, where there are supposedly more of their skeletons than any place on the planet.

While riders are not likely to find remains of mastodons along the suggested routes, they will find that all roads are paved and, for the most part, have little automobile traffic. During the fall, colorful foliage erupts along the routes.

For additional biking suggestions, check with the local bike shop or one of the local groups, Orange County Bike Club or Mid-Hudson Bicycle Club, that organize regular rides. Or you could pick up a copy of our sister publication, *RIDE GUIDE: Hudson Valley New Paltz to Staten Island*, available for $10.95 from Anacus Press (call 908/604-8110 or visit www.anacus.com). Both the Orange County Bike Club and Bryan's Bikes also offer cue sheets through their web sites, although without a detailed local map it can be difficult to figure out the routes.

Local Bike Shop
Bryan's Bikes Inc.
240 Main Street
Cornwall, NY 12518
(914) 534-5230
www.bryansbikes.com
Sales, service, and accessories. Rents hybrids and tandems. Will deliver rentals to inn.

Mountain Biking Opportunities
One of the most popular mountain biking destinations in the area is the buffer zone of **Stewart Airport**, a 7000-acre site set aside to shield the surrounding neighborhoods from air traffic noise. Most of site has been designated as a cooperative area for outdoors enthusiasts, including hunters. Referred to as "the holy land" by local riders, there are trails to suit all abilities. It's also the site of an annual NORBA-sponsored race in the spring. Because it's so large it's also easy to get lost. Ask for a map at Bryan's Bike Shop and get the required permit, free at the airport in Building #138, (914) 564-2100 (then dial 8), to avoid getting fined. The trails are accessible off Routes 207 and 17K. Because the area is also used for hunting, riders can enjoy safe riding between April and the end of September, when hunting season opens. As this book goes to press, however, there is some talk of selling the land to developers.

Another favorite area with lots of technical uphill and downhill riding is **Black Rock Forest**, (914) 534-4517, which requires membership in the Black Rock Forest Mountain Biking Club. Bryan's Bikes can provide guest day passes. The Forest, which is just west of West Point, offers plenty of rocky fireroads and challenging singletrack within its 3,780 protected acres. Trails are accessible from Route 9W.

RIDE GUIDE: Mountain Biking in the New York Metro Area, another Anacus Press title ($14.95; call 908/604-8110 or visit www.anacus.com), includes maps and cue sheets for rides in neighboring Putnam and Westchester Counties.

Other Resources
Orange County Tourism
30 Matthews Street, Suite 111
Goshen, NY 10924
(914) 291-2136 or (800) 762-8687
(914) 291-2137, fax
www.orangetourism.org

Mid-Hudson Bicycle Club
P.O. Box 1727
Poughkeepsie, NY 12601
www.mhv.net/~mhbc

Orange County Bike Club
P.O. Box 122
Warwick, NY 10990
www.sussexonline.com/ocbc/

NY/NJ Trail Conference
232 Madison Ave., #802
New York, NY 10016
(212) 685-9699

Hudson Valley Magazine
Regional magazine published by Suburban Publishing, 40 Garden St., 2nd Floor, Poughkeepsie, NY 12601-3106; (800) 562-1973. Publishes annual "Insider's Guide."

Hudson Valley Guide
Tourist guide published by Taconic Media, Box 316, Millbrook NY 12545; (914) 677-8241 or (800) 709-8818. http://northeast-travel.com

West Point via Old Storm King Highway (19.9 miles)
Easy to Moderate

Once riders get beyond the main street of Cornwall, this ride offers incomparable, breathtaking views of the Hudson River.

Before getting to Main Street, however, they pass through a quiet, tree-lined "boulevard" that's home to one of two installations of the **Museum of the Hudson Highlands** (the other one being Kenridge Farm, across the field from the inn), (914) 534-7781. A little off the beaten track, Museum of the Hudson Highlands, with a stream flowing beneath its galleries, is dedicated to the study the natural and cultural history of the Hudson Valley. Its collection includes preserved fishes, reptiles and amphibians, Indian artifacts, and geological specimens indigenous to the region. Self-guided nature trails lace its 70 acres of deciduous forest.

Hardly a mile from here riders get their first glimpse of the Hudson as they descend to the scenic riverfront Donahue Park at Cornwall Landing. A short climb from the landing takes them to **Old Storm King Highway**, also Route 218, a portion of which is closed in winter. The narrow winding road, carved along a rocky ledge on the eastern side of Storm King Mountain, offers unbelievable unobstructed views of the river. Several pull-offs provide perfect perches from which riders can ponder the massive waterway's natural beauty or capture souvenir photos.

The road leads to **West Point Military Academy** and the small town of Highland Falls. The Academy, which has turned out military heroes such as Eisenhower, Patton, and Schwartzkopf, hosts a number of special programs and concerts (in the chapel and by the U.S. Military Academy Band) throughout the year. Its **Visitors' Information Center**, (914) 938-2638, and **Museum** in Olmsted Hall are opened daily, where the collections include items such as pistols that belonged to George Washington and Napoleon, a section of the Berlin Wall, uniforms, flags, and tanks. The **Cadet's Chapel**, a gothic structure with castellated towers and buttresses, represents one of the most outstanding pieces of architecture at the Academy and houses what it claims to be, with 18,000 pipes, the world's largest church organ. Guided tours of the Academy are available.

From the south dock of West Point a ferry departs for **Constitution Island**, (914) 446-8676, where visitors can tour the Revolutionary fortification and a Victorian farmhouse once the home of prolific 19th-century authors Susan and Anna Warner. Anna also was a knowledgeable and accomplished gardener, and the garden she called Fairyland laid the foundation for the colorful, lush landscaping on the island today. During the Revolutionary War a huge chain was draped across the river between the island and West Point to prevent the ascent of British ships.

By skirting the river between Cornwall and West Point, the route avoids the more imposing hills to the west, providing a gentle route with just a few moderate climbs. Route 218 has little or no shoulder, but has little traffic. Through West Point, the volume of traffic will depend on the day of the week and the season. In any case, the traffic is controlled, moves slowly, and poses no problem. All roads are paved.

Pt.-Pt.	Cume	Turn	Street/Landmark
0.0	0.0	**L**	**Angola Rd.** from drive of Cromwell Manor Inn
0.8	0.8	**R**	Onto traffic circle at stop sign, then sharp turn onto **Continental Rd.**
0.9	1.7	**L**	Unmarked **Boulevard Rd.** Pass **Museum of the Hudson Highlands.**
1.5	3.2	**L**	Unmarked **Payson Rd.** at three-way stop sign
0.3	3.5	**S**	Cross Rt. 218 at stop sign onto **Wood Ave.** Steep descent.
0.3	3.8	**R**	Unmarked **Shore Rd.** at stop sign. Follow to Cornwall Landing.

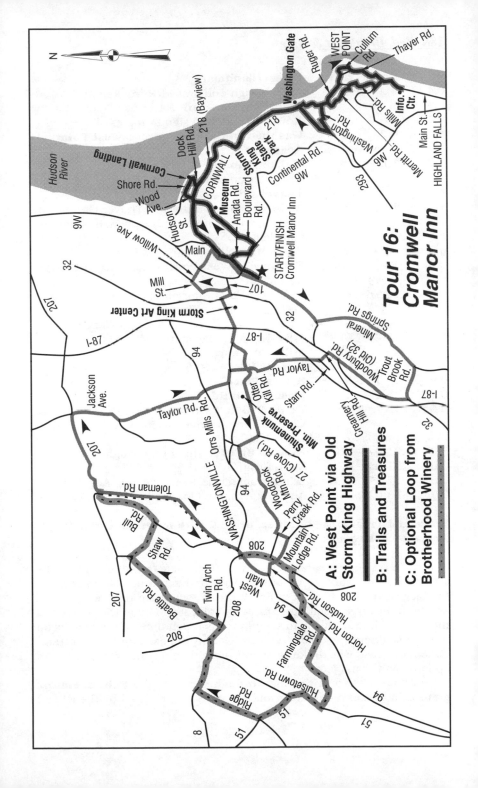

Tour 16: Cromwell Manor Inn

A: West Point via Old Storm King Highway

B: Trails and Treasures

C: Optional Loop from Brotherhood Winery

PtPt.	Cume	Turn	Street/Landmark
0.4	4.2	R	At yield sign and cross RR tracks onto unmarked **Dock Hill Rd.**
0.4	4.6	L	**Route 218** at stop sign at top of hill.
4.6	9.2	L	**Washington Gate** entrance to **West Point Academy**
1.3	10.5		**Washington Rd.** at stop sign. Follow road, which becomes **Ruger Rd., Cullum Rd.,** then **Thayer Rd.**
1.6	12.1	S	At 4-way stop sign, toward Thayer Gate entrance. Pass Hotel Thayer, which is on your left.
0.3	12.4	S	Enter **Main St.** of Highland Falls.
0.3	12.7		Entrance to **West Point Information Center** on the left
0.0	12.7	R	Exit West Point Information Center onto **Main St.**, toward West Point.
0.3	13.0	S	Enter **Thayer Gate** entrance to **West Point**.
0.3	13.3	L	**Mills Rd.** at 4-way stop sign
0.1	13.4	BR	**Mills Rd.** at split
0.8	14.2	L	**Merritt Rd.**
0.9	15.1	R	**Sladen Place**
0.1	15.2	L	**Washington Rd.**
0.5	15.7	R	**Route 218** at Washington Gate exit. Follow to Cornwall and bear left where Rt. 218 becomes **Bay View.**
5.3	21.0	BL	**Hudson St.** at flashing yellow light.
0.6	21.6	L	**Main St.** at light
0.5	22.1	L, R	Left on traffic circle, then right onto **Angola Rd.**
0.9	23.0		Arrive at Cromwell Manor Inn

Trails and Treasures (32 miles, or 45.2 with longer optional loop)
Moderate, Rolling hills

Nature and art lovers can mix it up with a visual feast of lush farmlands and mountain vistas, as well as artwork and sculptures from some of the biggest names in modern art. With an expansive nature preserve, and both the largest sculpture park and oldest winery in the U.S. along the route, riders are likely to spend just as much time off the bike as on it while soaking up some of Orange County's most interesting attractions. For those who'd like to spend more time on the bike there's an optional additional loop.

About a third of the way through the ride, the **Schunnemunk Mountain Preserve** offers 30 miles of trails, maintained by the NY/NJ

Trail Conference, over its 2400 acres. From here, the ride continues through picturesque open pastures filled with cows and horses toward the small town of Washingtonville, where there are a number of eating and shopping options. **Moffatt Library**, an elegant piece of architecture on Main Street with six Tiffany stained glass windows, was built in 1887 and offers local history exhibits. The town, however, is probably best known as the home of **Brotherhood Winery**, (914) 496-9101, which has been in continuous operation since 1839, having survived prohibition by producing sacramental wines. Despite a devastating fire in January 1999 that destroyed some of the original buildings, it continues to offer guided wine tasting tours through its newer wine-making facilities and vineyards.

Continue pedaling over rolling hills and rural roads to **Storm King Art Center**, 500 hilltop acres of rolling lawns, terraces, and fields where more than 120 works by sculptors such as Alexander Calder, Henry Moore, Louise Nevelson, David Smith, and Isamu Noguchi dot the landscape. There are no set trails, so visitors can roam freely over the grassy grounds and enjoy the spectacular views of Storm King Mountain and the Schunnemunk Mountain Preserve. Outdoor concerts are held in the summer, and the park is closed from mid-November through March, (914) 534-3115.

For the most part the roads are lightly traveled with good surfaces. However, traffic tends to be heavier on the short stretches on Routes 32, 208 (outside Washingtonville), and 207. All roads are paved except less than ¼ mile on Woodbury Rd. The terrain is marked by lots of rolling hills, but nothing terrible.

Pt.-Pt.	Cume	Turn	Street/Landmark
0.0	0.0	**R**	**Angola Rd.** from drive of Cromwell Manor Inn
1.7	1.7	**BL**	**Mineral Springs Rd.**
2.9	4.6	**R**	Unmarked **Trout Brook Rd./Rt. 34**
1.0	5.6	**R**	**Rt. 32** at stop sign
0.5	6.1	**R**	**Woodbury Rd. (Old State Hwy. 32)**
0.7	6.8		Turns to dirt
0.2	7.0	**L, R**	Left on **unmarked road**, then right onto **Rt. 32** at stop sign
1.0	8.0	**L**	**Creamery Hill Rd.** *Be careful* crossing highway.
0.2	8.2	**BR**	At split onto unmarked **Starr Rd.**
0.2	8.4	**L**	Unmarked **Taylor Rd.**
1.6	10.0	**L**	**Otter Kill Rd.** at T. Pass trailheads for **Schunnemunk Mountain Preserve**, on the right just after RR trestle.

PtPt.	Cume	Turn	Street/Landmark
1.5	11.5	R	**Clove Rd./Rt. 27** at yield at T
0.6	12.1	L	**Woodcock Mtn. Rd.**
2.4	14.5	L	**Perry Creek Rd.**
0.4	14.9	R	**Mountain Lodge Rd.** at stop sign
0.4	15.3	S	Cross Rt. 208 at stop sign onto **Hudson Rd.**
0.4	15.7	R	Unmarked **West Main St./Rt. 94**
0.7	16.4	S	**East Main St.** at stop light
0.3	16.7	L	**Brotherhood Plaza Dr.** (optional longer loop departs from here)
0.4	17.1	L	**Ahern Blvd.**
0.1	17.2	R	**North St.** at stop sign
0.2	17.4	BR	**Toleman Rd.** at split
3.2	20.6	R	Unmarked **Rt. 207** at stop sign (optional loop rejoins here)
1.8	22.4	R	**Lake Rd./Jackson Ave.**
1.1	23.5	BL	**Jackson Ave.**
2.2	25.7	S	Cross Rt. 94 to stay on **Jackson Ave.**
0.4	26.1	L, R	Left onto **Orrs Mills Rd.**, then quick right onto **Taylor Rd.**
0.5	26.6	L	**Otter Kill Rd.**
0.9	27.5	R	Unmarked **Orrs Mill Rd./Rt. 20** at stop sign
0.6	28.1		Entrance to **Storm King Sculpture Garden** on Pleasant Hill Rd. Ride 0.2 miles to entrance
0.5	28.6	R	**Rt. 32** at stop sign
0.2	28.8	L	Unmarked **Route 107** at stop light
0.1	28.9	L	**Mill St.**, which becomes **Willow Ave.**
2.0	30.9	R	**Main St.** (Bryan's Bike Shop is on your left)
0.2	31.1	L, R	Left on circle, then quick right onto **Angola Rd.**
0.9	32.0		Arrive at Cromwell Manor Inn

Optional Loop from Brotherhood Winery
Moderate

Pedal through lush farmlands and quiet country roads at the base of Schunnemunk Mountain. Aptly named Ridge Road provides breathtaking ridgetop views. All roads are paved with good surfaces and cover lots of undulating terrain. The busier numbered routes have good shoulders.

0.0	0.0	L	From Brotherhood Winery onto **Brotherhood Plaza Dr.**
0.1	0.1	L	**Ahern Blvd.**
0.1	0.2	L	**North St.** at stop sign

Pt.-Pt.	Cume	Turn	Street/Landmark
0.3	0.5	R	**East Main St.** at stop sign
0.1	0.6	L	**Rt. 208S** at light
1.2	1.8	R	**Horton Rd.**
1.1	2.9	L	**Rt. 94** at stop sign
0.7	3.6	R	**Farmingdale Rd.**
2.3	5.9	R	**Hulsetown Rd./Rt. 51** at stop sign
0.8	6.7	L	**Rt. 51** at split
1.0	7.7	R	**Ridge Rd.**
1.6	9.3	R	Unmarked **Sarah Wells Trail/Rt. 8**
1.3	10.6	BR	**Rt. 208** at stop sign
0.4	11.0	L	**Twin Arch Rd.**
0.5	11.5	R	**Beattie Rd.**
2.4	13.9	R	**Shaw Rd.**
1.1	15.0	L	Unmarked **Bull Rd.** at stop sign
1.4	16.4	R	Unmarked **Rt. 207**
0.3	16.7		Rejoin Storm King loop at intersection of 207 and Toleman Rd.

Inn at Silver Maple Farm, Canaan, New York

Inn at Silver Maple Farm

Meg and Bill Stratton, Innkeepers
P.O. Box 358, Route 295
Canaan, NY 12029
Rates: Budget-Deluxe, B&B
Open all year

Phone: (518) 781-3600
Fax: (518) 781-3883
Web: www.silvermaplefarm.com
E-mail: info@silvermaplefarm.com

The Inn at Silver Maple Farm sits nestled in a secluded corner of Columbia County, New York, in the foothills of the Berkshire Mountains, southeast of the state capital of Albany and just west of the Massachusetts border. Its quiet, out-of-the-way setting seems like it's miles from nowhere. But, to a cyclist's delight, it's a pleasant pedaling distance to a crystal-clear lake and many of the Berkshire's most popular destinations, including noteworthy museums (three of which provide a glimpse at life in Shaker villages of yesteryear), historic sites, and outdoor attractions.

It's also just minutes from several quintessential Hudson River Valley villages that reflect the simple, unassuming life of their rural communities. Often the town centers don't consist of much more than a white-steepled church, a post office in a clapboard house, a general store, a simple town hall, and maybe an antique shop or two. To guests' delight, the same quiet country charm that marks these communities is reflected in the ambiance of the Inn at Silver Maple Farm.

When Meg and Bill Stratton bought their farmhouse, barn, and adjacent 10 acres of property some five years ago with a vision of converting it to a B&B they didn't know what they would call it. They found the name for their future lodgment at a town zoning meeting. There, a long-time resident referred to their property, which hadn't operated as a farm for decades, as the "old Maple Leaf Farm". Today, the inn is surrounded by lots of maples and other deciduous trees, but most of the delicate silver maples that once dotted the property have not survived the decades. Bill and Meg, however, have planted a few new specimens.

The young couple continues to live in the farmhouse, but they've converted the former barn, according to plan, to quarters for their guests. They recently expanded the structure to add two new suites and a second common room. Much of the construction and carpentry work was done by Bill himself.

The centerpiece of the inn is the bright, spacious Great Room with its impressive barn-high ceilings, post and beam construction and wide board pine floors. This room, like the rest of the inn, is decorated in a refreshing, crisp Shaker-influenced country style: gingham-patterned wing-back chairs; stenciled tabbed curtains and decorative window swags anchored with twigs; woven rag area rugs; pots and baskets filled with dried flowers and plants; and lots of candles and other country accessories. Adding to the country charm, many of the inn's walls have been decorated with murals and freehand borders created by the light brush strokes of local artist Susan Leal.

The Great Room is a perfect place for relaxing in front of a crackling fire on cold days, or for sipping Meg's iced tea on a summer afternoon while indulging in homemade cookies that would make Grandma jealous. And, if you're not sure what to do with your day, there's a painted pine cupboard full of literature about local attractions.

Outside, there are also plenty of spots to relax, including porch rockers, a hammock tied under a big shade tree, Adirondack chairs scattered throughout the grounds, and a secluded whirlpool sunk in a huge cedar deck wrapped around a 200-year-old maple tree.

Along a long hall off the Great Room are seven guestrooms individually decorated with wide-plank floors, custom-made cupboards, antique trunks, decorative linens, and other country furnishings and accessories, many from local artisans. An upper level in the barn, accessible by a separate outside entrance, houses two spacious, more private rooms: the Upper Lodge Room and the King Room, one of the inn's favorites. This generous quarter has a king-size bed, separate sitting area with a pull-out sofa, and a small refrigerator and TV tucked into its built-in cupboards. All of these rooms have either a large walk-in shower or full shower and bath.

The newest addition to the barn includes two private suites. The Loft Suite, which features a cathedral ceiling and fireplace, is furnished with a king-size bed, sofa, and comfortable chairs. The two-story Pines Suite boasts post and beam construction in the first floor living room, which also has a fireplace. Upstairs is the bedroom, with cathedral ceiling, and a spacious bath. Both suites have deep soaking tubs and separate showers.

All rooms have air-conditioning and telephones.

In the morning, guests are treated to a scrumptious, beautifully presented breakfast of homemade breads and muffins, granola, and fresh fruits, along with items such as baked French toast, quiche, eggs, or apple pie pancakes.

Having worked together in the hotel business in Albany before launching their own enterprise, Meg and Bill are gracious and attentive hosts and, obviously, picked up many hospitality and service tips. Whether you need help securing dinner reservations, deciding which attractions to explore, or getting a box lunch or picnic basket, the Strattons are eager to help.

Biking from the Inn at Silver Maple Farm

Canaan, New York, officially sits in the Hudson River Valley; however, its terrain is that of the Berkshire Mountains, normally associated with Massachusetts. It's hard to get too far from the Inn at Silver Maple Farm without having to climb some hills, although none of them are really terrible. If you enjoy pedaling your way to the top of rollers and flying down the other side, you'll love the riding in this region.

If, on the other hand, you simply want to embark on a leisurely ramble, you'll find the easy ride around Queechy Lake to your liking.

Most of the roads in the area are lightly traveled, lined by picturesque farmlands, and offer fantastic mountain vistas from the many hilltops. During the fall, the scenery can't be beat. In the summer the area attracts performing arts fans who throng to Tanglewood, Jacob's Pillow, and a thriving array of summer stock theaters. Outdoor enthusiasts head to area lakes, state parks, and forests.

Cyclists who would like to tackle longer routes can combine the Museums ride with the Josh Billings loop from the Windflower Inn in Great Barrington, Massachusetts **(see page 133).**

Bike Shops in the Region

Plaine's
55 W. Housatonic St.
Pittsfield, MA 01201
(413) 499-0294
www.plaines.com
Sales, service, accessories. Mountain bike and hybrid rentals.

Ordinary Cycles
247 North St.
Pittsfield, MA 01201
(413) 442-7225
Email: ordinarycycles@taconic.net

Arcadian Shop
91 Pittsford Rd.
Lenox, MA
(413) 637-3010

Bash Bish Bicycles
Copake Falls, NY
(518) 329-4962

Mountain Biking Opportunities

There's a whole network of dirt roads lacing the hills around the Inn for riders who want to enjoy some invigorating, scenic off-road riding without all the roots and rocks of more technical mountain bike terrain. A small book from the Inn's library entitled *Loops, Strings, and Balloons*, by Edward Gibson, features 16 walks on country roads in Columbia County, several of which are nearby and make ideal mountain bike rides.

Kennedy Park, in nearby Lenox, Massachusetts, provides easy to moderate riding on about 6 miles of single- and doubletrack trails. Enter behind the shopping center on Route 20. Maps are available from the town of Lenox, (413) 637-5530, or at Arcadian Shop.

For more challenging riding, check out one of the ski areas or state-owned properties that permit mountain biking. Both Bousquet and Jiminy Peak provide lift-assisted access to their ski trails.

Bousquet Ski Area, (413) 442-8316, is located off Dan Fox Drive in Pittsfield, Massachusetts. Take Route 20 East to Route 7 South. Go about 2 miles and follow the sign for the Pittsfield Airport. **Jiminy Peak**, is located off Corey Road in Hancock, Massachusetts. For more information: (413) 738-5500 or www.jiminypeak.com.

Among the nearby areas managed by Massachusetts' Department of Environmental Management that allow mountain biking are **Beartown State Forest** and **October Mountain**, both east of Lenox, the **Pittsfield State Forest,** and **Mt. Greylock State Reservation.** Contact the department at (617) 727-3180 for additional information and maps.

Beartown, in Monterey, (413) 528-0904, offers dirt roads, logging roads, ORV, and snowmobile trails for easy to difficult riding. The Appalachian Trail, which intersects the forest's trails, does not allow bikes. You can swim in 35-acre Benedict Pond. The main entrance is off Blue Hill Road.

October Mountain, in Lee, (413) 243-1778, is the largest state forest in the state. Rocky logging roads and ATV trails are open to bikes. The trailhead is at the park's headquarters. From Mass Pike take 20 West, then right on Center Street and follow signs.

Pittsfield Forest, (413) 442-8992, offers plenty of technical climbing along the Taconic Ridge. The trailhead is off Circuit Road.

Mt. Greylock, the highest peak in Massachusetts, and Greylock Glen, (413) 499-4262/4263, in the Lanesborough/New Ashford area, offer a variety of trails accessible from a number of different points; many them begin off West Road, just northwest of the State Police station on Route 8.

Other Resources

Columbia County Tourism Dept.
401 State St.
Hudson, NY 12534
(518) 828-3375 or (800) 724-1846
www.columbiacountyny.com

Berkshire Visitors Bureau
Berkshire Common, Plaza Level
Pittsfield, MA 01201
(800) 237-5747 or (413) 443-9186
www.berkshires.org

SEE the Berkshires Magazine
P.O. Box 687
Sheffield, MA 01257
(413) 528-4002 or (800) 683-1000

Hudson Valley Magazine
Regional magazine published by Suburban Publishing, 40 Garden St.,
2nd Floor, Poughkeepsie, NY 12601-3106; (800) 562-1973. Publishes
annual *Insider's Guide.*

Hudson Valley Guide
Tourist guide published by Taconic Media, Box 316, Millbrook, NY
12545; (914) 677-8241 or (800) 709-8818. http://northeast-travel.com

Warm Up and Cool Down (21 miles)
Moderate

Riders can warm up their climbing legs during the first half of this ride,
with Routes 9, 34, and 5 offering lots of rolling hills and scenic hilltop
vistas. The rest of the ride covers relatively flat terrain as riders circle
Queechy Lake, reputed to be one of the cleanest lakes in the country.
Although it's a private lake community, and popular for pontoon boating
and fishing, there's a private beach where guests of the inn can swim. Be
sure to ask for a beach pass from the innkeepers before leaving the inn. A
visit to the General Store at the intersection of Route 295 and Queechy
Road is like taking a heavenly trip back in time. It's also a great place to
pick up a picnic lunch or get an ice cream cone before heading to the lake.
On Old Queechy Road you pass a house where prolific 19th-century writers Susan and Anna Warner spent several summers. The sisters authored
some 85 books, and scenes from *Wide, Wide World* and *Queechy* are set
around the house. All of the roads are paved, and traffic is very light.

PtPt.	Cume	Turn	Street/Landmark
0.0	0.0	R	**Rt. 295** from drive of Inn at Silver Maple Farm
2.3	2.3	R	**Rt. 9**, following signs for West Lebanon
5.0	7.3	R	**Rt. 34**
2.9	10.2	R	**Rt. 5** at stop sign
3.3	13.5	L	**Rt. 295** at flashing light/stop sign
0.0	13.5	R	**Old Queechy Rd.**
1.1	14.6	BR	**Rt. 295**
1.3	15.9	L	**Rt. 22** at light
1.5	17.4	L	**Queechy Lake Rd./Rt. 30**
1.4	18.8	R	**Rt. 295** at stop sign by the general store
2.2	21.0		Arrive at Inn at Silver Maple Farm

Museums, Museums, and More Museums (43.5 miles)
Moderate to Challenging, Hilly terrain

There's so much to see and do along this scenic and history-rich route that you'll want to do it twice. Riders start off following quiet, rolling back roads in Columbia County, New York. Then cross into Berkshire County, Massachusetts, where the Stockbridge/Lenox area offers a rich array of museums and attractions, one of the first along the route being the **Berkshire Botanical Gardens**, 15 acres of landscaped gardens, woodland paths, and picnicking areas, west of Stockbridge.

Just beyond the gardens is the **Norman Rockwell Museum**, (413) 298-4100, which houses the largest collection of original paintings by the famed artist. The 36-acre site overlooking the Housatonic River, where Rockwell bicycled on its trails with his wife Molly, includes his Linwood Cottage studio, outdoor sculptures by his son Peter, a reference library, and a museum store. Hardly a stone's throw away is **Chesterwood**, (413) 298-3579, the summer estate of sculptor Daniel Chester French, best known for *The Minute Man* and his sculpture of a seated Abraham Lincoln for the Lincoln Memorial. His Colonial Revival residence and studio house nearly 500 pieces of sculpture, and are open to the public.

Just after entering the town of Stockbridge, at the corner of Main and Sergeant Streets, is **The Mission House Museum**, built in 1739 by Rev. John Sergeant, the first missionary to the Mahicans. Heading north on Prospect Hill, riders pass a number of impressive private "cottages," one of which is open to the public: **Naumkeag**, (413) 298-3239. Designed by Stanford White and built in 1885 for Joseph Choate, former ambassador to Great Britain, the 26-room mansion and its furnishings offers visitors a glimpse into the Gilded Age.

The road meanders by the **Stockbridge Bowl**, a mile-wide pond that offers swimming, boating, and fishing—and a fantastic fireworks

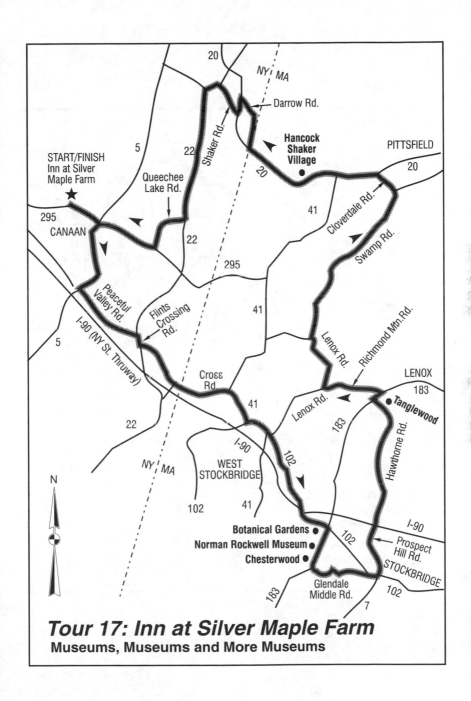

Tour 17: Inn at Silver Maple Farm
Museums, Museums and More Museums

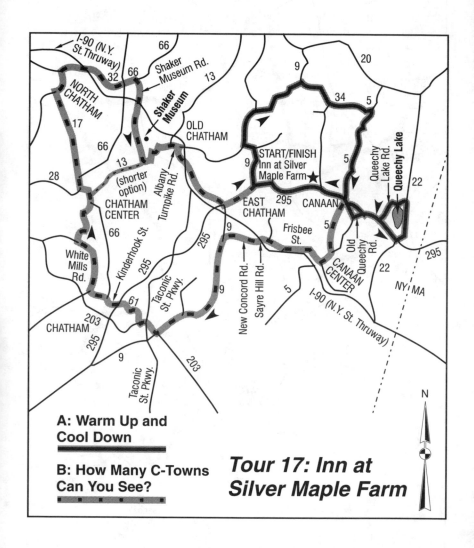

I-90 (N.Y. St. Thruway)

66

Shaker Museum Rd.

13

66

32

66

NORTH CHATHAM

17

66

13
(shorter option)

28

CHATHAM CENTER

66

White Mills Rd.

Kinderhook St.

295

61

203

CHATHAM

295

9

Taconic St. Pkwy.

203

Taconic St. Pkwy.

Shaker Museum

OLD CHATHAM

Albany Turnpike Rd.

295

9

EAST CHATHAM

295

9

New Concord Rd.

Sayre Hill Rd.

5

9

START/FINISH
Inn at Silver Maple Farm

9

34

5

20

5

Queechy Lake Rd.

Queechy Lake

22

CANAAN

295

Frisbee St.

5

Old Queechy Rd.

22

CANAAN CENTER

I-90 (N.Y. St. Thruway)

NY | MA

295

N

A: Warm Up and Cool Down

B: How Many C-Towns Can You See?

Tour 17: Inn at Silver Maple Farm

finale for the music season at **Tanglewood**, summer home of the Boston Symphony.

From the northern end of Stockbridge Bowl, riders tackle the most difficult climb on the route, Richmond Mountain Road. This long climb comes at about the midway point of the ride, with the second half offering the opportunity to visit two more museums, both preservations of the heritage of the nearly extinct Shaker sect. **Hancock Shaker Village**, off Route 20 in Massachusetts, maintains 20 restored buildings and a farm with a variety of livestock and plants. **Mt. Lebanon Shaker Village**, (518) 794-9500, across the border in New York, was founded in 1787 and served as a model community for the society. It features 25 restored buildings housing Shaker crafts and artifacts.

Riders return to the Inn along the west shore of serene **Queechy Lake**.

Depending on their conditioning, riders will find this ride to be of either moderate or challenging difficulty. But there are plenty of opportunities for rewarding breaks along the way. The route covers undulating terrain with rewarding ridgetop views, and a significant climb on Richmond Mountain Road. With the exception of a one-mile stretch on Shaker Road near the end of the ride, all roads are paved. Most of the roads are little traveled; Routes 20 and 22 present heavier traffic but offer wide paved shoulders.

Stronger riders who would like to do more mileage can combine this ride with the Josh Billings Loop from the Windflower Inn in Great Barrington, Massachusetts.

Pt.-Pt.	Cume	Turn	Street/Landmark
0.0	0.0	L	**Rt. 295** from drive at Inn at Silver Maple Farm
0.9	0.9	R	**Rt. 5** at flashing light
2.3	3.2	L	**Peaceful Valley Rd.**
2.5	5.7	R	**Rt. 22** at stop sign
0.2	5.9	L, R	Left onto **Flints Crossing**, just before gas station, then quick right after crossing RR
1.2	7.1	BL	Unmarked **Cross Rd.**
1.0	8.1	BR	**Dean Hill**
0.1	8.2	L	**Baker St.**, just after going under RR tracks
0.3	8.5	R	**Rt. 41S** at split in road
1.3	9.8	S	**Rt. 102**
0.2	10.0	BL, R	Stay on **Rt. 102** in W. Stockbridge
0.1	10.1	BL	**Rt. 102**
3.0	13.1	R	**Rt. 183 S** at flashing light. **Botanical Gardens** are at this intersection.
0.6	13.7	L	Entrance to **Norman Rockwell Museum**

Pt.-Pt.	Cume	Turn	Street/Landmark
0.3	14.0	-	Entrance to **Chesterwood** is on your right. Follow signs to museum entrance, **Willow St.** Approximately ½ mile to museum.
0.2	14.2	L	**Glendale Middle Rd.** Bear left after RR tracks to stay on road.
0.9	15.1	BL	Go through bridge to stay on **Glendale Middle Rd.**
0.8	15.9	L	**Pine St.** at obelisk, an **Indian burial ground monument**. (Turn is one block after Mission House Museum, where Rt. 7 goes right. To explore town of Stockbridge, continue straight)
0.1	16.0	BL	**Prospect Hill Rd.**, which becomes Hawthorne Rd.
5.3	21.3	R	**Rt. 183 N.** Gould's Meadow is on your left.
0.1	21.4	L	**Richmond Mtn. Rd.**, which becomes **Lenox Rd.**
3.0	24.4	BL	**Lenox Rd.**
0.2	24.6	R	**Swamp Rd.** at flashing light/stop sign.
4.1	28.7	L	**Cloverdale Rd.**
1.2	29.9	L	**Rt. 20**
1.1	31.0	-	Entrance to **Hancock Shaker Village**
3.6	34.6	L	**Darrow Rd.** to Mt. Lebanon Shaker Village
0.5	35.1	R	Unpaved **Shaker Rd.**
1.1	36.2	L	Unmarked **Rt. 22**
0.1	36.3	L	**Rt. 22** at split at flashing light
3.6	39.9	R	**Queechy Lake Rd./Rt. 30**
1.5	41.4	BR	**Rt. 295** at stop sign
2.1	43.5		Arrive at Inn at Silver Maple Farm

How Many C-Towns Can You See?
(36.2 miles, or 29.8 miles shorter option)
Moderate, rolling hills

It seems like this corner of Columbia County is dominated by towns and hamlets whose names contain words beginning with the letter C. This route through quiet farm country takes riders through Canaan, Canaan Center, New Concord, Chatham, Chatham Center, North Chatham, Old Chatham, and East Chatham.

Most of the towns aren't much more than crossroads around which are clustered a few picturesque colonial structures. However, the largest of them, Chatham, was once a major railroad hub and offers a number of specialty and antique shops, eateries, and even a movie theater.

Just before entering Old Chatham, riders have the opportunity to visit a **Shaker Museum and Library**, (518) 794-9100. The institution, which has built an outstanding reputation for its collection of artifacts depicting Shaker life and culture, houses over 18,500 objects spanning more than 200 years of Shaker history.

Across the road is another extraordinary site: **The Old Chatham Sheepherding Company**, which claims to be the largest sheep dairy in America. A flock of more than 800 ewes is managed on the 500-acre property, as well as a state-of-the-art milking parlor and creamery. The farm sells its "authentic artisanal handmade" sheep milk yogurts and cheeses, which carry names such as Hudson Valley Camembert, Mutton Buttons, and Mini Wheel, as well as items such as sheep skins and sheep fleece duvets. An inn and highly regarded restaurant are also on the property.

Down the road, a small general store in the center of Old Chatham commands a visit. It's like visiting a bygone era. Pick up a sandwich or a snack and enjoy it on the rockers on the front porch, surrounded by potted plants and antique collectibles.

Overall, the route is marked by lots of rolling hills through countryside dotted with lush pastures and rural scenery. All roads are paved, and traffic is very light.

Pt.-Pt.	Cume	Turn	Street/Landmark
0.0	0.0	**L**	**Rt. 295** from drive of Inn at Silver Maple Farm
0.9	0.9	**R**	**Rt. 5** at flashing light in Canaan
2.4	3.3	**R**	**Frisbee St.**, following signs to East Chatham
2.1	5.4	**L**	**Sayre Hill Rd.** Cross the interstate.
0.2	5.6	**R**	**New Concord Rd.** at stop sign.
1.4	7.0	**L**	**Rt. 9** at stop sign in New Concord at Y
2.1	9.1	**BR**	**Rt. 9**
2.5	11.6	**R**	Unmarked **Rt. 203** at stop sign
0.6	12.2	**R**	**Rt. 61** (just after crossing over the Taconic Pkwy.) Becomes **Austerlitz St.**
1.0	13.2	**S**	Cross RR track.
0.2	13.4	**S**	Go straight at fountain onto **Kinderhook St.** *(To explore town of Chatham, turn left.)*
1.2	14.6	**R**	**White Mills Rd.**
2.3	16.9	**R**	**White Mills Rd.**
1.7	18.6	**L**	**Rt. 66** at stop sign *(For shorter option, see cues below)*
0.3	18.9	**S**	**Rt. 66**
0.4	19.3	**BL**	**Rt. 17** at split from Rt. 66
3.0	22.3	**R**	**Rt. 203** at stop sign at T in North Chatham
0.6	22.9	**BR**	**Rt. 203** bends to the right

Pt.-Pt.	Cume	Turn	Street/Landmark
0.2	23.1	R	**Rt. 32**, following signs to Shaker Museum
2.2	25.3	L	**Rt. 66** at stop sign
0.7	26.0	R	**Shaker Museum Rd.**, just before church
2.2	28.2	-	**Shaker Museum and Chatham Sheepherding Company**
0.4	28.6	L	**Rt. 13** at stop sign at split
1.0	29.6	R	**Albany Tpk. Rd.**, in Old Chatham, following signs to NY 295
3.1	32.7	L	**Rt. 295** at stop
3.5	36.2		Arrive at Inn at Silver Maple Farm

Shorter option

-	18.6	L	**Rt. 66** at stop sign
0.2	18.8	R	**Rt. 13**, just before bridge
2.6	21.4	L	**Shaker Museum Rd.**
0.4	21.8	-	Visit **Shaker Museum and Sheepherding Company**. Turn around to return to Rt. 13
0.4	22.2	L	**Rt. 13** at stop sign at split
1.0	23.2	R	**Albany Tpk. Rd.**
3.1	26.3	L	**Rt. 295**
3.5	29.8		Arrive at Inn at Silver Maple Farm

Mill House Inn

Dan and Katherine Hartnett,
Innkeepers
33 North Main Street
East Hampton, NY   11937
B&B Rates:

Phone: (631) 324-9766
Fax: (631) 324-9793
Web: www.millhouseinn.com
E-mail: MillHouseInn@worldnett.att.net

Off season: Deluxe-Luxury; In season: Luxury
Open all year

East Hampton is best known for its exquisite vacation homes, celebrity seasonal residents, and prime beaches on Long Island's South Fork, known around the world as "The Hamptons." Majestic summer "cottages" have sprung up on—but not overwhelmed—East Hampton's landscape and Atlantic shoreline since affluent New Yorkers, taking advantage of advances in modern transportation, began vacationing here in the mid-1800s.

Today, East Hampton is a rich palette of contrasts. It remains steeped in the legacy and traditions of both its earliest residents, the farmers and fishermen who settled it in the mid-1600s when their boats landed on its shores, and the wealthy vacationers who came centuries later. Farm stands full of fresh fruits and vegetables still line the countryside during the growing season, potato fields dot the terrain, and local restaurants and markets feature fresh bounty from local waters.

In tribute to its early years, the tree-lined streets of East Hampton's meticulously-maintained historic district are graced with several museums, made possible by contributions from wealthy benefactors. Also prominent are Town Pond, which once served as a watering hole for cattle; a cemetery with tombstones dating to the 17th century; and an array of Colonial houses.

The business district of the well-manicured village boasts many specialty boutiques and restaurants, many charging Manhattan-like prices during the high season, along with many historic homes and buildings.

Mill House Inn, at the northern end of Main Street, claims a colorful past. It was built in 1790 by the Parsons family, one of the town's first settlers, and purchased in 1860 by Peter Lynch, one of 300 Irish immigrants shipwrecked at neighboring Amagansett in 1851. The house remained in the Lynch family for more than 100 years, but served a number of functions during those years, including that of a temporary Catholic church in the late 1800s and a butcher shop. Since the seventies it has operated as a guesthouse or B&B.

Dan Hartnett, an ex-priest, and his wife Katherine, a restaurant school graduate and ex-cook at the upscale Pierre Hotel in Manhattan, purchased the Mill House in 1994 and totally refurbished it top to bottom, adding a number of modern amenities. The Hartnetts also added a large, institutional kitchen, which fuels Katherine's passion for cooking, and separate living quarters to the back of the house. For part of the year, Katherine hosts gourmet cooking classes in the kitchen.

There's no pretense about this comfortable, homey B&B. A long front porch with French doors and white rocking chairs provides the perfect spot for breakfast on sunny mornings or for cocktails in the evening. A large landscaped garden with Adirondack chairs and garden tables invites cyclists to relax and unwind in the fresh air at the end of the day, or to enjoy the inn's scrumptious afternoon snacks and refreshments.

A brightly decorated common room on the first floor features comfortable sofas and chairs and a fireplace that crackles with a fire during the colder months.

As would be expected in a 200-year-old house, a few squeaks come from the floorboards. But the floors in the guestrooms have been covered with thickly-padded carpet to eliminate the noise between floors.

Most of the inn's eight rooms are small, but very comfortable. Many have closets, but some have only armoires, so if you're traveling with lots of gear, request one of the larger rooms with a closet. Better yet, travel light. All rooms offer amenities such as TVs, phones with voice mail, and private baths with a tub or shower.

The rooms are individually decorated and inspired by a Hamptons theme. The Patrick Lynch Room, for example, pays tribute to the former owner with a Gaelic flair played out in beige and hunter green Waverly fabrics and Irish lace. The Sail Away Room is decorated in shades of blue. And the Dominy Mill Room provides a view of the historic windmill across the street, built by Nathaniel Dominy IV in 1806. The picturesque mill, for which the inn is named, is open for tours in the summer.

The Garden Room is tastefully decorated in shades of pink, yellow, and green and offers a garden view, as well as a queen bed and bath with whirlpool. It sits just off the dining room.

The largest, most private rooms are on the third floor: Hampton Breezes and Hampton Holiday. They each have a fireplace and bath with whirlpool.

Six of the inn's eight rooms have fireplaces; four have baths with whirlpools, and all are spotlessly clean.

But what sets the Mill House apart is its bountiful gourmet breakfast. In fact, Katherine has assembled many of the Inn's best breakfast recipes—along with a collection of poetry, local information, and recipes from the area's top restaurants—in a book titled *Tasting The Hamptons.*

Indulge in delights such as pumpkin-cornmeal pancakes, cranberry-orange pecan scones, or potato and cheese frittata with southwestern chili sauce, either in the inn's dining room or al fresco on the front porch overlooking the windmill.

Biking from Mill House

Weather-wise, cycling on Long Island is enjoyable from late spring through autumn. However, as the seasons change, so does East Hampton's character—and the volume of automobile traffic. In contrast to the serene setting of the off-season, this popular, tony resort area is abuzz with New Yorkers escaping the concrete jungle of Manhattan to enjoy the unspoiled beaches, waterfront recreation, and summer social activities between Memorial Day and Labor Day.

The East End of Long Island offers an amazing mix of historic fishing villages, secluded harbors and inlets, beaches, preserved wooded areas, and farmland. For the most part, the terrain is flat, with some modest rolling hills along the northern part of the South Fork. In fact, the wooded area east of Sag Harbor presents some of the most pleasant riding in the region. What the area lacks in hills, however, can be offset by ocean winds, depending on weather conditions.

For beach lovers, biking is the only way to go. Parking permits for town beaches, restricted to residents only, are available to guests of the Mill House; but parking is nearly impossible during the busy season. Arriving by bike is hassle-free and provides the opportunity to explore more remote coves and beaches.

Organized road rides leave several times a week from BikeHampton bicycle shop in Sag Harbor.

Local Bike Shops

Cycle Path Bikes
330 Montauk Highway
Wainscott, NY 11975
(631) 537-1144
(631) 537-1081, fax
www.pinchflat.com
Sales, service, rentals, and accessories. Organized weekly mountain bike rides depart from shop.

BikeHampton
36 Main Street
Sag Harbor, NY 11963
(631) 725-7329
Sales, service, rentals, and accessories. Regular organized mountain
and road bike rides from shop.

Amagansett Beach & Bicycle Company
Montauk and Cross Highways
Amagansett, NY 11937
(631) 267-6325
www.amagansettbeachco.com
Sales, service, rentals, and accessories. Road bikes, hybrids, mountain
bikes, and tandems. Also rents surfboards, windsurfers, in-line skates,
and kayaks.

Other Resources
East Hampton Chamber of Commerce
79A Main Street
East Hampton, NY 11937
(631) 324-0362
(631) 329-1642, fax
www.easthamptonchamber.com

Sag Harbor Chamber of Commerce
P.O. Box 2810
Sag Harbor, NY 11963
(631) 725-0011
www.sagharborchamber.com

Long Island Convention and Visitors Bureau
330 Motor Parkway
Hauppauge, NY 11788
(877) FUN-ON-LI
www.licvb.com

East End Community Online
www.eastendcommunity.com

Bicycle Long Island
www.bicyclelongisland.org
Umbrella organization for five largest bike clubs on Long Island

Mountain Biking Opportunities
Off-road riders will find plenty of trails north of East Hampton and east of Sag Harbor in the area dominated by **Northwest Harbor** and **Cedar Point**, (631) 852-7620, County Parks. The dirt trails in Cedar Park are open to mountain bikers. And the entrance to 8-mile long **Northwest Path**, a favorite with experienced local riders, is at the intersection of Edwards Hole Road and Route 114.

Hither Hills State Park, (631) 668-2554 or 2461, off Old Montauk Highway east of East Hampton, offers 40 miles of poorly-marked double- and singletrack over diverse terrain suitable for beginner to intermediate riders. The 1059-acre park also features plenty of nature trails, sandy beaches, and horses for hire.

For additional suggestions, consult *RIDE GUIDE: Mountain Biking in the New York Metro Area* by Joel Sendek ($14.95 from Anacus Press; call 908/604-8110 or visit www.anacus.com). To join a scheduled group ride, contact BikeHampton in Sag Harbor or Cycle Path in Wainscott.

Water Mill, Bridgehampton, and more (29.3 miles)
Easy

This ride offers a little bit of everything: rich farmlands, including those ubiquitous potato fields, fashionable homes, a vineyard, museums, and dune-covered beaches. The terrain is flat, and the route is designed to wind along scenic roads north and south of busy Route 27.

Early in the ride, visit **Sagpond Vineyard**, (631) 537-5106, one of only a few vineyards on the South Fork. Most of eastern Long Island's vineyards are concentrated on its North Fork. Sagpond, once the site of a potato farm, is home to Wolffer Wines. Its picturesque 50 acres and Tuscan-style winery sit next to owner Christian Wolffer's Sagpond Farms, a premier equestrian facility. The Farms features an indoor ring, trails, and dressage and sand rings amidst 163 acres of rolling pastures. Sagpond's newest project is cheesemaking—thanks to Sunshine, Gutsy, Skittles, and Annabelle, cows kept on a neighboring commercial dairy farm.

Bridgehampton provides a chance to shop, eat, or visit the **Historical Museum,** housed in the circa 1770 August Corwith Homestead. In Water Mill, the 1644 gristmill at the **Old Water Mill Museum** has been restored so that it can grind the corn and grains grown in the area. Power is supplied by the flow from Mill Pond.

After passing through Water Mill, ride through the Mecox section, from which you can head to one of the sandy, dune-lined beaches on the open Atlantic.

Ride through the Georgica area of large, fashionable homes before returning through the historic district of East Hampton on James Lane, where there are a number of sites and museums near Town Pond.

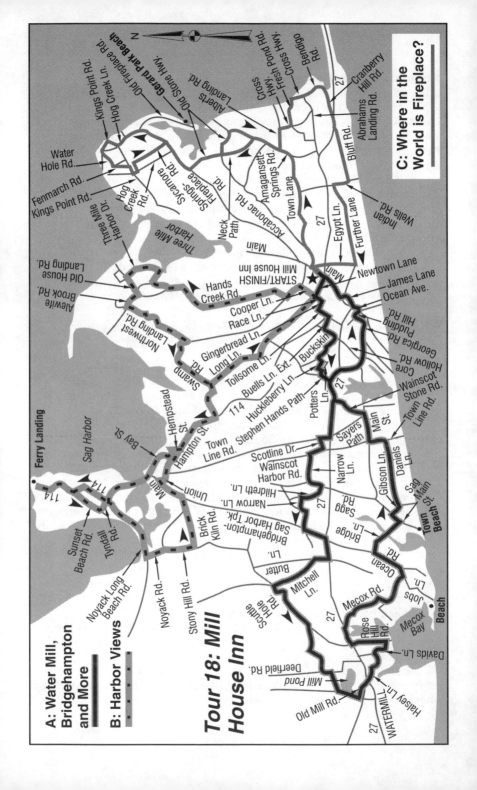

Tour 18: Mill House Inn

A: Water Mill, Bridgehampton and More

B: Harbor Views

C: Where in the World is Fireplace?

PtPt.	Cume	Turn	Street/Landmark
0.0	0.0	R	From Mill House drive onto **N. Main St.**
0.1	0.1	R	**Newtown Ln.** at light
0.5	0.6	L	**Race Ln.** at light
0.2	0.8	BR	**Gingerbread Ln.**
0.2	1.0	BL	**Toilsome Ln.**
0.3	1.3	R	**Buells Ln. extension** at stop sign
0.4	1.7	L	**Cove Hollow Rd.** at stop sign
0.3	2.0	R	**Buckskill Rd.**
0.7	2.7	L	**Mark Twain Ln.**
0.1	2.8	R	**Huckleberry Ln.**
0.3	3.1	R	**Potters Ln.**
0.0	3.1	L	**Stephen Hands Path** at stop sign
0.3	3.4	R	**Rt. 27W** at stop sign
1.4	4.8	R	**Town Line Rd.**
0.3	5.1	L	**Scotline Dr.**
0.2	5.3	R	**Wainscott Harbor Rd.** at stop sign
0.4	5.7	L	**Narrow Ln. East**, just before RR crossing
0.8	6.5	L	**Sagg Rd.** at stop sign
0.3	6.8	R	**Hildreth Ln.** (Just after Sagpond Vineyard.)
0.6	7.4	L	Unmarked **Narrow Ln.** at stop sign. Will go under RR.
0.9	8.3	L	**Bridgehampton-Sag Harbor Tpke.** at stop sign
0.3	8.6	R	**Rt. 27 W** at light, through center of Bridgehampton
0.6	9.2	R	**Butter Ln.**
0.3	9.5	L	**Mitchell Ln.**, just after going under RR
1.2	10.7	L	**Scuttle Hole Rd.** at stop sign
1.2	11.9	BR	**Head of Pond Rd.**
1.4	13.3	L	**Deerfield Rd.**
0.1	13.4	R	**Head of Pond Rd.**
1.0	14.4	L	**Old Mill Rd.**
0.4	14.8	S	Cross Montauk Hwy./Rt. 27 onto **Halsey Ln.** Use caution. Town of Water Mill is to your left
0.6	15.4	R	**Davids Ln.**
0.5	15.9	L	**Rose Hill Rd.** at stop sign
0.8	16.7	R	**Rt. 27E** at stop sign.
0.5	17.2	R	**Mecox Rd.**
1.3	18.5	L	**Mecox Rd.** (To go to beach, watch for signs at Jobs Ln.)
0.9	19.4	L	**Ocean Rd.** at stop sign.
0.7	20.1	R	**Bridge Ln.**
1.1	21.2	L	**Sag Main St.** (To go to Sag Main Town Beach, go right)

Pt.-Pt.	Cume	Turn	Street/Landmark
0.1	21.3	BR	Cemetery Rd.
0.1	21.4	R	Gibson Ln.
0.1	21.5	L	Daniels Ln.
1.6	23.1	L	Town Line Rd.
0.4	23.5	R	Main St.
0.7	24.2	L,R	Sayers Path, Wainscott Stone Rd.
0.8	25.0	R	Rt. 27E
1.1	26.1	R	Georgica Rd.
1.3	27.4	BL	Georgica Rd.
0.4	27.8	R	Pudding Hill
0.2	28.0	L	Unmarked **Ocean Ave.**
0.1	28.1	BR	**James Ln.**, before stop sign, which merges with Main St.
1.2	29.3		Arrive at Mill House

Harbor Views (32 miles)
Easy to moderate

Cycle on lightly traveled backroads, along the fringes of wooded parklands and preserves, skirting harbors and beaches to explore many of the South Fork's hidden treasures.

The first of these gems is the **LongHouse Reserve**, (631) 329-3568, on Hands Creek Road. Created by textile designer Jack Lenor Larsen, the Reserve's ground floor gallery houses changing exhibits by leading craftsmen. Its 16 acres showcase an amazing collection of sculpture surrounded by landscape that is itself an artform. Unfortunately, it has only limited visiting hours from May to September. Check the schedule. It also holds occasional performances and workshops.

Cover rolling hills as you ride the tree-lined roads that hug Three Mile Harbor, then **Cedar Point County Park**, Grace Estate Preserve, and Northwest Harbor Park, before reaching Long Island's former whaling center, Sag Harbor. Cedar Point, (631) 852-7620, bordered by Gardiners Bay on the north and Northwest Harbor on the west, offers hiking, picnicking, fishing, row boating, and swimming opportunities, plus views of Cedar Point Lighthouse. Its entrance is off Alewive Road.

In Sag Harbor, the **Whaling Museum** features memorabilia of the town's heyday as one of the largest whaling communities in the world. Today, this unassuming harbor village, with its historic colonial homes and buildings, houses a variety of restaurants, bookstores, antique shops, and boutiques. The tourist office is located in the windmill on Main Street.

From Sag Harbor, cross a narrow bridge to North Haven, from which, if you choose, you can take a ferry to Shelter Island.

Noyack Long Beach provides a great spot for sunbathing and swimming. All roads are paved with good surfaces.

Pt.-Pt.	Cume	Turn	Street/Landmark
0.0	0.0	R	**N. Main** from Mill House driveway
0.2	0.2	R	**Newtown Ln.** at light
0.4	0.6	R	**Cooper Ln.** at light
0.5	1.1	L	**Cedar St.**
0.2	1.3	R	**Hands Creek Rd.**
3.8	5.1	L	**Springy Banks Rd.** at stop sign
0.5	5.6	R	**Hands Creek Rd.**
0.6	6.2	L	**Three Mile Harbor Dr.**
1.0	7.2	L	**Old House Landing** at stop sign
0.5	7.7	R	**Alewive Brook Rd.** at crossroad
0.5	8.2	L	**Northwest Rd.**
1.8	10.0	R	**Old Northwest Rd.** at stop sign
0.1	10.1	L	**Northwest Landing Rd.** at T
0.5	10.6	L	**Swamp Rd.**
2.0	12.6	R	**Rt. 114/East Hampton-Sag Harbor Hwy.** at stop sign
1.2	13.8	R	**Hempstead St.**
0.2	14.0	R	**Bay St.**
0.7	14.7	S	Onto bridge at flashing light
1.3	16.0	R	**Rt. 114** at flashing light
1.9	17.9		Arrive at **ferry landing**. Turn around.
0.9	18.8	R	**Sunset Beach Rd.**
0.8	19.6	L	**Tyndall Rd.**
0.3	19.9	R	**Shore Beach Rd.** at flashing light. Becomes **Noyack Long Beach Rd.**
1.7	21.6	L	**Noyack Rd.** at stop sign
0.5	22.1	BR	**Stony Hill Rd.**
0.7	22.8	L	**Brick Kiln Rd.** at stop sign
1.4	24.2	L	**Main St.** at light in Sag Harbor
0.6	24.8	R	**Madison St.**
0.1	24.9	L	**Union St.** at 4-way stop
0.1	25.0	R	**Hampton St.** at light
1.9	26.9	L	**Swamp Rd.**
0.9	27.8	R	**Two Holes of Water Rd.**
2.0	29.8	S	**Long Ln.** at stop sign.
1.0	30.8		Road makes S and becomes **Newtown Ln.**
1.0	31.8	L	**Main St.** at light
0.2	32.0		Arrive at Mill House

Where in the world is Fireplace? (23.2 miles)
Easy

Ramble along quiet back roads around the ragged inlets and nature sanctuaries of Accabonac Harbor, through the tiny town of Springs and the residential area of Fireplace, at Hog Creek Point. Then pedal to Dennistown Bell Park at Alberts Landing, along the Promised Land section of Napeague State Park, through Beach Hampton, and past the impressive fairways of Maidstone Club and the luxurious summer homes along Egypt Lane.

In Springs, not much more than crossroads where times seems to stand still, you can visit the **Pollock-Krasner House and Study Center** at 830 Fireplace Road. Once the home and studio of famed abstract expressionist artist Jackson Pollock, the Center is now affiliated with the State University of New York and tours are offered Thursday through Saturday by appointment, (631) 324-4929.

Along Bluff Road view the grass-covered dunes of the Double Dunes Preserve or visit the **East Hampton Marine Museum,** (631) 267-6544, whose displays depict the economic, social, and political impact of fishing and whaling on the local community.

The route covers relatively flat, paved roads with light traffic and lots of opportunities to explore the natural beauty of the region.

Pt.-Pt.	Cume	Turn	Street/Landmark
0.0	0.0	L	**N Main St.** from drive of Mill House
0.2	0.2	R	**Collins Ave.** at light
0.1	0.3	L	**Accabonac Rd.** at stop
0.4	0.7	BR	**Town Ln.**
2.4	3.1	S	Unmarked **Amagansett-Springs Rd.** at stop
1.1	4.2	L	**Neck Path**
1.0	5.2	S	**Old Stone Hwy.** at stop sign
0.8	6.0	R	**Springs-Fireplace Rd.** at stop sign
1.7	7.7		****Optional: turn right onto Old Fireplace Rd. to go to Gerard Park Beach. Approximately 3 miles roundtrip to Gerard Point.*
0.5	8.2	L	**Hog Creek Ln.**
0.1	8.3	R	**Kings Point**
0.7	9.0	L	**Hog Creek Ln.**
0.1	9.1	R	**Water Hole Rd.**
0.5	9.6	R	**Fenmarch Rd.**
0.3	9.9	R	**Kings Point Rd.**
0.2	10.1	L	**Hog Creek**
0.1	10.2	L	**Sycamore Rd.**
1.0	11.2	R	**Spring Rd.** at stop sign

Pt.-Pt.	Cume	Turn	Street/Landmark
0.9	12.1	L	**Old Stone Hwy.**
0.9	13.0	BL	**Old Stone Hwy.**
2.0	15.0	L	**Albert Landing Rd.**
0.4	15.4	R	**Cross Hwy.**
0.4	15.8	L	**Fresh Pond Rd.** at stop sign
0.6	16.4	R	**Cross Hwy.**
0.3	16.7	R,L	**Abrahams Landing, Bendigo Rd.**
0.6	17.3	R	**Cranberry Hole Rd.** at stop sign
1.0	18.3	S	Cross Rt. 27 onto **Bluff Rd.**
1.5	19.8	R	**Indian Wells Rd.** at stop sign at T
0.3	20.1	L	**Further Ln.**
2.1	22.2	R	**Egypt Ln.**
0.8	23.0	S	Cross Rt. 27 onto **Accabonac Rd.** at light
0.1	23.1	L	**Hook Mill Rd.**
0.1	23.2	L	**N. Main St.**
			Arrive at Mill House

The Westchester House, Saratoga Springs, New York

The Westchester House

Bob and Stephanie Melvin,
Innkeepers
102 Lincoln Avenue
Saratoga Springs, NY 12866
B&B Rates: Budget-Moderate
Deluxe, Special Events
Luxury, Racing Season
Open all year

Phone: (518) 587-7613; (800) 581-7613
Web: www.westchester-bb.saratoga.ny.us

It's not unusual for towns like Saratoga that claim a rich and glorious past to erect memorials to their fallen heroes. This celebrated town, not far from the state capital, was, as American history buffs know, the site of a decisive Revolutionary War battle. Its buried heroes, however, include a peculiar "war" legend: Man O' War, that is. Big Red himself, the famous thoroughbred who was embalmed when he died, is buried across from the National Museum of Racing in the park that surrounds Saratoga's stunning historic race track, the oldest in America.

Long before Saratoga became the gathering ground of a well-to-do racing society, its mineral-water springs attracted visitors hoping to reap their restorative powers. George Washington supposedly visited the town after the Battle of Saratoga and tried to buy one of its springs.

Today, equestrian activities, the historic Saratoga Battlefield, and to a lesser extent the town's springs and spas, continue to attract visitors. So do the attractions of the 2200-acre Saratoga Spa State Park, which include the world-class programs of the Saratoga Performing Arts Center, summer home of the New York City Ballet, Philadelphia Orchestra, and Newport Jazz Festival. Another destination for a smaller set of visitors is the exclusive—and reportedly haunted—artists retreat Yaddo, which has served as a creative incubator for more than a century for the likes of Milton Avery, Aaron Copeland, Philip Roth, John Cheever, and Leonard Bernstein.

Saratoga's lake-dotted, rural countryside also entices of a variety of outdoor enthusiasts, including boaters, fishermen, and cyclists. In fact it's such an attractive cycling destination that the League of American Bicyclists (LAB) has held two GEAR rallies here in the past 10 years.

During GEAR, cyclists fill up local inns and B&Bs such as The Westchester House. Innkeepers Bob and Stephanie Melvin, a former government worker and opera singer respectively, have operated the Westchester House since 1986. In 1994, they bought the Greek Revival house next door, which they call the Lincoln House, and converted it to additional guest quarters. The Melvins offer a total of 11 guest rooms and suites in the two houses, which share a beautifully designed and maintained fenced perennial garden.

The houses sit just blocks from Saratoga's Congress Park, race track, attractive downtown commercial district, and famous boulevards lined with capacious Victorian and Tudor "cottages" and mansions.

The Westchester House, a large Queen Anne Victorian with complementary Victorian furnishings, serves as the heart of the inn. Outside, this painted lady is distinguished by its wraparound porch, decorative cupola and balcony, and a subdued seven-color paint scheme. Inside, guests find plenty of gathering spots in the inviting common rooms. They can research the region's offerings in the books lining the shelves in the front parlor or foyer, tap out a tune on the baby grand piano in the back parlor, or simply enjoy the afternoon's refreshments, or a glass of wine or sherry from the decanter near the stereo and games collection.

In any event, guests are encouraged to make themselves at home amidst the warm woody atmosphere of Eastlake influence created by the original owner, Almeron King. King, a master carpenter, built the house in 1885 and his exquisite woodworking sensibilities are on display throughout: elaborate carved fireplace mantels in the front and back parlors; beautiful newel posts on the staircase banister; handcrafted chestnut moldings; and a unique wood-framed arched doorway that leads from the dining room to the garden.

Upstairs, six guest rooms are decorated with a heavy Victorian influence, including lace curtains and bed canopies and floral print wallpaper and bed linens. In a nod to modern conveniences, all rooms have air conditioners, telephones with voicemail, private baths, and ceiling fans. The spacious Jefferson Room, on the most quiet side of the house, has a king-size iron bed and a large bath with a tub. The smaller Spring Room is a bright cheery corner room decorated in pastel colors. The large Sun Room has a king-size iron bed with lace canopy and several comfortable chairs in a small seating area. The Lookout Room, uniquely shaped because of the balcony off one corner, has two rare ¾ beds, a marble topped dresser and a large bath.

The four guest quarters in the Lincoln House are decorated with a hint of the Yankee touch, with furnishings that lean toward traditional colonial. The large two-room Porch Suite earned its name because it has its own private porch. It also has a private entrance off the garden. Beth's Room, on the second floor, boasts the best bathroom in the inn, with its clawfoot tub, shower, and pedestal sink. The spacious, private Hideaway Suite tucked into the back of the house on the top floor has a summer cottage-like feel. It features built-in cabinets and drawers and a brass bed in the sleeping room, and a pull-out love seat, desk, and rocking chair in the second room.

The Melvins serve as gracious and friendly hosts, available to make recommendations or engage in conversation at just the right times, but otherwise affording guests their privacy. Over breakfast, and before he snaps photos of departing guests for his collection, Bob enjoys spending time with guests to help plan their day or simply to talk about various cultural, historic, or current affairs.

There are no hot food items at breakfast, but there is a filling array of cold items. Guests, who dine together around the large table in the dining room or smaller table in the back parlour, are treated to fresh fruit and juices, a selections of cereals, including granola, and an assortment of wholesome baked goods and breads, such as fresh scones and muffins. And they're served with a dizzying array of specialty spreads and toppings, such as pumpkin butter, flavored cream cheeses, and jams.

Bicycling from Westchester House

The Saratoga area, which sits not far from the Hudson River just southeast of the Adirondack Mountains, is a bicycling mecca. Why else would LAB have held two GEAR events here in the last 10 years? The well-organized Mohawk-Hudson Cycling Club, which hosted the events, generated some three dozen route options for the events, many of which it posted on the Web. The club has nearly 700 members in the greater Albany area and organizes regular road and mountain bike rides and events in the region.

A smaller, but more local club, the Saratoga Freewheelers Bicycle Club, also organizes evening and weekend road and mountain bike group rides. Check Blue Sky Bicycles for details.

A number of century rides also are organized by local clubs and organizations, including one sponsored by bicycle manufacturer Serotta, (518) 587-2992, which is based just a few miles north in South Glen Falls.

Innkeeper Bob Melvin also can provide additional route suggestions, cue sheets, and descriptions, and can help guests locate the 40-mile paved Saratoga Springs bicycle path, part of the Saratoga Springs Open Space Project (518) 587-5554.

One of the reasons cyclists love the Saratoga region is that there is a multitude of options in terrain and distance to suit cyclists of all abilities. For touring cyclists there are also lots of attractions to break up the day. Another reason is, quite simply, that Saratoga is a downright pleasant and picturesque town. In fact, the well-preserved town recently won two national awards: The Great American Main Street Award, through the National Trust for Historic Preservation, and *American Heritage* magazine's "Great American Place" Award.

However, a few words of caution: Saratoga's famous thoroughbred racing season runs from the end of July through August. The town's population swells almost beyond its capacity during that time, so unless you like paying double-the-normal price for almost everything, or plan to make it up at the races, don't even think of trying to book a room during that time.

Local Bike Shops
Blue Sky
71 Church St.
Saratoga Springs, NY 12866
(518) 583-0600
Sales, service, and acccessories. Rents hybrids. Saratoga Freewheelers meets at shop for regular road and mountain bike rides.

The Bike Shop
35 Maple Ave.
Saratoga Springs, NY 12866
(518) 587-7857
Sales, service, accessories

For Bike Rentals
Recycled Recreation
80 Henry Street
Saratoga Springs, NY 12866
(518) 581-8103
Rents used bikes.

Mountain Biking
Off-road biking opportunities in the Saratoga area are just as diverse as the road riding options. To find more remote local trails, inquire at local bike shops or try joining one of the rides organized by the Saratoga Freewheelers or Mohawk-Hudson Cycling Clubs.

Near the Westchester House, there's a network of relatively easy yet enjoyable trails through **Saratoga Spa State Park,** (518) 584-2535. The massive park also is home to the Gideon Putnam Resort, the Saratoga Performing Arts Center, and the National Museum of Dance, as well as an Olympic-size swimming pool complex and two golf courses.

The **North Woods Trails**, off the campus of Skidmore College, offer options for riders of all abilities, from beginner to experienced, on everything from old carriage roads to challenging singletrack. They're accessible from the corner of Clinton Avenue, near the horse stables.

Grafton Lakes and Cherry Plains State Parks, in Grafton, are also popular local destinations. In fact, the Mohawk-Hudson Cycling

Club has sponsored an annual Mountain Bike Festival at Grafton Lakes, which offers rocky singletrack, mud holes, rock ledges, and severe climbs and descents. The park, (518) 279-1155, which is located on a forested mountain ridge, features nearly 10 miles of trails and five ponds, including the Martin-Durham Reservoir. Cherry Plains Park, (518) 733-5400, in addition to biking trails, has a sandy beach on Black River Pond.

Additional Resources
Saratoga Convention and Tourism Bureau
480 Broadway Suite LL-24
Saratoga Springs, NY 12866
(518) 584-1531
(518) 584-2969, fax
www.meetinsaratoga.org

Saratoga Chamber of Commerce
28 Clinton St.
Saratoga Springs, NY 12866
(518) 584-3255
(518) 587-0318, fax
www.saratoga.org/chamber/

Urban Cultural Park Visitor Center
297 Broadway
Saratoga, NY 12866
(518) 584-2110

Mohawk-Hudson Cycling Club
P.O. Box 12575
Albany, NY 12212-0575
www.mohawkhudsoncycling.org

Saratoga Freewheelers Bicycle Club
P.O. Box 3180
Saratoga Springs, NY 12866
http://hometown.aol.com/VeloJunkie/index.html

"Mohawk-Hudson Bike-Hike Trail"
Albany County Dept. of Planning
112 State St., Room 1006
Albany, NY 12207

Saratoga Battlefield (27.5 or 38 miles)
Moderate, rolling hills

This route over gentle rolling hills and quiet countryside takes riders to the site of two pivotal Revolutionary War battles and where British General John Burgoyne surrendered to American General Horatio Gates. It is now the 2800-acre **Saratoga National Historical Park**, (518) 664-9821, which has a small museum in the visitors center and a number of hiking paths. A one-way 10-mile road in the park winds through old farm fields, woodlands, and a bluff overlooking the Hudson River. Along the road, which is ideally suited for touring by bicycle, there are 10 interpretive stations highlighting the Battle of Saratoga. The park suggests allowing two to three hours for a visit. Bring a picnic and camera.

After leaving the park, ride along undulating terrain to Saratoga Lake, then back to the inn.

All roads are paved and the traffic is relatively light.

Pt.-Pt.	Cume	Turn	Street/Landmark
0.0	0.0	L	Turn left leaving driveway of Westchester House Inn, cross Lincoln onto **Clark St.**
0.2	0.2	R	**Union Ave./Rt. 9P South** at stop sign
2.2	2.4	L	**Meadowbrook Rd./Rt. 65**
2.4	4.8	R	**Staffords Bridge Rd./Rt. 67** at stop sign
0.3	5.1	L	**Rt. 68/Burgoyne Rd.**
3.8	8.9	R	**Rt. 32S** at stop sign
4.2	13.1		Turnoff for **Saratoga National Historic Park** is on your left. Loop road in park adds approximately 11 miles
2.2	15.3	R	**Rt. 423W** at stop sign at T
3.9	19.2	R	**Rt. 9P North**
4.3	23.5	L	**Rt. 22/Crescent Ave.**
2.5	26.0	R	**Nelson Ave.** at 4-way stop
1.3	27.3	L	**Lincoln Ave.** at stop light
0.2	27.5	L	**Jefferson Ave.** Enter driveway of Westchester House Inn

Moreau State Park (40 miles, or 45.5 with optional loop to Serotta factory)
Easy to moderate

This pleasant route to the recently-expanded **Moreau Lake State Park** provides an opportunity to picnic and swim at the lake, or make an optional loop to the Serotta Bike Factory, where if you call ahead they'll provide a tour, (518) 747-8620.

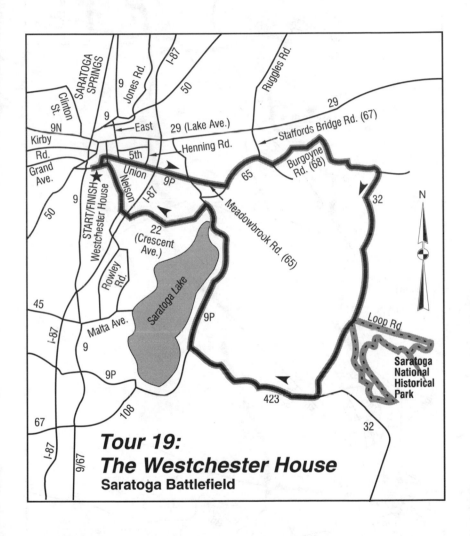

Tour 19:
The Westchester House
Saratoga Battlefield

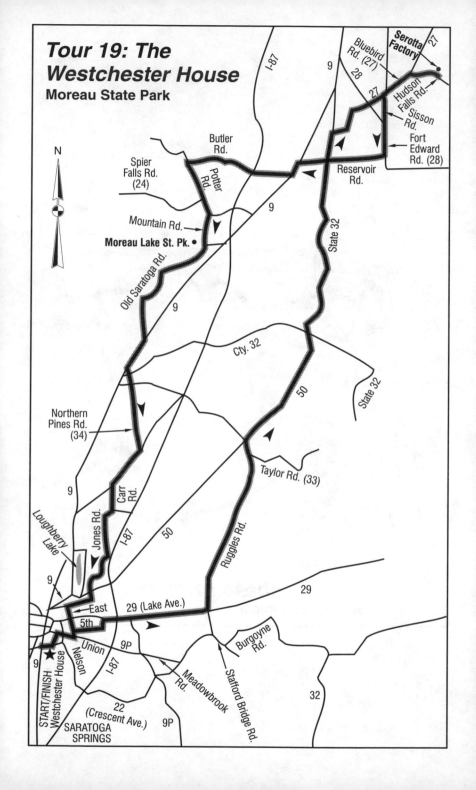

Tour 19: The Westchester House
Moreau State Park

Serotta Factory

Bluebird Rd. (27)

27

28

27

Hudson Falls Rd.

Sisson Rd.

I-87

9

Fort Edward Rd. (28)

Butler Rd.

Reservoir Rd.

Spier Falls Rd. (24)

Potter Rd.

9

N

Mountain Rd.

Moreau Lake St. Pk. •

State 32

Old Saratoga Rd.

9

Cty. 32

State 32

50

Northern Pines Rd. (34)

Taylor Rd. (33)

9

Carr Rd.

Jones Rd.

I-87

50

Ruggles Rd.

Loughberry Lake

9

East 5th.

29 (Lake Ave.)

29

Union

9P

Burgoyne Rd.

9

Nelson

I-87

Meadowbrook Rd.

Stafford Bridge Rd.

32

START/FINISH Westchester House

22 (Crescent Ave.)

9P

SARATOGA SPRINGS

The ride covers gently rolling terrain along scenic farmlands in the foothills of the Adirondack Mountains north of Saratoga. In the tiny town of Gansevoort, there's an ice cream and snack shop. Moreau Lake State Park, (518) 793-0511, which lies amid hardwood forest and pine stands with shady groves for picnicking, offers a sandy beach for swimming, lots of hiking trails, and boat rentals.

All roads are paved and traffic is light, except for sections near the town of Saratoga.

Pt.-Pt.	Cume	Turn	Street/Landmark
0.0	0.0	L	Turn left from drive of Westchester House. Cross Lincoln Ave. onto **Clark St.**
0.2	0.2	R	**Union Ave.** at stop sign
0.5	0.7	L	**East Ave.** at light
0.3	1.0	R	**Fifth Ave.**
0.7	1.7	L	**Henning Rd.** at stop sign at T
0.3	2.0	R	**Rt. 29E/Lake Ave.** at light
2.7	4.7	L, R	Turn left, following sign to **Ruggles Rd.**, then right to stay on Ruggles Rd.
4.6	9.3	L	**Taylor Rd./Rt. 33** at stop sign at T. Becomes **Ballard**
0.2	9.5	R	**Rt. 50** at light
3.5	13.0	L	**NY State Rt. 32 N** at stop sign
0.1	13.1	R	On **NY State Rt. 32 N** after crossing RR tracks (Do not take County Rt. 32)
4.9	18.0	S	At intersection with Reservoir Rd. (To go to Moreau Lake Park, without going to Serotta Factory, turn left onto Reservoir Rd. and pick up cues below at mile 27.0)
0.7	18.7	R	**Bluebird Rd./Rt. 27** at light
2.6	21.3	R	**Hudson Falls Rd.**
0.4	21.7		**Serotta Factory** is on the left in Building 23
0.0	21.7	R	Return via **Hudson Falls Rd.** Turn right leaving factory
0.4	22.1	L	**Bluebird Rd./Rt. 27** at light
0.9	23.0	BL	**Sisson Rd.**
0.7	23.7	L	**Fort Edward Rd./Rt. 28** at stop sign
0.9	24.6	R	**Reservoir Rd.**
2.4	27.0	L	**Rt. 9** at stop sign (Pick up cues here)
0.2	27.2	R	**Butler Rd.**
2.9	30.1	L	**Potter Rd.** at stop sign
1.0	31.1	L	**Spier Falls Rd./Rt. 24** at stop sign
0.4	31.5	R	**Mountain Rd.**
0.8	32.3	R	**Old Saratoga Rd.** at stop sign

Pt.-Pt.	Cume	Turn	Street/Landmark
0.3	32.6		Entrance to **Moreau Lake State Park**
0.0	32.6	R	Leaving park turn right onto **Old Saratoga Rd.**
3.1	35.7	R	**Rt. 9** at stop sign
0.9	36.6	L	**Northern Pines Rd./Rt. 34**
3.6	40.2	L	**Carr Rd.**
0.5	40.7	R	**Jones Rd.** at stop sign
2.4	43.1	S	**Veteran's Way** at light, crossing Rt. 9
0.1	43.2	R	Unmarked **Excelsior Ave.** at stop sign at T
0.5	43.7	L	**East Ave.**
0.4	44.1	S	**East Ave.** at stop, crossing Lake St.
0.6	44.7	R	**Union Ave.** at light
0.3	45.0	L	**Nelson Ave.** at light
0.1	45.1	R	**Lincoln Ave.** at light
0.4	45.5		Arrive at Westchester House

Lakes, Lakes and more Lakes (40.3 miles)
Easy

This generally flat route passes five scenic lakes. The first is Ballston Lake, once part of the Mohawk River. At its southern end is Lakeside Farms Cider Mill, a perfect snack stop. The next lake, Round Lake, also was once part of the Mohawk River. Lake Number 3, Saratoga Lake, is the largest of the five and a major destination for water sports enthusiasts. West of Lake Saratoga are Lake Lonely, then, in Saratoga Springs, Loughberry Lake, the city's water source.

Overall, the route is lightly traveled and relatively flat, with just a few small hills. On Dugans Hill Road, there's a very short, steep hill.

0.0	0.0	R	**Lincoln Ave.** from front of Westchester House
0.2	0.2	R	**Nelson Ave.** at light
1.3	1.5	S	**Nelson Ave. Ext.** at 4-way stop sign
0.9	2.4	L	**Nelson Ave. Ext./Rt. 64**
0.4	2.8	R	**Rowley Rd./Rt. 61** at T
2.2	5.0	R	**Malta Ave. Ext./Rt. 63** at stop sign
0.5	5.5	S	**Malta Ave.** at stop sign, crossing Rt. 9
0.7	6.2	L	**Van Aernum Ave.**
1.2	7.4	S	**Brownell Rd.** at stop sign
2.0	9.4	L	**East Line Rd./Rt. 82** at stop sign
0.2	9.6	S	**Rt. 82** at light
0.6	10.2	R	**Lake Rd.** Lake #1: **Ballston Lake**
3.2	13.4	R	**Round Lake Rd./Rt. 80** at stop sign

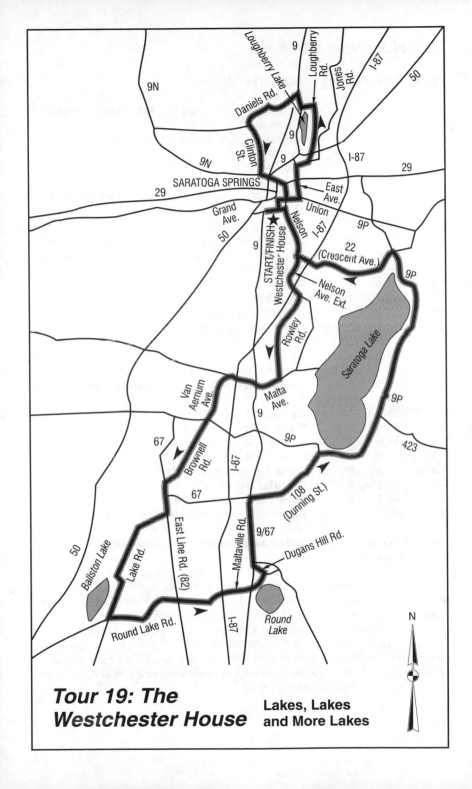

Tour 19: The Westchester House

Lakes, Lakes and More Lakes

N

Pt.-Pt.	Cume	Turn	Street/Landmark
2.0	15.4	S	**Rt. 80** at stop sign
0.8	16.2	S	At light. Continue on **Rt. 80**, passing under interstate
1.0	17.2	S	**Maltaville Rd.**, crossing Rt. 9. Lake #2: **Round Lake**
0.6	17.8	L	**Dugans Hill**
0.2	18.0	L	Unmarked **Rt. 67** at stop sign
0.1	18.1	L,R	**Rt. 67 W**, then quick right onto **Rt. 67W/9N** at flashing light and stop sign
1.6	19.7	R	**Dunning St./Rt. 108**
2.2	21.9	R	**Rt. 9P** at stop sign. Lake #3: **Saratoga Lake**
6.5	28.4	L	**Rt. 22/Crescent Ave.** Lake #4: **Lake Lonely**
2.6	31.0	R	**Nelson Ave.** at 4-way stop
1.4	32.4	R	**Union Ave/Rt. 9P**
0.3	32.7	L	**East Ave.** at light
0.6	33.3	S	At light, crossing Lake Ave.
0.4	33.7	R	**Excelsior Ave.** at 4-way stop
0.1	33.8	S	At 4-way stop sign
0.4	34.2	L	**Veteran's Way**
0.2	34.4	S, L	Go through light, then quick left onto **Loughberry Rd.** Lake #5: **Loughberry Lake**
1.6	36.0	R	**Rt. 9** at stop sign
0.2	36.2	L	**Daniel Rd.**
1.4	37.6	L	**Clinton St.**
1.4	39.0	S	**Clinton St.** at light
0.1	39.1	L	**Church St.** at light
0.2	39.3	S	Cross Broadway at light
0.2	39.5	R	**Circular St.** at light
0.6	40.1	L	**Park Place** at stop sign
0.2	40.3		Arrive at Westchester House

Lester Park and the Petrified Sea Gardens (32.8 miles)
Easy to Moderate

This moderately easy route covers gently rolling terrain interspersed with flat stretches as riders make their way to the **Petrified Sea Gardens**, an impressive example of fossilized stromatolite ocean-reef more than 500 million years old. The Gardens, which are a registered national natural landmark, include a small park with walking trails and self-guided tour and a picnic area. Hours vary from mid-May through October, (518) 584-7102. Neighboring **Joseph Lester Park** also includes examples of the frozen sea plants.

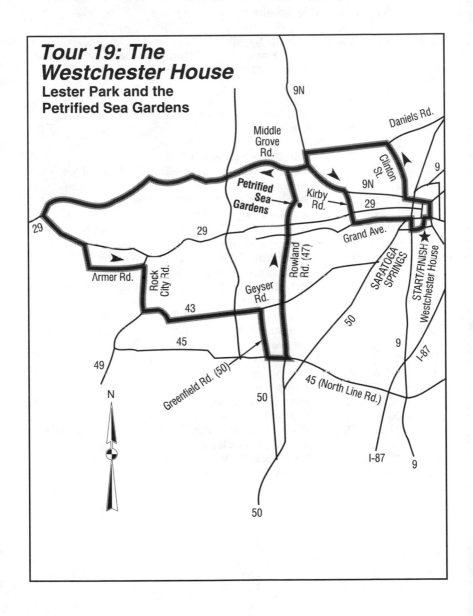

Tour 19: The Westchester House

Lester Park and the Petrified Sea Gardens

9N

Daniels Rd.

Middle Grove Rd.

Clinton St.

9

Petrified Sea Gardens

Kirby Rd.

9N

29

29

29

Grand Ave.

29

Armer Rd.

Rock City Rd.

Rowland Rd. (47)

SARATOGA SPRINGS

START/FINISH Westchester House

Geyser Rd.

43

50

9

45

I-87

49

Greenfield Rd. (50)

50

45 (North Line Rd.)

N

50

I-87

9

All roads are paved and, with the exception of the areas close to the center of Saratoga, traffic is light.

Pt.-Pt.	Cume	Turn	Street/Landmark
0.0	0.0	L	Onto **Park Pl.** from front of Westchester House
0.2	0.2	R	**Circular St.** at stop sign
0.6	0.8	L	**Lake St.** at light
0.4	1.2	R	**Clinton St.** at light
1.6	2.8	L	Unmarked **Daniels Rd.** at stop sign at T
1.5	4.3	S	4-way stop
0.7	5.0	L	**Rt. 9N** at stop sign at T
0.3	5.3	R	**Middle Grove Rd./Rt. 21**
7.8	13.1	L	**Rt. 29** at stop sign at end of Middle Grove Rd.
1.5	14.6	R	**Armer Rd.**
2.4	17.0	R	**Rock City Rd./Rt. 49** at stop sign
1.6	18.6	BL	**Rt. 43** at split in road
1.2	19.8	S	At 4-way stop, road becomes **Geyser Rd.**
1.5	21.3	R	**Greenfield Ave./Rt. 50**
1.3	22.6	L	**Northline Rd./Rt. 45** at 4-way stop
0.5	23.1	L	**Rowland Rd./Rt. 47** at light
3.6	26.7	S	**Petrified Sea Gardens Rd.** at light. Becomes **Lester Park Rd.**
0.5	27.2	-	Entrance to **Petrified Sea Gardens**
0.9	28.1	R	Unmarked **Middle Grove Rd./Rt. 21** at 4-way stop sign
0.5	28.6	R	**Rt. 9N South** at stop sign at T
0.8	29.4	S	At stop light
0.6	30.0	R	**Kirby Rd.**
0.5	30.5	S	**Pine Rd.** at light
0.4	30.9	L	Unmarked **Grand** at stop sign at T
0.6	31.5	R, L	Right onto **West Ave.** at light, then quick left onto **W. Circular** at light
0.8	32.3	R	**Hamilton St.**, crossing over Ballston
0.2	32.5	L	Unmarked **Lincoln** at stop sign
0.3	32.8		Arrive at Westchester House

WhistleWood Farm B&B

Maggie Myer, Innkeeper
11 Pell Road
Rhinebeck, NY   12572
Rates: Budget-Deluxe, B&B
Moderate-Luxury, cottage suites
Open all year

Phone: (914) 876-6838
Fax: (914) 876-5513
Web: www.whistlewood.com
E-mail: whistlwd@epix.net

Named for the way the wind softly whistles through its woods, Maggie Myer's WhistleWood Farm seems more like a rustic, casual retreat than a bed and breakfast. Located on 13.5 rolling acres outside the village of Rhinebeck, the Farm's location off quiet Pell Road is a perfect starting point for exploring by bicycle the back roads that lace this portion of the history-rich Hudson Valley. Best of all, WhistleWood's informal atmosphere and serene setting invite relaxation—after a long day of cycling, of course.

The sprawling main ranch house portrays Maggie's personality in its eclectic, yet comfortable, decor where she successfully intermingles country quilts with an unexpected array of collectibles and equestrian paraphernalia. The house is full of Maggie's garage sale and antique shop finds. That means one's eyes never take a rest, or know what to expect, as they pass over the large collection of items adorning the walls, accenting the furnishings, and hanging from the ceilings. Baskets, pans, and utensils hang from the wood beams in the kitchen and dining area, and in the spacious Wyoming guestroom an antique Old Town canoe hangs unobtrusively above the window and fireplace.

WhistleWood is ideal for travelers who enjoy informal lodgings with character. The principal structures on the property include the main house, a converted barn that houses two suites, and the stables. There are a number of smaller outbuildings, along with lots of walking trails, a pond (a favorite playing ground for Maggie's dogs), and informal gardens with lots of tables, chairs, and artistically-placed conversation pieces such as sculptures, bird baths, wagon wheels, and the like. One of the trails behind the house even leads to the new Rhinebeck Center for Performing Arts, a year-round facility for productions by regional theater groups.

Guests get the first hint that WhistleWood is not your ordinary B&B when they turn at a colorfully-decorated rural mail box onto the long dirt driveway that passes the farm's horse-filled pastures and stables. They enter the house through an enclosed front porch and past a sunken living room with fieldstone fireplace, passing along the way oversized acorn rockers, comfortable stuffed furniture, and everything from cowboy boots, saddles, and bridles to colorful Indian blankets and quilts.

WhistleWood offers six guestrooms: four whimsically-decorated quarters in the main house and two extra-large rooms in the converted barn, called the Guest Cottage. All rooms have private baths.

In the main house, the large Wyoming Room is furnished with a queen-size handmade pine fourposter bed, an antique iron twin bed, and a comfortable sitting area with a fireplace. The Juniper Room features sliding doors and a deck facing a wooded area. Sweet Violet, a bright corner room decorated in lavender, white, and green, has a queen-size Sheraton bed and Birdseye maple furnishings. Tumbleweed features warm yellow and floral patterns, with a large private bath across the hall.

The Guest Cottage, with wood floors, wood beam cathedral ceiling, and fireplaces, houses the Morningside and NorthWind rooms. The accommodations share a kitchen complete with refrigerator and stove, a living area with comfortable chairs, and a small library. Sliding doors lead to a bluestone patio, and a hot tub is nestled in the garden area. Morningside features a fourposter queen-size bed and its own sitting area in front of a stone fireplace. Its large bath has a Jacuzzi, tub, and shower. NorthWind also has a queen-size bed and fireplace, and private bath with a Jacuzzi tub and shower, as well as French doors leading to a private patio overlooking the horse pastures.

Maggie also rents out, by the day or week, Lake Cliff Cottage at Beaver Point in the nearby town of Pine Plains. The two-bedroom cottage, with modern kitchen, living and dining areas offers pristine lake views.

Back at WhistleWood, energy-burning cyclists will find plenty of delicious homemade treats in the afternoon and at breakfast. In fact, with advance notice Maggie will arrange a delicious four-course dinner or prepare picnic baskets for afternoon or evening outings. And she's got lots of suggestions for outings.

A huge farm table and 1904 Gold Coin cookstove in the dining room are stocked all afternoon with fresh-baked deep-dish pies and delicious cakes, as well as fresh fruit, coffee, teas, and juices. In the morning, guests enjoy hearty breakfasts of items such as fresh muffins, pancakes, French toast, or eggs and bacon, plus fresh fruit and juices, at the antique round oak pedestal tables in the dining room or on one of the sunny patios.

If the fine food and laid-back atmosphere leads you to let down your hair and test your vocal chords at the end of the day, you can launch a sing-along with other guests around the old player piano in the sitting area off the kitchen.

A plus for dog owners: With advance notice, WhistleWood will board guests' pets during their stay.

Bicycling from WhistleWood Farms

WhistleWood Farm sits just a few miles outside the quaint Hudson River village of Rhinebeck, which is worth spending time exploring. Originally settled by the Dutch, the town was given its name around 1713 by German settlers who were reminded of the countryside near their native Rhine River ("beck" means cliffs). The village, whose streets are lined with picturesque Colonial, Greek Revival, and Victorian homes, also claims to be home to the oldest continuously operated inn in America: the Beekman Arms, which was established in 1766. The town's commercial district also boasts a number of specialty shops and restaurants.

As cyclists pedal through the countryside and along the river banks, they don't need to stretch their imagination—even today—to see what inspired the Hudson River School of landscape painters in the mid 1800s. During the fall, in particular, colorful views of the Catskill Mountains offer a striking backdrop to the Hudson River.

The river's banks are lined with opulent estates from the Gilded Age, once owned by some of the biggest names in American enterprise, including the Livingstons, Astors, Vanderbilts, and Roosevelts. Many of them are now museums and public parks. The surrounding lush rolling hills are dotted with picturesque farms and remnants of America's earliest years. History buffs will be pleased to learn that the region claims 437 sites on the National Register of Historic Places.

There is little traffic on either the country roads or most of the numbered county routes. The numbered state routes, however, including 9—a designated state bike route—and 9G are heavily traveled in areas. There are plenty of relatively flat, easy stretches, but many roads twist and turn and wind up and down the gently undulating countryside. Allow time to stop along the routes to soak up the local history and natural beauty.

The Dutchess County Tourism Agency, (800) 445-3131, publishes a Bike Tours map recommending additional tours in the area. Also, ask for a copy of the Mid-Hudson Bicycle Club's ride book at local bike shops. The club also organizes regular group rides and special events, including its annual MHBC Century ride. Another popular annual ride is the Tour de Dutchess.

Local Bike Shop
Rhinebeck Bicycle Shop
Route 9, Astor Square
Rhinebeck, NY   12572
(914) 876-4025
Sales, service, and accessories.

Other Information Sources
Dutchess County Tourism Promotion Agency
3 Neptune Road, Suite M-17
Poughkeepsie, NY   12601
(914) 463-4000
(800) 445-3131
www.dutchesstourism.com

Rhinebeck Chamber of Commerce
19 Mill Street, P.O. Box 42
Rhinebeck, NY   12572
(914) 876-4778
www.rhinebeckNYchamber.org
Mid-Hudson Bicycle Club
P.O. Box 1727
Poughkeepsie, NY   12601
www.mhv.net/~mhbc

Mountain Biking Opportunities
Mills-Norrie State Park, actually two connected state parks, covers more than 1000 acres and offers incomparable views of the Hudson River. The diverse terrain makes it a great destination for riders of all abilities, with lots of roots and rocks, as well as faster fire roads. The scenic riverside trail runs from Norrie Point to Ogden Mills. Access from Old Post Road off Route 9 in Staatsburg. Trail maps are available at the park, which also offers fishing, hiking, a marina, an environmental museum, and the Mills Mansion State Historic site (see Mills Mansion ride).

Another popular local destination is **Ferncliff Forest Preserve**, (914) 889-4646, off Mt. Rutsen Road in Rhinebeck. It offers diverse beginner to intermediate riding on its 200 acres.

Also, not far from Rhinebeck is **Hereford State Preserve**, off the Taconic State Parkway in Pleasant Valley. It's fondly referred to as **"909"** by local riders, an abbreviated reference to its 909 acres. Its trails offer long climbs and descents, lots of gnarly, technical singletrack, as well as gentler grassy trails and hardpacked dirt. The preserve is encircled by a loop of gentle fire roads. Avoid riding the multi-use preserve during hunting season. For information, contact the Taconic Region State Park Office, (914) 889-4100, or Pleasant Valley Town Clerk, (914) 635-3274. Entrance is at the end of Tyrell Road.

James Baird State Park, (914) 452-1489, off Freedom Road in Pleasant Valley offers a relatively easy 3-mile loop on packed dirt through its forested land.

Fats in the Cats Mountain Bike Club, based on the opposite side of the Hudson River in Kingston, New York, organizes regular MTB rides, trail clean-up, and social events in the region. For information, check with Kingston Cyclery or www.angelfire.com/ny/fatsinthecats/.

Mills Mansion (31.5 miles)
Moderate, gently rolling hills

The gently-rolling terrain leading to Mills Mansion and the associated State Park takes riders through several tiny rural towns with interesting landmarks: Schultzville's general store is a favorite stopping point for local farmers and residents; Pleasant Plains is dominated by its Presbyterian Church, a picturesque Greek Revival structure; and in Frost Mills, parts of an old mill dam and sluice are still visible.

Staatsburg, home of both **Norrie Park** and **Mills Mansion State Historic Park**, (914) 889-8851, sits on the banks of the Hudson River. But, unlike other estates along the Hudson, the Mills Mansion is not separated from the river by railroad tracks. Its parkscape abuts the river and offers panoramic vistas. A country retreat, built by New York's third governor and his wife in 1792, the mansion remained in their family until 1938 when it was given to the state. The imposing 79-room Beaux-Arts structure was enlarged for Ruth Livingston and her husband, financier Ogden Mills, by Stanford White in 1895.

After leaving the Mills-Norrie Park area, which offers plenty of outdoor recreational opportunities, riders pass several more impressive estates as the route skirts the Hudson River.

Just north of Staatsburg sits **The Wilderstein**, a 35-acre estate owned by the Suckley family until 1983. Built in 1852, its name means "wild man's stone," a reference to a nearby Indian petroglyph. The original Italianate villa experienced a number of transformations over the years and its mansion, grounds, and trails are open to the public, (914) 876-4818.

Continue north through the hamlet of Rhinecliff, where a newly renovated dock provides a view of the 1912 Rondout Lighthouse and the river. Just north of Rhinecliff, ride past the "Ankony Farms," named for one of the six Sepasco Indian chiefs from whom Rhinebeck was originally purchased. On Route 103, pass Ferncliff, a former estate of William Astor, now run as a nursing home. Return to WhistleWood via quiet, little-traveled back roads north of Rhinebeck.

All roads are paved, and the terrain covers gently rolling hills. Most roads have little traffic, with the heaviest traffic found on the short stretch on Route 9, which has a wide paved shoulder.

Pt.-Pt.	Cume	Turn	Street/Landmark
0.0	0.0	L	**Pells Rd.** from end of driveway of WhistleWood Farms
0.2	0.2	S	Cross Rt. 308 onto **White Schoolhouse Rd.** at stop sign
2.4	2.6	L	Unmarked **Quarry Rd.** at stop sign
2.8	5.4	R	**Rt. 18**
2.3	7.7	R	**Fiddlers Bridge Rd.** at 4-way stop sign in Schultzville by general store
4.2	11.9	R	**Rt. 14** at stop sign
1.1	13.0	L	**Rt. 9G** at stop sign
1.3	14.3	R	**Rt. 37/North Cross Rd.**
1.4	15.7	S	Cross Rt. 9 at stop sign, onto unmarked **Hughes Ave.**
0.3	16.0	L	Unmarked **Mulford St.** at stop sign at T
0.2	16.2	R	Unmarked **Old Post Rd.** at stop sign
0.6	16.8		Entrance to **Mill Mansion.** Worth a visit.
0.9	17.7	L	**Rt. 9** at stop sign
0.8	18.5	L	**South Mill Rd.**, which becomes **Rt. 85**
2.1	20.6	L	**Morton Rd.** Follow route through Rhinecliff, past RR station
3.3	23.9	L	**Ryan Rd.** (immediately before Rt. 103 turnoff)
0.8	24.7	L	**Rt. 103** at stop sign
2.1	26.8	R	**Lower Cross Rd.**
0.4	27.2	BR	**Hook Rd.**
1.2	28.4	L	Unmarked **Old Post Rd.** at stop sign
0.1	28.5	S	Cross Rt. 9G onto **Old Post Rd.** at stop sign
0.1	28.6	S	Cross Rt. 9 onto **Wey Rd.** at stop sign
1.1	29.7	L	Sharp turn onto **Cedar Heights Rd.**
1.3	31.0	R	**Pells Rd.** at stop sign
0.5	31.5		Arrive at Whistle Wood Farms

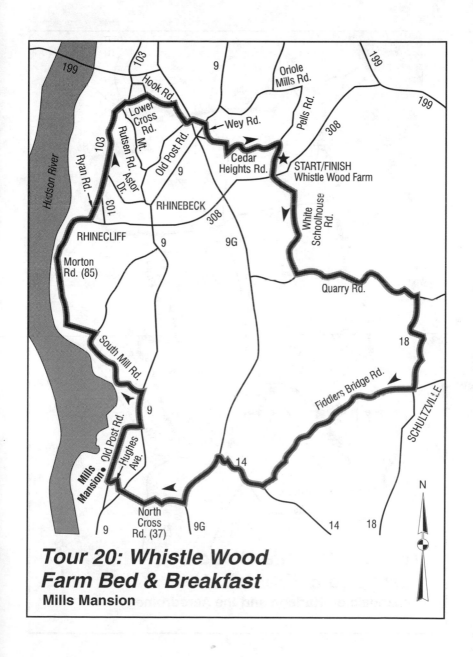

Tour 20: Whistle Wood
Farm Bed & Breakfast
Mills Mansion

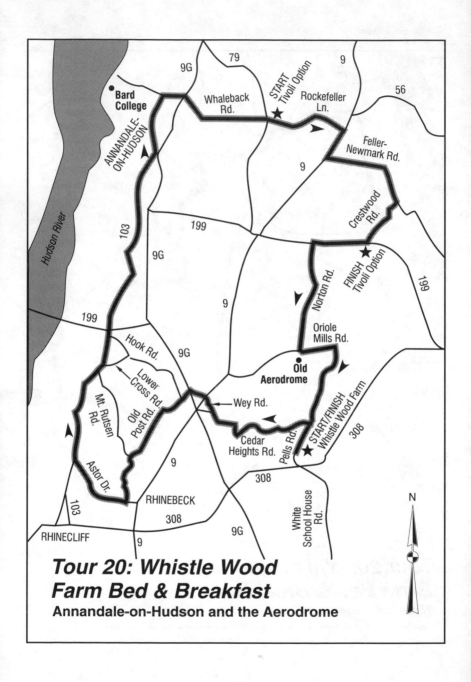

Tour 20: Whistle Wood
Farm Bed & Breakfast
Annandale-on-Hudson and the Aerodrome

Annandale-on-Hudson and the Aerodrome (23.9 miles)
Easy to Moderate, gentle rolling hills

Pedal one of the most scenic routes along the Hudson River, the River Road (also Route 103) between Rhinebeck and Annandale-On-Hudson. Along the way pass Rokeby, a working family farm still in the family of its original owners; the tiny enclave of Barrytown Corners, and **Montgomery Place**, one of the finest examples of Federal architecture in the Hudson Valley. This 434-acre riverfront estate is open to the public, (914) 758-5264, and contains working orchards, herb and rose gardens, and scenic walking trails.

Annandale is best known as the home of **Bard College**, which features an extraordinary mix of architectural styles. The campus houses two River estates: Blithewood, a Georgian Revival mansion with exquisite gardens, and Ward Manor. There's also an English Gothic-style chapel, Dutch stone farmhouses, a Victorian hexagonal gatehouse, and more modern Center for the Arts building. Visitors can tour the campus and attend public programs, (914) 758-6822.

From Annandale, return to WhistleWood via farm-lined country roads and the **Old Rhinebeck Aerodrome**, (914) 758-8610. The antique aircraft museum, just 2 miles from WhistleWood, features displays, air shows, and barnstorming rides in an open cockpit biplane. Riders interested in a more challenging, longer tour—or who haven't experienced enough of the region's Gilded Age architecture—can continue with an optional loop to two additional museum estates, Clermont and Olana.

All roads are paved and the terrain covers gently rolling hills mixed with long flat stretches. Overall, traffic tends to be light. Pack a lunch and enjoy a picnic on one of the scenic riverfront sites.

Pt.-Pt.	Cume	Turn	Street/Landmark
0.0	0.0	**R**	**Pells Rd.** from end of driveway at WhistleWood Farms
0.5	0.5	**L**	**Cedar Heights Rd.**
1.3	1.8	**R**	Unmarked **Wey Rd.** at T
1.0	2.8	**S**	Cross Rt. 9 at stop sign onto **Old Post Rd.**
0.1	2.9	**S**	Cross Rt. 9G at stop sign onto **Old Post Rd.**
1.7	4.6	**L**	**Mount Rutsen Rd.**, which becomes **Montgomery St.** at stop sign
0.5	5.1	**R**	**Astor Rd.** (If you continue straight, then turn left, you will go into town of Rhinebeck)
1.3	6.4	**R**	Unmarked **Rt. 103N** at stop sign
2.2	8.6	**S**	Cross Rt. 199 at light; continue on **Rt. 103**

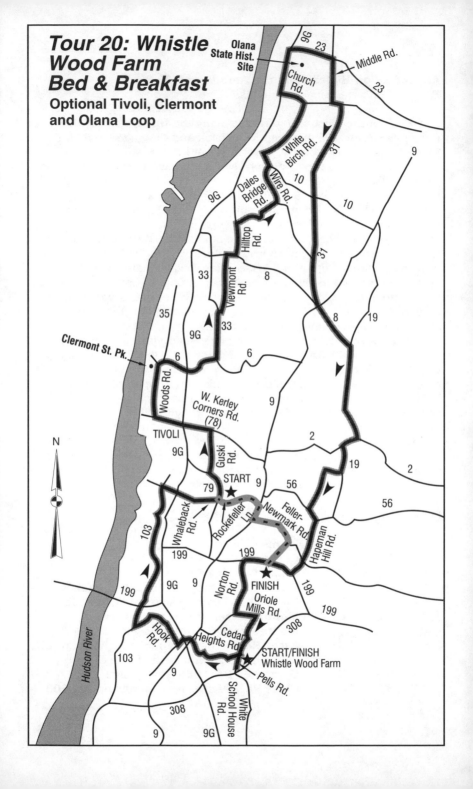

Tour 20: Whistle Wood Farm Bed & Breakfast

Optional Tivoli, Clermont and Olana Loop

Olana State Hist. Site

Middle Rd.

Church Rd.

9G 23

23

White Birch Rd.

31

9

Dales Bridge Rd.

Wire Rd.

10

10

Hilltop Rd.

31

33

Viewmont Rd.

8

9G 33

8

19

Clermont St. Pk.

6

6

35

9

Woods Rd.

W. Kerley Corners Rd. (78)

2

TIVOLI

9G

Guski Rd.

19

2

START

9

56

56

79

Rockefeller Ln.

Feller-Newmark Rd.

Whaleback Rd.

Hapeman Hill Rd.

103

199

199

FINISH

9G

9

Norton Rd.

Oriole Mills Rd.

199

199

199

Hook Rd.

308

103

Cedar Heights Rd.

START/FINISH Whistle Wood Farm

9

Pells Rd.

N

White School House Rd.

308

9

9G

Hudson River

Pt.-Pt.	Cume	Turn	Street/Landmark
2.1	10.7	S	Cross Rt. 92; continue on **Rt. 103**; ride through **Bard College Campus**
2.3	13.0	S	**Whaleback Rd.** at stop sign (cross Rt. 9G)
0.4	13.4	L	Unmarked **Whaleback Rd.** at stop sign
1.0	14.4	S	**Rockefeller Ln.** at stop sign
			***For optional loop to Olana turn left here.*
1.4	15.8	R	Unmarked **Rt. 9** at stop sign
0.4	16.2	L	**Feller-Newmark Rd.**
1.5	17.7	R	**Crestwood Rd.**
0.8	18.5	R	**Rt. 199** at stop sign
0.2	18.7	BL	**Unmarked road** at split with Rt. 199
			***Claremont/Olana loop joins here*
0.1	18.8	R	**Unmarked road**
0.6	19.4	L	**Norton Rd.**
1.9	21.3	L	Unmarked **Oriole Mills Rd.** at stop sign at **Old Rhinebeck Aerodrome**
0.7	22.0	R	**Pells Rd.**
1.9	23.9		Arrive at Whistle Farm Rd.

Optional Tivoli, Clermont and Olana Loop (additional 37 miles)
Moderate, rolling hills

This additional loop takes riders through the unassuming town of Tivoli, to two more impressive Hudson River estates that are now museums, and over miles and miles of rural farmland.

Tivoli, the unrealized vision of a perfect planned community following the French Revolution, today offers several eateries, small shops, and a bookstore. From its northern edge, Woods Road, lined with the entrances to a number of former estates, leads to **Clermont State Historic Park**, (914) 537-4240. The park, once the property of Chancellor Livingston, a drafter of the Declaration of Independence, features a small museum, historic gardens, trails, and wonderful river views in addition to its architectural masterpieces. The oldest of the Hudson River Estates, it covers 485 acres.

From here riders continue through picturesque countryside to **Olana**, a majestic hilltop estate created by Frederic Edwin Church, one of the foremost Hudson River School landcape artists. Today a state historic site, its grounds overlooking the Hudson are open to the public; (518) 828-0135.

All roads are paved. However, there is plenty of undulating terrain. The one-mile climb to Olana is a challenge. Ride with caution along sections of Routes 9 and 23 near Olana. Traffic moves fast and can be heavy. Otherwise, the roads are relatively lightly traveled and cover scenic, sprawling farmlands.

Pt.-Pt.	Cume	Turn	Street/Landmark
0.0	0.0	L	**Rt. 79** at stop sign (Intersection with Whaleback Rd.)
0.8	0.8	R	**Guski Rd.**
1.6	2.4	L	Unmarked **W. Kerley Corners Rd./Rt. 78** at stop sign
1.1	3.5	S	Cross **Rt. 9G** at stop sign, toward Tivoli
1.0	4.5	R	**Woods Rd.**, which becomes **Rt. 35** in Columbia County
1.6	6.1		**Entrance to park** is on the left. It's 0.7 miles to the mansion
0.4	6.5		Continue on **Rt. 6**
0.8	7.3	S	Cross Rt. 9G onto **Rt. 6** at stop sign
1.4	8.7	L	**Rt. 33**
1.4	10.1	R	**Viewmont Rd.**
2.1	12.2	R	**Rt. 8** at stop sign
0.1	12.3	L	**Hilltop Rd.**
0.9	13.2	BR	Unmarked **Dales Bridge Rd.** at yield
1.5	14.7	L	**Wire Rd.**
1.3	16.0	L	**Rt. 10** at stop sign
0.2	16.2	R	**White Birch Rd.**, which becomes **Howe Rd.**
2.3	18.5	L	Unmarked **Church Rd.** at stop sign
0.7	19.2	R	**Rt. 9G** at stop sign
0.4	19.6		Turnoff to **Olana**. Approximately 1-mile climb to mansion.
0.9	20.5		**Rt. 9** merges with **Rt. 23**
0.2	20.7	BR	**Rt. 23E**
0.9	21.6	R	**Middle Rd.**
1.3	22.9	L	Unmarked **Church Rd./Rt. 17** at stop sign
0.2	23.1	R	**Rt. 31** at 4-way stop sign
3.1	26.2	S	Cross Rt. 10 at 4-way stop onto **Rt. 31**
3.3	29.5	S	Cross Rt. 9 onto **Rt. 8** at stop sign in Blue Stores
1.6	31.1	R	**Rt. 19** at stop sign
3.1	34.2	BR	**Rt. 19** merges with Rt. 2 at Y
0.4	34.6	BL	Stay on **Rt. 19**
1.6	36.2	BL	Bend in road
1.3	37.5	L	**Rt. 56** at stop sign
0.4	37.9	R	**Hapeman Hill Rd.**
1.7	39.6	BR	At split in road
0.5	40.1	R	**Rt. 199** at stop sign
0.9	41.0	BL	**Unmarked road** at split (_pick up cues from Aerodrome loop_)

Rhode Island Inn and Rides

Rhode Island likes to claim that it was America's first vactionland and venue of the first two-week vacation with pay. It supposedly earned this distinction when Italian navigator Giovanni de Verazzano was so taken by the beauty of Narragansett Bay when exploring for France in 1524 that he lingered a fortnight.

Whether or not Verazzano's sojourn was truly a "vacation," Narragansett Bay is today a popular destination for boaters and explorers, including those who prefer overland exploration on two wheels. The area, like the Ocean State itself, offers an interesting blend of geography and history, and the Bay is one of the largest saltwater recreational areas in New England.

The Richards, a small B&B in a huge granite manor, in the seaside town of Narragansett makes a perfect home base for exploring the area on or off the bike. Ocean lovers will love mixing up cycling with swimming, boating, fishing, whalewatching, or surfing.

Those who prefer to stick to their bicycles will find that this tiny state boasts a number of scenic bikeways, bike routes, and bike paths. The state's Department of Transportation publishes a free map and "Guide to Cycling in the State," and the Rhode Island Greenways Council's Greenways Map is a useful guide to bikeways, rivers, trails, and natural areas.

Resources
Rhode Island Tourism Division
1 Exchange Street
Providence, RI   02903
(401) 222-2601 or (800) 556-2484
(401) 273-8270, fax
www.visitrhodeisland.com

Rhode Island Greenways Council
One Capital Hill
Providence, RI   02908
(401) 222-6479
www.planning.state.ri.us/GreenCouncil/GWCHOME.HTM

Rhode Island Department of Transportation
Bicycle Program Coordinator
(401) 222-4203, ext. 4042
www.dot.state.ri.us

Department of Parks and Recreation
2321 Hartford Avenue
Johnston, RI 02919
(401) 222-2632
(401) 934-0610, fax
http://www.riparks.com/

The Richards

Nancy & Steven Richards,
Innkeepers
144 Gibson Avenue
Narragansett, RI 02882
Rates: Budget-Moderate, B&B
Moderate-Deluxe, suites
Open all year

Phone: (401) 789-7746

Narragansett, with its long sandy beaches and captivating coastline, blossomed as a posh miniature Newport during the Victorian Era. Most of the huge Victorian resort hotels that once lined its shore are gone, but remnants of the town's heyday abound. One of the most notable of these is the imposing ocean-side "Towers," actually a stone arch spanning Ocean Road that is the remnant of the once-fabulous Narragansett Pier Casino, designed by Stanford White that sadly was destroyed by fire in 1900. The Towers now house a photographic exhibit featuring Narragansett during the Guilded Age, when huge summer "cottages" sprung up throughout the town and visitors arrived by steamship and train.

The Richards B&B, like many of the splendid remaining structures of the era, is defined by the detail work of fine craftsmen. Unlike its counterparts, however, it is built of granite. The original owner, Joseph Hazard, named the mansion Druid's Dream (a moniker that's carved into its façade) when he had it built in 1885 using granite from his own quarry at Seaside Farms.

Other than the Hazard family, the house had just one other owner before Steven and Nancy Richards, seasoned Narragansett innkeepers, bought it in 1987. The property was a bit rundown at the time, but they've restored the magic that its original name implies.

The Richards performed much of the restoration and decorating work themselves. In fact, when I arrived, Steve—whose day job is providing financial consulting services for large-scale transactions—was putting a new roof on a shed behind the house where, incidentally, guests can store their bikes.

Glancing beyond Steve's handiwork with the shed, one notes that the Richards have created an inviting, tastefully decorated inn that almost belies Druid's Dream's grandness. They've successfully created a *House and Garden* feel in an oversized manor that might otherwise feel imposing.

No matter where one steps in the 8500-square-foot mansion, a sense of spaciousness takes over. From the entrance foyer to the capacious second floor landing to the high ceilings, the house screams "grand."

The Richards have decorated the house with a mix of antique and traditional furnishings, using luxurious decorator fabrics for window treatments, table covers, lampshades, and pillows to provide the tasteful finishing touch that brings together the decor. Brightly polished hardwood floors are covered with oriental carpets and other area rugs. Large fireplaces are everywhere, enhancing the inn's warm atmosphere.

First floor common guest areas include a library and dining room, both with fireplaces, and an oversized furnished foyer with French doors leading to a sunny landscaped garden. From the gardens, which feature rose bushes and an array of perennials, guests can take a stroll on a walking path.

The second floor houses four spacious guest quarters, all of which have fireplaces. Some of the rooms have king or queen-size beds, and invite romance. They also invite guests to pour a complimentary snifter of brandy and to sit back and unwind. One of the guest rooms has twin beds and a suite layout that is perfect for a small group or family. Some rooms have private baths and some have a shared bath.

While there are no phones in the guestrooms, visitors have access to a shared phone in a small room on the second floor, where there's also a guest refrigerator and ironing board.

The Richards live on the third floor, which also is the home base of daughter Kristina's fashion accessories business. She manufactures brightly colored handbags of silk, decorated flowers, beads, and lace, that are sold in specialty clothing stores and have been featured in major fashion magazines.

In the morning, the Richards are happy to spend time with guests at the big dining room table to share their knowledge of the area and to help them plan their day. This, of course, is done over one of Nancy's gourmet breakfasts—which feature lots of fresh fruit and baked goods as well as tasty hot dishes—as the couple seamlessly shuttles in and out of the kitchen to attend to the needs of guests.

Bicycling from The Richards

Summertime is beach time in Narragansett, home to miles of sandy beaches and a mesmerizing coastline. But cyclists shouldn't be put off. A wide paved bike lane parallel to Route 1A in Narragansett provides plenty of room for cyclists to share the coastline with drivers.

At first glance, South County, where Narragansett sits, seems like it's flat as a pedal wrench. However, there is some diversity in the terrain as riders explore inland roads. There are certainly no mountain passes to climb, but there's enough variety to offer something for everyone.

Short sections of major road around Wakefield and Narragansett can be heavy with traffic, so riders should proceed with caution.

Novice cyclists who dislike traffic altogether can explore the bike path that runs between Kingston and Wakefield and which will soon continue to Narragansett.

In addition to the routes included here, cyclists can ride approximately 4.5 miles south from Narragansett along Ocean Road to Point Judith and its picturesque light house. From here ferries leave daily for Block Island; call (401) 783-4613.

Riders who prefer to ride with knowledgeable local cyclists can check the ride schedule of the Narragansett Bay Wheelmen, www.nbwclub.org, or join a day trip or hire a guide from Coastal Cycling Tours. Contact www.coastalcycling.com or (401) 788-0346 or (800) 701-6422.

Local Bike Shop
Narragansett Bikes
1153 Boston Neck Road
Narragansett, RI   02882-1734
(401) 782-4444

Mountain Biking Opportunities
Arcadia Management Area, a 14,000-acre park with some 60 miles of trails, is considered to be Mountain Biking Central in Rhode Island. It offers a wide variety of trails from fire roads to technical singletrack.

The area, which has been the site of a number of EFTA/NORBA races, offers something for everyone. Those looking for challenging technical riding should head to the Mt. Tom trail. Maps are available at the main parking lot off Route 165. Local bike shops often have Sunday morning rides that meet at the same lot.

The **Burlingame State Park**, west of Narragansett, also opens its trails to mountain biking. For information contact Burlingame State Park, Sanctuary Road, Charlestown, RI 02813; phone (401) 322-8910.

For additional information on off-road riding in the area contact the Rhode Island chapter of the **New England Mountain Biking Association.** Its website is http://members.aol.com/rinemba/.

Other Sources and Services
Narragansett Bay Wheelmen
P.O. Box 41177
Providence, RI   02878
(401) 435-4012
(401) 435-6343, fax
www.nbwclub.org

Rhode Island Greenways Council
One Capital Hill
Providence, RI   02908
Publishes Rhode Island Greenways Map, guide to a network of bikeways, rivers, trails, and natural areas

South Kingstown Chamber of Commerce
328 Main Street
P.O. Box 289
Wakefield, RI 02880
(401) 783-2801
(4010 789-3120, fax
e-mail: skcc@netsense.net
www.skchamber.com
Publishes excellent detailed map of South Kingstown and Narragansett

South Country Tourism Council
4808 Tower Hill Road
Wakefield, RI   02879
(800) 548-4662 or (401) 789-4422
(401) 789-4437
e-mail: scrc@netsense.net
www.southcountyri.com

Narragansett Tourist Information Center
The Towers
35 Ocean Road
Narragansett, RI   02882
(401) 783-7121
e-mail: narragansettcoc.com

Three Dubyas: Wordens Pond, Wakefield, and Westerly (39.3 miles or 25.4 miles shorter option)
Moderate with some hills

This scenic ride takes cyclists through varied landscape from farmland and wooded hills to some of South County's most scenic beaches.
    Pedal through the quaint downtown area of Wakefield, which sits on the bank of the Saugatucket River, and past Wordens Pond, the second largest fresh water pond in the state. On the longer route, ride to the beautifully preserved historic village of Wicksford. Take a detour off the route sheet and explore its authentic fishing port and handsome 17th- and 18th-century homes. The Old Narragansett Church, on Church Lane off Main Street, is one of the oldest Episcopal churches in America

and houses what is believed to be the oldest church organ (dating to 1680) in America.

From Wicksford, the ride parallels Narragansett Bay along Route 1, offering the chance to pedal off the beaten track to visit the **Gilbert Stuart Birthplace and Museum**, (401) 294-3001. Stuart, a master portrait painter and native of the area, is most famous for his portrait of George Washington that appears on the dollar bill.

Back on Route 1A, pass Casey Farms, (401) 295-1030, a working organic farm and museum dating to the 1750s.

Riders then get off Route 1A again to cycle along the headlands of Bonnet Shores. Back on Route 1A, they pass the turnoff for **South Shore Museum**, (401) 783-5400, at Canonchet Farm, where visitors step back in time to experience the region's rural heritage. It includes a picnic area, exercise course, and hiking trail.

The shorter option loops around Wordens Pond and the Great Swamp and returns to Narragansett via the Bike Path that begins at the historic Kingston Railroad Station.

Riders should use caution when riding along Woodruff Road, which has a narrow shoulder, and through the town of Wakefield. Route 1A has a wide shoulder. Route 2 has a wide shoulder and not much traffic.

Pt.-Pt.	Cume	Turn	Street/Landmark
0.0	0.0	R	From drive of The Richards onto **Gibson Ave.**
0.5	0.5	L	**S. Pier Rd.** at stop sign
1.1	1.6	S	Cross Rt. 108 at light onto **Woodruff Rd.** *Use caution*—busy intersection
1.2	2.8	L	**Main St.** in Wakefield
1.4	4.2	R	**Tuckertown Rd.**
2.4	6.6	S	**Wordens Pond Rd.** at flashing light, crossing Ministerial Rd./Rt. 110
2.6	9.2	R	**Biscuit City Rd.**
1.3	10.5	L	**New Biscuit City Rd.**, toward Rt. 2
0.4	10.9	R	**Rt. 2** at stop sign
3.4	14.3		****For shorter option, turn right onto Liberty Lane and follow cues below**
2.3	16.6	R	**Exeter Rd.**
1.8	18.4	L	**Lafayette Rd.**
2.8	21.2	R	**Rt. 102** at stop sign
1.4	22.6	S	**Rt. 102**, crossing Rt. 1 at stop light
0.6	23.2	R	**Rt. 1A S** toward Narragansett. (To explore town of Wicksford, go left)
2.3	25.5	R	**Gilbert Stuart Rd.**, which becomes **Snuff Mill Rd.**

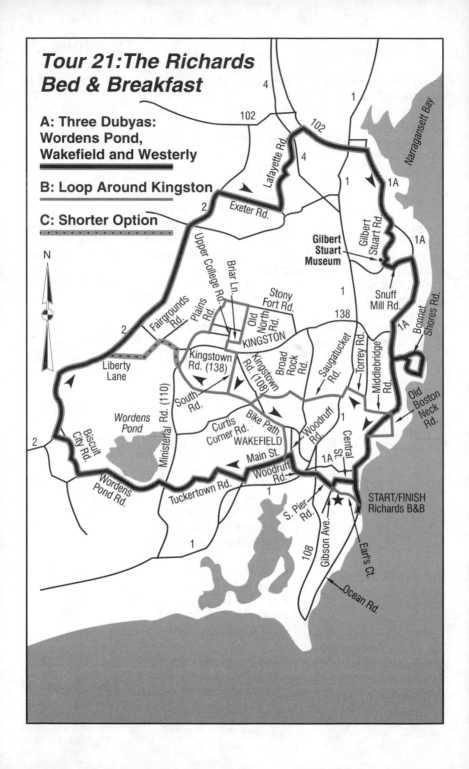

Tour 21: The Richards Bed & Breakfast

A: Three Dubyas: Wordens Pond, Wakefield and Westerly

B: Loop Around Kingston

C: Shorter Option

PtPt.	Cume	Turn	Street/Landmark
			(**Gilbert Stuart Museum** is off the road on the right after 1.5 miles)
2.5	28.0	R	**Rt. 1A S** at stop sign
3.1	31.1	L	**Bonnet Shores Rd.** at stop light
0.1	31.2	BL	At split in road
0.8	32.0	R	At stop sign and follow road along shore
2.1	34.1	S	**Bonnet Shores Rd.** at stop sign
0.1	34.2	L	**Rt. 1A S/Boston Neck Rd.**
3.8	38.0	S	At stop light
0.4	38.4	R	**Central St.** at stop sign
0.1	38.5	L	**Boon St.** at stop sign
0.8	39.3		Arrive at The Richards

Alternate return to The Richards, for 25.4 mile ride

PtPt.	Cume	Turn	Street/Landmark
0.0	0.0	R	**Liberty Lane**
1.2	1.2	BL	Road changes name to **Fairgrounds Rd.**
0.6	1.8	R	**Kingstown Rd./Rt. 138** at light
0.2	2.0	R	Turn into **Kingston RR station** and go to the end of the parking lot
0.2	2.2		Enter **bike path**
4.1	6.3	R	Exit bike path onto unmarked **Rodman St.** in Peace Dale
0.5	6.8	S	Changes name to **Willard St.** at stop sign
0.5	7.3	L	**Highland Ave.**
0.4	7.7	R	**Unmarked street**
0.1	7.8	L	**Main St.** at stop sign
0.4	8.2	R	**Woodruff Rd.** at light
1.3	9.5	S	Cross Rt. 108
1.1	10.6	R	**Gibson Ave.**
0.5	11.1		Arrive at The Richards

Loop around Kingston (24.1 miles)
Moderate with a couple short hills

This pleasant scenic route takes riders to Kingston, home of the University of Rhode Island. It's also home to the Pettaquamscutt Historical Society/Old Washington County Jail and the Fayerweather Craft Center.

Riders pedal north from Narragansett along the coast, then head inland crossing the salt water inlet of the Pettaquamscutt River and then the Saugatucket River. Pleasant South Road leads to Kingston and the university campus. Return to Wakefield via the scenic, car-free bike path, which eventually will continue to Narragansett.

Overall, there is not much traffic on the route. However, there is a tricky 0.2-mile segment where riders cross Route 1 from Torrey Road and another busy 0.5-mile section at the far end of Main Street in Wakefield on the return. (When the bike path is complete, riders will circumvent this section.)

Pt.-Pt.	Cume	Turn	Street/Landmark
0.0	0.0	R	**Gilbert Ave.** from drive of The Richards
0.3	0.3	R	**Earl's Court**
0.2	0.5	L	**Ocean Rd**. at stop sign
0.9	1.4	R	**Rt. 1A N** at light
1.4	2.8	R	**Old Boston Neck Rd.**
0.3	3.1	BL	**Old Boston Neck Rd.**
0.3	3.4	S	Cross Rt. 1A at stop sign
0.3	3.7	L	**Middlebridge Rd.** at stop sign
1.1	4.8	L	**Torey Rd.** Short (0.2 mile), steep hill.
0.5	5.3	U	Turn right at stop sign; go onto jug handle, then turn left onto **Rt. 1S** at light
0.3	5.6	R	**Saugatucket Rd.**
1.2	6.8	S	At stop sign cross Broad Rock
1.2	8.0	S	Cross Kingstown Rd. at light, onto unmarked **Curtis Corner Rd.**
0.7	8.7	L	Enter **Bike Path**, just after S. Kingstown Jr. High School
2.0	10.7	R	Unmarked **Ministerial Rd./Rt. 110**
0.6	11.3	S	**Plains Rd.**, crossing Rt. 138, at light
0.7	12.0	BR	Road bends right
0.3	12.3	L	**Plains Rd.**
1.1	13.4	R	**Stony Fort Rd.**
0.8	14.2	R	**Old North Rd.** at stop sign
1.3	15.5	R	**Briar Lane**
0.3	15.8	L	**Upper College Rd.**
0.2	16.0	L	**Rt. 138** at light
0.1	16.1	R	**South Rd.**
1.3	17.4	L	**Bike Path**, just after South Road School
1.3	18.7	R	Unmarked **Rodman St.**, at end of bike path in Peace Dale (Future plans call for continuing the path to Narragansett)
0.5	19.2	S	Changes name to **Willard St**. at stop sign

Pt.-Pt.	Cume	Turn	Street/Landmark
0.5	19.7	L	**Highland Ave.**
0.4	20.1	R	**Unmarked street**
0.1	20.2	L	**Main St.** at stop sign
0.8	21.0	R	At light. This is a very busy area—*use caution*
0.5	21.5	S	**Narragansett Ave.** at stop sign, after crossing over highway
			Becomes **Mumford St.**
0.8	22.3	R	Cross Kingstown Rd. onto **Larchwood Dr.**
0.4	22.7		**S. Pier Rd.**
1.0	23.7		**Gibson Ave.**
0.4	24.1		Arrive at The Richards

Vermont Inns and Rides

Vermont—without question—is bed, breakfast and bike heaven. The state must have more B&B's than France has vineyards. And its scenic, cyclist-friendly country roads seem to attract more cyclists and cycle touring companies than the Tour de France does spectators. All right, that may be an exaggeration—despite Vermont's French legacy (its name is derived from *Vert Mont*, French for Green Mountain.) Fortunately, its roads are not over-crowded with cycling enthusiasts. Yet cyclists, no matter where they travel in the state, are guaranteed to meet plenty of others who share their passion for two-wheel adventure.

Rich in both American history and a natural beauty that has inspired many of the country's greatest artists, writers, and explorers, Vermont invites adventure. Today, adventurers don't have to go far to discover the state's landmark covered bridges, cow-filled pastures (immortalized by the marketing efforts of Ben & Jerry's), and country lanes lined with maple trees, maple sugaring houses, and cider mills. In the fall, from border to border the state blazes with the colors of foliage.

Most of the state's 251 towns feature picturesque colonial architecture, village greens, and white-steepled churches, and emit an inviting, informal small-town atmosphere. All of the featured inns are located in or near one of these small villages, with the sister inns of **Edson Hill Manor** and **Ten Acres Lodge** located in the most developed of these towns: the popular ski resort of Stowe.

Like Edson Hill and Ten Acres, many of our cyclist-friendly inns are located near ski resorts. In fact, no matter where one travels in the Green Mountain State, a ski resort is not far away. The spectacular mountains that dominate the state—and give it its nickname—create varied cycling terrain that offers something for everyone. Demanding mountain passes test hard-core riders, while those who prefer more temperate riding terrain can stick to the flatter river valleys and enjoy the surrounding peaks that rise up from them.

In the nearly traffic-free, more remote Northeast Kingdom, not far from the Canadian border, the **Black Lantern Inn** sits at the base of Jay's Peak in a small town that has no less than three covered bridges. To its southwest, **The Inn at Mountain View Creamery**—once a working creamery and dairy farm—sits on a hilltop that provides fantastic views of Burke Mountain, an outdoor enthusiast's heaven. Further south, in the heart of the Mad River Valley, the beautifully landscaped and well-appointed **Inn at the Round Barn Farm** is barely a stone's throw from Sugarbush Mountain. The Green Mountain Cultural Center, located in its unique round barn, also serves as the heart of local music and arts activities.

Closer to the middle of the state, the **October Country Inn** serves as a popular way station for cyclists, most of whom keep coming back to enjoy the innkeepers' jovial camaraderie and bountiful repasts.

Within a day's cycling distance from October Country Inn, to the southeast, the majestic **Juniper Hill Manor** is perched on a hilltop above the town of Windsor, birthplace of Vermont.

Southwest of Windsor, on the western border of the Green Mountain National Park, the **Silas Griffith Inn** and its hometown of Danby transport visitors back in time.

Before departing for a cycling vacation in Vermont, be sure to contact the well-organized Vermont Department of Tourism and Marketing or the Vermont Chamber of Commerce for additional details on local attractions and scheduled events. Their *Vermont Traveler* guide even includes a two-page listing of cycling resources, such as bike shops and tour companies.

Another useful source of information about Vermont is the www.linkvermont.com web site.

Resources

Vermont Department of Tourism and Marketing
123 State Street
Montpelier, VT 05601-1471
1-800-VERMONT or (802) 828-3237
(802) 828-3233, fax
www.1-800-vermont.com
Free travel guide and official state map.

Vermont Chamber of Commerce
P.O. Box 37
Montpelier, VT   05601
(802) 223-3443
(802) 223-4257, fax
email: vtchambr@together.net
www.vtchamber.com

State Travel Division
61 Elm Street
Montpelier, VT   05602
Publishes list of commercial bicycle tour companies for the state and a Vermont tour map showing 23 one-day tours and seven regional tours.

Central Vermont Chamber of Commerce
P.O. Box 336
Barre, VT 05641
(802) 229-4619
(802) 229-5713, fax
Publishes free *Back Road Bike Tours: A guide to Day Trips in Central Vermont*

Vermont Life Magazine
6 Baldwin St.
Montpelier, VT 05602
(802) 828-3241
Publishes *Bicycle Vermont Map and Guide.* $2.95, plus postage.

Green Mountain National Forest
231 North Main Street
Rutland, VT 05701
(802) 747-6700
(802) 747-6766, fax
http://www.fs.fed.us/r9/gmfl/

Department of Forests, Parks & Recreation
Vermont Agency of Natural Resources
103 South Main St. – 10 South
Waterbury, VT 05671
(802) 241-3655

Green Mountain Bicycle Club
P.O. Box 563
Waterbury, VT 05676
(802) 583-8188
www.gmbc.together.com/

Vermont Mountain Bike Advocates (VMBA)
www.vmba.org

Mountain Bikers of Vermont
Route 1, Box 1450
Waterbury, VT 05676
(800) 628-4040 or (802) 244-5067

The Black Lantern Inn, Montgomery, Vermont

The Black Lantern Inn

Allan & Rita Kalsmith,
Innkeepers
Route 118
Montgomery, VT   05460
Rates: Budget-Moderate B&B
MAP plan available
Open all year

Phone: (800) 255-6661; (802) 674-5273
Fax: (802) 326-4077
Web: www.blacklantern.com
E-mail: blantern@together.net

When The Black Lantern Inn first opened its doors in 1803, it provided lodging for weary guests arriving by stagecoach. Today, it welcomes adventurous travelers and outdoor enthusiasts arriving by more modern means of transportation. And innkeeper Allan Kalsmith, an avid cyclist, extends a particularly friendly reception to fellow wheelmen.

This quiet, unspoiled corner of the Green Mountains, near the Canadian border, is a cyclist's paradise. Except for the business districts in the small towns in the region, the roads are nearly traffic-free. And the landscape and countryside around Montgomery epitomize Vermont, from the imposing Jay Peak which towers above the tiny village to the ubiquitous maple trees and dozens of sugar houses to Montgomery's six covered bridges (two of which are barely a stone's throw from the inn).

Allan and his wife Rita have operated the inn for more than 20 years, and their restaurant has earned a reputation as one of the finest dining establishments in the area.

The inn's 10 rooms and six suites are housed in two separate buildings: the main house, which is listed in the National Register of Historic Places as The Montgomery House, and the Burdett House, believed to have been built about the same time as the main house.

On the first floor of the inn are a common sitting room with a woodstove, a cozy bar, and the dining room, all decorated with antiques and country furnishings. On the top floor of the main building are individually decorated rooms with private baths. While all of the rooms have been renovated, some of them are small and not as cheery or as inviting as either Room #10, which has a gas fireplace and private porch, or the attractively decorated suites in the Burdett House.

The well-appointed suites in the newly renovated Burdett House offer a nice combination of historic charm and modern conveniences. All of them have working fireplaces, whirlpool tubs, and queen-size beds; some have private porches. Suite 3B, a duplex, has a nicely furnished seating area in front of the wood-burning fireplace on the first floor, with a bedroom and bath on the second floor.

In addition, a 3-bedroom suite at the back of the main house is suitable for a family or small group traveling together.

At the end of the day, guests can enjoy a cocktail on the front porch or on one of the Adirondack chairs on the lawn behind the inn. Or, they can relax their weary muscles in the outdoor hot tub as they take in the countryscape.

The dining room, with its French provincial print wallpaper and country furnishings, provides a comfortable spot for guests to enjoy the Black Lantern's hearty country breakfasts: Fresh muffins, fruit, cereals, and all kinds of hot items from the kitchen, such as pancakes, French toast, eggs, bacon, and potatoes.

In the evening the dining room fills with candlelight and the aromas of the Black Lantern's enticing dinner menu, which features items such as spinach-stuffed mushrooms or Gravlax for starters, and Filet Mignon, Lam Marguerite or Shrimp with Salmon Mousse as entrees.

Biking from The Black Lantern Inn
The Northern Kingdom is lightly populated and offers heavenly, traffic-free cycling for riders of all interests and abilities. Although the terrain overall is marked by rolling hills, cyclists find everything from gentler routes, usually running north-south along river valleys, to the thigh-burning climb around Jay's Peak.

The cyclist-friendly "Loyalists Region" of Canada, just over the border, is marked by scenic bike routes, many of which will be part of the trans-Quebec 3,000-kilometer "Route Verte" (green route) bike "path", when it is completed by year 2005. The Sutton area is home to several annual competitive cycling events including the women's international Grand Prix of Canada and Coupe des Amériques, a stage race for veteran cyclists. For information on the more leisurely Rallie Ton Vélo, a June weekend of guided bicycling tours, or Le Tour des Couleurs, a popular mountain (or hybrid) bike tour in September, call 800-565-8455.

Bike Shops in the Region
Velo Sutton
19, Principale Nord
Sutton J0E 2K0, Quebec, Canada
(450) 538-6997
Sales, service, accessories. Mountain bike rentals.

Power Play Sports
64 Portland Street, P.O. Box 1307
Morrisville, VT 05661
(802) 888-6557
Sales, service, accessories. Mountain bike rentals.

Chuck's Bikes
10 Main Street
Morrisville, VT 05661
(802) 888-7642

North Star Cyclery
16 S. Main Street
St. Albans, VT 05478
(802) 524-2049

Bike It Bicycle Shop
179 Pearl Street
St. Albans, VT 05478
(802) 524-9678

Porter's Bike Shop
116 Grand Avenue
Swanton, VT
(802) 868-7417

Rentals available at:
Jay Peak Mountain Bike Center
(800) 451-4449 or (802) 988-2611
Also offers regularly-scheduled mountain bike tours.

Mountain Biking Options

Dirt roads outnumber paved roads in the Northeast Kingdom. So there's no shortage of mountain biking opportunities on a mix of class 4 roads, ATV trails, and singletrack.

Popular destinations include the lift-accessed trails of **Jay Peak**, where its 60-passenger tram transports riders to the top. There are 44 miles of mountain biking trails, and maps are available. For information call the Mountain Bike Center at (800) 451-4449 or (802) 988-2611, e-mail jaypeak@together.net or visit www.jaypeakresort.com. Or, explore the trails in the nearby **Hazen's Notch** and **Sugarloaf Mountain** area.

Local Information

Northeast Kingdom/Montgomery
Northeast Kingdom Travel & Tourism Association
The Historic Railroad Station
Box 355, Main Street
Island Pond, VT   05846-0355
(888) 884-8001
www.vtnek.com

Northeast Kingdom Chamber of Commerce
30 Western Avenue
St. Johnsbury, VT 05819
(800) 639-6379 or (802) 748-3678
www.vermontnekchamber.org

Montgomery Town Association
P.O. Box 18
Montgomery Center, VT 05471

Canada
Sutton Tourist Association
Place Sutton
C.P./P.O. 418
Sutton, Quebec, JOE 2K0 Canada
(514) 538-2646
Publishes a cycling map, with distances and road classifications for
Sutton and Eastern Township area.

"Cycling Southern Québec"
Brochure highlighting routes in the Monteregie and Eastern townships available from their Tourism Associations: Monteregie (514)
674-5555; Eastern Townships (800) 355-5755.

Sutton: Region des Loyalistes (39 miles)
Moderate; Don't forget your passport—and your French dictionary

Pass the town lattice-style Longley and Hopkins covered bridges as you
cycle along gentle Route 118 toward Richford, a once flourishing furni-
ture-manufacturing town. Upon entering Quebec, pass the lush farmlands of its Eastern Township en route to the pristine town of Sutton,
where you can enjoy the small shops or buy lunch. This area's "Loyalists
Region" moniker dates back to the late 1700s when Americans wanting to

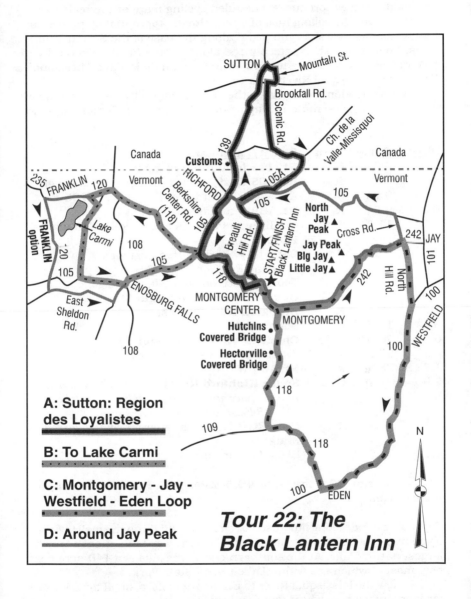

SUTTON — Mountain St. — Brookfall Rd. — Scenic Rd. — Ch. de la Valle-Missisquoi

Canada — Vermont — Canada — Vermont

235 — FRANKLIN — 120

Customs — 139 — RICHFORD — Berkshire Center Rd. (118) — 105A — 105

FRANKLIN option — Lake Carmi — 108 — Breault Hill Rd. — START/FINISH Black Lantern Inn — 105 — 105 — **North Jay Peak** ▲ — Cross Rd. — 242 — JAY — 101

'20 — 105 — 105 — **Jay Peak** — **Big Jay** ▲ — **Little Jay** ▲ — North Hill Rd. — 100 — WESTFIELD

East Sheldon Rd. — ENOSBURG FALLS — 118 — **MONTGOMERY CENTER** — 242 — **MONTGOMERY** — 100

108 — **Hutchins Covered Bridge** — **Hectorville Covered Bridge**

A: Sutton: Region des Loyalistes

109 — 118

B: To Lake Carmi

C: Montgomery - Jay - Westfield - Eden Loop

118

D: Around Jay Peak

100 — EDEN

N

Tour 22: The Black Lantern Inn

remain loyal to the British Crown settled here. Sutton's tourism office in the middle of town produces a detailed cycling map for the region.

Ride over the rolling hills of Scenic Road, appropriately named for its spectacular views, as you pedal along the base of the Sutton Mountains. There's one short, steep piece along Scenic Road, followed by a nice downhill, just before turning onto Chemin de la Valle-Missisquoi. Follow the Missisquoi River back to the U.S.

Return to Montgomery via either the slightly hillier—but extremely scenic and remote—route through South Richford, or Routes 105 and 118.

Pt.-Pt.	Cume	Turn	Street/Landmark
0.0	0.0	L	**Rt. 118** from Inn parking lot
4.7	4.7	R	**Rt. 105 East**, toward Richford, at stop sign
4.5	9.2	S	At flashing light to continue on **Rt. 105 East**
0.3	9.5	R	**Rt. 139 N** at flashing light at T
1.5	11.0	S	Go through customs and pick up Canadian **Rt. 139 N**
6.8	17.8	R	**Cemetery St.** in Sutton, just after A La Fontaine Restaurant & B&B. If you pass the Tourist Office on your left, you've gone too far
0.0	17.8	R	Quick right onto **Mountain St.**
1.3	19.1	R	**Brookfall Rd.** at stop sign
0.6	19.7	L	**Scenic Rd.**
6.3	26.0	R	**Ch. de la Valle-Missisquoi**
1.2	27.2	S	Enter U.S. on **Rt. 105A West**
1.7	28.9	R	**Rt. 105 W**
2.9	31.8	L	**South Richford Rd.** (also **Breault Hill Rd.**) *(For an alternate return route you can follow Rt. 105 East to Rt. 118 South)*
7.1	38.9	R	Onto **Rt. 118 North**, after crossing covered bridge
0.1	39.0		Black Lantern Inn

To Lake Carmi (33.3 miles, or 40.5 miles with Franklin option)
Easy to moderate

Enjoy a quiet ride along little-used back roads and through small towns— if you blink you're bound to miss them—on the way to Vermont's fourth-largest natural lake. At the southern end of the lake is a 140-acre peat bog, most of which lies within Lake Carmi State Park.

Follow the Missisquoi River to Enosburg Falls, a small town known for its dairy festival, where you can buy lunch or refreshments.

All routes are paved, except about 1 mile along the lake. There is little traffic on the routes, except around Enosburg. There are gently rolling hills along Berkshire Center Road and Route 120 South. On the longer options, there are a couple notable short climbs.

Pt.-Pt.	Cume	Turn	Street/Landmark
0.0	0.0	L	From Inn parking lot onto **Rt. 118N**
4.7	4.7	L	**Rt. 105 West** at stop sign at T
0.1	4.8	R	Unmarked **Berkshire Center Rd./Rt. 118**
7.5	12.3	L	**Rt. 120 S**
0.6	12.9	BR	To stay on **Rt. 120 S**
1.2	14.1	L	Unpaved **Dewing Shore Rd.**
			***For longer option, continue straight on Rt. 120 S and pick up cues below*
0.9	15.0	R	**Rt. 236 South**
5.2	20.2	L	**Rt. 105 East** at stop sign
3.0	23.2	L	To continue on **Rt. 105 East** at stop sign in Enosburg Falls
5.3	28.5	R	**Rt. 118 South**
4.8	33.3		Black Lantern Inn

Franklin option

0.0	14.1	S	On **Rt. 120 S** at turnoff for Dewing Shore Rd.
3.1	17.2	L	Continue on **Rt. 120 South**
5.5	22.7	S	Onto **Kane Rd.** at stop sign
1.1	23.8	L	**East Sheldon Rd.** at T
4.5	28.3	L	**Unmarked road** at stop sign
1.4	29.7	L	Onto **Rt. 108 North** at stop sign
0.1	29.8	R	Onto **Rt. 105E/Rt. 108 N** at stop sign
5.9	35.7	R	**Rt. 118 South**
4.8	40.5		Black Lantern Inn

Montgomery-Jay-Westfield-Eden Loop (50.4 miles)
Challenging

If you like long climbs—and short climbs—you'll love this route. Get the serious climbing out of the way during the first 10 miles, then enjoy lots of moderate riding, with an occasional hill, as you ride in the shadows of the imposing Jay Peaks and Belvidere and Haystack Mountains. Great scenery and road conditions. Several small country stores provide opportunities for nourishment; Lake Eden, Long Pond, and rivers and brooks crossing the route serve as great picnic sites.

PtPt.	Cume	Turn	Street/Landmark
0.0	0.0	R	From Inn parking lot onto **Rt. 118S**
2.5	2.5	L	Onto **Rt. 242** toward Jay at split in road. Climb for next 7 miles
11.5	14.0	R	Unmarked **North Hill Rd.**, just after Jay General Store
4.1	18.1	BR	Onto **Rt. 100S** at fork in Westfield
15.6	33.7	R	**Rt. 118N** at Eden General Store
6.5	40.2	BR	Continue on **Rt. 118N** toward Montgomery Center
6.0	46.2		*Optional side trip:* Go left onto **Gibou Rd.**, and continue several hundred yards to see **Hectorville Covered Bridge**
0.8	47.0		*Optional side trip:* Go left on **Hutchins Bridge Rd.** and go 0.2 miles to see **Hutchins Covered Bridge**
1.4	48.4	L	Continue on **Rt. 118N**
2.0	50.4		Black Lantern Inn

Around Jay Peak (39.2 miles)
Challenging

Get a look at Jay Peak—and Little Jay, Big Jay, and North Jay—from all sides as you enjoy several nice climbs. Opportunities for food and beverage are few and far between in this remote mountainous corner of the Northern Kingdom. The scenery is exhilarating.

0.0	0.0	R	From Inn parking lot onto **Rt. 118S**
2.5	2.5	L	Onto **Rt. 242** toward Jay at split in road. Climb for next 7 miles, then enjoy the downhill
11.5	14.0	L	**Cross Rd.**
1.6	15.6	L	**Rt. 105W** at stop sign. A 3.5-mile climb on this stretch.
10.4	26.0	S	Continue on **Rt. 105W** at junction with Rt. 105A
3.2	29.2	BR	Continue on **Rt. 105W** at junction with S. Richford Rd.
0.7	29.9	L	Onto **Rt. 105W** at stop sign
4.5	34.4	L	**Rt. 118 South**
4.8	39.2		Black Lantern Inn

The Inn at Mountain View Creamery

Marilyn and John Pastore, Hosts
Laurelie Welch, Innkeeper
Darling Hill Road, Box 355
East Burke, VT 05832
Rates: Moderate-Luxury, B&B
Open all year

Phone: (802) 626-9924 or (800) 572-4509
Web: www.innmtnview.com
E-mail: innmtnvu@plainfield.bypass.com

The Inn at the Mountain View Creamery and its idyllic setting make an ideal base for cycling the remote byways of Vermont's Northeast Kingdom. This former working creamery, with its pastoral setting and fantastic 360-degree mountain views, exudes both the majesty of a kingdom and the authenticity of rural Vermont. The 460-acre property atop Darling Hill includes the inn, a carriage house, an enormous picture-perfect cow barn, Morgan Horse stable, and a farmhouse.

The inn, a red brick Georgian colonial building with a butter churn cupola, was built in 1890 as the creamery on Elmer Darling's quintessential gentleman's farm. Darling, an East Burke native son, was a lifelong bachelor who studied architecture at MIT and was proprietor of the elegant Fifth Avenue Hotel in New York City. The Mountain View Farm supplied his hotel with beef and dairy products.

When Marilyn and John Pastore, a retired Russian teacher and cardiologist respectively, purchased the neglected creamery, surrounding buildings, and farmland in 1989, the property was in need of repair. Today, the gentrified Creamery is filled with elegant antiques and decorative furnishings, with authentic remnants of its early days amidst the tasteful decor.

The property that surrounds the inn and series of red and white barns around its courtyard is beautifully maintained and dotted with organic vegetable and perennial gardens. The ability to explore and enjoy the property is one of the best parts of staying here. Adirondack chairs throughout the garden, and a front patio with chairs and umbrella tables, provide perfect vantage points for soaking up the spectacular mountain views. Guests can sip afternoon tea or a glass of wine as they gaze at Willoughby Gap or the Burke Mountains. They can hike or mountain bike (or, in the winter, cross-country ski) on the Darling Hill Trail system that laces the property. Or, visitors with Dr. Dolittle-like afflictions can talk to the managerie of animals on this genteel farm, which includes pigs, pheasants, turkeys, and Rhode Island red hens and roosters, in addition to John's cows, three horses, and Roxie, a Scottish terrier.

Ten guest rooms, all with private baths with either a tub or shower, are located on the second floor of the creamery. They are tastefully furnished—each in a different color scheme—with country antique and wicker furnishings, chintz fabrics, and handmade quilts. A wall of white painted embossed tin tiles lines the upstairs hall, where there's a small, cozy reading corner.

On the first floor of the Creamery, two large manor-style sitting rooms provide comfortable corners to relax in after a long day of riding. One features a huge fireplace, large stuffed sofa, a TV, video player, and a collection of videos, some of which highlight local history and culture—or, like "Spitfire Grill," include scenes shot locally.

All of the downstairs rooms, including the dining room—which is home to Darling's Country Bistro—have charmingly stenciled floors and attractive window treatments. Floor-to-ceiling windows in the dining room, which once served as the center of the Creamery's butter and cheese production, provide fantastic views of the courtyard. The full country breakfast includes a broad array of items to satisfy appetites of all sizes—fresh fruit and baked goods, yogurt, granola, eggs, and specialties such as apple pancakes—all attractively presented.

The Bistro is open for lunch and dinner Friday through Sunday and, as with breakfast, the dishes incorporate lots of fresh ingredients—many from the inn's garden. The menu features items such as slow roasted beet and boursin gateau or smoked Atlantic salmon with chives and chevre for appetizers, and roasted rack of New Zealand lamb, pork tenderloin with rhubarb ginger chutney and a layered polenta terrine as entrees.

For small groups or a family, a beautiful townhouse, in the farmhouse next to the inn, offers a full kitchen, living room with fireplace, two bedrooms (one with Jacuzzi), and two baths. Inquire about its special rates.

Whether in the townhouse, Creamery, or amidst the open spaces of the surrounding gardens and meadows, guests are treated to a magnificent country setting and inspiring environs.

Biking from The Mountain View Creamery

Vermont's bucolic northeastern corner is a cyclist's heaven. The roads are virtually traffic-free and the towns are just far enough apart to provide pleasant break spots. Vince or John, at The East Burke Sports Shop, just down the hill from the inn, can offer additional local cycling tips or provide area maps and ride descriptions. Across the street from the shop, in quaint Bailey's General Store (a popular stop for provisions and local information), an information binder also contains suggested bike tours in the area.

The region's diverse terrain—from moderate to extremely hilly, mixed with long flat stretches—offers enjoyable pedaling for cyclists of all abilities.

Local Bike Shop
East Burke Sports
Route 114, P.O. Box 189
East Burke, VT 05832
(802) 626-3215
(802) 626-1223, fax
Sales, service, accessories for road and mountain bikes. Rents mountain bikes. Provides road and mountain bike guide service for a few hours or for the day.

Also in the Region
Burke Mountain Base Lodge
Trailside Shop
(802) 626-1443
Mountain bike rentals.

Village Sport Shop
Route 5
Lyndonville, VT 05851
(802) 626-8448

Mountain Biking Opportunities
They're everywhere. The East Burke area boasts literally hundreds of miles of mountain biking trails.

The closest options are just behind the barns of the Mountain View Creamery, where the **Darling Hill** trails offer miles of everything from easy to difficult singletrack riding.

Nearby **Burke Mountain**, which rises 2,000 vertical feet from its base lodge, is a mountain biking mecca. It's in the middle of what it claims is "the largest and most sophisticated trail network in New England," where there are 300 miles of singletrack, cross country, and mountainside trails for riders of all abilities. Stop at the Trailside Shop for more information, call (802) 626-3305, or visit www.burkemountain.com. In September Burke is home to the Kingdom Classic Mountain Bike Race, billed as one of the hardest races on the NORBA circuit.

Kingdom Trails Association publishes a trail guide for the East Burke region that includes loops along Darling Hill and on Burke Mountain. The contour map highlights more than 75 miles of easy to expert trails, plus indications for paved and unpaved roads, rivers, and lakes. Pick up the map at East Burke Sports Shop or write: Kingdom Trails Association, P.O. Box 204, East Burke, VT 05832.

East Burke Sports Shop also offers guided mountain biking services.

Other Resources
The Northeast Kingdom Travel & Tourism Association
The Historic Railroad Station
Main Street, P.O. Box 355
Island Pond, VT 05846-0355
(802) 723-9800 or toll-free in U.S.: (888) 884-8001
Email: info@travelthekingdom.com
www.travelthekingdom.com

Northeast Kingdom Chamber of Commerce
30 Western Avenue
St. Johnsbury, VT 05819
(800) 639-6379 or (802) 748-3678
www.vermontnekchamber.org

To Sutton: Off the beaten track (24.9 miles)
Moderate, lots of easy rolling hills and one significant climb

Enjoy "real" Vermont countryside—lots of farmland and mountain views as you pedal over scenic rolling terrain. Ride through the high pastures of Sutton and take in the unspoiled meadows and sparsely populated farmland along remote country roads.

About two miles north of West Burke off Route 5, near Sutton Station, is **Ledge in Thyme** gardens, where hundreds of perennials and herbs grow among rock and ledge terraces. **LaPlant's Sugar House** is just a bit further up the road. After passing through the village of Sutton you'll pass the **Don Sim III Farm** which has a rotary milking parlor where you can watch the process if you pass at milking time.

Except for a portion of Darling Hill Road, all roads are paved with good surfaces.

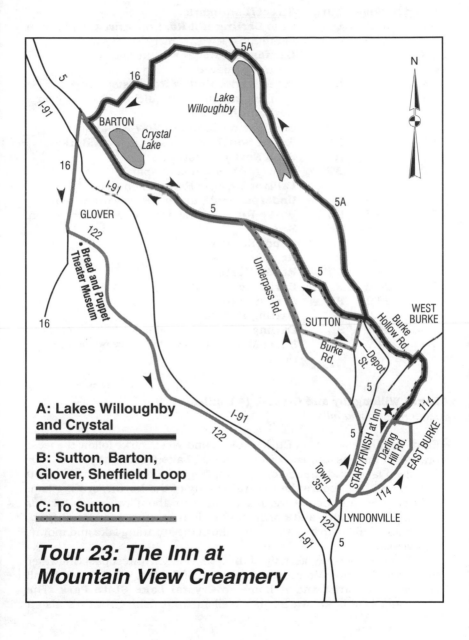

N

5A

16

Lake
Willoughby

I-91

BARTON

Crystal
Lake

16

I-91

GLOVER

122

5

5A

5

• Bread and Puppet
Theater Museum

Underpass Rd.

16

SUTTON

Burke
Hollow Rd.

WEST
BURKE

Burke
Rd.

Depot St.

**A: Lakes Willoughby
and Crystal**

**B: Sutton, Barton,
Glover, Sheffield Loop**

C: To Sutton

I-91

122

5

5

114

START/FINISH at Inn

Darling Hill Rd.

EAST
BURKE

Town
35

114

LYNDONVILLE

*Tour 23: The Inn at
Mountain View Creamery*

122

I-91

5

Pt.-Pt.	Cume	Turn	Street/Landmark
0.0	0.0	**L**	Onto **Darling Hill Rd.** from driveway of Inn at Mountain View Creamery
0.4	0.4	**BR**	**Darling Hill Rd.** at split in road
0.2	0.6		Road is unpaved
1.4	2.0	**L**	Paved **Burke Hollow Rd.** at stop sign
0.7	2.7	**BL,R**	Bear left at split, then quick right to stay on **Burke Hollow Rd.**
0.9	3.6	**BR**	Continue on **Burke Hollow Rd.** at split
1.2	4.8	**L**	**Rt. 5A South** at stop sign in West Burke
0.1	4.9	**R**	**Rt. 5 North** at stop sign
0.0	4.9	**BR**	Stay on **Rt. 5 North** at split
2.8	7.7		**LaPlant's Sugar House** is on right
3.7	11.4	**L**	**Underpass Rd.**, under RR, toward Sutton
5.3	16.7	**BL**	**Burke Rd.**, at 4-way intersection after Sutton School
2.8	19.5	**BL**	**Depot St.** at Y
0.3	19.8	**R**	**Rt. 5** at stop sign
0.1	19.9	**L**	**Rt. 5A North**
0.1	20.0	**R**	**Burke Hollow Rd.**
2.2	22.2	**BR**	At split in road
0.7	22.9	**R**	**Darling Hill Rd.**
1.6	24.5	**S**	**Darling Hill Rd.** at stop sign
0.4	24.9		Inn at Mountain View Creamery is on your right

Lakes Willoughby and Crystal (41 miles)
Moderate, rolling hills

From the tiny enclaves of Burke Hollow and West Burke follow the west branch of the Passumpsic River to glacial **Lake Willoughby**. The 300-foot-deep lake, and the imposing Mts. Pisgah and Hor that rise 1,000 feet above it, symbolize the natural beauty of the Northeast Kingdom. Off Route 5A just before the lake, and then about two miles further north, are the south and north trailheads respectively for Mt. Pisgah, which lures hikers to its summit to take in the stunning lake and mountain vistas.

From the northwestern tip of the lake, ride southwest past Stillwater Swamp and Barton Mountain to the town of Barton, which has a small commercial district and is home to **Crystal Lake State Park**. The clearwater lake is known for its excellent trout fishing, but it's also a great place to swim. Pierce's Pharmacy in Barton has an old-fashioned soda fountain. Follow Route 5 along Crystal Lake's shore to West Burke, then through back roads to East Burke.

All routes are paved, except a short stretch on Darling Hill Road, and there is little traffic.

Pt.-Pt.	Cume	Turn	Street/Landmark
0.0	0.0	L	Onto **Darling Hill Rd.** from driveway of Inn at Mountain View Creamery
0.4	0.4	BR	**Darling Hill Rd.** at split in road
0.2	0.6		Road is unpaved
1.4	2.0	L	Paved **Burke Hollow Rd.** at stop sign
0.7	2.7	BL,R	Bear left at split, then quick right to stay on **Burke Hollow Rd.**
0.9	3.6	BR	Continue on **Burke Hollow Rd.** at split
1.2	4.8	R	**Rt. 5A North** at stop sign
11.3	16.1	L	**Rt. 16 South**
0.3	16.4	BR	At split to stay on **Rt. 16 South/Willoughby Lake Rd.**
6.4	22.8	L	**Rt. 5 South** at stop sign in Barton
13.2	36.0	L	**Rt. 5A North** in West Burke
0.1	36.1	R	**Burke Hollow Rd.**
2.2	38.3	BR	At split in road
0.7	39.0	R	**Darling Hill Rd.**
1.6	40.6	S	**Darling Hill Rd.** at stop sign
0.4	41.0		Inn at Mountain View Creamery is on your right

Sutton, Barton, Glover, Sheffield Loop (47.4 miles)
Challenging, Hilly

A favorite loop among local cyclists, this route offers plenty of hilltop vistas and passes through several typical regional hamlets. In total, this challenging route includes approximately 2,000 feet of climbing. Enjoy a swim in cool Crystal Lake or visit the **Bread and Puppet Theater Museum**, housed in a former dairy barn on Route 122 outside Glover. The Bread and Puppet Circus, known for its huge puppets and political theater with a leftist bent, has toured the world. The Museum's collection includes hundreds of masks.

Pt.-Pt.	Cume	Turn	Street/Landmark
0.0	0.0	**R**	**Darling Hill Rd.** from drive of Mountain View Creamery
0.3	0.3		Unpaved surface begins
1.6	1.9		Pavement begins again
1.4	3.3	**R**	**East Burke Rd./Rt 114 South** at stop sign
0.5	3.8	**R**	**Rt. 5 North** at stop sign and flashing light
2.7	6.5	**L**	At bottom of small hill, **unmarked road**, follow signs to Sutton
3.8	10.3		Begin 1-mile steep climb
0.6	10.9	**S**	At 4-way intersection in Sutton toward Sutton School. Unmarked **Underpass Rd./ Sutton Rd.**
5.4	16.3	**L**	After underpass, onto **Rt. 5 North**
3.7	20.0		Swimming at **Crystal Lake**
2.6	22.6	**L**	At Barton General Store and E.M. Brown & Sons onto **Rt. 16**
0.2	22.8	**L**	**Rt. 16 South**
3.0	25.8		**General Store** in downtown Glover is cyclist-friendly
1.4	27.2	**L**	**Rt. 122,** after cemetery
7.6	34.8		Village of Sheffield
2.0	36.8		Village of Wheelock
5.0	41.8	**L**	Unmarked **Town Hwy. 35**, following sign to Rt. 114. Do not cross covered bridge.
0.5	42.3	**S**	**Rt. 114 North** at stop sign
4.4	46.7	**L**	At Burke Hollow sign, to cross river in East Burke. (Just before East Burke Sports shop.)
0.1	46.8	**BL**	**East Darling Hill Rd.** at split in road
0.6	47.4	**L**	**Darling Hill Rd.** Inn at Mountain View Creamery is on your right

The Inn at The Round Barn Farm

Anne Marie DeFreest, Host
Tim O'Brien & Tracie Kaslin,
Innkeepers
RR 1, Box 247, East Warren Road
Waitsfield, VT   05673
Rates: Moderate-Luxury, B&B
Open all year

Phone: (802) 496-2276
Fax: (802) 496-8832
Web: http://Innattheroundbarn.com
E-mail: roundbarn@madriver.com

The Inn at The Round Barn Farm, nestled among more than 200 glorious acres of mountains, meadows, and ponds in the heart of the Mad River Valley, offers incomparable lodging for outdoor enthusiasts of all sorts—and bicyclists in particular.

Owners Jack and Doreen Simko, who moved to Waitsfield from New Jersey, purchased the old Joslin Farm with its historic, 12-sided round barn in 1986. Over the next six years they renovated the 19th-century farmhouse, adjacent carriage storage area, and 1910 Round Barn to create a magnificent 11-room inn. From pouring a new foundation for the barn to the creation of the sunny breakfast room, the massive and painstaking renovations are well-documented in a collection of bronze-plaqued photo albums in the library.

The Shakers, according to folklore, built round barns (only five of which still stand in Vermont) so that the devil couldn't "catch you in the corners." Folklore or not, there's absolutely no sign of the devil at the Inn at The Round Barn Farm.

In fact, it's more like heaven on earth. And its list of heavenly features and amenities is endless: Superb furnishings and tasteful decor, with immaculate attention to detail. A 60-foot lap pool in the lower level of the barn that extends into a bougainvillea and hibiscus-filled greenhouse. Fresh cut flowers and plush terry robes in the rooms. Cow-filled meadows. Beautifully landscaped grounds, reflecting the Simko's background in the floral industry—complete with water lilies and ducks afloat on a pond. A cozy library with fireplace. A game room with antique pool table, organ, television, VCR, and a refrigerator stocked with complimentary juices and soda.

All of the rooms are luxuriously decorated and have private baths, and the inn's spacious "Luxury" rooms in the converted carriage area offer cathedral ceilings, mountain views, gas fireplaces, phone jacks, and relaxing steam showers or oversized whirlpool tubs. The inn's rooms are named after local families, with the Richardson, Sherman, Dana, and English rooms being the ones in the carriage area. The spacious Joslin room, namesake of the original owners, is located on the ground floor at the front of the main house and features a fireplace and king-size cano-pied bed, as well as an oversized whirlpool tub and steam shower. The rooms at the back of the inn offer serene mountain and meadow views and several rooms have skylights—perfect for stargazing.

Anne Marie DeFreest, the Simko's daughter, is a gracious, multi-talented hostess and a major supporter of the Green Mountain Cultural Center, which is housed in the Round Barn. Throughout the year the Center features performing arts programs, art and photography exhib-its, and workshops.

Attending to the details of innkeeping is enough to keep anyone busy. Yet Anne Marie recently co-authored, with her friend Annie Reed Rhoades, a cookbook/storybook: *Recipes & Reflections, A Journey of Food and Friendship.* The book features "cooking from the Heart of The Round Barn," where the gourmet breakfasts provide an almost deca-dent start to a hard day of cycling. Specialties such as cottage cheese pancakes, Belgian waffles, and homemade muffins are served in the breakfast room or on the terrace overlooking the gardens.

And when riders return to the inn after a long day of cycling they find equally decadent afternoon treats that include tea and sweets, such as the Round Barn Chocolate Chip Revolution Cookies or hors d'oeuvres such as smoked salmon pinwheels with cucumber salsa. The open de-sign of the kitchen, just off the breakfast room, also provides guests an opportunity to see these culinary masterpieces in the making.

Innkeepers Tim O'Brien and Tracie Kaslin not only keep things running smoothly in the kitchen and the rest of the inn, but, along with Anne Marie, can provide plenty of suggestions for activities and dining in the area. Tim, an avid cyclist and river guide, can help with road and off-road suggestions, or if you're looking for a change of sport, can rec-ommend hiking spots or canoeing and kayaking options.

Or, if you just need a day of R&R after climbing the Appalachian and Middlebury gaps, settle into a comfortable chair or hammock in the garden and spend the afternoon basking in the tranquil surroundings or testing your horticultural knowledge by identifying the many species in the perennial and annual garden of one of New England's most beau-tifully landscaped inns.

Biking from the Inn at The Round Barn Farm

The surrounding Green Mountains offer plenty of passes to challenge the serious cyclist, while the Valley itself, and Route 100 along the Mad River, provide more moderate terrain. However, it's hard to avoid hills altogether. After all, this is Vermont.

This cyclist-friendly region offers a wide variety of both road and mountain biking opportunities. In fact, the local phone book (available at the Chamber of Commerce) includes six pages of recommended regional and local bicycle tours and mountain biking routes—36 suggestions in all. It also includes suggested walks and hikes and information about regional points of interest, museums, and state forests, as well as 32 pages of historic information covering the life of town founder Benjamin Wait.

In August several major cycling events keep things rolling in Waitsfield. Early in the month, the Mad River Valley Road Race, known as one of the toughest US Cycling Federation road races in the Northeast, takes riders on a 67-mile route through Waitsfield and over the Middlebury and Appalachian Gap passes. At the same time, the Wicked Witch of the East Mountain Bike Race is held at Sugarbush Mountain. Later in the month, the Mad River Valley Century, voted "Coolest Century" by *Bicycling* magazine in October 1997, offers participants 25-, 50-, and 100-mile options. The century ride routes participants through the mountains and the state capitol of Montpelier. For information on the century or road race, contact Mad River Cyclery (below) or The Hyde Away at (802) 496-2322 or (800) 777-4933.

Local Bike Shops
Mad River Cyclery
Routes 100 and 17
Waitsfield, VT
(802) 496-9996
Sales, service, and accessories for road and mountain bikes. No rentals.

Clearwater Sports
Route 100
Waitsfield, VT   05673
(802) 496-2708
Rents mountain bikes; limited sales, service, and accessories. Also offers canoe and kayak rentals, plus guided trips and clinics.

Sugarbush Cycling Center
Sugarbush Access Road
Lincoln Peak, Gate House Lodge
Warren, VT   05674
(802) 583-6572 or 6516
www.sugarbush.com
Sales, accessories, and repairs. Front- and full-suspension mountain bike rentals.

Mountain Biking Opportunities

Old logging trails and dirt roads throughout the region afford plenty of mountain biking opportunities. Innkeeper Tim O'Brien, the local telephone book, the National Forest Service in Rochester, and bike shops are all sources for additional recommendations.

By the cemetery in Waitsfield Common (at the intersection of Cat Joslyn, Common, East, and North Roads) is the entrance to more than 25 miles of singletrack and doubletrack trails for intermediate to advanced riders.

Lincoln Peak at nearby **Sugarbush Mountain** offers miles of lift-serviced trails for mountain bikers of all abilities—from on-road beginner to expert singletrack—accessed by the Gatehouse Quad Chairlift. There's a dual slalom course and a "Moto Park" that offers terrain diversions. The **Sugarbush Cycling Center** provides guided tours and instruction.

In the Green Mountain National Forest, **Leicester Hollow Trail** offers scenic doubletrack and singletrack riding. From Waitsfield, go south on Rt. 100, then west on Rt. 73 (Brandon Gap Road), cross the gap and Forest Road 53 and go to one of the parking areas. The trails (which are north of Route 73 and east of Route 53) go around Silver Lake and The Falls of Lana area and offer great views. Other popular easy to moderate National Forest loops include **Steammill Road** and the **Natural Turnpike**, both of which begin off Forest Road 59 (Steammill Road) at the Break Loaf campus of Middlebury College.

Other Resources

Sugarbush Chamber of Commerce
General Wait House
Route 100
Waitsfield, VT 05673
(800) 828-4748 or (802) 496-3409
www.sugarbushchamber.org
Email: chamber@madriver.com

US Department of Agriculture
Green Mountain National Forest
Rochester Ranger District
Rt. #2, Box 35
Rochester, VT 05767
(802) 767-4261, fax: (802) 767-4777
Publishes road and mountain bike tour suggestion sheet, in addition to general information about the National Forest. Sells USGS maps.

Warren Loop (14.4 miles)
Moderate terrain

This popular local loop provides a nice introduction to the area's diverse terrain. Route 100, which follows the Mad River, is relatively flat with a good shoulder and, although a major artery, is not heavily traveled. Exiting Warren there is a gradual climb following Freeman Brook before you reach the farm-lined route that leads past the Morgan horse farm back to the Inn.

The route also offers several attractions and distractions. The Village or Great Eddy Covered Bridge, which crosses the Mad River in Waitsfield, is the second-oldest covered bridge in Vermont and the oldest in continuous operation. Just below it is a popular swimming hole. The Lareau Swimming Hole, just across from the Lareau Farm Inn on Route 100 south of Waitsfield, provides another opportunity to swim on the river. And if you forgot your suit, the Punch Bowl, also on the Mad River off Route 100 south of Butternut Hill, is reportedly a popular nude swimming spot.

The hamlet of Warren, like Waitsfield, is listed on the National Register of Historic places. Its covered bridge, at the far end of the village, was built in 1879. The Warren Store, a former stagecoach inn, is a good place to stop for provisions.

To combine this short ride with another activity, consider soaring over the route in a sailplane from the Sugarbush-Warren airport by taking a detour on Airport Road, (802) 496-2290 or (800) 881-7627. You also can picnic there in the gazebo, play volleyball or have lunch at the airport restaurant as you watch other brave souls glide through the air.

Pt.-Pt.	Cume	Turn	Street/Landmark
0.0	0.0	**R**	**East Warren Rd.** from drive of Inn at the Round Barn Farm
1.7	1.7	**L**	**Rt. 100S** at stop sign
0.9	2.6	**BL**	Stay on **Rt. 100S** at Y
4.9	7.5	**BL**	**Brook Rd.**, toward Warren village. Pass Pitcher Inn. (Continue down Main Street to see the **covered bridge**.)
0.3	7.8	**L**	**Unmarked street** just before white church
0.1	7.9	**R**	At stop sign. Unmarked **Brook Rd.** becomes **East Warren Rd.**
6.5	14.4		Arrive at Inn at the Round Barn Farm

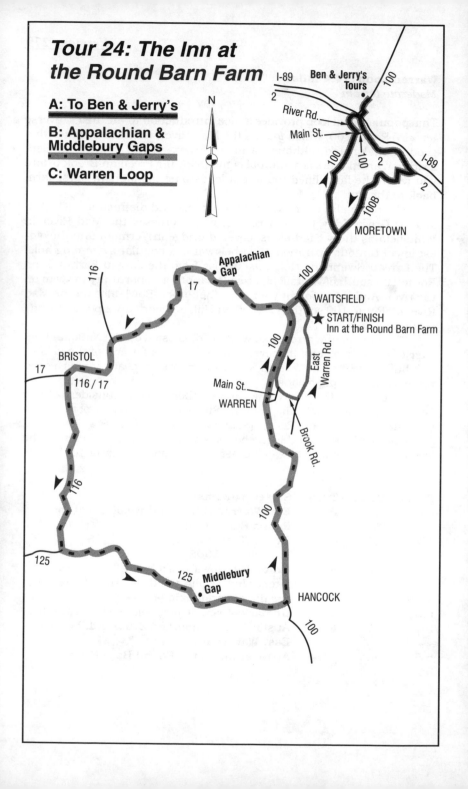

To Ben & Jerry's (36.5 miles)
Moderate terrain; a few moderate climbs

(Note: *Can be combined with Waterbury trip from Ten Acres Lodge for longer ride.)*

As the Mad River winds its way along Route 100 for the first part of the ride, you enjoy gentle terrain before hitting the rollers that take you to Waterbury. From Waterbury back to Waitsfield you again have some gentle hills. With the exception of a busy ½-mile stretch on Route 100 between Waterbury and Ben & Jerry's, the traffic is relatively light. The route is paved with good surfaces, except for one scenic mile of packed dirt along River Road.

The Ben & Jerry's tour ends with free samples, or you can visit the scoop shop that features all 34 tempting flavors. If for some reason you can't satisfy your ice cream craving here, look for regional favorite Maynard's Snack Bar among the farm fields on Route 100B in Morestown.

Waterbury offers several shops, coffee houses, and restaurants where you can pick up lunch or picnic items to enjoy at the Kenneth Ward Access area, a public river swimming hole on Route 100B.

Pt.-Pt.	Cume	Turn	Street/Landmark
0.0	0.0	R	**East Warren Rd.** from drive of Inn at the Round Barn Farm
1.7	1.7	R	**Rt. 100N** at stop sign
4.5	6.2	L	To stay on **Rt. 100N**, at split for Rt. 100B
6.3	12.5	L	**Main St.**
0.4	12.9	L	At fork in the road, onto unpaved **River Rd.**
1.0	13.9	R	Cross metal bridge
0.4	14.3	R	**N. Main Street/Rt. 2 East** at stop sign
0.1	14.4	L	**Stowe St.** at stop light
0.8	15.2	R	**Rt. 100N** at stop sign
0.6	15.8	L	Into **Ben & Jerry's**
0.0	15.8	R	**Rt. 100S**, from parking lot of Ben & Jerry's
0.6	16.4	L	**Stowe St.**
0.8	17.2	L	**Rt. 2 East** at stop light
5.4	22.6	R	**Church St./Rt. 100B South** (approximately 3 miles after turn is **Kenneth Ward Access Area**)
7.8	30.4	S	Onto **Rt. 100 South**
4.4	34.8	L	**East Warren Rd.**
1.7	36.5		Inn at the Round Barn Farm

Appalachian & Middlebury Gaps (75.2 miles)
Challenging; covers 2 demanding mountain passes

This route, which covers one of the USCF's most challenging road race courses, includes stretches of steep and winding hills with sometimes narrow shoulders. During the first half of this ride, you climb from the 400-foot elevation of Waitsfield, over the Appalachian Gap (elevation 2356 feet), descend to the town of Bristol, and travel south along the western edge of the Green Mountain National Forest before climbing to the 2149-foot summit of the Middlebury Gap pass.

The route, however, will reward you with sweeping views, scenic stream valleys, waterfalls, and lush forests. The Appalachian Gap is the state's northernmost mountain gap, and the Middlebury Gap marks the divide between the Lake Champlain and Connecticut River watersheds. Several miles east of Middlebury sits Ripton, the former home of poet Robert Frost, and along the interpretive trail that bears his name are posted commemorative poems. The Moss Glen Falls, north of Granville on Route 100, and the nearby spruce and hemlock stand command a stop to take in Mother Nature's wonders.

When passing through Hancock, stop at the Big Rock Bike Stop to refuel with an energy bar or cold drink—or to pick up local cycling advice.

Pt.-Pt.	Cume	Turn	Street/Landmark
0.0	0.0	R	**East Warren Rd.** from drive of Inn at the Round Barn Farm
1.7	1.7	L	**Rt. 100S** at stop sign
0.9	2.6	BR	**Rt. 17** over the Appalachian Gap
16.0	18.6	L	**Rt. 116S**
4.0	22.6	S	Enter town of Bristol
1.0	23.6	L	Continue on **Rt. 116S**
13.0	36.6	L	**Rt. 125** to climb Middlebury Gap
16.0	52.6	L	**Rt. 100N** in the town of Hancock
20.0	72.6	R	To stay on **Rt. 100N**
0.9	73.5	R	**East Warren Rd.**
1.7	75.2		Arrive at the Inn at the Round Barn Farm

Juniper Hill Inn

Robert and Susanne Pearl,
Innkeepers
Juniper Hill Road, RR #1, Box 79
Windsor, VT 05673
Rates: Budget-Deluxe
Open all year, except April

Phone: (800) 359-2541; (802) 674-5273
Fax: (802) 674-2041
Web: www.juniperhillinn.com
E-mail: innkeeper@juniperhillinn.com

The stately Juniper Hill Inn exudes elegance and, at the same time, the unassuming comfort of a country home. Its secluded perch above the historic town of Windsor, birthplace of Vermont, provides incredible views of Lake Runnemede and Mount Ascutney—and a hilltop window on the inviting cycling terrain that lies along the Upper Connecticut River Valley.

The majestic Colonial Revival mansion was built in 1902 by Maxwell Evarts, chief financial officer of the Union Pacific Railroad. Evarts was a close friend of President Theodore Roosevelt, and Juniper was once known as "the summer White House" because Presidents Roosevelt, Benjamin Harris, and Rutherford B. Hayes were his frequent guests. Today, it retains its original splendor and holds a place on the National Register of Historic Places.

Corporate escapees Robert and Susanne Pearl bought the 14,000-square-foot, 28-room mansion and adjacent 12 acres in 1990 after combing New England for the perfect inn. They've added their own special touches to create an inviting and idyllic retreat.

Upon entering the oak-paneled, 30'x40' Great Room that once served as a ballroom, guests immediately get a sense of the expansive, well-appointed rooms with stately fireplaces that await them. An afternoon treat of ice tea and cakes or cookies is served here. Enjoy them in one of the room's cozy wing chairs or sofas, or under the adjacent white-columned portico overlooking the manicured lawn and swimming pool framed by a white picket fence and perennials.

Or unwind at the end of the day in front of one of the fireplaces in the Library or the Sitting Parlor, where, if you really think you need contact with the hurried outside world, you'll find the inn's only TV with its "weather dependent" reception.

Juniper Hill's 16 luxurious guest chambers, all with mountain, lake, or woodland views, have private baths, many with clawfoot tubs. Eleven of them have fireplaces, nine wood- and two gas-burning. All of the individually decorated rooms feature comfortable beds and antique furnishings. In-room welcoming touches include bedside chocolates, fresh flowers, and brandy or sherry with crystal glassware.

Two spacious grand chambers above the library are in a secluded wing of the house, offering extra privacy. One of them has its own porch.

The Pearls' three corgis, Tucker, Jane, and Cuddles, add to the homey atmosphere. Longer-term residents Tucker and Jane, no doubt, could lead the way to Paradise Park, a little known local haven in front of the inn. Along its 3.5 miles of wooded trails are several secluded waterfalls.

Other Windsor attractions include the Old Constitution House, where Vermont was born; the Vermont State Craft Center; Catamount Brewery and visitor center; Simon Pearce Glass Blowing center; and the American Precision Museum.

The Pearls and their staff serve up a hearty Vermont breakfast in the inn's sunny dining room, decorated in warm Colonial colors and floral Waverly window treatments; they'll serve breakfast in bed by special request. Breakfast specialties include items such as poached egg with tomato, cheese, and white sauce on toast, served with side dishes of fresh banana bread and fruit slices. In the evening, four-course dinners are served by reservation at candlelit tables in front of the dining room's period fireplace. The menu, which changes daily, features culinary delights such as herb-crusted rack of lamb and grilled halibut with pineapple cilantro salsa, followed by dessert temptations such as chocolate raspberry truffle cheesecake and Vermont carrot cake with cream cheese topping.

Biking from Juniper Hill Inn

Juniper Hill is surround by quiet country roads and the rolling hills that line the Connecticut River. The varied terrain presents plenty of opportunity for pleasant day trips, easy and difficult alike. However, as in other parts of the state, if you veer from the designated route sheets you may find a paved road turning to dirt before you know it.

Route 5, one of the principle arteries in the region, is more heavily traveled than other roads, but it has a wide paved shoulder.

The Pearls have several 18-speed bikes for rent and can provide alternative route suggestions. They also offer their own 2-day Yankee Rambler Pedal & Paddle Package, which combines lodging and fine dining at the Inn with a day of cycling and a four- to five-hour paddling excursion.

Bike Shops in the Region
Tom Mowatt Cycles
213 Mechanic St.
Lebanon, NH 03766
(603) 448-5556
(603) 448-6327, fax
www.sover.net/~tmc/
Sales, service, accessories. Racing, touring and mountain bikes.

Woodstock Sports
30 Central
Woodstock, VT 05091
(802) 457-1568
Sales, service, and accessories for road and mountain bikes. Rentals.

The Cyclery Plus
36 Route Four
West Woodstock, VT
(802) 457-3377
Sales, service, and accessories for road and mountain bikes. Rentals and free route maps.

Morris Brothers Mountain Bikes
20 Bridge St.
White River Junction, VT 05001
(802) 296-2331
Sales, services, and accessories.

Mountain Biking Opportunities
While both Vermont and neighboring New Hampshire are popular mountain biking destinations, few destinations are close to Juniper Hill Inn. However, the many dirt roads near the inn present easy, enjoyable off-road riding for less experienced riders.

MTB riding at nearby Ascutney Mountain is an on-again, off-again proposition, so it's worth inquiring about the current situation. Also, see the references under October Country Inn and Moose Mountain Lodge for popular destinations within a reasonable driving distance.

Other Resources
Chamber of Commerce
Mt. Ascutney Region
P.O. Box 5, Main Street
Windsor, VT 05089
(802) 674-5910

Woodstock Area Chamber of Commerce
18 Central Street, P.O. Box 486
Woodstock, VT 05091
(802) 457-3555 or (888) 4WOODST
(802) 457-1042, June to October
www.woodstockvt.com

Quechee (33.5 miles)
Easy to moderate

*(**Note:** Can be combined with Bridgewater Corners Quechee ride for longer option.)*

The ride to Quechee takes you on a trip through the quiet backroads of quintessential Vermont, featuring covered bridges, lush pastures, and a spectacular river gorge.

Highlights of the tour include **Quechee Gorge**, a 165-foot chasm above the Ottauquechee River that is known as "Vermont's Little Grand Canyon;" the riverside **Simon Pearce** restaurant and glass blowing facility in Quechee, where the power of the river has been harnessed to generate energy; and the **Taftsville Covered Bridge**, which was built in 1836.

Undulating County and Quechee Hartland Roads are marked by a few short climbs, and there are small hills on Dewey Mills Road and Route 12. With the exception of 1½ miles of packed dirt on Quechee Road, the roads are paved.

Note: *Route begins at the end of Juniper Hill Inn driveway*

Pt.-Pt.	Cume	Turn	Street/Landmark
0.0	0.0	**R**	**Juniper Hill Rd.**
0.7	0.7	**L**	**County Rd.** at stop sign
3.9	4.6	**R**	Unmarked **Brownsville Rd.** at stop sign at T
0.8	5.4	**L**	**Rt. 12N** at stop sign in Hartland Four Corners
6.1	11.5	**L**	**Rt. 4 W/Rt. 12 N** at stop sign/flashing light
0.6	12.1	**R**	**Taftsville Covered Bridge Rd. East**; then quick turn right to go over the bridge
0.0	12.1	**BR**	After crossing bridge, onto unmarked **River Rd.**; go up short hill
3.4	15.5	**BR**	At yield sign, onto **Quechee W. Hartford Rd./Main Street**
0.9	16.4	**S**	At end of **Main St.** (Waterman Hill Rd. and **Quechee covered bridge** are on your right. On opposite side of bridge you get a great view of the river.)

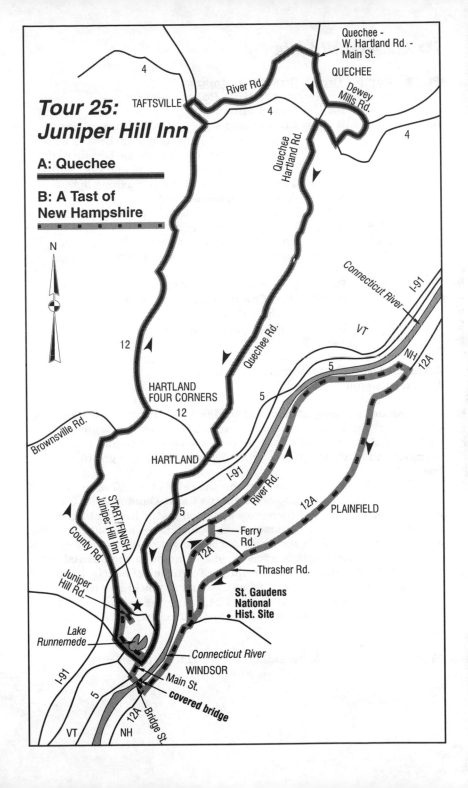

Tour 25:
Juniper Hill Inn

A: Quechee

**B: A Tast of
New Hampshire**

N

Quechee -
W. Hartland Rd. -
Main St.

QUECHEE

River Rd.

4

TAFTSVILLE

4

Dewey
Mills Rd.

4

Quechee
Hartland Rd.

Connecticut River

I-91

VT

NH

12A

Quechee Rd.

5

12

HARTLAND
FOUR CORNERS

12

5

Brownsville Rd.

5

HARTLAND

I-91

River Rd.

12A

PLAINFIELD

START/FINISH
Juniper Hill Inn

5

Ferry
Rd.

12A

Thrasher Rd.

County Rd.

St. Gaudens
National
Hist. Site

Juniper
Hill Rd.

Lake
Runnemede

Connecticut River

WINDSOR

I-91

5

Main St.

covered bridge

VT

NH

12A

Bridge St.

Pt.-Pt.	Cume	Turn	Street/Landmark
0.1	16.5	S	**Dewey Mills Rd.** at stop sign
0.9	17.4	BR	**Dewey Mills Rd.**
0.8	18.2	R	**Rt. 4** at stop sign. (*note:* Most people view the **gorge** from the highway bridge. Best views are not from the road, but from the bottom of the hiking trail. Get off your bike and take a hike.)
0.9	19.1	L	**Quechee Hartland Rd.** at flashing light
1.0	20.1	BR	To stay on **Quechee Rd.**
3.3	23.4		Pavement ends. Turns to packed dirt road.
1.4	24.8		Pavement starts again.
1.7	26.5	S	Onto **Rt. 5 South**, cross over Rt. 12 at stop sign in Hartland and again at second stop sign.
4.8	31.3	R	Onto **State St**. at light
0.7	32.0	R	Onto **County Rd.** Hospital sign.
0.8	32.8	R	**Juniper Hill Rd.**
0.7	33.5	L	Juniper Hill Inn driveway

A Taste of New Hampshire (24.7 miles)
Easy to moderate

Cross **America's longest covered bridge** for a scenic a ride along the Connecticut River that also offers spectacular mountain vistas. A well-weathered sign on the two-span, 460-foot wooden structure connecting Vermont and New Hampshire warns, "Walk your horse or pay two dollars fine."

One of the primary attractions on the ride is the 150-acre estate of American Renaissance sculptor **Augustus Saint-Gaudens**. His Cornish home, gardens, and studio are now operated by the National Park Service, (603) 675-2175. The landscaping, architecture—and naturally, the artwork—are well worth the short ascent to get to the entrance. Cornish, once a thriving artists enclave, also is home to the **Cornish Artists Colony Museum,** and in the simple Town Hall of nearby Plainfield rests an impressive 1916 set design by artist Maxfield Parrish.

Except for one climb on Route 12A, with an extremely rewarding view, the overall route, which follows the Connecticut River, is relatively flat.

Note: *Mileage begins at the end of Juniper Hill Inn driveway.*

Pt.-Pt.	Cume	Turn	Street/Landmark
0.0	0.0	R	**Juniper Hill Rd.**
0.7	0.7	L	**County Rd.** at stop sign
0.8	1.5	L	**Hunt Rd./State St.** at stop sign
0.7	2.2	R	**Rt. 5/Main St.** at light
0.3	2.5	L	**Bridge St.** toward **Cornish-Windsor covered bridge** at stop sign
0.3	2.8	L	**Rt. 12A North** (Route continues to the left, but best photo opportunity of bridge is from the right after crossing it.)
3.7	6.5	L	**Ferry Road,** which becomes **River Rd.** (Just after Townline Equipment Company)
6.3	12.8	R	**12A South** at stop sign
4.2	17.0	S	**Plainfield General Store**. A good place to buy lunch
1.0	18.0	L	**Thrasher Rd.** Just after you begin to descend
1.8	19.8	L	**Rt. 12A South**
0.7	20.5		Optional side trip to **Saint Gaudens National Historic Site**. Entrance to the left. ½-mile climb, but well worth it.
1.7	22.2	R	**Bridge St.**
0.0	22.2	R	**Main St.** at light.
0.3	22.5	L	**State St.** at light
0.7	23.2	R	**County Rd.** Hospital sign
0.8	24.0	R	**Juniper Hill Rd.**
0.7	24.7	L	Juniper Hill Inn driveway

October Country Inn, Bridgewater Corners, Vermont

October Country Inn

Richard Sims and
Patrick Runkel, Innkeepers
Upper Road, P.O. Box 66
Bridgewater Corners, VT 05035
Rates: Budget-Moderate,
          MAP for two
Closed early November and April

Phone: (800) 648-8421; (802) 672-3412
Fax: (802) 674-2041
Web: www.vermontel.net/~oci/
E-mail: oci@vermontel.com

October Country Inn, known for its homemade baked goods and gastronomical delights, is a favorite stop for touring cyclists, many of whom return over and over again. During the cycling season there are sure to be bicycles propped against the log fence that borders the property or against the house next to the spacious courtyard patio.

The converted 19th-century farmhouse and serene five acres of pastures and gardens in quiet Bridgewater Corners sits seven miles from the more crowded tourist destination of Woodstock.

Richard Sims, the "people" person, and Patrick Runkel, the quiet "chef extraordinaire," have operated the popular bed and breakfast since 1987. The rustic farmhouse is decorated with a mix of country and antique furnishings, and abounds with interesting knickknacks and conversation pieces. But there's nothing pretentious about the decor. It's the kind of place where you can kick off your cycling shoes, put up your feet and relax next to the fireplace in the living room. Both the living room and the patio are favorite spots for cyclist and other guests to exchange thoughts and adventures. And, when Richard joins the conversation, they're sure to share a laugh as he keeps their cups and glasses filled.

Ten double sleeping rooms are spread throughout the first and second floors of the rambling house. Each is comfortably decorated with small homey touches, such as stenciling, lace trimmed curtains, and decorative door numbers. Eight rooms have private baths or showers.

A few resident animals add to the country ambiance: Zoe, the cat, purrs away while three sheep graze in the grass near the barn. Richard and Patrick also cultivate beautiful flower and vegetable gardens, with the latter serving as a source of fresh herbs and vegetables for Patrick's feasts. Perched on a mound beyond the garden is an in-ground swimming pool where guests can swim or unwind at the end of the day.

A guest refrigerator is stocked with soda and beer, and in the afternoon Patrick puts out hot and cold drinks and his scrumptious home-baked cookies.

Meals are served family-style around large tables in the dining room, adding to the friendly, at-home atmosphere. The breakfasts are hearty, including such delights as home-baked rhubarb muffins, homemade granola, sour cream dollar pancakes, French toast, or scrambled eggs and bacon. Dinners are themed, with a different cuisine featured each night: Mexican, Italian, Greek, French, and more. Portions are generous and desserts are heavenly.

Richard, an easy conversationalist and gracious host, can offer suggestions on area sites, artists, artisans and other distractions. During the theater season, he and Patrick, enlightened theater buffs, have been known to lure an inn full of guests to join them for a pre-show picnic and performance at the nearby Weston Playhouse, Vermont's oldest professional theater.

Biking from October Country Inn
October Country Inn sits off Route 4, west of the 100-year old vacation community of Woodstock, not far from historic Plymouth and top New England ski resorts Killington and Okemo. The pictorial countryside is typical of Vermont—dotted by farms and pastures, with scenic mountain views and the occasional covered bridge. And the roads, except those running parallel to rivers, are typically undulating. With the exception of busy Route 4, there is little traffic along the routes. About one-third of the Quechee route takes riders over hard-packed dirt suitable for a regular road bike (but not skinny racing tires).

Local Bike Shops
The Cyclery Plus
36 Route Four
West Woodstock, VT   05091
(802) 457-3377
Sales, service, and accessories. Rents hybrids and provides local biking maps.

Woodstock Sports
30 Central
Woodstock, VT   05091
802-457-1568
Sales, service, and accessories. Rentals.

Vermont Ski & Sports
Bridgewater Mill
Bridgewater, VT 05034
(802) 672-3636
Bicycle sales, limited accessories and service. No rentals at Bridgewater store, but rents mountain bikes from its Northern Ski Works stores at Killington, (802) 422-9675, and Okemo, (802) 228-3344.

Other Shops in the Region
Mountain Cycology
P.O. Box 527 (Route 100)
Ludlow, VT 05149
(802) 228-2722
Sales, service, accessories. No rentals. Local Killington Pico and Black River Bike Clubs meet for weekly rides at shop. Call for details.

Mountain Biking Opportunities
Nearby ski and mountain resorts offer both a multitude of mountain biking opportunities and extraordinary vistas.
    Killington, about 5 miles west of the Inn, boasts a 41-mile trail system for cyclists of all abilities from easy to challenging, tight, technical singletrack. The K1 Express Gondola transports riders and their bikes to Killington's 4,241-foot peak, where on a clear day the panoramic view spans five states. The Killington Mountain Bike Center offers guided group clinics and tours, for beginners and experts alike, and its on-site shop rents standard and high performance bikes and performs repairs. In July, Killington hosts the Beauty & The Beast Fat Tire Festival, part of the Trail 66 Mountain Bike Series. For details, call (800) 621-MTNS or visit www.killington.com.
    Hawk Mountain Resort, on Route 100 in Plymouth, allows non-guests to use the trails on its 1,200-acre property. Mountain bikes can be rented at its recreation office where the director can also make trail recommendations—from novice to extremely technical. (800) 685-HAWK.

Other Resources
Killington-Pico Cycling Club
PO. Box 522
Pittsfield, VT 05762
(802) 746-8076

Woodstock Area Chamber of Commerce
18 Central Street, P.O. Box 486
Woodstock, VT 05091
(802) 457-3555 or (888) 4WOODST
(802) 457-1042, June to October
www.woodstockvt.com

Ludlow Area Chamber of Commerce
P.O. Box 333
Ludlow, VT 05149
802-228-5830

Off the beaten path, to Woodstock and Quechee (41.1 miles)
Easy to moderate terrain; approximately 10 miles are unpaved

*(**Note:** Can be combined with the Quechee ride from Juniper Hill Inn for longer ride.)*

Follow secluded River Road past the Lincoln Covered Bridge (the only remaining bridge in Vermont using a Pratt-type truss) to 200-year-old Woodstock. The village's central Green and well-preserved early 19th-century architecture and Federal homes reflect the prosperity of earlier settlers. Just outside Woodstock, pass the **Billings Farm and Museum**, and pick up again the little used River Road that follows the Ottauquechee River, passing the Taftsville Covered Bridge and Lake Pinneo.

Ride through the picturesque Main Street of Quechee, a good stop for lunch or to pick up picnic items. A major attraction in Quechee is the former mill, which was restored by Irish glassblower **Simon Pearce** and converted to a restaurant and glassblowing studio. The mill's hydroelectric turbines use water from the river to supply power to the building.

Continue though Dewey's Mill and Dewey's Pond, where the Ottauquechee takes an abrupt turn before plunging into the 165-foot-deep **Quechee Gorge**, known as "the Little Grand Canyon" of the Northeast.

Pt.-Pt.	Cume	Turn	Street/Landmark
0.0	0.0	**L**	From drive of October Country Inn onto **Upper Rd.**
0.4	0.4	**L**	**Rt. 4 W**
3.6	4.0	**R**	To cross metal bridge
0.0	4.0	**L**	Onto **bike path/Bridges Rd.** (unpaved)

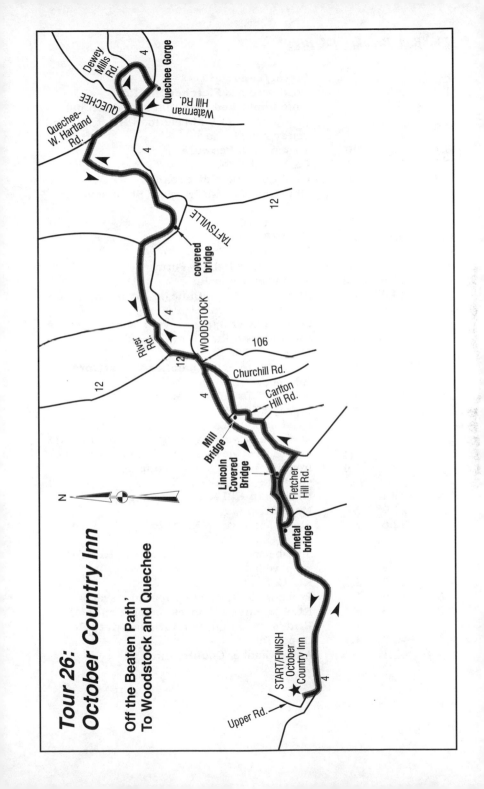

Tour 26:
October Country Inn

Off the Beaten Path'
To Woodstock and Quechee

PtPt.	Cume	Turn	Street/Landmark
1.0	5.0	**S**	Road becomes **Fletcher Hill Rd.**
0.6	5.6	**L**	Onto **unmarked road** that goes down hill (If you arrive at V at Peterman Hill/Churchill you've gone too far)
0.7	6.3	**BR**	To stay on **bike route**
0.5	6.8	**L**	**Carlton Hill Rd.**
1.2	8.0	**BR**	Onto **unmarked dirt road**
0.2	8.2	**L**	Onto **Church Hill/Prospect St.** at stop sign at T
1.4	9.6	**R**	Onto **Rt. 4E**
0.1	9.7	**L**	**Rt. 12N**
0.3	10.0	**BR**	**Rt. 12N**
0.3	10.3	**R**	**River Rd.** at Billings Farm
1.6	11.9	**BR**	To stay on **River Rd.**
2.5	14.4	**L**	At stop sign to continue on **River Rd.**; road immediately turns right and goes uphill. (**Taftsville Bridge** is on your right. Just over the bridge on Rt. 4 E in Taftsville is a general store)
3.4	17.8	**BR**	At yield sign, onto **Quechee W. Hartford Rd./Main St.** in Quechee.
1.0	18.8	**S**	**Dewey Mills Rd.** at stop sign
0.9	19.7	**BR**	**Dewey Mills Rd.**
0.8	20.5	**R**	**Rt. 4** at stop sign. Most people view the **gorge** from the highway bridge. Best views are not from the road, but from the bottom of the hiking trail. Get off your bike and take a hike.
0.9	21.4	**R**	**Waterman Hill Rd.**, at flashing light
0.3	21.7	**L**	**Main St.**
0.9	22.6	**L**	Sharp left to go on **River Rd.** (West Hartford Rd. goes to right)
2.3	24.9	**R**	Just before bridge to continue on **River Rd.** (unpaved)
4.1	29.0	**L**	**Rt. 12 S,** at stop sign
2.6	31.6	**L**	**Prosper Rd.** (turns to unpaved surface)
2.0	33.6	**R**	**Rt. 4 W** (after 0.1 miles turn left onto **Mill Bridge**; then right to return via **River Rd.**)
7.1	40.7	**R**	**Upper Rd.**
0.4	41.1		Arrive October Country Inn

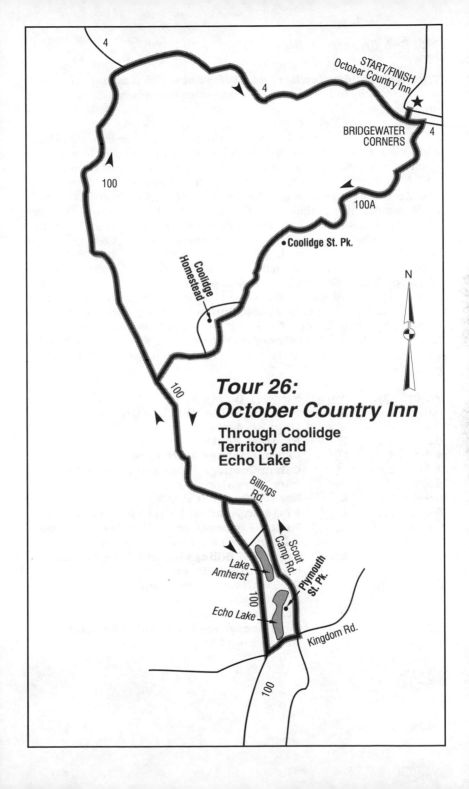

START/FINISH
October Country Inn

4

4

BRIDGEWATER
CORNERS

4

100

100A

• Coolidge St. Pk.

Coolidge
Homestead

N

100

Tour 26:
October Country Inn

Through Coolidge
Territory and
Echo Lake

Billings
Rd.

Scout
Camp Rd.

Plymouth
St. Pk.

Lake
Amherst

100

Echo Lake

Kingdom Rd.

100

100

Through Coolidge Territory and Echo Lake (28.2 miles)
Moderate, with one long climb; paved except approximately 1 mile of packed dirt

The Coolidge Range and prominent peaks such as Salt Ash, Bear, and Killington mountains form a backdrop as riders travel through unspoiled forest lands, along rippling rivers and past quiet lakes and ponds.

After a short flat warm-up ride along Broad Brook, climb easily and steadily for several miles past the entrance to **Coolidge State Park** to **Plymouth**, the birthplace of Calvin Coolidge. The restored village, where he was sworn in as President, is worth a stop. It includes the Union Christian Church, the Vermont Farmers Museum, Calvin Coolidge Memorial Center, a cheese factory, and a small, cozy restaurant.

Descend a steep, short hill (known as Hysteria Hill), then follow the Black River past Echo Lake to Tyson, where you can buy lunch at the general store, then pick a picnic spot on the east side of the lake in Camp Plymouth State Park. Follow Route 100 and the Black River north through Plymouth Union, past Black Pond and Woodward Reservoir to Route 4. Route 4, which follows the Ottauquechee River, is more heavily traveled than the other roads, but offers a wide paved shoulder with a good surface.

Pt.-Pt.	Cume	Turn	Street/Landmark
0.0	0.0	R	From drive of October Country Inn
0.1	0.1	L	**Onto Rt. 4** at stop sign
0.2	0.3	R	**Rt. 100A South**
4.4	4.7		**Calvin Coolidge State Park**
1.7	6.4		**Calvin Coolidge Homestead**. Steep downhill from here to next turn.
0.9	7.3	L	**Rt. 100 South** at stop sign
5.0	12.3	L	**Kingdom Road** (at Echo Lake Inn in Tyson)
0.6	12.9	L	Toward **Plymouth State Park/Scout Camp Rd.** (unpaved after park entrance)
1.4	14.3	BR	Unmarked **Billings Rd.** at Y (after passing Meadow Hawk Rd. on right)
0.6	14.9	R	**Rt. 100 North** at stop sign
2.5	17.4		Pass turnoff for 100A
5.3	22.7	R	**Rt. 4 East**
5.5	28.2	L	Enter **access road to October Country Inn** (across from Long Trail Brewery)

Silas Griffith Inn

**Paul and Lois Dansereau,
Innkeepers
South Main Street,
RR 1, Box 66F
Danby, VT   05739
Rates: Budget, B&B
Open all year, except April and Dec. 1-20**

**Phone: (800) 545-1509; (802) 293-5567
Fax: (802) 293-5559
Web: www.silasgriffith.com
E-mail: sginn@together.net**

Silas Griffith Inn, in the quiet, vintage town of Danby, provides a peaceful resting spot for bicyclists, hikers, paddlers, and auto tourists alike. Set about ¼ mile off Route 7 and nestled in the midst of the Green Mountains and thousands of acres of cow-filled pastures, Danby offers a welcome retreat from the busy tourist and commercial center of nearby Manchester, with its abundance of factory outlet stores.

Danby, settled in 1765, is known for its marble, which has been used to build, among other notable buildings and monuments, the Jefferson Memorial in Washington. It also was the home of Silas Griffith, a 19th-century lumber baron and Vermont's first millionaire, who built for his bride in 1891 the mansion now known as Silas Griffith Inn. While there's no pretense about today's inn, it's clear that Mr. Griffith didn't spare expenses. The house is filled with elegant architectural features such as embossed tin ceilings, original leaded stained glass windows, and, of course, handsome handcarved woodwork in bird's eye maple, curly maple, and cherry. A stunning 8-foot wide semi-circular "Moon gate" sliding pocket door separates the game room and parlor, which now serves as a common TV room.

The mansion and separate carriage house have been renovated and updated with modern conveniences. And the amiable and accommodating innkeepers Lois and Paul Dansereau have created many cozy gathering areas, as well as quiet nooks—inside and out—where guests can enjoy the understated charm of the house and its surrounding 11 acres.

In addition to the game and TV rooms, the first floor of the mansion features a separate dining room, where guests find brownies, iced tea, and lemonade in the afternoon, and a combination living room and library. A fireplace dominates the huge living room, which has a number of nicely clustered seating areas with stuffed sofas, chairs, and tables, as well as a piano.

Outside, a huge wrap-around porch provides an ideal spot to unwind at the end of the day. Or guests can retreat to the swimming pool, which is wedged on the side of a grassy hill and enveloped by delightful herb and flower gardens. A barbecue grill and picnic table sit next to the pool.

The 17 guestrooms—14 with private baths—are divided between the main house and the converted carriage house. Most of the rooms have queen-size beds and are decorated with period furnishings. Guests also find small special touches, like vases of wildflowers or a small basket of apples. All of the rooms in the mansion, featuring lots of floral wallpaper, hardwood floors covered with area rugs, and Victorian furnishings, are on the second floor. Room #14 has a small circular porch that offers a great view of the Green Mountains.

The rooms in the renovated carriage house have a more modern feel, but offer plenty of country charm and comfort. The main floor of the carriage house contains the inn's dining room and bar, where guests are treated to a bountiful Vermont country breakfast, which includes assorted fruit juices, freshly-baked muffins or scones, cereal, and hot items such as almond French toast or multi-grain pancakes—with Vermont maple syrup, of course—or Spanish omelets and homefries. Dinner is served by the fireplace in the carriage house most evenings during warm-weather months, and on special occasions in the winter.

While in Danby, visitors should check out the small shops in town and the Peel Gallery and its outdoor sculpture garden, on Route 7, a short bike ride away. Follow North Main Street (Old Route 7) to the end then turn right to get on 7 North.

Bicycling from Silas Griffith Inn

Danby sits in a Green Mountain valley formed by the Otter Creek, which runs parallel to Route 7. There are plenty of traffic-free, rural roads where the most serious traffic obstacle might be a herd of cows crossing the road. The region is somewhat hilly, with the undulating roads providing a nice balance of moderate climbing followed by exhilarating downhill coasting. Routes running north-south tend to be flatter, with east-west routes forcing cyclists to pedal over a few "humps" in the road.

Route 7 and the roads around Manchester are fairly heavily traveled; however, for the most part, they have good shoulders for cycling.

Silas Griffith Inn is a popular overnight stop for cycling groups, whose members are happy to share their travel experiences.

Huntington Graphics (P.O. Box 163, Huntington, VT 05462) publishes a Recreation Map & Guide for Bennington County that includes 12 road biking routes and 9 mountain biking suggestions, in addition to hiking, swimming, canoeing, and fishing information, for the Manchester-Bennington area. Battenkill Bicycle Shop and the Manchester Tourist Office also can provide local cycling information.

Closest Bike Shops

Battenkill Sports Bicycle Shop
1240 Depot Street, Stone House
Exit 4 off 7/Intersection Rt. 11 & 30
Manchester Center, VT 05255
(802) 362-2734 or (800) 340-2734
battbike@sover.net
Road and mountain bike sales, service, and accessories. Mountain, hybrid, and road bike rentals. Immediate tourist repairs. Organized mountain bike rides from shop twice a week.

Equipe Sport/Mountain Riders Bikes and Boards
Junction Routes 30 & 100
Rawsonville, VT

-and-

Stratton Village Square
Stratton Mountain, VT 05155
(800) 282-6665
www.equipesport.com
equipe@vermontel.net

Great Outdoors Trading Co.
Routes 11/30
Manchester Center, VT 05255
(802) 362-0410

-and-

219 Woodstock Avenue
Rutland, VT
(802) 775-9989

Stratton Mountain Resort
RR 1, Box 145
Stratton Mountain, VT 05155
(800)-STRATTON or (802) 297-4000
www.stratton.com
Mountain bike sales and service. Gondola transports riders to Stratton summit. Full- and front-suspension mountain bike rentals, tours, maps.

Mountain Biking Opportunities

The region's many unpaved town roads, carriage and logging trails, and ski resorts offer a broad range of mountain biking opportunities.

Local bike shops are a good source of information. Organized mountain bike tours leave from Battenkill Bike Shop twice a week, and Equipe Sport publishes a free pocket map guide with mountain biking (plus hiking, swimming, and paddling) suggestions.

Stratton Mountain's gondola transports bikers to its summit, or they can enjoy its network of wooded trails in the Sun Bowl. There's parking at the top of the Stratton Mountain Access Road; continue straight following signs for the Sun Bowl. **Mount Snow** provides access to its trails for a small fee, with lift service on the Canyon Chair beginning in July. The Mount Snow Mountain Bike Center, (802) 464-3333, also rents bikes, runs a mountain bike school, and provides maps.

The **Equinox Mountain** and Equinox Pond area, just west of Manchester, is a favorite destination of local stump jumpers. Riders park by the water tower at the western end of the Union Street extension.

Or head to **Mount Tabor** (see road ride below), where Forest Road #10 continues for 14 miles to Landsgrove. To access from the Landsgrove side: From the center of Peru, take a left onto Hapgood Pond Road, which is also Landsgrove Road. Riders can pick up Forest Road #10, or explore the trails around the tiny town of Landsgrove. Forest road maps are available from the Green Mountain Ranger District Office.

The Rutland area, north of Danby, is another destination for local riders. Trails in the **Muddy Pond/Rocky Pond** area can be accessed from Evergreen Street, Watkins Street, and Giogetti Park. A little further north, **Chittenden Dam** trails, which vary from easy to advanced, can be accessed on the left past the Lieferts Pond entrance to the Chittenden Reservoir.

Local Information

Manchester and The Mountains Chamber of Commerce
RR2, Box 3452
Manchester Center, VT 05255
(802) 362-2100
www.manchesterandmtns.com

Green Mountain National Forest
Manchester Ranger District
RR 1, Box 1940
Manchester Center, VT 05255
(802) 362-2307

Warm-up Those Climbing Legs (5.4 Miles)

This short, sweet climb takes riders up the west side of Mt. Tabor through the tiny town of the same name, which was called Griffith around the turn of the century after the local lumber baron who operated a large logging and charcoal operation here. Most of the town is now incorporated into the Green Mountain National Forest and the out-and-back ride crosses the Appalachian Trail, where it skirts the White Rocks National Recreation Area. It also connects with Forest Road #10, which leads to Landsgrove.

Pt.-Pt.	Cume	Turn	Street/Landmark
0.0	0.0	L	**Main St.** from Silas Griffith Inn
0.1	0.1	R	**Mt. Tabor Rd.**
0.1	0.2	S	Cross Rt. 7
2.5	2.7		Arrive at picnic area after steady climb; turn around in parking lot and return by same route
2.5	5.2	S	Cross Rt. 7
0.1	5.3	L	**Main St.**
0.1	5.4		Silas Griffith Inn

Around Tinmouth Mountain (36.5 miles)
Moderate, with one notable climb

(Note: *Can eliminate initial climb, for a 28.1-mile ride, by starting at Danby Four Corners)*

This ride through quintessential, rural Vermont begins with a climb. It's steep for just a short stretch in the beginning and levels out to a mild, steady 3.5-mile ascent. The rest of the route follows gentle back roads through picturesque, lush farmlands, where the summer air fills with the aroma of fresh fields and the autumn brings the crisp air and brilliant colors of the changing fall foliage.

Enjoy the gentle rollers on Tinmouth Road, then the easy downhill as Brook Road winds along Mill Brook to Danby.

There are limited opportunities to buy food or beverage along the loop's wonderfully remote country roads. Danby Four Corners Store at the top of the first hill presents the last opportunity to buy food or drink before Middletown Springs.

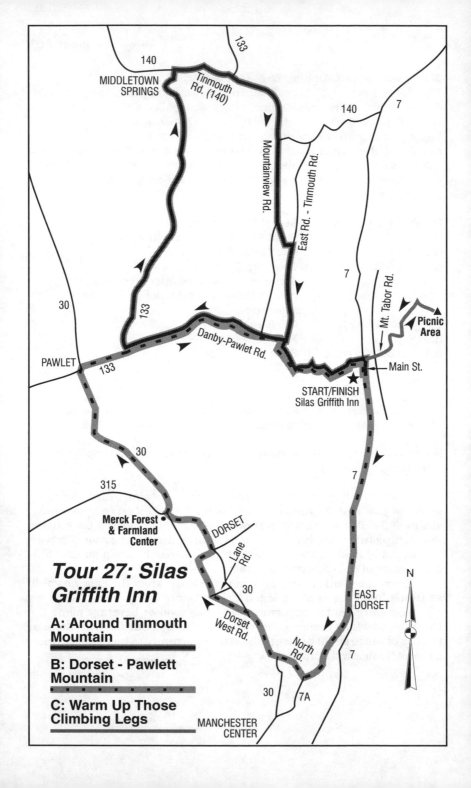

Tour 27: Silas Griffith Inn

A: Around Tinmouth Mountain

B: Dorset - Pawlett Mountain

C: Warm Up Those Climbing Legs

Pt.-Pt.	Cume	Turn	Street/Landmark
0.0	0.0	L	**Main St.** from drive of Silas Griffith Inn
0.1	0.1	L	**Brook Rd.**
4.1	4.2	L	**Danby-Pawlet Rd.**
5.9	10.1	R	Unmarked **Rt. 133 North**
10	20.1	R	**Rts. 133 North/140 East.** Also **West St.- East St.** in Middletown Springs
2.3	22.4	R	**Tinmouth Rd./Rt. 140 East**
3.2	25.6	S	Toward Danby on unmarked **Mountainview Rd.** (Rt. 140 turns to the left)
3.5	29.1	R	**East Rd./Tinmouth Rd.** at stop sign
3.2	32.3	S	**Brook Rd.** toward Danby at stop sign
4.1	36.4	R	**Main St.**
0.1	36.5		Silas Griffith Inn

Dorset-Pawlett Loop (36 miles)
Moderate, with challenging hill

Enjoy a nice combination of Vermont's farming tradition and inviting country villages. An otherwise easy-to-moderate route includes one long, steady climb over Paris Hill.

South on Route 7, pass Emerald Lake State Park, an area historically known for its marble quarrying. Today the coldwater-filled lake is used by swimmers, boaters, and fisherman alike. There are also nature trails and a natural bridge. A little further south, East Dorset's claim to fame is that Alcoholics Anonymous founder Bill Wilson was born, ironically, behind the barroom of the nearby inn.

From West Road, popular with local cyclists, take an optional side trip to Dorset, where the state's first marble quarry opened in 1796. Although it's better known today for its inns, playhouse, and Peltier's country store, two swimming holes at the quarry offer the option of bathing with or without clothes. To find them: from West Road, turn right onto Lane Road 0.2 miles beyond Marble West Inn. Go 0.6 miles to stop sign and turn right onto Vt. Route 30; go 0.5 miles and, across from a single-story white building on the right, follow a path that leads to the Dorset quarry. Approximately 20 yards further is a swimming hole; 100 yards to the nude beach.

In East Rupert-Pawlet ride through the fertile farmlands of the Mettowee Valley. There are a country store and two restaurants in Pawlet.

A couple miles outside Pawlet is the only notable climb on the route; then it's smooth pedaling to Danby.

Pt.-Pt.	Cume	Turn	Street/Landmark
0.0	0.0	R	**Main St.** from Silas Griffith Inn
0.8	0.8	R	**Rt. 7**
7.0	7.8	R	**Rt. 7A**
3.2	11.0	R	**North Rd.**
1.7	12.7	R	**Rt. 30** at stop sign
0.9	13.6	L	**Dorset West Rd.** *(Lane Rd., to visit quarries, is to the right after approximately 3 miles—0.2 miles beyond Marble West Inn. Church St., which leads to the center of Dorset, is on the right about 1 mile further.)*
4.8	18.4	R	At stop sign. (The Merck Forest and Farmland Center is off Route 315 to your left.)
0.0	18.4	L	Quick left after stop sign onto **Rt. 30 N** toward Pawlet
6.2	24.6	R	**133 N** at Y
1.3	25.9	S	**Danby Rd.** (includes 3.5-mile climb)
5.9	31.8	R	**Brook Rd.** at T at Danby Four Corners
4.1	35.9	R	**Main St.**
0.1	36.0		Silas Griffith Inn

Ten Acres Lodge

14 Barrows Road
Stowe, VT 05672
(800) 327-7357 or (802) 253-7638
Fax: (802) 253-6589
Rates: Budget-Moderate, B&B

Edson Hill Manor

1500 Edson Hill Road
Stowe, VT 05672
(800) 621-0284 or (802) 253-7371
Fax: (802) 253-4036
Rates: Moderate-Deluxe, B&B

MAP Add $20 pp

Jane & Eric Lande, Innkeepers
William O'Neil, General Manager

Sister inns Ten Acres Lodge and Edson Hill Manor offer cyclists comfortable accommodations, scenic surroundings and award-winning dining. Situated on expansive properties on the perimeter of the picturesque village of Stowe, the inns provide lodging with breakfast or a Modified American Plan (MAP), which includes gourmet dinner at either inn's restaurant.

The Landes have created two inviting, well-maintained and manicured inns and General Manager William O'Neil keeps operations running smoothly at both. Due to the demands of running the two facilities and their restaurants, however, they aren't as accessible as owners and innkeepers at smaller establishments. But a friendly staff and a stream of guests who are outdoor enthusiasts, including cyclists, hikers, and equestrians, will share tips on local attractions and distractions.

Edson Hill Manor

Built in the 1940s by Vernan Reed as a gentleman's estate, Edson Hill Manor maintains a stately presence and ambiance befitting the 225 hilltop acres it commands. Its brick walls came from the former Sherwood Hotel in Burlington, Vermont; antique fireplace tiles were imported from Holland; and the living room beams were hewn for Ethan Allen's barn.

Reed's country retreat was converted, around 1950, into a country inn by Lawrence and Dorothy Heath, whose family operated it until 1991 when Eric and Jane Lande took it over.

The wood floors, adorned with oriental carpets, rich wood paneling and wood-beamed ceilings in the common areas create a warm and inviting environment complemented by elegant furnishings and accessories.

The nine guestrooms in the Manor house feature fireplaces framed by Dutch tiles, plus canopy beds and comfortable sitting areas. The bathrooms are decorated with whimsical hand-painted murals. In addition there are four Carriage Houses, each with three or four guestrooms. The spacious, modern rooms feature either a king or two queen-sized beds, fireplaces, and sitting areas perfect for relaxing after a day of cycling.

It's hard to decide which is more enjoyable: the breathtaking view from the dining room windows, or the view from the ground as your explore the gardens, trails, and woodlands—complete with trout-stocked ponds—surrounding Edson Manor. Hand-painted murals by Gail Kiesler add to the charm of the restaurant, which earned a place among the top six "Best Inns in North America" for Inn dining by *Country Inn* magazine. A lounge below the main restaurant serves as a meeting place and extra dining room.

While the inn serves as a perfect retreat for weary cyclists, it's actually a favorite among riders of another sort. From the Manor's stables, equestrians—from novice to extremely skilled—find plenty of riding options through the narrow wooded paths, carriage trails, dirt roads, and wildflower-filled meadows that envelop the inn. Guests can book a riding lesson or a carriage ride from the stables in the summer—or a sleigh ride in the winter.

The Manor also boasts a swimming pool surrounded by a well-groomed garden.

Ten Acres Lodge

Ten Acres offers a variety of lodging options, from individual rooms in the main Lodge to larger, more private rooms in its Hill House, to two cozy cottages in the garden next to the swimming pool.

Eight guest rooms in the main lodge, a red clapboard New England farmhouse built in 1840, are individually furnished with a mixture of country furniture and antiques, and all have private baths. On the main floor are two cozy salons with fireplaces, overstuffed sofas and paintings by 19th-century American artists; the restaurant; and a recently redecorated bar lounge where guests can enjoy a drink or casual dining. In the afternoon, chocolate chip cookies and coffee are served next to one of the fireplaces.

Ten Acres also offers larger, private accommodations in its more modern Hill House, which sits on a shady knoll overlooking the main lodge. Room features include fireplaces, balconies, private baths, a sitting area, cable television, and in-room phones. After a long, hard day of cycling, guests can relax in the outdoor hot tub on the second floor of the hilltop retreat.

Two red clapboard cottages with white shuttered windows—one with two bedrooms and one with three bedrooms—provide a perfect option for families or small groups who want to share accommodations. The cozy little poolside houses each have a living room with fireplace and kitchenette, and are surrounded by shade trees and expansive green lawn.

Sunshine pours into the dining room in the main Lodge in the morning, where guests are served from a menu of traditional breakfast items: French toast, pancakes, eggs, bacon, cereals, yogurt, and the like, plus a selection of juices, hot beverages and fresh whole and sliced fruits. In the evening the room is turned into an elegant candlelit dining spot that has received accolades from *Gourmet* and *Bon Appetit* magazines. The restaurant's extensive and impressive wine list earned it *Wine Spectator* magazine's Award of Excellence.

Other amenities include tennis courts and access to nearly 25 miles of walking trails (cross country ski trails in the winter) at Edson Manor. Ask for a trail map. And if you've had a body-bruising day of cycling, you can arrange for a massage in the privacy of your room.

Biking from Ten Acres Lodge and Edson Hill Manor

Stowe, which sits at the foot Mt. Mansfield, Vermont's highest peak at 4,494 feet, offers terrain for riders of all abilities. Whether tackling the challenging climb around "The Notch", part of the once-famous Stowe Bike Race, or meandering along the beautifully maintained 5.5-mile paved recreation path, cyclists are rewarded with beautiful vistas. It's this diversity and cycling friendliness that placed Stowe among the "Top 10 Bike Towns in the Northeast" by *The Ride* magazine in 1998.

Ten Acres Lodge is located just 0.3 miles from the entrance to the Stowe Recreation Path and at the foot of Trapp Mountain Road, a perfect short climb for warming up your legs to catch breathtaking views of the Worcester Range and Nebraska Notch.

The climb up Edson Hill to get to the Manor that bears its name can be challenging for the inexperienced cyclist, but you'll be rewarded with spectacular views. The road is only partially paved. Alternatively, park your car at Ten Acres Lodge, where all of the cue sheets begin. The two inns are 3 miles apart.

Local bike shops and the Stowe Visitor Information Center on Main Street can offer additional suggestions for both road and mountain biking. They also carry the *Northern Vermont Biking Map and Guide* for the Mt. Mansfield/Stowe area, which includes 32 mountain bike trails and road rides with topographic information, trail descriptions and ratings. It costs $4.95 and is published by Map Adventures, 846 Cottage Club Rd., Stowe; (802) 253-7489; www.mapadventures.com.

Local Bike Shops
Mountain Bike Shop
Mountain Road (Route 108), P.O. Box 478
Stowe, VT   05672
(802) 253-7919 or (800) 682-4534
www.mountainbikeshop.com
Sales, service, accessories. Mountain bike and hybrid rentals.

A.J.'s Ski and Sport Shop
P.O. Box 456, Mountain Road
Stowe, VT   05672
(802) 253-4593 or (800) 226-6257
Email: ajssports@pwshift.com
www.ajssports.com
Sales, service, accessories. Tandem, hybrid and front- and full-suspension mountain bike rentals. Mountain bike tours.

Action Outfitters
Mountain Road
Stowe, VT   05672
(802) 253-7975 or (800) 244-7975
Sales, service, accessories. Mountain bike and hybrid rentals.

Boots 'n Boards
430 Mountain Road
Stowe, VT   05672
(802) 253-4225 or (800) 298-5574
Sales and accessories. Hybrid and mountain bike rentals.

Mountain Biking Opportunities
Stowe, home of Fat City Cycles, is a stump jumper's heaven.

The area's varied terrain, dirt roads, and hundreds of miles of mountain trails offer a multitude of mountain biking opportunities. There's plenty of singletrack through **Bolton Valley** and **Mt. Mansfield State Forest**. At **Smuggler's Notch Resort** there's no trail usage fee for its 12 miles of singletrack and forest roads.

Less than two miles from Ten Acres Lodge, the **Cotton Brook Region**, part of Vermont State Forest land, has 15 miles of mountain bike trails, from easy to expert. **Green Trails**, a series of marked singletrack trails with some steep roller coaster hills, runs parallel to Cotton Brook Road. To get there, bear right on Barrows Road from the main parking lot in front of the Ten Acres; at 1.7 miles turn right onto Moscow Road, cross a bridge and turn left onto Cotton Brook forest road. (0.2 miles).

There's a bike trail information board at the first parking area on the right.

At **Mount Mansfield Mountain Bike Center** the high-speed gondola to the Cliff House transports you to some of "the most thrilling trails you'll ever blast down." Access easy rolling singletrack from Alpine Double Lift on Spruce Peak, or more challenging cross country trails from near the Midway Lodge at the base of Mt. Mansfield. For information about trail passes and prices, call the Center at 800-253-4754.

For other suggestions visit local bike shops or pick up Map Adventures' *Mountain Bike Map and Guide* for 11 suggested rides between 8 and 18 miles.

A.J.'s Mountain Bike Center offers regularly scheduled guided mountain bike tours.

Other Resources
Stowe Information Bureau
Main Street
Box 1320
Stowe, VT   05672
(800) 247-8692, fax: (802) 253-2159
www.stoweinfo.com
stowe@sover.net

Ben & Jerry's via Moscow (24.3 miles or 26.3 for longer option)
Moderate to hilly terrain; approximately 8 miles of unpaved road (not suitable for skinny racing tires)

*(**Note:** Can be combined with Ben & Jerry's loop from Inn at the Round Barn Farm for longer ride.)*

The terrain may be a little rough at times, with a few short, rugged climbs on packed dirt, but the rewards are plenty: panoramic mountain views, an ice cream break at the factory that put Vermont on the ice cream lovers' map, a cider mill, a haunted covered bridge, and an abundance of unspoiled countryside and picture postcard views.

Begin the ride by either taking flat, easy Barrow Road, or by climbing past the Trapp Family Lodge (yes, these are the Trapps of *Sound of Music* fame, who built this hilltop lodge after fleeing the Nazis in the 1930s because the surroundings reminded them of their native Austria). The road turns to dirt before beginning a steep, but short, descent into Little River valley.

Although busy Route 100 provides a straight shot between Stowe and Waterbury, the home of **Ben & Jerry's**, the route is designed to minimize the miles cycled on it—and maximize the miles covered on scenic, virtually traffic-free back roads. It passes through the unspoiled hamlets of Moscow, named after Russia's capital, and Waterbury Center, both of which have small country general stores. Catch spectacular views of Mount Mansfield and the Green Mountains from Barnes Hill Road, before crossing Stowe Hollow, or Emily's Covered Bridge, which spans Gold Brook. The brook is supposedly gold-bearing, or at least Old Indian Pete used to buy his necessities in the village with gold he found in it. The bridge is named after a young woman who died there, and whose spirit haunts it.

Pt.-Pt.	Cume	Turn	Street/Landmark
0.0	0.0	R	**Barrows Rd.** from in front of Ten Acres Lodge *(Note: For longer, more challenging route turn left on Luce Hill Rd. toward Trapp Lodge and follow cues for Trapp Family Lodge option below)*
1.7	1.7	L	Onto unmarked **Moscow Rd.**, toward Rt. 100, at stop sign
1.0	2.7	BR	**Moscow Rd.**, toward Rt. 100, at Y
0.6	3.3	R	**Rt. 100 South** at stop sign
1.0	4.3	BR	Unpaved **Gregg Hill Rd**.
2.9	7.2	-	**East Lagoon** or **Little River Reservoir** is on your right.
1.0	8.2	R	**Rt. 100 South** at stop sign
0.6	8.8	L	**Hollow Rd.**, just after the Cider Mill, before bend in road.
0.2	9.0	S	**Hollow Rd.** at stop sign, toward Guptil Rd.
0.1	9.1	BR	**Guptil Rd.**
2.0	11.1	L	**Rt. 100 South** at stop sign
0.3	11.4		**Ben & Jerry's** is on your right
0.0	11.4	R	Leaving Ben & Jerry's drive onto **Rt. 100 N**
0.3	11.7	R	**Guptil Rd.**
2.0	13.7	BR	**Guptil Rd.** at Y. Guptil changes name to **Maple St.**, then **Barnes Hill Rd.**, then **Stowe Rd.** Part of Barnes Hill Rd. is unpaved.
5.3	19.0	S	Cross **Gold Brook Rd.** at stop sign. Go through **covered bridge** onto unpaved **Covered Bridge Rd.**
0.9	19.9	L	Stowe Hollow Rd., paved, at stop sign

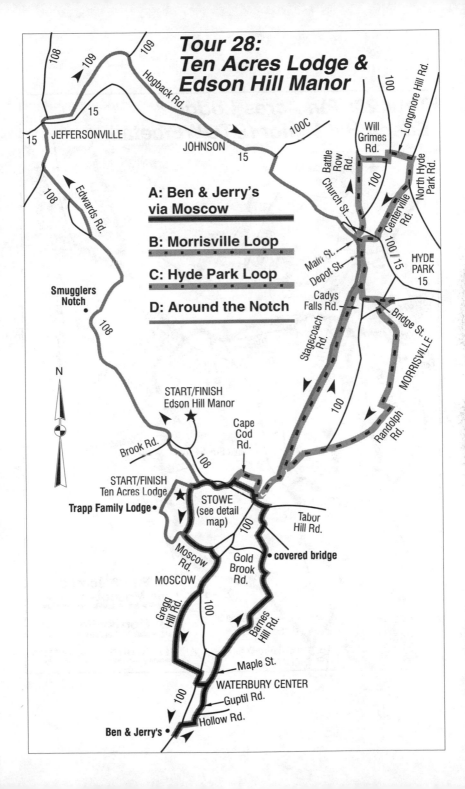

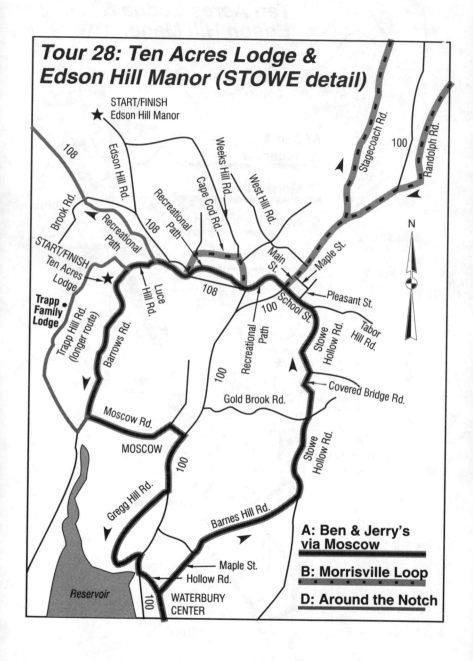

Tour 28: Ten Acres Lodge & Edson Hill Manor (STOWE detail)

START/FINISH
Edson Hill Manor

108

Edson Hill Rd.

Brook Rd.

Recreational Path

START/FINISH
Ten Acres Lodge

Trapp Family Lodge

Recreational Path

108

108

Cape Cod Rd.

Weeks Hill Rd.

West Hill Rd.

Stagecoach Rd.

100

Randolph Rd.

N

Main St.

Maple St.

Pleasant St.

School St.

Tabor Hill Rd.

Stowe Hollow Rd.

Trapp Hill Rd. (longer route)

Luce Hill Rd.

Barrows Rd.

100

Recreational Path

Covered Bridge Rd.

Moscow Rd.

MOSCOW

Gold Brook Rd.

Stowe Hollow Rd.

100

Gregg Hill Rd.

Barnes Hill Rd.

Reservoir

Maple St. Hollow Rd.

100

WATERBURY CENTER

A: Ben & Jerry's via Moscow

B: Morrisville Loop

D: Around the Notch

Pt.-Pt.	Cume	Turn	Street/Landmark
0.8	20.7	L	Unmarked **School St.** at stop sign (intersection with Taber Hill)
0.2	20.9	R	**Pleasant Rd.**
0.1	21.0	L	**Maple St.** at stop sign
0.1	21.1	L	**Main St.**
0.0	21.1	R	Between Hardware Store and Community Church, enter **Recreational Path**
3.0	24.1	L	Exit Recreational Path (shortly after going under a bridge) and go **through parking lot**
0.0	24.1	R	Onto **Luce Hill Rd.** at stop sign leaving the parking lot
0.2	24.3		Ten Acres Lodge is on your left

Trapp Family Lodge option

0.0	0.0	L	On **Trapp Hill Rd.**
0.7	0.7	L	Stay on paved road
0.9	1.6	S	Summit. **Trapp Family Lodge** on right. Road is unpaved for next 1.6 miles
1.6	3.2	L	Unmarked **Moscow Rd.**, toward Rt. 100
0.5	3.7	S	**Moscow Rd.**, toward Moscow (Barrows Rd. is to left) Pick-up cues above, following Moscow Rd. to **Rt. 100 South**

Morrisville Loop (24.8 miles, or 36.2 miles with optional Hyde Park loop)

Hilly terrain

The Old Stagecoach Road, between Stowe and Morristown Corners, was built following the high ground (thus, the term "highway"), where there was less mud to hamper early travelers. Today, the route is paved and presents cyclists with several rewarding climbs as they ascend and descend "the Stagecoach Hills" and take in the pastoral landscape and impressive views of Mount Mansfield.

Pass through the tiny hamlet of Morristown Corners with its general store and notable used bookstore, before crossing the south end of Lake Lamoille to enter Morrisville.

Return to Stowe via scenic Randolph Road, where the terrain is flatter and the countryside is dotted by dairy farms and pastures.

Pt.-Pt.	Cume	Turn	Street/Landmark
0.0	0.0	R	**Luce Hill Rd.** (toward Stowe)
0.3	0.3	L	Enter **parking lot** for Recreation Path
0.0	0.3	R	Onto **Recreation Path**
0.5	0.8	S	Exit Recreation Path and enter **Cape Cod Rd.**, after crossing Rt. 108
1.1	1.9	R	**Weeks Hill Rd.**
0.2	2.1	R	**Mayo Farm Rd.**
0.4	2.5	R	**West Hill Rd.** at stop sign
0.7	3.2	L	**Rt. 100 North** at stop sign
0.9	4.1	S	**Stagecoach Rd.** at split (Rt. 100 bears right)
5.6	9.7	S	**Stagecoach Rd.** at stop sign at Morristown General Store
1.3	11.0	R	**Cadys Falls Rd.** at stop sign
			***for Hyde Park Loop, turn left and follow cues below.*
0.4	11.4	L	Unmarked **Bridge St.**
0.7	12.1	S	At stop sign
0.1	12.2	R	**Portland St./Rt. 100 S** at T
0.1	12.3	R	**Main St./Rt. 100 S** at stop sign
0.2	12.5	BL	**Rt. 100 S**
0.1	12.6	L	**Randolph Rd.** Be careful crossing traffic.
6.4	19.0	L	**Rt. 100 S** at stop sign
2.6	21.6	R	Enter **Recreational Path**, behind Community Church
3.0	24.6	R	Exit Recreational Path (shortly after going under a bridge) and go **through parking lot**
0.0	24.6	R	Onto **Luce Hill Rd.** at stop sign leaving the parking lot
0.2	24.8		Ten Acres Lodge is on your left

Hyde Park Loop

Pt.-Pt.	Cume	Turn	Street/Landmark
0.0	0.0	L	**Cadys Falls Rd.** at stop sign
1.4	1.4	L	**Main St.** at stop sign
0.1	1.5	R	**Church St.**
0.3	1.8	S	Cross Rt. 15 at stop sign
0.1	1.9	L	**Battle Row Rd.**
2.5	4.4	R	**Will Grimes Rd.**
1.4	5.8	L	**Rt. 100 N** at stop sign
0.1	5.9	R	**Longmore Hill Rd.**, unpaved
0.2	6.1	BR	**Longmore Hill Rd.**
0.7	6.8	R	**North Hyde Park Rd.**

Pt.-Pt.	Cume	Turn	Street/Landmark
0.7	7.5	R	**Centerville Rd.**
2.3	9.8	S	**Cross Rt. 15**
0.1	9.9	R	**Unmarked street** at stop sign
0.1	10.0	L	**Cadys Falls Rd./Depot St.**
1.8	11.8	L	Unmarked **Bridge St.**
			Pick up cues above

Around "The Notch" (47 miles)
Extremely challenging

This scenic and challenging route covers part of the annual Stowe Bike Race, a 90-mile Olympic development race that includes two grueling rides through Smugglers' Notch.

The route begins with a little warm up along the recreation path followed by a steep climb up The Notch; then a fast descent into Jeffersonville; relatively flat and rolling terrain through the towns of Johnson, Hyde Park, and Morrisville; more moderate climbing through the "Stagecoach Hills", and finally an easy return to the Inn

Route 108 through Smugglers' Notch is the oldest and narrowest pass crossing the main range of the Green Mountains. The Notch earned its name during the Embargo Act of the War of 1812, when smugglers brought contraband from Canada through the region to avoid revenue officers. Blind curves and switchbacks wind around huge boulders, trees, and overhanging cliffs at the steepest part of the climb as riders grind their way to the road's summit at 2,152 feet. The road widens as the descent begins and passes a waterfall, which pours water across the road in the spring.

Johnson, with its shops and restaurants, makes a good rest stop. Check out the Johnson Woolen Mills, the Vermont Studio Center, or the Debden Center for the Arts at Johnson State College.

Pt.-Pt.	Cume	Turn	Street/Landmark
0.0	0.0	R	**Luce Hill Rd.** (toward Stowe)
0.3	0.3	L	Enter **parking lot** for Recreation Path
0.0	0.3	L	Onto **Recreation Path**
2.6	2.9	R	At end of Recreation Path, right onto **Brook Rd.**
0.1	3.0	L	**Rt. 108 N**
5.2	8.2		Summit
0.1	8.3		Parking area on left is across from trailhead, if you're up for a hike.
6.4	14.7	R	**Edwards Rd.**

Pt.-Pt.	Cume	Turn	Street/Landmark
1.5	16.2	R	**Rt. 108** at stop sign
2.8	19.0	R	**Rt. 108 N**, toward Rt. 109 at stop sign
0.2	19.2	BL	**Rt. 108 N**
0.1	19.3	S	Cross Rt. 15 at flashing light to stay on **Rt. 108 N**
0.5	19.8	R	**Rt. 109 North**
3.8	23.6	R	**Hogback Rd.**
4.6	28.2	L	**Rt. 15 East** at stop sign
6.0	34.2	R	Unmarked **Sylvan Hill Rd.** (across from cemetery)
0.2	34.4	L	**Main St.**
0.3	34.7	BR	**Depot St.**, toward Cadys Fall
1.3	36.0	R	**Stagecoach Rd.**
1.3	37.3	S	**Stagecoach Rd.** at stop sign
5.7	43.0	R	**Rt. 100 South** at stop sign
0.8	43.8	R	**West Hill Rd.**
0.7	44.5	L	**Mayo Farm Rd.**
0.4	44.9	R	Unmarked **Weeks Hill Rd.** at stop sign at T
0.2	45.1	L	**Cape Cod Rd.**
1.1	46.2	S	Cross Rt. 108 at stop sign and enter **Recreational Path**
0.6	46.8	R	Exit Recreational Path (shortly after going under a bridge) and go **through parking lot**
0.0	46.8	R	Onto **Luce Hill Rd.** at stop sign leaving the parking lot
0.2	47.0		**Ten Acres Lodge** is on your left

Selected Recipes

Lemon Blueberry Corn Muffins
Allen House
Amherst, MA

Sift together:
1 cup cornmeal
2 cups flour
1 teaspoon baking soda
2 tablespoons baking powder
½ cup sugar
Zest from one lemon

Whisk together:
½ cup honey
½ pound melted butter
2 cups buttermilk
1½ cups blueberries

Topping
Zest of 1 lemon
Mix with sugar

Whisk wet into dry. Fold in blueberries. Sprinkle with lemon sugar. Bake at 375 degrees for 15 to 25 minutes.

Granola
Amerscot House
Stow, MA

42 ounces old fashioned oats
2 cups wheat flakes (18-ounce package)
1 package coconut
Sunflower seeds
1 pound honey
½ cup oil
Cinnamon and nutmeg to taste

Mix above ingredients in a large roasting pan. Bake at 225 degrees for 1 hour, stirring every 15 minutes.

Add any or all of the following ingredients:
16 ounces Grapenuts
18 ounces Allbran
14 ounces walnuts
16 ounces peanuts
2 packages raisins
2 packages dates
Remaining wheat flakes
Almonds

Walnut-Crusted Sole
The Black Lantern Inn
Montgomery, VT

4 sole fillets
1/3 cup flour
Salt and pepper
2 egg whites
3 tablespoons crushed saltine crackers
3/4 cup chopped walnuts
4 tablespoons butter
1 tablespoon oil

Combine flour, salt, and pepper on a plate. Put egg whites in a bowl and beat lightly. Combine walnuts and crushed saltines on another plate.

Rinse fish and dry; dip in flour, then egg whites and crumbs. Sauté fish in melted butter and oil over medium flame for about 3 minutes per side, until golden brown. Serve with sautéed cherry tomatoes and lemon over rice; yields 4 servings.

Hancock Shaker Village Pumpkin Loaves

Black Swan Inn
Tilton, NH

2 cups sugar
1 cup melted butter
3 eggs
2 cups canned heated pumpkin
2 cups sifted flour (½ white, ½ wheat or all white)
½ teaspoon salt
½ teaspoon double acting baking powder
1 teaspoon baking soda
1 teaspoon ground cloves
1 teaspoon cinnamon
1 teaspoon nutmeg
½ cup chopped pecans or walnuts
½ cup golden raisins

In a bowl beat sugar, butter, and pumpkin to blend. Beat in eggs one at a time and continue beating until blended. In a separate bowl sift together flour, salt, baking powder, baking soda and all spices. Beat into pumpkin mixture. Divide batter between 3 greased loaf pans (7½" x 3½"x 2¼"). Bake at 325 degrees for 60 minutes or until straw test comes out clean. Cool in pans for 10 minutes. Remove and cool on wire racks.

Orange Butter

Beat together 1 container of sweet whipped butter with ½ jar of orange marmalade. Serve with pumpkin bread, toast, or French toast.

Apricot-stuffed French Toast with Orange Syrup

Captain Jefferds Inn
Kennebunkport, ME

1 one-pound loaf unsliced French bread
2/3 8-ounce package cream cheese, softened
1/3 cup part skim ricotta cheese
1/3 cup apricot preserves
5 eggs
1¼ cups milk
1/2 teaspoon vanilla
1/4 teaspoon ground cinnamon
Dash ground nutmeg
2 tablespoons butter

Cut the French bread into diagonal slices about one inch thick. Then cut pocket in each slice, cutting from the top-crust side almost to the bottom-crust side. In a small mixing bowl stir together softened cream cheese, ricotta cheese, and apricot preserves. Spoon about 1 tablespoon of the cheese mixture into each pocket. In a mixing bowl beat eggs, milk, vanilla, cinnamon, and nutmeg until combined. Dip stuffed bread slices into egg mixture. On a griddle or skillet heat butter. Add stuffed bread slices. Fry over medium heat until golden brown, turning once (allow about 1½ minutes for each side). Serve with orange syrup.

Orange Syrup
Yields: ¾ cup
½ cup butter or margarine
½ cup sugar
½ of a 6-ounce can frozen orange juice concentrate

Cook and stir ingredients over low heat just until butter is melted. Do not boil. Remove from heat and cool for 10 minutes. Using a rotary beater, beat until slightly thickened. Serve warm.

Pineapple Bread Pudding with Bourbon Sauce

Captain Jefferds Inn
Kennebunkport, ME

2 cups hot water
1½ cups sugar
1 (12 ounce) can evaporated milk
4 large eggs
1 cup flaked coconut
1/2 cup crushed pineapple, drained
1/2 cup raisins or chopped nuts
1/3 cup butter or margarine, melted
1 teaspoon vanilla
1/2 teaspoon nutmeg
9 slices white bread with crust cut into 1/2-inch cubes. (Pepperidge Farm Hearty White or about 2/3 large loaf of crusty French bread)

Combine water and sugar. Stir to dissolve. Add milk and eggs. Stir with whisk until blended. Stir in coconut and next five ingredients. Add bread cubes. Let stand, stir occasionally, for 30 minutes. Pour into greased 13"x9"x2" baking dish. Bake at 350 degrees for 45 minutes or until knife inserted in middle comes out clean. Serve warm.

Bourbon Sauce
1 cup light corn syrup
¼ cup butter or margarine
¼ cup bourbon
½ teaspoon vanilla

Bring syrup to boil. Remove from heat and cool lightly. Stir in butter, bourbon, and vanilla with whisk. Serve warm.

Non-Fat Blueberry Oatmeal Pancakes
Colby Hill Inn
Henniker, NH

Mix together in a medium bowl:
1 cup all-purpose flour
½ cup oatmeal (not instant)
2 teaspoons baking powder
2 tablespoons granulated sugar
Pinch of salt
1 teaspoon cinnamon
Stir in 1 cup skim milk. Beat 2 egg whites until soft peaks form. Fold in beaten egg whites. Preheat griddle or frying pan to medium heat (about 350 - 375 degrees). Using butter-flavored, non-fat cooking spray, grease griddle or frying pan. Spoon batter onto griddle and sprinkle about 2 tablespoons Wyman's Wild Blueberries (rinsed from can or drained if defrosted) over each pancake before turning. Turn when small bubbles appear on surface. Serve hot with maple syrup or blueberry sauce.

Cromwell Manor Quiche
Cromwell Manor Inn
Cornwall, NY

In a ready made pie crust, place a light layer of fried diced onion and ½ package of broccoli spears lightly sautéed. Layer a cup of shredded sharp cheddar cheese on top.

Whisk together vigorously the following ingredients and pour into pie crust:

4 eggs
2 cups heavy cream
1/4 teaspoon salt
1/8 teaspoon nutmeg
Dash of cayenne pepper

Bake 15 minutes at 425 degrees. Reduce to 350 degrees and continue to bake another 30 minutes.

Chilled Oysters on the Half Shell
With Cucumber Radish Salad and Cilantro Pepper Mignonette
Edson Hill Manor
Stowe, Vermont

26 fresh oysters, washed and chilled
2 limes

Cucumber Salad
2 whole cucumbers, peeled and sliced thin
1 bag large red radishes, washed and sliced thin
1 large red onion, peeled and sliced thin
½ cup rice wine vinegar
2 tablespoons chopped parsley
3 tablespoons sesame oil
Salt and fresh ground black pepper

Cilantro Pepper Mignonette
4 tablespoons chopped cilantro
4 tablespoons fine diced jalapeno peppers, halved and seeded
4 tablespoons cracked black pepper
¼ cup fine diccd red pepper
¼ cup fine diced yellow pepper
2 cups rice wine vinegar

For the salad: In a large stainless steel mixing bowl, combine sliced cucumbers, radishes, red onion, and chopped parsley. Finish with vinegar and sesame oil and toss. Season with salt and pepper and chill. For the cilantro pepper mignonette: Combine all ingredients in a mixing bowl and let rest for 2 hours.

On a large serving platter, place crushed ice and the 24 open oysters. In a small serving bowl, place the cucumber salad and put in the center of oyster platter. Spoon a tablespoon of mignonette onto each oyster and serve with lime wedges. Yields 4 servings.

Butternut Squash Bisque with Crab Meat
Griswold Inn
Essex, CT

1 large butternut squash, peeled and diced
1 shallot, finely diced
1 Spanish onion, finely diced
½ teaspoon white pepper
1 teaspoon nutmeg
1 teaspoon granulated garlic
Bouquet garni*
2 quarts chicken stock
4 ounces butter or margarine
4 ounces flour
Half and half

Combine in large sauce pan squash, shallots, onion, white pepper, nutmeg, garlic, bouquet garni, and chicken stock. Cook over medium heat until squash is tender. Once tender, remove squash from liquid and puree.

To prepare roux, melt butter or margarine in separate sauce pan. Add flour and cook for 15 minutes on low heat. Once roux is cooked, add stock and pureed squash. Let simmer for 30 minutes.

When ready to serve, thin out with half and half. Add ounce of crab meat to center of each bowl. Serve immediately.

*parsley sprig, bay leaf, teaspoon thyme, 5 peppercorns, all wrapped in cheesecloth

Shaker Cranberry Pot Roast
The Hancock Inn
Hancock, NH

Note: The Inn's secret is in a veal stock that is reduced three times before being used to create this house specialty. Below is a simplified recipe of a dish that's been on its menu for more than 20 years.

½ cup of canola oil
1 five-pound shoulder roast
6 garlic cloves, minced
Shallots, minced
Salt and pepper
1 quart cranberry juice
4 bay leaves
2 quarts of beef broth
1 pound cranberries (whole cranberry sauce can be used)
¾ cup of sugar

Heat pan with canola oil. Rub meat with garlic, shallots, salt and pepper. Sear meat on all sides. Deglaze pan with cranberry juice; add bay leaves and beef broth. Cover and braise at 350 degrees for 2-3 hours or until fork tender. Strain liquid and reduce by half. Add cornstarch to thicken if desired.

Cranberry Sauce
In a medium saucepan add cranberries and sugar. Fill pan with water until half the ingredients are covered. Simmer until cranberries just begin to pop. Let cool. Refrigerate. To serve add a generous tablespoon of cranberries to top the pot roast and cover with sauce.

Vegetable Terrine with Boursin And Tomato-Basil Vinaigrette
Inn at Mountain View Creamery
East Burke, VT

2 eggplants, ½-inch slices
4 Portobello mushrooms, sliced
2 zucchinis, ½-inch slices
2 red peppers, roasted and peeled
1 shallot, minced
2 large red onions, French cut
4 ounces Boursin cheese
Fresh basil leaves
Olive oil
Salt
Fresh ground black pepper

Preheat oven to 375 degrees.

Sauté the mushrooms in olive oil with shallots, and set aside. Cut red peppers in half and drizzle with olive oil. Place under the broiler until the skin is charred. Put the roasted peppers into a sealed container to sweat the skins off. Peel the peppers when cool enough to handle. Place eggplant slices on baking sheet. Drizzle with olive oil and sprinkle with salt and pepper. Broil the slices until lightly brown on both sides. Remove from heat and set aside. Repeat this process with the zucchini. Toss the onions with olive oil and salt and black pepper and place under the broiler; continue stirring the onions to prevent burning; remove from heat when they are soft and golden brown. Remove and set aside.

Spray four 8-ounce soufflé dishes with non-stick spray. Lay a roasted red pepper half in the bottom of dish. Then place two eggplant slices, then several zucchini slices, then 1 ounce Boursin, 3-4 fresh basil leaves, roasted onions, sautéed mushrooms, and finish with a couple of eggplant slices.

Wrap each soufflé dish in foil and bake in the oven 25 minutes. Remove foil and invert soufflé dish to reveal the colorful layers of this tempting vegetarian delight.

Smoked Salmon Pinwheels With Cucumber Salsa
The Inn at Round Barn Farm
Waitsfield, VT

Salmon Filling
16 ounces cream cheese, softened
¼ cup chopped red onion
1 ounce smoked salmon
1½ tablespoon lemon juice
1 tablespoon drained capers
2 sprigs fresh dill, stems removed

Process the cream cheese, red onion, salmon, lemon juice, capers, and dill in a food processor until smooth. Transfer to a bowl. Refrigerate, covered, for 1 hour.

Cucumber Salsa
1 cup peeled, seeded and minced cucumber
2 tablespoons minced red onion
2 tablespoons minced red bell pepper
2 tablespoons minced yellow bell pepper
2 tablespoons chopped fresh dill
½ cup rice wine vinegar
¼ cup sugar

Combine the cucumber, red onion, red pepper, yellow pepper and dill in a bowl. Bring the vinegar and sugar to a boil and cook until clear. Cool completely. Add the vinegar mixture to the cucumber mixture. Refrigerate, covered, until ready to use. Drain before using.

Assembly
6 (8-inch) flour tortillas

Lay the tortillas in a row. Spread 1/3 cup salmon evenly over the bottom 1/4 of each tortilla. Starting at the bottom, tightly roll up each tortilla. Wrap each tightly in plastic wrap. Refrigerate for 2 hours or until firm.

Unwrap the tortillas. Slice both ends off each tortilla and discard. Then slice each crosswise at 1/2-inch intervals to form pinwheels. Arrange the pinwheels in a concentric pattern on a serving platter. Place 1 teaspoon cucumber salsa on 1 side of each pinwheel.

Note: The leftover salmon filling makes a delicious dip. Refrigerate, covered, for up to 1 week.

Baked Apple French Toast
Inn at Silver Maple Farm
Canaan, NY

1 large loaf of Italian bread, sliced 1 ½" thick
8 eggs
3 cups milk
¾ cup of sugar divided
1 tablespoon vanilla extract
2-3 Granny Smith apples
2 teaspoons cinnamon
2 tablespoons butter

Spray glass baking dish with Pam and place sliced bread in one layer.
Beat together eggs, milk, vanilla, and just ¼ cup of sugar.
Pour ½ the batter over bread slices.
Peal, core, and slice apples into thin rings and place over batter.
Pour remaining batter over the apples and bread.
Mix remaining sugar with cinnamon and sprinkle on top.
Dot with butter.
Refrigerate overnight allowing the bread to soak in the batter.
Bake at 350 degrees for 35-40 minutes until puffed. (You may want to place foil lightly over top of pan so apples do not burn.)

Herbed Leek & Spinach Soup

Juniper Hill Inn
Windsor, VT

¼ cup butter
4 medium leeks, sliced
1 medium onion, thinly sliced
2 stalks celery, thinly sliced
6 cups canned chicken broth
1 bay leaf
1½ teaspoon salt
2 tablespoons snipped parsley
1½ tablespoon snipped fresh thyme
¼ teaspoon ground white pepper
1 pound fresh spinach, washed and drained
1 cup half and half
Croutons, for topping

Melt butter over low heat in a skillet. Add leeks, onion, and celery. Cook
for 10 minutes, stirring. With slotted spoon, transfer to 5- or 6-quart
pan. To large pan, add chicken broth, bay leaf, 1 tablespoon parsley,
thyme and pepper. Remove heavy stems from spinach. Add to pan.
Bring mixture to a boil. Reduce heat, cover and simmer for 20 minutes.
Remove bay leaf. In blender, puree mixture in three batches, 15 sec-
onds each.

Serve topped with croutons and a dollop of sour cream or crème fraîche.

Berry Special French Toast

The Maine Stay
Camden, ME

16 slices Pepperidge Farm white bread
1 eight-ounce package whipped cream cheese
1 teaspoon vanilla
½ cup chopped walnuts

Combine cream cheese, vanilla, and chopped walnuts. Spread on eight slices of bread, making eight sandwiches. Cover with wax paper and refrigerate overnight.
When ready to fry, dip sandwiches in mixture of:
3 beaten eggs
1 cup half and half
¼ teaspoon nutmeg
¼ teaspoon vanilla

Sauce
1 eight-ounce jar apricot jam
½ cup orange juice

Heat jam and juice. Bring to a boil and stir until sauce is mixed well. Keep warm on hot plate. Serve toast with hot sauce and a variety of fruit. The Maine Stay uses bananas and seasonal fresh fruit. Serves 8.

Breakfast Bread Pudding

Manor House Inn
Bar Harbor, ME

4 eggs
¾ cup sugar
3 cups low-fat milk
1 cup half-and-half
½ cup butter
1 tablespoon vanilla
¾ cup raisins
2 apples, thinly sliced
1 teaspoon nutmeg
1 loaf Texas Toast (French toast bread) cut up

Combine all ingredients except bread. Allow bread to soak up liquid (about 20 minutes). Lightly grease 9"x12" glass baking pan, and pour bread mixture in pan. Bake at 350 degrees for about 45 minutes.

Apple Cider Sauce

Combine:
1 cup sugar
2 tablespoons corn starch
½ teaspoon pumpkin pie spice

Add:
2 cups cider
2 teaspoons lemon juice
¼ cup butter

Cook until thickened and serve with bread pudding.

Orange Waffles

Manor House
Norfolk, CT

2 cups sifted all-purpose flour
3 teaspoons baking powder
2 tablespoons sugar
½ teaspoon salt
4 eggs, lightly beaten
4 tablespoons melted butter
1 cup milk
3 tablespoons grated orange rind
Dash of nutmeg

Sift together the dry ingredients. Set aside. Combine eggs, milk, and butter. Add orange rind. Add the sifted dry ingredients, ½ of the total amount at a time. Beat well after each addition until the batter is smooth. Pour about ¾ to 1 cup of batter at a time onto a preheated waffle iron, following the manufacturer's directions. Bake until the waffles are golden brown. Serves 8.

Miles River Country Inn Yogurt Pancakes

Miles River Country Inn
Hamilton, MA

Sift together dry ingredients: (you can do this the night—or day—before and store in a ziplock bag)
1 cup flour
2 teaspoons baking powder
1 teaspoon baking soda
½ teaspoon salt
2 tablespoons sugar

Mix together wet ingredients:
3 eggs
¾ cup yogurt
1 cup milk
4 tablespoons oil or melted butter

Combine with a few swift strokes. (Do *not* mix thoroughly. Leave lumps.) Cook on hot grill adding to each pancake whatever fruit you might like in it.

Sweet Potatoes

Moose Mountain Lodge
Etna, NH

6 large sweet potatoes or yams
Fresh ground nutmeg
Maple syrup
Half and half cream, or orange juice
Salt and pepper to taste

Peel and slice the potatoes. Cover with cold water and cook until soft. Drain, using the same pan and a hand mixer or a potato masher, mix until smooth. Add nutmeg, maple syrup, salt and pepper, to taste. Add half and half or orange juice until they have the consistency of loose mashed potatoes. Scoop sweet potatoes into a casserole. Reheat in either a microwave or a 350-degree oven before serving. Serves 8.

Zucchini Curry Soup
October Country Inn
Bridgewater Corners, VT

4 zucchinis, cut into thick slices
1 onion, chopped
1 tablespoon good curry powder
3 cups chicken stock
Salt and pepper
¾ cup half and half

Garnish
½ cup crème fraîche, sour cream, or yogurt
½ cup chopped chives
Chive blossoms (if available)

Put zucchini, onion, curry powder, and chicken stock in a saucepan. Bring to a boil, cover and simmer for 25 minutes, stirring occasionally. Puree mixture in blender, strain, and add half and half. Season to taste with salt and pepper. Reheat to serving temperature.

Serve with a dollop of the crème fraîche, yogurt, or sour cream, a sprinkle of chopped chives, and chive blossoms if available. Serves 6.

Blueberry Muffins
The Richards
Narragansett, RI

½ cup butter
1 cup sugar
Eggs
1 teaspoon vanilla
2 cups flour
½ cup milk
2 cups blueberries

Beat butter until creamy. Add sugar and beat until fluffy. Add eggs one at a time, beating well after each addition. Beat in vanilla extract. Fold in half of flour, then add half of milk. Repeat. Fold in blueberries.

Bake at 375 degrees for 25 minutes.

The World's Best Cookies
Silas Griffith Inn
Danby, VT

1 cup margarine, softened
1 cup sugar
1 cup firmly packed brown sugar
1 egg
1 cup vegetable oil
1½ cups oatmeal
1 cup Grape Nuts cereal
1 cup shredded coconut
1 cup chopped walnuts
3½ cups flour
1 teaspoon vanilla
½ teaspoon salt

Preheat oven to 350 degrees.

Cream margarine and sugars together until light and fluffy. Beat in egg and oil. Add oats, cereal, coconut, and nuts, mixing well. Add flour, baking soda, and salt, add vanilla. Form into balls the size of small walnuts and place on ungreased cookie sheet. Bake for 12 minutes or until light brown. Allow to cool on cookie sheets a few minutes before removing to wire racks.

Makes approximately 100 cookies.

Apple & Mushroom Bisque with Pistachio Cream
Snowvillage Inn
Snowville, NH

1 tablespoon olive oil
1 large onion, finely diced
1 large pack of domestic mushrooms, chopped
3 large apples (Granny Smiths are best), peeled and sliced
2 Yukon Gold potatoes
6 cups of water or chicken stock
1 tablespoon Tamara soy sauce
1 cup heavy cream
Kosher salt & pepper to taste

Sauté onions in oil in a covered stock pot. When these are soft, add chopped mushrooms and apples. Sauté briefly, then add stock. Bring to a boil and add potatoes. Reduce heat and simmer for 10 to 15 minutes or until potatoes are soft. Add tamari, season with salt and pepper. Process in food mill until smooth. Add cream and adjust flavor. Keep warm.

Pistachio Cream
¼ cup shelled pistachios
¼ - ½ teaspoon salt (to taste)
1 cup of heavy cream

Process nuts until they are very finely ground. Scrape down and add salt and cream, process until smooth. Serve dollops on soup.

Serves 6-8.

Whistle Wood's Buttermilk Pancakes
Whistle Wood Farm
Rhinebeck, NY

1 egg
1¼ cups buttermilk
2 tablespoons oil
1 teaspoon sugar
2 teaspoons baking powder
1/3 cup cornmeal
1/2 teaspoon baking soda
2/3 cups all-purpose flour
1/2 teaspoon salt

In a large mixing bowl, beat the egg with a fork. Beat in buttermilk and oil. Combine the flour, cornmeal, sugar, baking powder, soda, and salt. Add the dry ingredients. Stir the mixture until blended but slightly lumpy.

Pour 1/4 cup of batter onto a hot slightly greased griddle or heavy skillet. Turn the pancakes over when they start to bubble.

Serve with maple or berry syrup for breakfast. They are also great with fresh fruit, and if you have leftovers, store them in the refrigerator and reheat in the microwave for short time and serve them with ice cream and chocolate syrup or sauce.

Upside Down Pear Cranberry Cake

Windflower Inn
Great Barrington, MA

1 ½ cup all purpose flour
1 ½ teaspoons baking powder
1 ½ sticks (6 ounces) softened sweet butter
3 tablespoons softened sweet butter
1/2 cup granulated sugar
3 eggs, room temperature
2/3 cup lightly packed dark brown sugar
4 medium-sized sweet ripe pears (peeled, cored, sliced)
1/3 cup whole cranberries—fresh or frozen
2 teaspoons vanilla
2 tablespoons cranberry liquor
Cinnamon and nutmeg

Place pear slices in glass pie plate, sprinkle lightly with cinnamon and nutmeg, and soften in microwave for 2 minutes. (If you don't have a microwave, the cake will still be fine as long as the pears are ripe and soft.)

Mix flour and baking powder in a small bowl. In mixing bowl, beat 1 ½ sticks of butter until pale and creamy. Add granulated sugar and beat until light and fluffy. Add the eggs, one at a time, beating after each one. Add the two teaspoons of vanilla. Fold the flour into the batter just until no white streaks remain, add the two tablespoons of cranberry liquor.

In a nine-inch, oven-proof, non-stick skillet, melt remaining three tablespoons butter. Add the brown sugar and cook over moderate heat until melted and bubbly.

Remove from heat and toss cranberries into pan. Arrange pear slices in circles over the melted butter, sugar, and cranberries. Begin with the outer circle and work in. Spread batter evenly over the pear slices.

Bake in pre-heated 375-degree oven approximately 25 minutes or until cake tester comes out clean. Allow cake to cool for five minutes and then invert onto large platter. Serve warm, garnish with whipped cream or vanilla ice cream.

Look for these other
Bed, Breakfast & Bike books:

Bed, Breakfast & Bike Pacific Northwest
(Oregon, Washington, British Columbia)

Bed, Breakfast & Bike Western Great Lakes
(Illinois, Minnesota, Wisconsin)

Bed, Breakfast & Bike Midwest
(Ohio, Indiana, Michigan)

Bed, Breakfast & Bike Mississippi Valley
*(Following the Mississippi River from
New Orleans to St. Louis)*

www.anacus.com